THE BEACH BOYS

PET TRACKS

The Stories Behind 100 of Their Greatest Songs

MICHAEL FRANCIS TAYLOR

NEW HAVEN PUBLISHING

Published 2023
First Edition
NEW HAVEN PUBLISHING LTD
www.newhavenpublishingltd.com
newhavenpublishing@gmail.com

All Rights Reserved
The rights of Michael Francis Taylor, as the author of this work, have been asserted in accordance with the Copyrights, Designs and Patents Act 1988.
No part of this book may be re-printed or reproduced or utilized in any form or by any electronic, mechanical or other means, now unknown or hereafter invented, including photocopying, and recording, or in any information storage or retrieval system, without the written permission of the
Author and Publisher.

Front Cover Image ©wikimedia
Back Cover Image©wikimedia
Cover Design © Pete Cunliffe

Copyright © 2023 Michael Francis Taylor
All rights reserved
ISBN: 978-1-912587-98-8

Introduction

As long as I can remember I always wanted to write a book about the Beach Boys. Growing up mid-60's England, where the only Surf I knew was Mum's washing powder, it was all about the Beatles and the Rolling Stones, so when I first laid my eyes on an album called *All Summer Long* (still one of my favourites), it was like a glimpse into another world - a sun-kissed playground so far removed from middle England where long hot summers were a premium and beaches were a 100-mile, once-a-year drive away, with fingers and toes crossed in the hope of a little sunshine.

Only later did I know that this was their sixth album in a little under two years, and the first that did not have a cover that focused on either ocean waves or souped-up cars. The difference was plain to see. These five guys were not boys anymore; in fact, all but one were now in their 20's, but, as the rear cover showed, they were no longer portrayed as a group, but more like confident individuals, here promoting the sunny California dream as a way of life; one that no longer just revolved around surfing and hot-rods, but much more about the attraction of young women.

It was only a matter of time before I sought out the other five albums (thanks to my generous dad), and continued to enjoy each and every album of theirs that came along over the next thirty years or so, until, sadly, we lost two of the brothers, and their magic for me began to slowly fade-away.

The Beach Boys made some of the finest music in pop history; an album still considered today as one of the greatest ever made, and even one described as one of the finest albums never heard. Although not all of their music hit the mark, their extensive back catalog has been one of the most celebrated in the history of popular music, leading some of the finest biographers and music academics in the world to bring their incredible story to life.

The Beach Boys recorded hundreds of songs and no one really knows how many more are hidden somewhere in the vaults. But for each song we did get to hear, whether it made your playlist or not, there was a story behind it that was waiting to be told - their inspiration, the writing and recording process, the infighting and controversies, and their ultimate success or failure - all factors in creating what became a musical legacy unparalleled in American popular culture.

In choosing my hundred "pet tracks," the ones that I believe are their "greatest," there's little doubt that my best will not necessarily be the same as yours. I know for sure that Beach Boy fans are among the most loyal and discerning in the world. Not all your favourite songs will be mentioned in these pages, although a good many will, but I am certain that we will agree more than we will disagree.

Apart from personal reflection I have included excerpts from scores of published interviews and the work of some of the top writers in the music business in order to validate my claim for a song's inclusion on the list. For that reason I am indebted to the likes of David Leaf, Steven Gaines, Timothy White, Keith Badman, Craig Slowinski, Jon Stebbins, Andrew G Doe, Domenic Priore, Philip Lambert, Peter Carlin, Jim Fusilli, James B Murphy, and a host of others, whose descriptive writing puts my meagre effort to shame. I implore you to seek out their work to gain a much broader and informative picture.

I never had the chance to see the Beach Boys or Brian Wilson in concert and I envy all who did. But I hope by reading this book it will make you seek out these wonderful songs again (or even for the first time), and give you that feeling of joy and amazement they gave me all those years ago.

I feel privileged to have been around to share their incredible journey. Their music continues to be reevaluated by music gurus every year, but each time their legacy remains firmly intact, if not enhanced. They were one of a kind, and we'll never see their like again. I firmly believe that when debating their place in the history of popular music, the Beach Boys should no longer be called America's Band, but a band for *everyone,* every living soul who still feels the enormous power that music has to give.

Michael Francis Taylor
England, September 2023

A guide to contents
The songs are listed 100-1
Song title (Parent album and year of US release)
(Songwriters in parentheses)
Recording
Dates and studio where known, with session details
Producer
Engineer
Band members
No particular order, but lead vocalist usually first.
Session musicians
Inc. guests and friends at the recordings
Album release date
US release only
US Single release date
Inc. flip-side, label number, and chart position on Billboard Hot 100 (chart position refers to the A-side)
UK Single release date
Inc. flip-side, label number, and UK chart position
Film/TV Performances
Not comprehensive, but some of the most notable filmed performances in movies, television, and concerts
Description of the song
Footnotes refer to the relevant source

Images
All image are in the public domain and supplied via Wikimedia Commons

Acknowledgements
To Teddie Dahlin at New Haven, for bringing to life the book I always wanted to write.
To Peter Cunliffe, for the cover artwork
To Angela, for her tolerance and continuing support
To Brian and Tony, for giving "God Only Knows" to the world.

By the same author
Harry Chapin: The Music Behind the Man (New Haven 2019)
Songs From the Vineyard: The Music of Carly Simon (New Haven 2020)
Taylor Swift: The Brightest Star (New Haven 2021)
Taylor Swift: Stolen Lullabies (New Haven 2023)

California Dreaming

The Wilsons

Murry Gage Wilson was born in Hutchinson, Kansas on July 2nd 1917, the third of what would be eight children for William Coral "Buddy" Gage and Edith Sophia Sthole. They gave Murry his middle name from the doctor who delivered him. Due to economic hardship and having to raise a large family, Buddy, a master plumber by trade, always found ways of avoiding the ban on liquor and regularly got drunk on badly fermented moonshine. By all accounts that drunkenness soon led to frustration, rage, and physical abuse. It also made him unreliable and at times unemployable.

In 1921 Buddy left his family behind and like so many others headed west to California to find his fortune, apparently with the false hope of becoming a professional baseball player. After finding odd jobs on the way to the coast he finally made it to Escondido, California, and secured a plumbing job. While there he called for his wife and children to join him. To help with the burden three-year-old Murry and his one-year-old sister Emily were sent to stay with Edith's cousin near San Diego. The following year the rest of the family joined them. After finding various work as a journeyman Buddy and the family moved close to Inglewood but were so impoverished they camped for two months in a tent on the beach alongside thousands of other victims of the Depression. His frequent bouts of alcohol-fuelled abuse left Murry having to protect his mother and siblings from him.

By 1929 Buddy, Edith and their three boys and four girls had moved into a modest house, and with Buddy able to find continuous work with a modest income the family were at last able to spend some leisure time, including singing together around the piano. Young Murry was found to be good at sports, especially baseball and football, but he also had some musical talent.

Two years later Murry was enrolled at George Washington High School in Los Angeles and it was there that he first met fellow student Audree Neva Korthof. Born in Minneapolis on September 28th 1917 she was the second child of Carl Arie Korthof and Ruth ("Betty") Finney. In the spring of 1928 salesman Carl moved his family west and rented a house on West 52nd Street in LA, before moving into a bigger property on West 84th Street in Inglewood. Murry and Audree shared a love for music, both being members of their respective glee clubs, although she was the more accomplished musician. Three years after graduating they married on March 26th 1938 and moved into a house on West 18th Street. Murry worked as a clerk for a gas company while Audree earned extra money giving piano lessons to local children, and by 1941 they had moved to a small rented bungalow at 8012 South Harvard Boulevard. On June 2nd 1942 their first child **Brian Douglas Wilson** was born at Centinela Hospital.

Meanwhile 52-year-old Buddy had continued with his hard drinking, and Murry was the one who often came to blows with him. Soon after Brian's birth Murry secured a job as junior supervisor at the massive Goodyear Tire & Rubber Company in central LA, enjoying all the perks that came with the job, and instilling in him a new-found vitality. On December 4th 1944 Audree gave birth to a second son **Dennis Carl Wilson**. With the need for a larger house and with mortgages easier to come by Murry put a down payment of $2,300 on a new two-bedroom bungalow at 3701 West 119th Street in the South Bay area of Hawthorne, some 12 miles from central LA. 3

> *"When I was twenty-five, I thought the world owed me a living. When I lost my eye, I tried harder, drove harder, and did the work of two men..."*

Murry was promoted in 1945 to instruct new trainees on the assembly line. Shortly after, he lost his left eye in an accident at work, and although incapacitated and fitted with a prosthetic eye it only served to motivate him: "When I was twenty-five, I thought the world owed me a living. When I lost my eye, I tried harder, drove harder, and did the work of two men in the company and got more raises."3 After leaving Goodyear he worked as a foreman for AiReseach, the manufacturing arm of Garrett Aeronautics Corporation but resigned after five years, telling his wife that he could no longer stand working for someone else.

Unlike his father Murry was keen to engage his family in his dreams and ambitions, playing his favourite songs on the piano (though rather badly), and teaching his two young sons to sing the words. Audree did her bit by singing them nursery rhymes and playing them classical albums. On December 21st 1946 their third child **Carl Dean Wilson** was born.

After leaving AiReseach Murry became a junior partner in his brother's machinery business but realised he could do much better. In 1955 he risked his mortgage on the Wilson home, took out a $20,000 loan, and established his own company, ABLE (Always Better Lasting Equipment) Machinery Company, importing quality tools from a British manufacturer, and operating out of a rented storefront. Within a few years he would acquire much larger premises, due to the growing need for better tools from businesses like the nearby Northrop Aircraft Company. At the best of times it would earn him an annual after-tax profit of $15,000 from the rentals of tools and machinery.

As the three boys reached school age they were enrolled two blocks from home at York Elementary School and taken to Sunday School at nearby Inglewood Covenant Church, despite the Wilsons not being considered avid churchgoers. Audree recalled that even at such a young age Brian had a beautiful singing voice - a precocious natural talent that his parents said dated back to his ability to hum melodies at the age of two. A natural shyness would soon give way to unashamed confidence when singing solo with a local church choir, with the director praising his clear soprano for having perfect pitch.

But it was also a time when they first noticed Brian was having a problem with his right ear. While singing in the choir he tended to tilt his head to hear better. Murry recalled how he kept turning his head to listen and wondered whether it was due to an injury, maybe while playing football. In an interview for *Rolling Stone* Audree revealed: "Brian thinks his deafness happened when he was ten. Some kid down the street whacked him in the ear. It's a damaged nerve so he could have been born that way."11

"Deep down, [Murry] was a ruthless egomaniac whose parenting philosophy was skewed by his own experience as a child of an abusive, alcoholic father"

Over the years, there have been many stories of Murry's alleged physical and verbal abuse toward his boys, especially Brian and Dennis, all of which he later denied.122 But in a televised interview in 1999 Brian revealed: "My Dad was a very inspirational person in my life, but he was also the worst person I ever met in my life. He yelled so loud, you could have sworn the devil was in the room…He beat us so badly that we had no choice but to lay on our beds and cry after we got beat…He hit me with a two by four, right to the side of my head. He totally put my right ear out. He made me so deaf."11

Beach Boy historian Charles Granata wrote: "As a father, Murry Wilson was an inscrutable failure. On the surface, he appeared to be a strict disciplinarian who wanted the best for his children. But deep down, he was a ruthless egomaniac whose parenting philosophy was skewed by his own experience as a child of an abusive, alcoholic father. Life in the Wilson household wasn't easy, and each of the boys dealt with the dysfunction in a different way."74

According to biographer Kingsley Abbott, "Murry was an extremely strict disciplinarian. Though he loved his sons, Murry was prepared to use physical punishment and other tactics of intimidation to assert his will. He was also a firm believer in traditional masculine values, and expected his sons to follow suit."75

But it was rebellious Dennis who endured the most punishment dealt out by his father, and with his own quick temper there was always going to be friction between them for years to come. With Brian being the golden boy in the family, and Carl the innocent babe, it was inevitable that Murry would turn to Dennis for his punch bag. As time went on Dennis's only ambition was to be as different to his father as he possibly could, but Murry's hair-trigger anger towards him infected his maverick son like a cruel virus that only time would cure.

Brian described Murry as "violent" and "cruel" in his most recent memoir, but his writing also suggests that some of the stories had been overstated or unfounded.35

One way to divert the beatings and gain Murry's affection was through the boys' mutual love of music, and their access to it was totally unrestricted, with both parents doing their utmost to saturate them with guidance. With his family now considered complete, Murry managed to indulge more in his long-held ambition to be a songwriter, but to his frustration it never came easy. He had seen how sheet music sales earned authors like Irving Berlin and George M Cohan large amounts of money, and in 1952, in order to allow him to concentrate more away from the children, he converted the garage into a music room for his upright piano and a jukebox, and bought on credit an electric Hammond organ for Audree.

Someone else who needed to escape was Brian. To distance himself from family conflicts and the pressures of school (where he was only achieving average results), Brian took every opportunity to spend time alone, especially when the three brothers had outgrown their shared bedroom. He also found time to go to the music room as a way of bonding with his mother, who was more than happy to sing and play along with him. With Murry footing the bill for instruments and records, Brian took lessons on a toy accordion, while Carl received brief guidance with a guitar. They would then have Audree accompany them on the organ with high-pitched renditions of "When You Wish Upon a Star," one of Brian's favourite songs from *Pinocchio*.

By sharing her small record collection with her son, Audree exposed Brian to the kind of music that was at least more interesting than Murry's, who would try banging out his latest creations on the piano that now seemed to everyone to be a decade out of date. Of course, Murry couldn't really play the piano well at all, and could only manage simple melodies or ask Audree to play the organ for him.

One of the first pieces of serious music that had a marked influence on Brian was Gershwin's "Rhapsody in Blue," perhaps heard on one of Audree's records. It showed him how complex emotions could be expressed through music. According to writer Andrew Doe, it became Brian's "emotional anchor…an expression of the power of music to touch the deepest reaches of his being."[75]

But as interesting as this was for Brian, his favourite companion was the tiny transistor radio he kept under his pillow, and every evening after dinner he would go to his room and tune in. He recalled: "My favourite [station] was KFWB in Hollywood. Every record had something you would listen to; every record had some kind of twist in it that gave you that feelin', and you'd say 'Oh Man.' You'd go to the piano and say, 'Now, how do they do that?' You'd start learning about it - it's an education. Anybody with a good ear is gonna pick up on those records."[74]

Although Brian's voice was in the high alto range, he was able to sing in a clear falsetto, a skill perhaps developed by singing Audree's favourite Rosemary Clooney songs for her. But having such a high voice made him feel insecure about his own masculinity. He still endured occasional taunts from other boys for "singing like a girl," but woe betide anyone who dared to do it with young Dennis around to knock them to the floor.

In 1951 Murry found people who at least would take his songs seriously. Husband and wife Hite and Dorinda Morgan owned a modest recording and publishing business called Guild Music on Melrose Avenue in Hollywood. With their help, Murry managed to get his material accepted by several little labels. He wrote the kind of music that was being played by the big dancehall bands at the time, like those of Tommy Dorsey and Duke Ellington, with the belief that there would always be a demand for that kind of music - a belief that was somewhat validated with the success of his novelty piece, "Two Step, Side Step," recorded by Johnny Lee Wills, the Bachelors and Bonnie Lou, and performed to his utter delight on a local radio show by the Lawrence Welk Orchestra in 1953. That was Murry's crowning glory as a songwriter, but the market for his kind of music would soon be disappearing, and taking its place would be rhythm & blues.

Like his own father had done with him, Murry began to see in Brian the potential for a budding athlete who would achieve some success in sport. He was not only a top tetherball player at York Elementary but also excelled at baseball, joining the Little League "Seven Up" squad. However, when Murry came to coach and criticise him in front of other parents, Brian switched to left field to escape the embarrassing side line heckling. Although he did had some degree of sporting talent, he lacked what was most important - confidence, no doubt exacerbated by the expectations and pressure put on him by his dad.

Dennis was the polar opposite of Brian, always seeking adventure, and, according to noted biographer Timothy White, "a chronic victim of acute nervous tension, free-floating anxiety that seized him with a force verging on violence."[29] He was the naughty kid on the block, starting fights for no reason, tormenting his brothers, and even causing unnecessary damage to other people's property. Young Carl, by comparison, was just happy watching his favourite shows on television.

The Wilsons also enjoyed the company of many friends, and there were a number of cousins living in the immediate area, with Murry and Audree both having siblings close at hand. They were a 15-minute drive away from Audree's sister Glee Love in Baldwin Hills, where she lived with husband Milt and their six children, including Mike and his sister Maureen. Every Christmas they would be invited there for elaborate parties, harmonising carols around the piano, with Brian and Mike finding a quiet place where the two cousins could practice vocal harmonies.

Mike remembered how the many singalong sessions helped ease some of the tension between Murry and his sons: "We loved all the songs with falsetto and bass parts...I would sing the bass, Brian had high, and Carl the middle part. Maureen or my Aunt Audree would take up the fourth part. It was always a search to find the person to sing that fourth part with us. It wasn't a formal group at the time - it was just me and Brian getting together at his house or mine."[74]

"Something Magical happened in my head, I instantly transcended. It came out of me...It was magic. Total magic"

The more time Brian spent with cousin Mike helped exposed him to R&B music, and the two of them regularly tuned into the Johnny Otis Show on KVOX Radio, which increased Brian's awareness of other forms of pop, especially the power of black R&B artists like Otis Redding and James Brown.

June 13th 1955, a week before his thirteenth birthday, would prove to be a momentous day for Brian. It was the day the Four Freshmen released their new single, "Day By Day," and after being encouraged by his mother to listen to it on the radio for the first time, he was captivated by their incredible four-part harmonies. He even begged his mother to take him to a record store where he could listen in the booth to the whole of their album, *The Four Freshmen And the Five Trombones*. Almost mirroring the future Beach Boys lineup, the quartet who hailed from Indiana consisted of two brothers, a cousin and a friend. Brian recalled: "Something Magical happened in my head, I instantly transcended. It came out of me...It was magic. Total magic."[303]

From that day on those harmonies became a fixation for Brian, and one he tried to emulate or even take it to the next level: "It brings a feeling of love inside me," he admitted, "It does, it really does. That feeling of harmony." Carl recalled: "He would listen to their records and play the harmonies on the piano. What he would do is sit at the piano and figure out each part. Then he would teach Mom and me a part. He would sing the third part, record the three of us singing together, and then he would sing the playback to hear the fourth part."74

Brian liked nothing more than teaching his two siblings vocal arrangements in their bedroom. In the spring of 1956, he taught them a vocal arrangement of "Ivory Tower," a chart hit for Cathy Carr earlier that year. Brian called it "his special song." Carl remembered how most bedroom sessions ended in horseplay and laughter, but only until their father came in - then it was lights out and goodnight. There were also times when Dennis was reluctant to join in the singing, and by his mid-teens he would find more pleasure in outdoor pursuits.

For Brian's 16th birthday on June 20th 1958 his parents bought him a Wollensak 1500 two-track reel-to-reel tape recorder. This would open up a whole new sonic world for Brian and kick start his development as a record producer. Now he could record his four-part vocal arrangements on tape and even overdub in order to structure the layered harmonies: "For the first time he could record the harmonies himself. First he taught Audree the simplest part and sang harmony with her into the tape recorder. Then he would play it back and he and Audree would sing live to it, creating four parts."123 Not wishing to leave his eager dad out, Brian would expand the parts to not only include him, but Carl as well. It was the finest present Brian had ever received, and just one more token of appreciation from his parents who could now see that their talented son just might have a future in music. That Christmas, Brian's parents would also buy him his first car - a 1957 Ford Fairlane 500.

Although Dennis appeared at times determined to do as little as possible other than annoy his father, he also craved his affection, and there were times when he behaved himself long enough for Murry to buy him a surf board. Once he met up with the surfing community, he relished the bohemian lifestyle they had, fuelled by drink, marijuana and easy-going girls. It proved to be the perfect escape mechanism for his wild ways. Here were the kind of people he could relate to, ones that Murry would probably refer to as beach bums, but for his son it would shape the rest of his short life.

The music room now looked more like a recording studio. Brian would enlist both parents and Carl for the additional voices he required for four-part harmonising. Sadly, Dennis now had more interesting things on his mind, but then there was always cousin Mike. Apparently, Brian and Mike were not friends to begin with. Vickie Amott, a classmate of Brian's, recalled that when they started the group, "Mike just came in and took over. Brian was so laid back and Mike had such a dominant personality. Brian was kind of in the clouds."3

In his senior year at Hawthorne High, Brian enrolled in a piano and harmony course run by the school's Fred Morgan, who would later teach Carl to play saxophone and Dennis to play drums (albeit short-lived). Young Carl was just as interested as Brian when it came to music, but that passion soon became focused in playing guitar. In a 1996 article for *Tiger Beat,* he recalled: "A friend of my parents, a fantastic guitarist, often dropped by to play…Whenever he put down the guitar I'd grab it and start messing around…The instrument fascinated me…My folks bought me a guitar when I was 12."187 Carl practiced all the time, copying riffs from favourites like Chuck Berry, which "were really thrilling for me to hear."

It was due to guitar playing that he began a friendship with young David Marks, Dennis's partner in neighbourhood misdemeanours, and another budding guitarist who lived just across the street.

That fall, Brian wrote a campaign song for classmate Carol Hess, who was running for student body president. It was a reworking of "Hully Gully," and Brian and some pals sang it at a rally. This led to a request for him to form a combo and play at a special student rally, so Brian, Mike, and schoolmates Bruce Griffin and Robin Hood got together to perform. When Hood dropped out at the last minute, Brian cajoled a reluctant Carl to take his place. To placate his nerves, Brian named the combo Carl and the Passions. Although the nerve-jangled performance led to some ridicule from members of the audience, later ones would be more appreciated.

It was alleged that 18-year-old Brian received a failing F grade for submitting a rock music melody instead of the requested sonata for his final music project (later changed to an A grade in 2018 when Brian was 75!) While one account has his submission eventually being reworked to become, "Surfin,'" others, including Audree, later disputed it. The fact is we will never know the truth. After graduating Hawthorne High in June 1960, Brian elected to go to El Camino Community College, a local tuition-free institution. Taking courses in psychology and music appreciation, he found to his dismay the music teacher was disdainful of rock & roll and hesitant to make a clean break from chamber music.

One afternoon Brian ran into fellow student Alan Jardine, and it wasn't long before Al, who had a folk combo known as the Tikis, cajoled him into jam sessions in the college's music room, singing hits by the Four Freshmen and Kingston Trio.

In July 1961, the 3,000-capacity Rendezvous Ballroom in Balboa became a hot spot and the place to go to when the hugely popular surf group Dick Dale and the Del-Tones began a summer residency there. Budding musicians travelled there to see what they could learn, and they included Dennis and his brother Carl, who had always been inspired by Dale's guitar playing. David Marks recalled for *Trouser Press*: "[Brian] and his cousin Mike, plus Al Jardine from the junior college, had a little group, Kenny & the Kadets. They weren't into surf music; they just played for parties and bar mitzvahs. Brian and Carl were on separate trips all the time. Brian with his group, Carl jamming with me and with another guy in the street who had an accordion."[11]

Although not knowing it at the time, the seeds were being sown for what would eventually become the Beach Boys.

Mike Love

Edward Milton ("Milt") Love first met Murry's younger sister, Emily Wilson (nicknamed "Glee") while attending George Washington High School. Glee was born in 1919 and enrolled at the school two years before him. Milt was a year older and had attended Hyde Park Elementary School. Handsome and athletic, he was the older brother of Stanley, and it was through him he got to know his classmate Glee. As a budding actor and singer, she often sang in the glee club with her future sister-in-law Audree Korthof.

Following Milt's graduation in 1934 the two of them dated for several years before finally getting married on September 10th 1938. Milt attended UCLA for a short time before working at Love Sheet Metal Service Company, which had been founded by his Louisiana-born father Edward in 1909. With the growing success of the business and the money earned, Milt and Glee had a Spanish-style house built in the affluent View Park -Windsor Hills area of LA. Not quite a mansion, but it still had 14 rooms and seven bedrooms, and was just ten miles from the Wilson home.

On March 15th 1941 Michael Edward Love was born, the first of six children, followed over the next eleven years by Maureen, Stephen, Stanley, Stephanie and Margie. Mike attended Susan Miller Dorsey High School and, like his father, he excelled in athletics, running long distance on the track team, and being a competitive member of the colleges basketball team. But while doing well at sports, he was disruptive in class and only received average grades. Nevertheless, he was seen as a well-liked, bright, quick-witted boy. Maureen Love described her strawberry-blond brother growing up: "He chose to sneak around a little and lie a little just to do the things he wanted to do. He rebelled and got into trouble, and so he had a reputation of being a liar and a sneak around our house. And my mother had a dark, kind of unforgiving side, and she and Mike just clashed...I remember him being so girl-crazy. Whenever my friends came over, he was always there, wanting to be around the girls. And he was charming and handsome, so he had fun."32

Like Brian, Mike had a keen interest in music, no doubt inherited from his mother, who had a wonderful, clear soprano voice. However, he was more interested in R&B, especially street-corner harmony groups like the Drifters.

Graduating in 1958, Mike left school without any prospects and took a menial job at his father's sheet metal company. However, on the eve of a Wilson-Love family holiday party in the autumn of 1960 he found out that his 18-year-old girlfriend Frances (Franny) St Martin was pregnant, with her outraged parents demanding he did "the right thing" by marrying her. Mike's mother took it worse, and when they discovered that he was planning to sneak off to Tijuana for a quick abortion, she banished him from the house. With a child now on the way, Mike's father fired him from his company, forcing his son to take a part-time night job pumping gas at a nearby station, although soon quitting after being held up at gunpoint during a robbery.

"Brian never had any other dream than writing and composing. Leading a pop-song group never entered his head"

The low-key wedding took place in January 1961 and the couple moved into a house on Eight Avenue. To settle his debts Mike took various jobs before finally working for another sheet metal company. Later that year, the Loves themselves lost their home in Baldwin Hills when Milt's business went bankrupt, forcing them to relocate to a dingy three-bedroom house in a crime-ridden area of Inglewood.

On July 15th 1961 18-year-old Frances Love gave birth to a daughter Melinda. Mike, having just dropped out of Los Angeles City College, was desperate to fix his financial troubles and continued banishment and reclaim his former lifestyle.

He believed the only way to achieve that was through a recording career, and began lobbying his cousin to follow in the footsteps of local college kids-come pop wannabees Jan Berry and Dean Torrence (Jan and Dean), who were on the cusp of stardom.

When Mike dropped by to take part in a singing session, he recalled: "Brian would memorise songs and deal out parts for us. It never ceased to amaze me. It would be hard to grasp one part, yet he'd have all four parts in his head. Brian, me, and Carl were the only ones who could sing the intricate harmonies. We didn't know anybody who had the ear to tune into those things. So, his mother, my aunt Audree, would sometime sing the top part of the melody and we'd sing three parts, well not on our records, but this is how we actually got together the first time singing."[3] In the conversations that followed, 18-year-old Brian wasn't sure what life had in store for him. According to Carl, "None of us had childhood dreams of growing up and singing for a living. Dennis wanted to be a racing-car driver, Mike didn't know what he wanted to do, and Brian never had any other dream than writing and composing. Leading a pop-song group never entered his head."[11]

But the facts were clear to see. Teenage kids all over the City of Angels were getting into rock & roll, and by doing so, making them very rich. All that was needed was something to sing about…and that's where young Dennis would come in.

Alan Jardine

Donald Charles Jardine was born in Toledo, Ohio, in 1912. His father had worked with Thomas Edison on developing the first electric automobile, and as a clarinet player in the University of Toledo's orchestra he met and began dating 18-year-old violin-player Virginia Louise Loxley, born in Ohio in 1915. After graduating in 1934, Don took a job as a government photographer, and three years later they were married. By the time America entered the war, he was working as a full-time photographer for the Lima Locomotive Works, with a three-year old son Neal, and another baby on the way, but was granted a deferment from military service when the company began making tanks.

Their second son, Alan Charles, was born on September 3rd 1942. Like the Wilsons, the Jardine children grew up in a house filled with music, and by the time he was six, Alan could sing and play his four-string toy ukelele.

In 1948 he enrolled at the local high school, but the following year the family moved to Rochester in upstate New York, with Don gaining employment as an instructor in a printing department at RIT. Three years later, the family moved again to Summerville near Lake Ontario where Al completed his fourth grade at the local elementary school. By the time he was ten, his father was offered a job as manager of the Royal Blueprint Company in San Francisco, and in 1955 was reassigned to LA to emulate the company's success there. For a time the family rented a house on 117th Street in Hawthorne, before finally moving into an apartment on El Segundo Boulevard.

Al followed his brother into Hawthorne High School, while Neal graduated and went on to El Camino College to study theatre arts before transferring to

UCLA. In 1958 both Al and Brian Wilson commenced their junior year at Hawthorne High. Al and his school friends, Gary Winfrey and Bob Barrow, played on the school football team, the Cougars, with Al being the starting fullback. He and Brian played together during the 1957 season, and would rekindle their friendship at El Camino College three years later. On November 7th 1957 Al fractured his leg in a playing-field collision with quarterback Brian, who apparently called one play and executed another. Because of Brian's wholehearted apology, the two of them became friends, at least until Brian's football career came to an end.

Like Brian, Al and his friends shared a love for the Kingston Trio, who had just released their chart-topping single "Tom Dooley." After football practice, they sang together in the locker room and decided to form a group called the Tikis, and they continued to play together and record folk songs onto a tape machine at Gary's house. In an interview for *Rolling Stone*, Al recalled: "I saw Brian in concert with his brother, Carl. I was quite impressed by what I heard . I persuaded Brian to start thinking about doing some singing. We had no basis or anything. We were just pals on the football field."[11]

In early 1960 Don Jardine was offered a teaching job at Ferris University in Big Rapids, Michigan. His wife joined him later, leaving Al, just short of his 18th birthday, to move in with the Winfreys at their home in Hawthorne, just two streets away from the Wilsons. Following his parents back to the Midwest in September, Al enrolled at Ferris Institute for the 1960-61 academic year with a plan to become a dentist. Completing his freshman year the following June, he hitchhiked his way back to LA and later registered as a student at El Camino College for his second-year pre-dental curriculum, which included a year of organic chemistry.

On his return, Al resumed his folk combo with Gary, but with Bob away, he brought in Gary's younger brother Don to complete the trio. Having heard that there was already a group called the Tikis, they decided to change their name to The Islanders. They rehearsed and recorded on tape an old folk song called "The Wreck of the Hesperus" (based on the Longfellow poem), with Gary on lead vocal, and Al and Don doing backing vocals.

This was the time when Al and Gary considered asking Brian to join their combo and went over to his house to ask him. Finding he was not at home, they struck up a conversation with Audree, and she mentioned that Murry knew someone who had a new recording studio called Stereo Masters on Melrose Avenue and suggested they get in touch with co-owner Hite Morgan. Transferring the song onto a three-inch tape reel, they were invited to go down and do a demo. With the Morgans still in the process of building their studio, they agreed to give the boys a listen. With Al on guitar and his two friends on banjos, they performed the song and tried out some Kingston Trio numbers. According to Dorinda, "they were imitators, not innovators," and turned them down. But if something different came up, they would get in touch.

In August 1961 something did come up. Gary got a call from Hite Morgan, asking them to come down and record a song that had been written by their son Bruce called "Down By the Rio Grande." Two sessions were held, with Keith Lent replacing the unavailable Don. After two unsuccessful attempts, Al decided to ask Brian for help, and although he came down and tried his best, the whole project was abandoned. But at least the Morgans had met Brian again. Having watched him grow from a young boy, they could still remember his beautiful voice.

Meanwhile, Brian, Al, Carl and Mike were still practicing Four Freshmen-style vocal harmonies themselves, joined for a time by Mike's sister Maureen.

David Marks

David Lee Marks was born in Hawthorne on August 22nd 1948. The son of Elmer and Josephine (Jo) Ann Marks, they had moved from New Castle, Pennsylvania in 1955, and a year later had bought a house in Inglewood. David enrolled at Andrew Bennett Elementary School and befriended local boys Carl and Dennis Wilson, who had previously been his playful tormentors when first arriving in the neighbourhood. Music was part of David's makeup, having a grandfather and two uncles who played guitar and mandolin.

His prayers were answered when one Christmas his parents bought him a Kentucky Blue guitar for $18.95. By the age of seven, David had moved to a house across the street from the Wilsons, with David often invited by the family to take part in their Sunday night singalongs. David began taking lessons from 15-year-old John Maus, whose mother, a friend of Jo Ann, had sometimes babysat David. Maus would later go on to become one third of the legendary Walker Brothers. By 1959 Carl was also taken guitar lessons with Johnny Moss, whose other pupil was David. Because of the lessons they shared, and his friendship with two of the Wilson brothers, David soon took part in music sessions in their music room or at his house, although no one yet had even mentioned the idea of forming a group. He recalled: "We would get together every day in my room and play records by Duane Eddy, Chuck Berry, Dick Dale, and the Ventures."[187]

For both of these budding guitarists, making records was still a distant dream…

Surfin'

One of the first ideas to form a group came from Mike, who while with Dennis on one of their visits to Malibu Beach in early 1961, discussed the possibility, and an excited Mike then urged Dennis to put the idea to Brian. When Al Jardine reunited with Brian at El Camino and spoke about the two of them forming a group, it was Brian who suggested it could also include Carl and Mike. With that, things would begin to move at a fast pace.

That same August, having failed to impress the Morgans with their music, Al asked Brian if he would join him at Stereo Masters to help record his version of the folk favourite, "The Wreck of the John B," along with other popular covers. Al recalled: "That was the pretense in which we went down to the studio. I called Brian and suggested to him we record some folk music."[3] Joined by Carl, Dennis and Mike, Al's performances once again failed to impress the duo, who recommended they come back with some original songs.

Dorinda recalled: "They weren't as smooth as the other group Alan had brought, but knowing Murry…we figured Brian had talent as a songwriter."[187] According to her, it was an excited Dennis who said, "No one has ever written a song about surfing!...It's new, but its bigger than you think." It was a pivotal moment, one that could have snuffed out their dreams there and then, if fate hadn't have intervened. The Morgans certainly hadn't heard of the latest craze, but it sounded interesting, and Dorinda asked Dennis to write down some surfing terms. As he did, Brian and Mike grabbed pens and immediately started writing down lyrics. With the guitar Al had brought along, a rough melody was hatched out before they left the office. Mike said to the Morgans, "Give us some time to come up with a song."3

"No one has ever written a song about surfing!"

On Labor Day weekend that August Murry and Audree Wilson went on vacation to Mexico City with some friends from England, leaving their sons a reputed $100 each for extra food and drink while they were away (both the time and the amount of money are disputed). While gone for less than half a day, Al suggested the boys rent musical equipment for the weekend in order to practice their new song, which they simply called "Surfin.'" One account has them taking the grocery money to Hogan's House of Music on Hawthorne Boulevard and renting two better guitars, drums, saxophone, stand-up bass, and amplifiers and microphones. However, according to Al, they had eaten all the food long before they rented the equipment, and it was actually his mother who loaned them $300. Meanwhile, 13-year-old David Marks, the neighbourhood friend of Carl and Dennis, had been keen to be part of the new group, but his parents had forbidden him to stay up late and rehearse with them. Unbeknown to them, his time would come in the very near future. David later recalled: "I wasn't really in the group then. I was practicing with them...I was just their kid friend from across going the street going, 'Hey guys, can I play too? Can I, huh, huh?'"3

During the same weekend Al celebrated his 19th birthday. For him it had been a frustrating year. The Islanders, now in their third year, had failed in their dream to have a song recorded, and during that time they had not written any new songs. Also, all attempts to steer Brian more toward folk music had fallen on deaf ears (or at least one).

The following five days were spent rehearsing song in Murry's music room, with the best parts recorded onto Brian's tape recorder. 14-year-old Carl recalled: "Well, I was going to play guitar, but we didn't know who was going to play the other instruments. Alan could play stand-up bass, Brian could play keyboards and had been hammering out arrangements since he was twelve. Dennis just chose the drums. And Brian said, 'Well look, I'm going to play the bass, and you play guitar, and then it will be like a rock sound.' Michael didn't play anything, but got a saxophone. He'd thought he'd play sax, but Mike never practiced. The group really learned how to play after we made records."3 Mike sang lead vocal while Brian duetted with him on the chorus.

Apparently, Al's voice is not audible on the tape, leading to suggestions that Brian intended the group to match the model set by the Four Freshmen. Al, who would quit the group the following February and be replaced by Marks, later recalled: "We were working on that song way back in 61. We all became instruments for Brian's barber shop concept. He said, 'Let's all do this, let's sing this idea.' Carl would be one instrument, I'd be another. Mike would be another instrument."33

The rehearsals didn't go without some tension, and arguments flared up over who would take credit for the writing, mainly between Brian and Dennis. Mike cooled things a little with his sardonic reply: "Don't sweat it. It's not worth arguing about until the coins start coming in because there won't be any coins at this rate."3

On September 11th Al and Brian started their second year at El Camino, with Dennis and Carl beginning their junior and sophomore years at Hawthorne High. While rehearsals continued, the boys decided to come up with a name for the group, and decided on The Pendletones, after the plaid woollen shirts favoured by surfers and surf groups. At Audree's behest, Dennis was also included in the group.

When the parents returned from vacation there was hell to play, with Murry allegedly throwing Brian against the wall for defying him. Brian then shouted: "Dad, just listen!" Once Audree had calmed her husband down, Brian was given the chance to play the recording of the song (another version of events is that the boys actually performed it for him). In an interview for *Rolling Stone*, Audree recalled: "They said 'We want to play something for you.' They were very excited about it and I thought the songs were darling. But I never thought anything would happen." Surprisingly, Murry was impressed enough to see it had potential and got in touch with his recording friends, the Morgans. After another day of rehearsing at the Wilson home, it was actually Al who managed to fix an audition.

Although the date has never been unverified, according to noted Beach Boy historian James B Murphy the boys went back to the Morgans' living room studio sometime in September or early October to cut demos of "Surfin,'" (1 take), and two other songs - Dorinda's a capella "Lavender," (4 takes) and Bruce Morgan's "Luau" (3 takes). The demo of "Surfin'" had only a guitar backing, finger clicks, and the voices of Brian, Mike, Carl, Dennis and Al singing the refrain, markedly slower than the later recording. According to Dorinda, the Morgans were anxious to record it for a potential single, and preferring to have one of their own songs for the flip-side.

With the demos finished Hite advised them to carry on rehearsing at home and he would arrange a studio session to record more professional versions of the songs. For the remainder of October, the boys continued practicing.

In early November Hite booked and paid for a session at a professional recording studio to record two masters for an intended single (Al later said the boys had to pay $100 for the recording). The Pendletones, along with Murry, accompanied Hite and his son Bruce to World Pacific Studio on West Third Street, and, with the help of engineer Dino Lappas, recorded masters of "Surfin'" (8 takes), as well as "Luau" (12 takes) and "Lavender" (4 takes) for the possible flip-side. Hite was particularly impressed with "Surfin,'" despite having little knowledge of the impact the sport was having on the West Coast teens.

> *"We were five green idiots the first time we went into a recording studio. We had a song and a dream, that's all"*

It was the first time the boys had set foot in a professional recording studio, and it proved to be a daunting experience. Carl recalled: "We didn't know anything about the sounds or how a record was made. We just lucked it…And the way it sounded was the way it sounded." Al, too, remembered: "We cut 'Surfin' real quickly. We did it all at one time. We sang and played. We just stood up in front of the microphone and basically played the song for Murry and the publisher, and that's the one they liked."33

Brian recalled: "We were five green idiots the first time we went into a recording studio. We had a song and a dream, that's all. We sang and played our song once through, paid the guy for the use of the hall, and walked out with the demo record clutched in our hot fist."307

According to Mike the group "manufactured an instant surfing song." That same day, the boys signed a songwriting contract with Guild Music, the Morgans' publishing company, guaranteeing Brian and Mike, as songwriters, to receive 50% of publishing income, 28.5% of the wholesale price of sheet music, and 6 cents per copy of sheet music sold. As for writing credits, Brian later recalled: "Dennis and Carl got the great idea. Mike and I just got a few ideas."

In mid-November Hite took the acetate to his friend Bill Angel, a record librarian at KFWB Radio, to ask his opinion. He not only liked it but suggested it could be a hit. He called Joe Saraceno, the top A&R (Artist & Repertaire) man at Candix Enterprises, a small independent record company on Hollywood Boulevard. The future of the Surfers, the name Hite had suggested the boys should call themselves, now lay in the hands of Saraceno. Once hearing it, he said, "I loved it. I always love group harmonies." Saraceno then called Robert Dix, co-owner of the company, and said: "I have a record here by these kids I want you to hear." Dix then played it to his two brothers, and when it finished, Robert Dix said: "Well, it's a little weak in the bridge, but we'll put it out immediately."3

There was one caveat - the name the Surfers had to go, as a group by that name already existed in Hawaii. Although accounts differ, it was Saraceno's friend Russ Regan, the label's accountant, who came up with an idea. He first offered surf-related names like the Woodies and the Hang Tens, which were immediately dismissed. Finally, he said, *"Then call them the Beach Boys."*

Apparently, the boys were unaware of the change until after the record was released. Brian recalled being told of the decision via a phone call from Regan, while Mike revealed that they were unaware until after the release: "We didn't even know we were the Beach Boys until the record came out. It was that kind of thing. We could have said 'No, we're not going to be the Beach Boys,' but it sounded pretty far out."187

On November 27th 1961 "Surfin" was released with the number Candix 331. Five days later it received its first ever play on the local KFWB Radio. Before long, it began to garner airplay outside of California, and, with sales of some 50,000 copies, managed to score a #75 spot on the Billboard Hot 100 in March 1962.

Despite Audree's fear that nothing would come of the recording, Dennis had convinced Brian that choosing to write about surfing would be something that local kids to relate to, and, of course, he was proved right. With Murry about to do a superb job in convincing one of the biggest record labels in the world to sign them up with a lucrative recording contract, the Beach Boys' incredible journey to worldwide fame was well and truly underway....

The 100 Greatest Songs

100. Shut Down (*Surfin' USA* 1963)
(Brian Wilson, Roger Christian)

Recording
05/01/63 Western Recorders, LA
Producer - Nick Venet
Engineer - Chuck Britz
Band members
Mike Love (lead vocal, sax); Brian Wilson (harmony & backing vocals, bass guitar); Carl Wilson (harmony & backing vocals, lead guitar); Dennis Wilson (harmony & backing vocals, drums); David Marks (rhythm guitar, lead guitar during fade-out)
Album released - 25/03/63
US single released -04/03/63 b-side to "Surfin USA" Capitol 4932 #23
UK single released - 07/08/63 b-side to "Surfin USA" Capitol 4932 #34
Film/TV performance
14/03/64 NBC Television Studios, Burbank (part of concert for screening in selected US cinemas; later released in 1998 as *The Lost Concert*

 After Gary Usher, Brian's second collaboration with someone outside of the group was with Buffalo-born Roger Christian (1934-1991), who moved to California to became a well-known radio personality on several stations in the L.A area and one of the original "Boss Jocks. Christian gained the nicknamed "Poet of the Strip" for his love of hot rods and for the poems he wrote about the sport.
 Murry Wilson had heard Christian on his popular late-night KFWB radio show explaining to listeners the lyrics of the Beach Boys latest single, "409," the sole hot rod song off their debut album *Surfin Safari*. Christian later recalled: "A 327 is really better…But the 409 was the big number they were pushing back them. Everybody who got one thought it was just the biggest thing around…So I was playing the record, and I said it was good song about a bad car." This was music to Murry's ears. Here was a guy who knew about cars and could write lyrics with Brian, and he arranged for the two of them to meet. This was also an opportunity for Murry to try and get rid of Brian's friend Gary Usher, who had co-written "409" and five other tracks on the debut album. Murry had a genuine dislike for the guy, firmly based on a burning jealousy that a former bank teller was now one of the chief collaborators with his talented son.

> *"So I was playing the record, and I said it was good song about a bad car"*

 At a café called Otto's, Christian chatted with Brian over hot fudge sundaes and showed him a notebook containing his car-related poems. One was called "Shut Down," and Brian was stirred by the dragster terminology, sadly missing from "409." It was a match made in heaven, and in no time at all he had composed a melody to accompany Christian's words. It became the first of a number of their collaborations, including "Little Deuce Coupe" and the much-revered, "Don't Worry Baby," while Christian also teamed up with Beach Boy friends Jan (Berry) and Dean (Torrence) on car classics such as "The Little Old Lady From Pasadena" and "Dead Man's Curve."

"Shut Down" describes a drag race between the narrator's fuel-injected 1963 Chevrolet Corvette Sting Ray and a Super Stock 413 cu.in-powered 1962 Dodge Dart, and the boast of winning the race by "shutting the other down." The end of the song sounds inconclusive with the 413 still ahead and the Sting Ray gaining ground, but the lyric *"shut it off, shut it off/Buddy now I shut you down,"* indicates the race has already been won. Although the song is over around the 1:30 mark, by repeating the last couple of lines it gives it a further 20 seconds before fade-out. On Mar 9th 1963 *Cash Box* reviewed the single's two sides: "More top rock-a-teen sounds on the powerful 'Shut Down' pairing. Can be a double-header."

At the first sessions for the next album *Surfin' USA*, "Shut Down" was one of three songs recorded, the others being the title track and "Lana." At that time Brian had decided to double-track vocals, bringing added power to these and future performances. Both "409" and "Shut Down" would be reprised on the *Little Deuce Coupe* album, while the instrumental track, "Shut Down, Part II" on *Shut Down Volume 2* has no connection with this song. According to Keith Badman, five days after the session the group departed on a seven-day tour of Eastern USA.[11]

David Leaf described the importance of "Shut Down" and "409": "The two songs illustrate two prime aspects of Brian's artistic personality: the competitive and driven hit maker in opposition to the kid who whom stardom came quickly and who honestly wondered whether his songs were that good."[6]

99. Good Time *(The Beach Boys Love You* 1977*)*
(Brian Wilson, Alan Jardine)
Recording
07/01/70 Beach Boys Studio, Bel Air (basic tracking for Spring version)
10/76 -11/76 Brother Studios, Santa Monica (remixing)
Producer - Brian Wilson
Engineer - Stephen Desper
Band members
Brian Wilson (lead vocal), The Beach Boys (backing vocals)
Session musicians - unknown
Album released - 11/04/77

Spring were a female duo consisting of sisters Marilyn (Brian's wife) and Diane Rovell, formed in 1971 after their cousin Ginger Blake left the Honeys to pursue a solo career. Their first and only album entitled *Spring* was produced by Brian at his home studio in Bel Air, with help from songwriter/producer David Sandler, a friend of Bruce Johnston, and engineer Stephen Desper. With recording sessions taking place during breaks from work on the Beach Boys' album *Carl and the Passions - So Tough*!, it soon became evident that he was spending a lot more time and focus on the girls' recordings (in fact, he had more involvement as producer of this than any released Beach Boys album since *Friends* in 1968 and remained as such until *15 Big Ones* in 1976).

According to Sandler, Brian "was definitely trying to establish some independence from the group, and the *Spring* album was part of that. He still had a lot of music in him, but I think he was depressed. And maybe some of the people who were supposed to be helping him were hacking away but not helping him much."32.

"A buoyant and cheerful counterweight to Brian's daily life outside the studio"

After producing their first single, a cover of Carole King's "Now That Everything's Been Said," Brian let them record the breezy "Good Time," a song written by Brian and Al Jardine but left off the 1971 *Sunflower* album. Apparently, during the tracking session, while either Brian or Bruce Johnston played piano, they segued into a version of the Beatles "You Never Give Me Your Money" (the audio was later made available on 2021's *Feel Flows* box set). Brian overdubbed the girl's vocals onto the instrumental track, adding horns and strings later, and included the short but catchy "*hey baby turn up the radio*" bridge (omitted from the later *Love You* version).

Both the single and album were released in May 1972 but resulted in disappointing sales. Later in the year the girls faced legal issues over their name, as there was already a UK group called Spring claiming they owned the rights to the name. Therefore, it was changed to American Spring. Peter Carlin described the lyrics as "nursery-rhyme erotica."32

Musicologist Philp Lambert wrote: "With its naked musical exuberance, unadorned chordal simplicity, effervescent vocals, brass, and percussion, and an ambiguous notion of how a 'good time' can be had, the song comes across as a buoyant and cheerful counterweight to Brian's daily life outside the studio."9

Seven years after "Good Time" was written came the album *Love You*. According to Brian, he was finding it difficult to come up with new songs: "Material is getting harder and harder to write all the time for me. I don't know why" (although he would later go on to admit some 28 songs were actually written for the album). He had fond memories of recording "Good Time," and in an interview for *Crawdaddy* in May 1977 recalled: "On the same tape was my lead vocal and Marilyn did her lead part too. They didn't even erase my lead, so when the *Spring* album wasn't that successful, I thought maybe the exposure of that song to people would be good. Why waste a song."40

So the song was resurrected, with synthesisers added, the "*hey baby*" bridge omitted, and no longer sounding like it belonged on *Sunflower*. One noticeable difference for those listening to the album was that on this one track, Brian's voice does not sound course like it does on the rest. Unfortunately, although well received by some critics, the album became another financial disaster.

Like Brian said, it would have been a shame to have wasted such a catchy song (although I still prefer the girls' version).

98. Pacific Coast Highway (*That's Why God Made the Radio* 2012)
(Brian Wilson, Joe Thomas)
Recording
02/12-03/12 Ocean Way Studio, Hollywood
Producer - Brian Wilson

Engineer - Frank Pappalardo
Band members
Brian Wilson & Jeffrey Foskett (lead vocals)
Session musicians
Probyn Gregory (French horn); Joe Thomas (piano); Nelson Bragg (percussion); Paul von Mertens (string arrangements, flute); 2 cellos; 6 violins
Album released - 05/05/12

Following on from the death of Dennis in 1983 and Carl in 1998, it was widely reported in the late 2000's that the surviving members of the band were planning to reunite for a 50th Anniversary album and tour. Not only that, the album would be the first by them to feature original songs since 1992's *Summer in Paradise,* and the first album to have Brian as producer since *Love You* in 1977. It would also see a welcomed return to the fold for former member David Marks since his last appearance on *Little Deuce Coupe*. Preceded by the title track, the album went on to score a #3 hit on the Billboard 100, their highest chart placing since 1974's *Endless Summer* (and highest studio album placing since *Summer Days* in 1965).

All but one of the tracks are collaborations with Brian, with Joe Thomas's name credited to the rest (Thomas had previously co-produced the band's album *Stars and Stripes Vol 1* and Brian's second solo album *Imagination (*one which had resulted in a lawsuit being filed against him by Brian, later settled out of court). Sometime between 2008 and 2010 Brian had reached out to him and invited him to work with him again on the new album.

> ***"If the Beach Boys, at their best, reminded us how great and painful and confusing it was to be young, it's a gift that they can provide the same soundtrack for getting old"***

The highlight of what, for me, is an uninspiring album comes with the final four songs, a *Smile*-inspired suite that originally was dubbed "Life Suite" and consisted of six tracks before being narrowed down to just four - "Strange World," "From There To Back Again," "Pacific Coast Highway," and "Summer's Gone," all Wilson-Thomas collaborations.

In early May 2012 Thomas recalled: "[Brian] really wanted to do like a kind of reflection of California from the standpoint of a...guy who's almost 70 years old. So its driving down Pacific Coast Highway and thinking about his life in retrospect. So this suite was a series of maybe one or two minute vignettes that he had, like, 15 of them that he would start and never finish...It just seemed like all these little pieces became like this theme, and instead of being Americana, or whatever *Smile* was, it was his drive down Pacific Coast Highway."[255]

Will Hermes of *Rolling Stone* also identified with the album's "suite": "If the Beach Boys, at their best, reminded us how great and painful and confusing it was to be young, it's a gift that they can provide the same soundtrack for getting old. *'Sunlight's fading, and there's not much left to say,'* Brian Wilson sings on this perfectly melancholy, *Smile*-ish ditty - part of the seriously moving medley that closes out the Beach Boys' new LP."[13] Ryan Hamm of *Under the Radar* summed it up perfectly: "Wilson has always been the guy who just wasn't made for these times. And these songs are his (and by extension, the Beach Boys) way of saying goodbye..."14

Although a number of tracks failed to impress, the *Guardian's* Alexis Petri disrated the album as "the best thing Brian Wilson has put his name to in the last 30 years."15 The *Beats Per Minute* website's noted: "The album as a whole isn't flawless, yet by sounding utterly enchanting during its climax it leaves the listener feeling genuinely touched,"16, while *Consequence of Sound* referred to the album as "a funeral dirge full of majesty," singling out "Pacific Coast Highway" for its "subtle flourishes of strings and plodding piano [that] drive the song into the darkening horizon."17

"Pacific Coast Highway," with its melancholic, slowed-down reflection on life, evokes a profound sense of isolation. Although the lyrics may seem mundane to some, this is Brian opening his bleeding heart perhaps one last time, maybe finally coming to terms that, although the fun was good while it lasted, this album is the last hurrah, the setting sun, for the surviving members of the Beach Boys, all now elder statesmen aging gracefully.

Despite the album's flaws, this final suite of four songs, and "Pacific Coast Highway" in particular, serve as a fitting way to pull the curtain down on what has been a legendary career.

97. Good Timin' (*L.A Light Album* 1979)
(Brian Wilson, Carl Wilson)
Recording
29/04/74 Brother Studios, Santa Monica
04/11/74 Caribou Ranch, Colorado
13/12/78 Britannia Studio, Santa Monica (vocals)
Producers - Bruce Johnston; The Beach Boys; James William Guercio
Engineer - unknown
Band members
Carl Wilson (lead & backing vocals); Mike Love (backing vocals); Brian Wilson (piano, harpsichord, organ); Dennis Wilson (drums); Al Jardine (backing vocals); Bruce Johnston (backing vocals, Fender Rhodes)
Guest
Jim Guercio (bass)
Album released - 16/03/79
US single released -04/79 b/w "Love Surrounds Me" Caribou ZS8 9029 #40
Film/TV Performance
Promo c1974

Blondie Chaplin had left the group in December 1973; Ricky Fataar and Bruce Johnston would depart the following year, but by January 1974 the group had developed a relationship (through Dennis) with 28-year-old Chicago-born Jim Guercio, a musician and producer who had helped steer the band Chicago to great success by the middle of the decade. Guercio, a huge fan of the Beach Boys, became their part-time manager and Blondie's replacement as bass player for live performances. Not only that, he owned Caribou Ranch, a recording studio outside of Denver, Colorado.

Guercio managed to bring order to what was a developing rift in the group, especially when it came to clashes over choosing between sticking to the old hits "formula" (in Mike's corner, of course), or recording new material (preferred chiefly by Carl and Ricky). First on Guercio's agenda was to get Brian back into the studio with the band, and in October 1974 he sent them up to his Caribou studio where sessions included preliminary work on two originals - Brian's "Good Timin," and Brian and Mike's "It's OK." However, the tapes were eventually shelved for four years, during which time the group would record three more studio albums.

> *"… stands as a startling reminder of the first class songwriting, performance, and production the Beach Boys drew on routinely in the sixties, then let slip away"*

Because of the criticism levelled at their dreaded disco-themed, "Here Comes the Night," it was decided to rush out "Good Timin" as their next single, with Carl and Bruce arranging the vocal overdubs. Bruce later recalled: "I'm not putting Al down or Mike but the real soldier who stuck with me the whole time was Carl. The two us sang the verses on "Good Timin," the two of us sang the four vocal parts."[18]

As one of the few tracks with joint songwriting credits to Brian and Carl, it was, according to Carl, slated to be on the next album, which turned out to be *15 Big Ones,* but it was left off, causing Dennis to lament and praise the song as "another "Surfer Girl."[19]

Often cited as the album's standout track, "Good Timin" peaked at #40 on the Billboard Hot 100, their first to reach that position since "It's OK" three years before. It also made an impressive #12 on the Adult Contemporary chart. In its review of the song, *Record World* described it as "a vintage Beach Boys ballad complete with rich layers of their trademark falsetto harmonies soaring behind Carl's warm vocals."[20] Rick Swan lamented on its short length, writing: "It vanishes just as we're reminded that this was the best vocal group on the planet…[and] stands as a startling reminder of the first class songwriting, performance, and production the Beach Boys drew on routinely in the sixties, then let slip away"[21].

96. Deirdre *(Sunflower* 1970)
(Bruce Johnston, Brian Wilson)
Recording
21/03/69 Gold Star Studio, LA (tracking & vocals - take #20 master)
18/08/69 Capitol Studio, Hollywood (reduction mix)
09/01/70 Beach Boys Studio, Bel Air (horns overdub)
Producer - Bruce Johnston
Engineer - Steve Desper
Band members
Bruce Johnston (lead vocals, opening multi-tracked harmonies, backing vocals); Brian Wilson (backing vocals); Carl Wilson (harmony & backing vocals); Mike Love (harmony & backing vocals); Al Jardine (harmony & backing vocals)
Session musicians/Guests
Ed Carter (guitar); Al Casey (guitar); Joe Osborn (electric bass); Jimmy Bond (double bass); Larry Knechtel (piano); John Guerin (drums); Frank Capp (tambourine); Michael Colombier (string arrangement);unknown (flutes, trumpet, French horns, trombones); Daryl Dragon (vibraphone)
Album released - 31/08/70
US single released -24/05/71 b-side to "Long Promised Road" Brother/Reprise 1015

UK single released - 18/06/71 b-side to "Long Promised Road" Stateside SS 2190
US single re-released - 11/10/71 b/w "Till I Die" Brother/Reprise 1047 #89

Along with the highly emotive "Tears in the Morning," "Deirdre" is one of two contributions Bruce Johnston made to the wonderful 1971 album *Sunflower*, both perfect examples of his penchant for middle of the road ballads and top-notch production skills. So who was this red-haired goddess? According to Bruce, the song is named after the sister of one of his ex-girlfriends, although Brian had a little part to play in the lyrics: "I tried to get Brian to do the lyrics. I gave him 50 per cent of the song and he wound up writing four lines. I said to myself, 'Most of this song is me, but what the hell, we'll just split it.'" In another interview, he recalled: "I gave [Brian] 50% of the song; it should have been 5%. He came up with two lines, that was it. When the money arrived, I said, that's all I get? He was suggesting lines like, *'My friend Bob/he has a job,'* and I was saying, 'No, Brian.' I was kinda disappointed, but maybe I sang flat once, and he was disappointed with me, who knows?"[22]

But there may be more to it than that, with some noted commentators suggesting that the song was actually "developed" from a musical theme Brian wrote for "We're Together Again," a leftover track from the initial *20/20* album sessions in 1968 (in my opinion, after listening to that track on the cd reissue, any similarities are hard to find).

Bruce Arthur Johnston was born Benjamin Baldwin in Peoria, Illinois on June 27th 1942. Growing up in LA with his adopted parents, he learned to play classical piano and in 1959 played on the instrumental single "Teen Beat," a Hot 100 #4 and UK #9 for Sandy Nelson. After producing a number of surfing songs for various artists, he joined up with Terry Melcher as part of the Rip Chords and together co-produced the million-selling car song "Hey Little Cobra" in 1963. On April 9th 1965 he officially joined the Beach Boys as both bass player and as a replacement for Glen Campbell, who had filled in for Brian while the band toured. For the next seven years he became a vital cog in the Beach Boys' machine, probably best remembered for being their voluntary spokesman and for his nostalgic song "Disney Girls (1957)" on the *Surf's Up* album. After certain disagreements, he quit the band in 1972, only to rejoin at Brian's request in late 1978. The year before, he had released his third solo album *Going Public*, which not only contained re-recordings of "Deirdre" and "Disney Girls", but also his "I Write the Songs," which had been a chart-topper for Barry Manilow in 1975 (long believed to be a Manilow composition). He later dispelled the rumour that he had written the song about Brian Wilson.

"The song floats by the listener like a Rogers & Hammerstein piece, crossed with the sunny air of the Beach Boys harmonies"

Reviewing the song, *Rolling Stone* noted how it "could be a Beach Boy-influenced anybody,"[23] while *AllMusic's* Matthew Greenwald compared it to the musicals of the 30's and 40's: "The song floats by the listener like a Rogers & Hammerstein piece, crossed with the sunny air of the Beach Boys harmonies, creating a fine synthesis."24 The instrumental track was later included on the 2021 *Feel Flows* box set.

In a later interview, Bruce declared his admiration for *Sunflower*, describing it at the time as the band's last "true" Beach Boys' album that featured Brian's active involvement and input. At the same time, however, he regretted having his two songs put on the album, stating that on refection he should have recorded "Deirdre" himself and that "Tears in the Morning" was just "too pop" for the album's theme.

95. Our Prayer (*20/20* 1969)
(Brian Wilson)
Recording - Smile version
19/09/66 CBS Columbia Studio, LA (initial dialogue)
04/10/66 Gold Star Studio, LA (vocals, mixing)
Recording - 20/20 version
17/11/68 Capitol Studio, Hollywood (additional vocals)
Producer - The Beach Boys
Engineer - Ralph Valentin? (*Columbia*); Larry Lavine? (*Gold Star*)
Band members
The Beach Boys (vocals)
Album released -10/02/69

The finest example of how the Beach Boys use just their voices to create something that is both magical and spiritual. Originally titled "Prayer" and pencilled in as the opening track to the abandoned *Smile* album, it was later resurrected as "Our Prayer" for the 1969 album *20/20,* with some vocal additions and double-tracking by Carl, Dennis and Bruce. It wasn't the first a capella song Brian had written, but it was most definitely different from anything that had gone before. Previous voice-only offerings included the dismal, "The Lord's Prayer" (*Christmas Album*), and "A Young Man is Gone" (*Little Deuce Coupe*), a reworking of Bobby Troup's "Their Hearts Were Full of Spring," which in itself became a concert favourite; but these were just sweet and simple imitations of Four Freshmen-style harmonising. With "Our Prayer" we have a sonic tapestry of voices, one which musicologist Philip Lambert describes as "every technique of chromatic harmony [Brian] had ever heard or imagined."9

An exquisite, spiritual, and graceful gift to the world from the troubled genius that is Brian Wilson

Brian recalled how the band were blown away with the arrangement: "I was sitting at my piano thinkin' about holy music. I poked around for some simple but moving chords. Later I sat down and wrote 'Our Prayer' in sections…I was definitely into rock church music."26. The song also became the only *Smile* track to have a defined placement on the proposed album.

For the long-anticipated 2004 release of *Brian Wilson Presents Smile*, "Our Prayer" was medlied with a brief, idiosyncratic adaptation of"Gee," a 1953 one-hit wonder by The Crows. Many biographers, included the esteemed David Leaf, were quick to compare the song to a Gregorian chant sung in some medieval castle.

Although originally intended for *Smile*, *Mojo* suggested: "It made perfect sense: like the saying of grace before the "Teenage Symphony to God"…there's a whiff of a Bach chorale, but emanating the warmth of the California sun rather than the interior cool of a Baroque *kirche.*"25

What their five voices create is something that should be studied in music class, not just as a blueprint for vocal harmonies, but as an exquisite, spiritual, and graceful gift to the world from the troubled genius that is Brian Wilson.

94. Surfin' Safari *(Surfin' Safari 1962)*
(Brian Wilson, Mike Love)
Recording
08/02/62 World Pacific Studio, LA (initial demo)
08/03/62 Stereo Masters, Hollywood (possible stereo overdub)
19/04/62 Western Recorders, LA (re-recording)
04/62 World Pacific Studio LA (spliced a Feb 8th take onto a demo reel)
Producer - Murry Wilson (on paper) more likely Brian
Engineers -Steve Hoffman (*World*), Chuck Britz (*Western*)
Band members/guest
08/02 - Brian Wilson (Fender bass), Dennis Wilson (drums), Al Jardine (possibly rhythm guitar),
19/04 - Mike Love (lead & backing vocals); Brian Wilson (backing vocals, bass guitar); Carl Wilson (backing vocals, lead guitar); Dennis Wilson (backing vocals, drums); David Marks (backing vocals, rhythm guitar), Val Poliuto (possibly piano)
Album released - 01/10/62
US single released - 04/06/62 b/w "409" Capitol 4777 #14
UK single released - 10/62 b/w "409" Capitol CL 15273
Film/TV performance
28/07/62 *One Man's Challenge* documentary, Azura Teen Club, Azura Ca.

The story of the Beach Boys' first single for Capitol and their first Top 30 hit on the Billboard Hot 100 is another one clouded with inconsistences and conflicting recollections over the passage of time. What is certain is that with the local success of the first record "Surfin," Murry Wilson knew his eldest son was on to something, and that conviction spurred him on to make it a reality. Taking out a small mortgage, he agreed to pay for studio time so the boys could cut demo tapes of new songs to be offered to record labels. When Candix, the label behind their debut single, fell into bankruptcy, Murry took advantage of a loophole in the contract and prepared to look for a better deal.

In the meantime Brian had collaborated with Gary Usher and had written two more songs, "409" and "Lonely Sea." But he had also got together with Mike to write "Surfin' Safari," which had all the makings of a follow-up single if a new label could be found. David Marks recalled: "When Brian sat down at the piano and played 'Surfin Safari,' and said this is our next hit, I got chills. Got goosebumps, man. We jumped around and pounded him on the back, "God, you're a genius, man!"11

> *"He was beautiful - all American kid who knew what he wanted, and was pretty sure of himself…"*

Inspired by Chuck Berry's style of combining in a song simple chord progressions with lyrical references to actual place names, Brian recalled it as being "a silly song with a simple-but-cool C-F-G chord pattern that I came up with one day while trying to play the piano the way Chuck Berry played his guitar."28. Among the Southern California names mentioned are Malibu, Rincon, Huntington, Laguna, Doheny and Sunset Beach, and many of the surf-related locations and terms were provided by surfer Jimmy Bowles, brother of Brian's then-girlfriend Judy.

Hite Morgan booked a session for the band at World Pacific Studio, and, on February 8th, Murry, accompanied by the Morgans, took Brian, Dennis and Al down to cut some potential follow-ups to "Surfin." The tracks recorded were "Surfin' Safari;" Brian and Mike's "Surfer Girl;" Brian and Usher's "409" and "Lonely Sea;" Brian's "Judy," and the instrumental "Beach Boys Stomp" (aka "Karate").

Apparently, Murry had little confidence in Dennis's drumming and Brian brought along Gene Krupa, who had been seen playing in a local club. As a result, Dennis stormed out and only returned when they found out that Krupa was unsuitable. There was also keyboardist Val Poliuto of the vocal group the Jaguars, who Hite had brought along and was well known to Brian. The only difference to this recording of "Surfin' Safari" to the single version is that David Marks plays guitar on the single (Al having decided to quit the band shortly after signing with Capitol).

According to audio engineer Steve Hoffman: "[The session] was recorded in an under-dub with just the rhythm guitar and an overdub which basically fed the first music back through the console while Carl added an overdubbed electric guitar."3. Despite Murry's usual interference during the sessions, Brian did accede to his suggestion of speeding up "Surfin' Safari" one whole tone so as to "put the song in a younger-sounding key."29. This would also be the first song to feature their distinctive counterpoint harmonies.

Usher, dubbed the motivating force behind the band's early success, recalled: "I kept telling Brian that you can't just sit around and wait for a company to come to you. I constantly urged, 'We should go in and cut some masters ourselves right away'. I was pushing him all the time to rehearse and cut more material"3.

On his recommendation the band went down to Western Recorders on April 16th and met up with the talented sound engineer Charles "Chuck" Britz (1927-2000), who not only struck up an immediate rapport with Brian, but would become the driving force in their recordings for years to come. During the session, their first at Western, they recorded a handful of Usher's own songs and four Usher/Wilson originals, most notably "Beginning of the End."

Three days later they were all back in the studio, along with Murry and Audree Wilson, to record "Surfin' Safari," "409," "Lonely Sea," and a re-recording of Brian's "Judy." David Marks recalled later that at Western there was a "little...soundstage that was used for radio shows. There was a little studio [13 x 34ft] at the back, Studio 3, where we did all our stuff. Western told us it was like it was, real funky sounding. The sound and the success of the group came out of that dinky little studio."11

Britz remembered the session: "Murry, Audree and myself were in Studio Three's control room. The booth had been built, but the studio wasn't completed yet. So they were in a big studio across the hall, and I talked to them on the intercom. As far as producing, indirectly Brian was producing everything even at that early stage. As far as I'm concerned, the total commitment of producing was from him. He was beautiful - all American kid who knew what he wanted, and was pretty sure of himself…"3. Brian also had a more vivid recollection, that of his dad standing next to Britz and yelling, "Give it more punch! Come on boys, give it more punch!"

David Marks recalled: "Brian would [make] all the settings on the control board and go out into the studio, and Murray would change everything. Then Brian would come back in and go, 'What the f**k happened? It sounds different!' They were fighting all the time. I guess Murry has trying to live through his sons. It was finally agreed that Murry wouldn't try to produce any more."11

Mike credits the distinctive "treblelly" guitar sound on the track to Murry. When Brian would leave the control room to record his bass parts, Murry would switch the sounds on the guitar to the treble he preferred, and Mike felt that the guitar sound really cut through and helped sell the record.

According to noted Beach Boy historian James B Murphy, the two April session dates have been recently challenged, with no official documentation to support it, and goes on to suggest the sessions took place earlier in the month.3

With the recordings done Murry took the tapes to several record labels without success. He then got in touch with his old business friend Ken Nelson, who was employed at Capitol Records as country music's A&R man. Through Nelson, Murry was able to get in touch with 22-year-old junior A&R guy Nick Venet (1936-1998) and arrange an interview and audition. With Venet out of town, Murry sent a box crammed with tapes of what must have been over a dozen songs, perhaps the band's entire recordings at the time, including their a capella version of Bobby Troup's "Their Hearts Were Full of Spring", which apparently he had spliced onto the February 8th demos without the boys' knowledge.

Murry, Brian and Usher met Venet at the Capitol Tower office on or about May 7th 1962. It was reported that Venet, on first listening to "Surfin' Safari," decided there and then he was hearing a number one single. Although other accounts have him sleeping on it for several days, Venet later recalled: "Before eight bars had spun around, I knew it was a hit record. I wasn't one to hide my feelings. I got all excited, and of course [Murry] got all excited, because he wasn't one to hide his feelings either. I knew the song was going to change West Coast music". An initial offer of $100 was tabled for the masters of "Surfin' Safari," "409," and "Lonely Sea," but, with Venet's help, Murry eventually struck a deal with the company heads for an impressive $300 per song master, plus 2.5% royalties, with proceeds split between Murry, Brian and Usher.

On May 24th Murry signed an interim contract with Capitol. Conflicting accounts followed over disagreements whether "Surfin' Safari" or "409" should be the lead single, with Venet allegedly favouring "409." Murry had insisted right from the start that it should be the surfing song, and that the company had put everything behind the hot-rod song. Venet hit back later, claiming: "If it was '409' I was interested in, why did I have the group take pictures at the ocean with a surfboard?" He had a point, and, as yet, no one has found a copy that has "409" on the A-side. Incidentally, the single had the band's name as just *Beach Boys*, maybe intentionally, but was soon corrected for the album and future singles.

With a touch of irony it turned out that sales of "Surfin' Safari" first took off in New York and the Mid-West, rather than on the West Coast. Venet reported: "We were getting reports from spots like Phoenix, Arizona, where you couldn't go surfing if you tried". In the July issue of *Billboard* magazine, Detroit was cited as the major market for the single's national "break-out." "Surfin' Safari" went on to sell some 900,000 copies, just short of having gold status. In its review, *Billboard* wrote: "The beach scene gets a rolling, rocking treatment on this side by the boys. Tune swings along neatly on lead singer's talent and support of the rest of the group."[27]

According to some reports Murry had kept it from the Morgans that the band were recording new material (which included the two re-recordings of Morgan-copyrighted songs), despite him having recently signed an exclusive contract with the couple. Once disclosed, the Morgans sued Capitol for using the songs they owned, resulting in a cash settlement of $80,000.

Just a matter of days after the single's release Capitol were inundated with calls about the band. Venet recalled: "...agents called and asked me for an introduction to the Beach Boys in order to represent them. I also received calls from producers who wanted to put the Beach Boys in movies."[11]

On July 16th 1962 the Beach Boys signed the contract with Capitol. It covered an initial period of one year, while also granting the company six additional consecutive option periods of one year each. In each successive year the band were obliged to produce a minimum number of masters, beginning at six and rising to twelve for the final three years. Royalties were set at 5%. For their part, Capitol agreed to release at least one single each period, and, if failing to do so, the band had the option to terminate the contract. For all his faults, Murry Wilson had pulled it off for the boys.

The die was cast. The Beach Boys, still with 13-year-old David Marks on board, were now on the threshold of what would be one of the most famous and successful careers in popular music.

Meanwhile, over in England, and perhaps unknown to anyone outside of the country, four young mop-tops from Liverpool had just released their first record, *Love Me Do*.

93. I Went to Sleep *(20/20* 1969)
(Brian Wilson, Carl Wilson)
Recording
04/06/68 Beach Boys Studio Bel Air (tracking - take #6 master)
c05/06/68 Beach Boys Studio Bel Air (vocals)
Producer - Brian Wilson
Engineer - Stephen Desper?
Band member inc.
Brian & Carl Wilson (lead vocals)
Album released - 10/02/69

The late 60's was a pivotal time for the Beach Boys. Brian's involvement in recordings had declined due to his latest bout of mental illness requiring hospital treatment, and to many in the business it appeared that the band's career could be on the wane, especially in the US, where two of the last three singles had failed to get into the top 60 of the Hot 100 (even the great nostalgia trip that was "Do It Again" just scraped into the top 20). Their three previous albums had also fared poorly, especially the last one, *Friends*, which had peaked at an unbelievable #126. Even though looked on by some as the "healing album" for the ailing band and one which Brian would later go on record to say it was his second favourite album after *Pet Sounds*, its odd mixture of music and mantras just didn't connect with the buying public. It even led to dwindling concert audiences and the cancellation of the so-called "Maharishi tour" after just a handful of dates. However, over in Europe, especially in the UK, things were quite different and their popularity and record sales were as strong as ever. Brian had even suggested they change their name to just Beach, claiming they were not boys anymore.

> ***A gently-rolling waltz full of divine chords and impeccable harmonising from the two brothers ...***
> ***Blissful in its gorgeous serenity***

Their current contract with Capitol was also about to expire and the next album would be their last before moving on to a new chapter with Warner Brothers (although Capitol would retain ownership of all previous albums up to and including *Party!*).

The new album was called *20/20*, apparently due to it becoming their 20th overall release (including live and compilation albums). With Brian's state of mind making him reluctant to engage with the recordings, it was left to Carl, Dennis and Bruce to step up to the plate and produce the new album. As a result it would be almost devoid of any input from Brian. Instead, it included recent singles, leftovers from previous albums, several covers, the infamous Charles Manson song, and, perhaps, its saving grace with a brace of gorgeous *Smile* tracks. According to Bruce, it was "a very un-Brian album, the first album where all the members got to do what they really wanted to do." Dennis wasn't impressed, calling it in a radio interview, "the only let down of the Beach Boys' career that embarrassed me through and through...It was the first album the group made that was completely disjointed."[234]

Despite that the album has since been re-evaluated. Richie Unterberger referred to it as "one of their better post-*Pet Sounds* records...The highlights, however, were a couple of *Smile*-session-era tunes...as hard as they were trying to establish their identity as an integrated band in the late 60's, their new recordings were overshadowed by the bits and pieces of *Smile* that emerged at the time."[256] Peter Carlin suggested that "whatever the album lacked in thematic coherence, it made up in the quality of the pieces contributed by each band member,"[32] and fellow biographer David Leaf called it, "one of the most artistically interesting releases of their career and certainly one of their stronger later LPs."[26] One musicologist called it "a resting place for sundry odds and ends."

"I Went to Sleep" was a song that had orginally been written for *Friends* but then rejected, apparently in favour of the dire "Transcendental Meditation" and "Anna Lee the Healer." It was resurrected for *20/20* probably because the band (and for that matter, more importantly, Capitol too) needed to have Brian songs on the new album, and there was just so little out there to choose from. But what an inspired decision it was. Written by Brian and Carl, it was another of Brian's "lifestyle" observations, a gently-rolling waltz full of divine chords and impeccable harmonising from the two brothers. Blissful in its gorgeous serenity.

92. Do You Wanna Dance? (*The Beach Boys Today!* 1965)
(Bobby Freeman)
Recording
11/01/65 Gold Star Studio, LA (tracking, backing vocals, lead vocal- take #3 master)
Producer - Brian Wilson
Engineer - Chuck Britz
Band members
Dennis Wilson (lead vocals); Brian Wilson (harmony & backing vocals, acoustic grand piano); Mike Love (harmony & backing vocals); Carl Wilson (harmony & backing vocals, electric lead & rhythm guitar); Al Jardine (harmony & backing vocals)
Session musicians/Guests
Hal Blaine (drums, wood blocks, claves); Steve Douglas (tenor sax); Plas Johnson (tenor sax); Larry Knechtel (bass guitar); Jay Migliori (baritone sax); Bill Pitman (acoustic & electric rhythm guitar Russell Bridges (Leon Russell) (Hammond B-3 organ); Billy Strange (electric mandolin); Tommy Tedesco (baritone guitar, mandolin); Julius Wechter (tambourine, timpani); Marilyn Wilson (harmony & backing vocals).
Album released - 08/03/65
US single released - 15/02/65 b/w "Please Let Me Wonder" Capitol 5372 #12
Film/TV performance
21/04/65 *Shindig!* ABC

This much-covered invitation to dance was written and first recorded as "Do You Want To Dance" by 17-year-old soul singer Bobby Freeman, a #5 Hot 100 hit in 1959. Cliff Richard then scored a UK #2 with the same title as the flip-side to "I'm Looking Out the Window," and four years later the Mamas and the Papas included it on their debut album, *If You Can Believe Your Eyes and Ears,* with the more familiar title, "Do You Wanna Dance?"

This superior version is one of two covers on the band's stellar album, *Today*! (the other being "I'm So Young.") Not just superior, but for many - definitive. Beginning with Dennis's slightly subdued double-tracked vocal on the first verse, the chorus explodes with multiple pianos, saxophones and timpani that wash over the listener like a tsunami, leading to a second verse where we have the boys showcasing their exquisite backing vocals. After a short bridge of jangling guitars, there's a break in the final chorus before the song fades out with a crescendo of voices, with Brian's breathtaking falsetto taking it into the stratosphere.

> *"The song fades out with a crescendo of voices, with Brian's breathtaking falsetto taking it into the stratosphere"*

Rick Swan wrote: "The chorus is a mini-symphony in itself, with timpani and pianos and saxes flying every which way, sweeping up the listeners and flinging them around the room."21

Cash Box reviewed the single, predicting that they "seem sure to skyrocket up the charts once again…the crew treats the rhythmic romantic oldie in an infectious neo-surfin' style complete with rapidly-changing, danceable riffs."30 Session examiners reveal that the lead and backing vocals were recorded simultaneously, a remarkable feat in itself. Although recorded in mono, a stereo mix of the song can be found on the 2012 stereo remaster of *Today!*

Musicologist Philp Lambert wrote: "While Brian hoped to retain and recapture the spirit of the original version of 'Do You Wanna Dance,' he also viewed the model as a springboard for invention, a set of ideas upon which he could exercise his own creative impulses. It highlights the difference between ' a song covered by the Beach Boys' and an existing song transformed into a 'Beach Boys song.'"9

Rocksucker described how "its chorus drenched in a gleaming mirror ball of harmonies…go a long way towards making the song their own."301

The band performed this song live on *Shindig* on April 21st 1965 with Brian in the line-up, despite having been replaced by Glen Campbell while on tour.

91. Lady Lynda (*L.A (Light Album)* 1979)
(Al Jardine, Ron Altbach, Johann Sebastian Bach)
Recording
19/09/78 Western Recorders, LA (re-make?)
11/10/78 Western Recorders, LA
16/10/78 Western Recorders, LA
18/10/78 Sounds Good Studio, LA
27/11/78 Britannia Studios, Santa Monica
18/12/78 Britannia Studios, Santa Monica
27/12/78 Super Sound, Monterey
Producer - Al Jardine
Engineers - Chuck Britz (*Western*), Armin Steiner (*Sounds*)
Band members
Al Jardine (lead & backing vocals, 12-string guitar); Brian Wilson (possible backing vocals); Carl Wilson (backing vocals); Mike Love (backing vocals); Bruce Johnston (backing vocals, possibly Fender Rhodes); Dennis Wilson (co-arranger)
Session musicians
Jimmy Bond (double bass); Verlye Mills Brilhart (harp); Ed Carter (guitar, bass guitar); Jim Decker (French horn); Bobby Figueroa (drums, tambourine, tubular bells); Dick Hyde (trombones & bass trombone); Charles Loper (French horn); Arthur Maebe (French horn); Jay Migliori (flutes); Ray Pizzi (bassoons); Jack Redmond (French horn); William Reichenbach (French horn); Lyle Ritz (double bass); Bobby Shew (trumpets); Sterling Smith (harpsichord, possible Fender Rhodes); Harry Betts (string arrangement), 12 violins; 4 violas, 4 cellos
Album released - 16/03/79
US single released - *06/79* b/w "Full Sail" Caribou ZS9 9030 #100
UK single released - *01/06/79*b/w "Full Sail" Caribou S CRB 7427 #6
Film/TV performances
15/09/79 *American Bandstand* ABC
21/06/80 Knebworth, England concert (later released on CD/DVD)
04/07/86 *Farm Aid II Concert*, Manor TX(as "Lady Liberty") VH-1

One of the few shining lights in the dimness of an album that was referred to by *Rolling Stone* as "worse than awful. It is irrelevant."31 It was a time when the band seemed to have reached an all-time low. In the wake of their disappointing *M.I.U* album, largely ignored by the label, there was internal squabbling within the band, especially between Carl and Dennis on one side, and Mike and Al on the other, no doubt fuelled by excessive drug and alcohol dependence by some of the members, and marital problems for both Carl and Dennis. Brian, suffering from mental illness and substance abuse, was admitted to Brotzman Memorial Hospital after attacking a doctor, and remained there from November 1978 to March 1979.

There was also added pressure from CBS, with whom they had signed an $8 million deal in March 1977, and were now expecting them to deliver the new album before January 1st 1978. Initial recordings for the album had begun at Miami's Criteria Studios with all members present, but it was soon apparent that Brian was in no state of mind to produce, and that other members had no desire to step up in his place. At Brian's suggestion they called in Bruce Johnston, who had left the group in 1972, persuaded him to re-join the band and help with the production, although the results would be disappointing to say the least. Brian, as feared, contributed little, as Peter Carlin recalled: "If Brian sang a note anywhere on the album, his voice is so far down in the mix as to be completely un-identifiable."32

"We always seemed to be five people making five different albums on the same album"

The album was to all intent and purposes a collection of almost-all individual solo performances, apart from the shocking 10-minute-plus disco disaster that was Brian and Mike's "Here Comes the Night."

But it was Al's "Lady Lynda" that turned out to be the most successful track in terms of chart success, especially thanks to their most loyal fans in the UK. This glowing tribute to Lynda Sperry, his wife of 14 years and mother of two children, was co-written with his close friend Ron Altbach (1946-2023), a songwriter and keyboard player who had co-produced the *M.I.U* album. For the spine of the instrumental track Al used Altbach's arrangement of Johann Sebastian Bach's Cantata 147 (a melody he himself had borrowed from German composer Johann Schop in 1716), which was then turned into the famous and more familiar hymn, "Jesu, Joy of Man's Desiring."

Speaking to *Goldmine*, Al recalled: "[Ron] and I decided to write something together. I was familiar with his love of classical music. I was at the Johann Sebastian Bach festival up here in Carmel which happens every summer up here. I heard this beautiful piece sung at the Mission Cathedral here in Carmel. Gorgeous piece…It was written for the church. When I heard the movement I went, "My God, that's too heavy! Maybe I can start the song with this thing…Ron is such a great player that it just worked. We had to hire a classical guy [Sterling Smith] to play an absolutely beautiful harpsichord that was brought in just for the occasion. It was a monster session with a 26-string orchestra…Harry Betts arranged the strings. I can't remember if Dennis played the drums. Dennis helped me with the track. We played it live a couple of places before we recorded it…I did that 12-string guitar…It would have worked better if it had been on my own album, but it certainly worked. We always seemed to be five people making five different albums on the same album."33

Although the US single, an edited version without the harpsichord intro, just managed to scrape into the Hot 100, the full version became the band's highest chart entry in the UK since "Cottonfields" in 1970.

Ironically, Al and Lynda's marriage only lasted another two years, with them divorcing in 1982. As a result the song was performed in subsequent concerts as "Little Lady." Four years later, as part of the "America's Band" rebranding campaign, and to honour the reopening of the Statue of Liberty on July 5th, the band re-recorded the song, with revised lyrics, as "Lady Liberty," releasing it as the flip-side to their "California Dreamin'" single.

Al and the band were given the honour of performing it on the statue's pedestal as part of the Liberty Weekend celebrations.

Musicologist Rick Swan, in his usual tongue-in-cheek manner, wrote: "Essentially a solo performance, it's good in a Barry Manilow sort of way - comforting to Manilow fans - until we get to the violins, which nudge it from Manilow to Mantovani."21

90. With Me Tonight (*Smiley Smile* 1967)
(Brian Wilson)
Recording - Smile
05/06/67 Western Recorders, LA (part of the "Vegetable" suite)
06/06/67 Western Recorders, LA
07/06/67 Western Recorders, LA
Recording - Smiley Smile
30/06/67 Beach Boys Studio, Bel Air (completed song)
Producer - Brian Wilson
Engineer - Chuck Britz
Band members
Brian Wilson (lead & backing vocals, electric harpsichord, finger snaps, handclaps); Mike Love (backing vocals); Carl Wilson (lead & backing vocals, bass guitar); Dennis Wilson (backing vocals); Al Jardine (lead & backing vocals)
Session musician
Chuck Berghofer (double bass)
Album released - 18/09/67

A song that had its genesis as a snippet of a tune recorded during the *Smile* sessions and originally titled "You're With Me Tonight," a near-three minute vocal chant with a stunning bass-driven intro, reputed to be a segment of the proposed multi-part "Vegetables" suite, which eventually became a stand-alone song. Brian later expanded it for inclusion on *Smiley Smile,* dropping the "You're" on the way. The result was a gentle piece of psychedelia, reminiscent of the band's earlier R&B influences, and consisting of an unusual arrangement where the title words are sung repeatedly in a revolving chorus. Showcasing Brian and Carl's amazing vocal harmonies, the song was described by one writer as "do it yourself acid casualty doo-wop music." Musicologist Brad Elliott wrote that the short *Smile* track "Barnyard," with its "hum-hum de doobie doo," has similarities with both "With Me Tonight" and "Heroes and Villains." 34

Apparently, during the *Smile* sessions for the song Brian brought to the studio a load off hashish as a "communal source of inspiration" for the band. Its effect can plainly be heard with the giggling as they try and sing "On and on she go dum-be-doo-dah," with Brian insisting that they all "sing with a smile...you wait and see what happens, I swear to God!"

"A gentle piece of psychedelia"

AllMusic's Matthew Greenwald described the song as "one of the better (or, more accurately defined) songs on the *Smiley Smile* album...the melody envelopes the listener in a graceful way, and in this sense, makes it quite different from many of the other songs on the album."24 Sharp ears will notice that around 0.26 seconds of the *Smiley Smile* version, you can hear someone say "good." This was the voice of Arnie Geller, Brian's friend and assistant in the studio. Maybe just for a laugh, he decided to leave it in the final take.

The early sessions for "Vegetables", which included just the original vocal chant, were later included on the 2001 anthology *Hawthorne, Ca,* while another longer version appeared on *The Smile Sessions* in 2011.

89. Don't Hurt My Little Sister (*The Beach Boys Today!*1965)
(Brian Wilson, Mike Love)
Recording
22/06/64 Western Recorders, LA (tracking - take #18 master; vocal overdubs)
18/01/65 Western Recorders, LA (vocals)
Producer - Brian Wilson
Engineer - Chuck Britz
Band members
Mike Love (lead & backing vocals); Brian Wilson (lead & backing vocals, upright piano); Carl Wilson (12-string lead/rhythm guitar, backing vocals); Dennis Wilson (tambourine, backing vocals); Al Jardine (electric Fender bass guitar, backing vocals)
Session musicians
Hal Blaine (drums); John Gray (grand piano); Ray Pohlman (baritone guitar, 6-string bass guitar); Tommy Tedesco (rhythm guitar).
Album released - 08/03/65

Two days after his 22nd birthday, Brian took time out from the sessions for the *Christmas Album* to record a new song he had written in the early spring called, "Little Sister," with the naïve intention of offering it to producer Phil Spector "for him to produce and Darleen Love to sing." At a nerve-jangled meeting in a Hollywood hotel room, Brian gave his hero a demo of the song, but was told bluntly that he didn't play it right. He was then invited to attend a session at Gold Star, Spector's favoured recording studio, where the producer "tinkered" with the backing track. Brian later recalled that session keyboardist Leon Russell was too drunk to play, and was asked by Spector to take his place. However, having to play under his rigid scrutiny, nerves got the better of him and he failed to impress his master, who described his playing as substandard. According to Brian, this episode took place the previous year during Spector's session for what would be the Crystals' "Santa Claus is Coming To Town."

In 1966, perhaps to rub salt in the wound, Spector would completely transform Brian's song, re-name it "Things Are Changing (For the Better)," and use it as a throwaway Public Service Announcement about equal-opportunity employment which was played on radio stations and sung by Darleen Love and the Blossoms. Other reports indicate that Brian was again present in the studio when Spector produced "Little Sister," with Darleen's voice overdubbed, although it was never released. Brian took it to heart. There would be no more attempts at achieving a professional link with Phil Spector.

Despite the setback, Brian knew the semi-autobiographical song was just too good to discard and renamed it "Don't Hurt My Little Sister." It was based on his relationship with 16-year-old girlfriend Marilyn Rovell (who he would marry six months later) and her two younger sisters Diane (aged 17) and Barbara (13). In his since-discredited 1991 biography *Wouldn't It Be Nice*, Brian recalls that her parents "assumed I liked Diane best, since she and I still spent the most time together talking. Deep down I still harboured feelings for cute little Barbara, though I continually reminded myself she was too young."28 In the more recent and reliable memoir, *I Am Brian Wilson,* he recalls "I wrote it from the perspective of one of them telling me not to treat another one of them badly."35

> ***"It was made up but based on the protective feeling that a brother would have. It was a fun song, a neat song…"***

Former collaborator Gary Usher gave a different view: "When Brian moved out of his apartment and began living at the Rovell's house, he fell madly in love with Barbara, Marilyn's and Diane's younger sister. I was over there many times, and I could see this scene happening and Brian becoming so frustrated because there was nothing he could do about it." Mike Love, whose successful lawsuit later won him co-writing credits for this and a number of Brian's compositions, remembered: "The Wilson brothers didn't have a sister, so that idea had to come from somebody else…I had three. It was made up but based on the protective feeling that a brother would have. It was a fun song, a neat song…"36

Scott Interrante saw the song as "an important reminder of Brian's musical debt to Phil Spector. As he continues to expand his own 'wall of sound' in more interesting and creative ways, the presence of a song written specifically for Spector shows not only his mastery of Spector's technique, but also the ways in which he is able to exceed his idol."37 Jonny Abrams of *Rocksucker* opined: [The] titular refrain-repeating chorus weaves in and out of keys in ways that may barely have seemed possible within the confines of rock and roll at the time…in ways that a thousand modern-day indie bands with a thousand guitars and pianos would be hard-pushed to come up with in even a thousand years."301

Most likely composed with innocent intentions, Brian had nevertheless produced a sophisticated and emotionally layered song, with its remarkable descending chorus pattern one of the key moments in his development, a refrain that would be echoed later in "California Girls." The song was also recorded by the Surfaris as the flip-side to their single "Catch a Little Ride With Me" in August 1965.

Like so many other songs on the album, "Don't Hurt My Little Sister" was responsible for placing Brian and the band on a different level, and another stepping stone on the way to even greater success.

88. California Saga/California (*Holland* 1973)
(Alan Jardine)
Recording
06/72 - 08/72 Baambrugge Centraal 2 Studio, Baambrugge, Utrecht
14/08/72 Baambrugge Centraal 2 Studio, Baambrugge, Utrecht
15/08/72 Baambrugge Centraal 2 Studio, Baambrugge, Utrecht (inc. Brian's intro)
09/72 - 10/72 Village Recorders L.A (inc horn overdubs & backing vocals)
19/09/72 Village Recorders, LA (possible overdub session)
Recording - "California Saga/ On My Way to Sunny Californ-i-a"
06/03/73 Village Recorders L.A (single mix, additional vocals)
08/03/73 Brother Studio, Santa Monica (remixing)
Producer - The Beach Boys (Carl & Al for the re-recording)
Engineers - Stephen Moffitt (Holland), Rob Fraboni (Village)
Band members
Mike Love (lead & backing vocals); Brian Wilson (intro vocal); Carl Wilson (backing vocals, Hammond B-3 organ, Moog synthesiser (bass); Al Jardine (backing vocals, banjos, electric 12-string guitar); Ricky Fataar (drums, pedal steel guitar); Blondie Chaplin (electric guitar with wah-wah pedal); Bruce Johnson (backing vocals)
Session musicians
Charles Lloyd (flute); Frank Mayes (baritone sax, horn arrangement); Unknown (tenor sax, trumpets, diatonic harmonica).
Album released - 08/01/73
UK single released - 03/02/73 b/w "Sail On, Sailor" Reprise K14232 #37
US single released - 05/73 b/w "Funky Pretty" Brother/Reprise 1156 #84 (re-recording)
UK single released - 05/73 b/w "Funky Pretty" (re-recording)
Film/TV Performance
21/07/77 Capital Centre, Washington DC

The Beach Boys' non-appearance as the headline act at the Monterey Festival in 1967, the reasons for which are legion, was a turning point in the band's fortunes, both financially and in terms of their popularity. Added to this was Brian's failure to complete *Smile* and his reduced involvement with the band due to increasing health and anxiety issues. Their next four albums (and last for Capitol) received good reviews but sales were disappointingly modest. Even the glorious *Sunflower* was seen as a financial misfire.

By the end of the decade, the media's focus on West Coast music had firmly shifted from LA to what was happening up in San Francisco. The band had become a victim of its own legacy, with their label, concert audiences, and even a certain band member, clamouring for them to retain their old "formula" of pre-*Pet Sounds* material and reluctant to embrace their current avant-garde type of music, even the much-welcomed input by new band members Ricky and Blondie.

If their popularity was waning in the States, it was a different story in the UK and other European countries, where their fanbase was as buoyant as ever. This was never more evident than when the band toured there toward the end of 1970. Although the UK dates were missing their panache, when they appeared in concert in Amsterdam they received a rapturous response, with the audience welcoming new songs as well as old ones.

> *"That was like the homesick blues for us. It kinda came out of my soul"*

New manager Jack Rieley spearheaded their artistic recovery in the US with a series of well-received concerts in which the band played a mix of old and new material, but the boys were still committed to playing and recording new music. With Brian's input still minimal, and certain band members squabbling, the next eco-themed album, *Surf's Up*, despite some of its gems, fared little better than *Sunflower*. The following album, *Carl and the Passions - So Tough!* was even coupled with *Pet Sounds* to avoid the anticipated poor sales.

Looking back on their recent success in Europe, Rieley had the idea of recording the next album in Holland, and then had the mammoth task of not only flying out there dozens of family members (including Brian), their friends and staff, but also finding suitable accommodation for them and flying out all the equipment necessary to create a studio from scratch outside of Amsterdam. According to Rieley, "I felt that the Beach Boys had to do a record outside of California, to get away from that whole scene, find a new scene, and create in that new scene."[11]

Recordings for the new album, simply called *Holland*, were carried out from June - September 1972, all under the supervision of Carl, his final album in that role. The results and response for what became another dark legend can be found further down this list.

Taking up most of side one is a trio of songs entitled "California Saga", the result of Mike and Al feeling a little homesick for their home state. The first one, subtitled "Big Sur," is Mike's dreadful poem-cum-song about driving along Highway One to find his spiritual home. This is followed by Al's "The Beaks of Eagles, derived from poet Robinson Jeffers' *Jeffers Country*, with additional lyrics by Al and his wife Lynda, certainly a step up from the previous track, but more like an outtake from *Surf's Up*.

Then we come to the final part, "California Saga / California," a beautifully produced ode to the world the Beach Boys had created and, like a tourist guide, a joyous romp through some of the state's most inspiring locations. Al recalled the song was recorded in just one take and the last thing done for the album. He also remembered Brian coming into the studio where the mix-down was being done: "That was like the homesick blues for us. It kinda came out of my soul. But then the uplifting part, Brian brought that home beautifully. I said, 'Brian, can you put your part on this? 'He just walked right in. I don't think he even heard the track more than once, and he started to singing 'On my way to sunny Californ-i-a.' He then left the microphone and walked right out."[11] Bruce, despite having officially left the band several months earlier, recalled: "I had to secretly come down and do vocals. Al told me, 'I've got this track 'California Saga' and I want you to sing on it.' That's a cool track and I sang background on that uncredited."[38]

This song was pencilled in to be the lead single from *Holland*, but when the album was presented to Warner's executives, they flatly rejected the whole thing, feeling there was no hit single. But thanks to Brian's old friend Van Dyke Parks, a solution was found with the inclusion of "Sail on Sailor." Al recalled: "['California'] was supposed to be the single but Warner Brothers didn't hear it. So when we came home [we] recorded 'Sail on Sailor.'"

However, when released in the UK in May 1973, Al's song was chosen as the A-side, maybe, as Mark Dillon surmised, because Al's "Cottonfields" had been their last hit there.[10] That same month, a remixed version of the song with overdubbed new vocals was released with a new title, "California Saga/On My Way To Sunny Californ-i-a." The new version was later included on the woefully inaccurately-titled *Ten Years of Harmony* compilation, but not the US cd version.

Record World wrote that the immaculately produced song "had all the sounds of many of their hits, complete with those legendary harmonies,"39 while in an April 2020 interview, Brian called it, "a great achievement in music" and one to "lift your spirits up."

87. Wonderful (*Smile* version 1967)
(Brian Wilson, Van Dyke Parks)
Recording (Smile)
25/08/66 Western Recorders, LA (version 1 - tracking; harpsichord -18 takes; backing vocals)
06/10/66 CBS Columbia Studio, LA (added instruments, Brian's lead vocal overdubbed, rough mix)
15/12/66 CBS Columbia Studio, LA (vocals inc. Brian's lead)
27/12/66 CBS Columbia Studio, LA (vocals)
09/01/67 Western Recorders, LA (version 2 - vocals, musical sequence insert)
10/04/67 Sound Recorders Studio, LA (version 3 - solo piano, vocals)
Recording (Smiley Smile)
12/07/67 Beach Boys Studio, Bel Air (piano, vocal overdubs on new version)
Producer - Brian Wilson
Engineers - Chuck Britz (Western), Armin Steiner (Sound)
Band members
25/08/66 - Brian Wilson (lead & backing vocals, harpsichord); Mike Love (backing vocals); Carl Wilson (backing vocals); Dennis Wilson (backing vocals); Al Jardine (backing vocals); Bruce Johnston (backing vocals)
09/01/67 - Brian Wilson (backing vocals, harpsichord); Carl Wilson (lead & backing vocals)
Session musicians (25/08/66)
Lary Knechtel (grand piano); Lyle Ritz (upright bass, overdubbed tenor ukelele); Alan Weight (trumpet); Henry David (unknown instrument).
Session musicians (09/01/67)
Hal Blaine (overdubbed drums); Carol Kaye (Danelectro fuzz bass); Ray Pohlman (overdubbed mandolin); Lyle Ritz (overdubbed upright bass)
Album released - 29/07/93

"There was an orchestra playing with a single clarinet singing softy over. The music slowly gave way to a harpsichord with two voices singing the word "won." I thought to myself, "Mike, you're coasting," so I picked up the needle and placed it at the beginning of the song. It sounded like a nursery rhyme through the memory of twenty years. The harpsichord and voice singing like sparrows. It is a song of discovery, like the first flower of spring finding the sun..."7

Just one person's description of what is considered to be one of the outstanding gems of *Smile!* Not only was this stunning collaboration with Van Dyke Parks one of the first songs Brian attempted for the abandoned project, it was also their only love song. Unfortunately, none of the original versions were completed. The title was derived from the pet name Brian used for his wife Marilyn with lyrics that relate to a young girl transforming into a woman and the effect it has on her both her devotion to God and her loving (but confused) parents.

> ***"I always believe that it would be wonderful to write the love song, like the great American novel"***

Parks wrote later: "Musically, it's entirely different from anything else [on *Smile*], and I thought that it was a place, an opportunity, to begin a love song. I remember Brian pressing me about the relationship between the mother and the father and the child. And this is the guy who wrote 'When I Grow Up (To Be a Man)', the guy who is becoming a man. I really think that he was thinking about his own personal progression from childhood. Now I thought, once we had gotten 'Heroes and Villains' done, we might have seen a boy/girl song emerge, other than 'Wonderful.' Honestly, I really thought we would do it, but I never found an opportunity to pursue that with the music I was given." [8]

Although Parks would not initially be given writing credit, it would later be awarded to him after raising with Brian in 2003. In another interview, he confessed: "It wasn't that we were trying to climb an ivory tower or get away from boy-meets-girl, I wanted to meet more chicks; that's why I was working for Brian Wilson. Truly, it couldn't have been something that hadn't occurred to me. I always believe that it would be wonderful to write the love song, like the great American novel, something that doesn't seem to have been written quite yet."[8] Brian gave his own description of the song: "A sweet song all about a girl who just stays in her little world, you know? And then she bumps into a boy, and then she gets her heart broken, then she goes back to her 'Wonderful'[9]. Incidentally, despite some of the tracks being spiritually-themed, this song is the only one that explicitly refers to God, something that music journalist David Zahl was quick to point out: "The Lord gets a mention…mainly as a somewhat creepy device to deal with adolescent sexuality."[10].

The original version of the song, recorded in August 1966, has a harpsichord-led arrangement, but problems with the instrument's keys resulted in it having 18 takes to perfect. Audio of the session reveals Brian shouting at engineer Chuck Britz, "Some of these notes are f*****g up. I swear to God. You push them and they don't go!"

The second version, recorded in January 1967, produced what was dubbed the "Rock with Me Henry version),"one that Keith Badman suggests was considered by Brian to be in the running for the flip-side of the "Heroes and Villains" single.[11] Following the final *Smile!* version in April 1967 (with Paul McCartney in attendance), publicist Derek Taylor reported the imminent release of "Vegetables" as the next single, with "Wonderful" on the flip-side. [11].

The final session for the *Smile!* project took place on May 18th 1967, with work commencing on *Smiley Smile* just over two weeks later. That album's simplified and poorly edited reinterpretation of "Wonderful" was completed in just one three-hour session at Brian's home studio, only saved from complete disaster by Carl's sweet lead vocal. Thanks to the original *Smile!* tapes resurfacing and the inclusion of Brian's original version of "Wonderful" on 1993's *Good Vibrations* box set, we can relish the love and innocence of the jewel-like ballad in all its harpsichord-driven glory.

Darain Sahanaja, co-founder of Brian's later touring band, the Wondermints, perhaps paid the song the greatest compliment: "I remember around 1984 or '85 getting one of the first cassettes with *Smile* bootlegs floating around and hearing this version of 'Wonderful' with Brian playing harpsichord. That pretty much changed my life. It sounded to me like the natural link between *Pet Sounds* and *Heroes and Villains*. So amazing. Even now, when I think of *Smile* I think of that piece."[12]

86. Little Honda (*All Summer Long* 1964)
(Brian Wilson, Mike Love)
Recording
02/04/64 Western Recorders, LA (tracking & vocals)
23/06/64 Western Recorders, LA (vocals for alternative version)
20/10/65 Western Recorders, LA(new backing vocals for tv appearance)
Producer - Brian Wilson
Engineer - Chuck Britz
Band members
Mike Love (lead vocal); Brian Wilson (backing vocals, upright or grand piano, Hammond B-3 organ); Carl Wilson (backing vocals, electric lead guitars, electric rhythm guitars); Dennis Wilson (opening voice, backing vocals, drums); Al Jardine (backing vocals, electric rhythm guitars, electric bass, guitar)
Session musician
Ray Pohlman (6-string electric bass guitars).
Album released - 13/07/64
US EP Four by the Beach Boys released - 21/09/64 Capitol 5267 #44
UK EP Four by the Beach Boys released - 11/64 EAPI #11
Film/TV performances
22/10/65 *The Andy Williams Show* NBC (performed as "Little Cycle")
05/65 *Girls on the Beach* movie intro
65 Promo

After paying homage to surfing, hot rods, and all manner of teenage fantasies, Brian turns his attention to the Honda 50, the Japanese motorcycle, dubbed "America's largest selling car (on two wheels)," priced in 1964 at around $245, and made popular due to its easy operation. Recorded the same time as the classic "I Get Around," the vibrant song is memorable for Dennis's "*Go!*" intro, Mike's dynamic lead, and the cluster of vocals imitating the sound of an engine warming up. Then there's Carl's guitar distortion emulating engine noise, one of the earliest examples of fuzz-tone in a rock song. In a 1976 interview for *Rolling Stone*, Carl recalled the session: "[Brian] does exactly what he wants to. I remember [sits back and laughs]- this is so funny - when we did 'Little Honda' Brian wanted me to get this real distorted guitar sound, real fuzzy. 'The guitar sounds like shit,' I said. 'Brian, I hate this.' And he goes, 'Would you f*****g do it? Just do it.' When I heard it, I felt like an asshole. It sounded really hot. That was before fuzz became a big deal."[41].

The April 2nd session for "Little Honda" and "I Get Around" was also memorable for Brian sacking his father as the band's self-appointed manager. For many months, Murry had continued to muscle in on sessions, ridiculously criticising Brian and his brothers for no particular reason, and generally undermining what little authority Brian had. To appease him, it was alleged they had the engineer set up a fake mixing box in the control room so he could twiddle knobs to his heart's content, but without having any effect on what the boys were doing.

> *"Up to this point we had milked every idea dry. We milked it f*****g dry... but we needed to grow artistically"*

Although pencilled in for a single the label thought otherwise, so a disappointed Brian offered it Gary Usher and his new band the Hondells. Ironically, it scored a #9 on the Hot 100.

The Beach Boys' version did eventually appear two months after the album's release as one of the two leading tracks on the band's first EP *Four by the Beach Boys* (the other being "Wendy"). The single version with new organ fills later appeared on the 2014 compilation *Keeping the Summer Alive*. A colour promo film was also recorded for the song, directed by Dennis and starring Carl messing around on a pushbike. The boys also sang it in the movie *Girls on the Beach* in May 1965, and it was one of three songs performed on the *Andy Williams Show* on Oct 22nd 1965. With Andy joining in the fun and singing along, they were obliged to sing "little cycle" as not to fall foul of tv advertisers. For the performance, Mike sang live over a new backing track recorded two days before.

Reviewing the song Alexis Petridis of *The Guardian* wrote: "...as close as the Beach Boys came to garage-rock toughness: nothing to scare the Shadows of Knight, but its vague hint of pounding aggression is really thrilling." 42. Andy Paley, co-producer of the *Good Vibrations* box set, described it as "one of the greatest rock n roll records of all time...what an incredible groove."

By now Brian was growing tired of writing songs about surfing, hot rods and cars. In an interview with Earl Leaf for *Teen Beat,* he admitted: "We needed to grow. Up to this point we had milked every idea dry. We milked it f*****g dry. We had done every possible angle about surfing and then we did the car routine. But we needed to grow artistically."11

After this album there would be no more, and now Brian would be focusing on new themes and striving for musical perfection.

85. Can't Wait Too Long (*Smiley Smile/Wild Honey* 1990)
(Brian Wilson)
Recording
28/10/67 Wally Heider Studio, Hollywood (tracking)
01/11/67 Wally Heider Studio, Hollywood (tracking overdubs & "Miss you baby" vocal overdub)
24/07/68 Beach Boys Studio, Bel Air (further tracking)
26/07/68 Beach Boys Studio, Bel Air
c30/07/68 Beach Boys Studio, Bel Air
Producer - Brian Wilson
Engineer - Jimmy Lockert or Bill Halverson (*Wally Heider*)
Band members
Brian Wilson (lead vocal), Carl Wilson (guitar, backing vocals); Mike Love (backing vocals); Dennis Wilson (drums?, backing vocals); Al Jardine (backing vocals); Bruce Johnston (backing vocals)
Session musicians inc.
Max Bennett (bass guitar); Frank Guerrero (percussion); Lyle Ritz (bass)
Album released - 09/90

By the fall of 1967 it appeared that Brian's creative juices had been seemingly sapped by the intensive work that had been done on both the abandoned album *Smile* and the subsequent *Smiley Smile*. But during the sessions for their next album

Wild Honey he began work on what turned out to be a highly intricate piece of music, originally known as "Been Way Too Long" and later, "Can't Wait Too Long."

In the first session at Wally Heider Studio in Hollywood, Brian recorded a tracking tape for the first two verses, the first featuring guitar and other instruments, and the second adding drums, guitar, xylophone, bass, and tambourine together with backing vocals by the band. A rough mix was then made of the two sections.

Four days later the band recorded vocal overdubs of "Miss you baby" at Brian's home studio in Bel Air, together with more instruments (piano, xylophone, organ, fuzz bass, bongos and tambourine) overdubbed onto the song's second section.

For the next few months Brian completed the *Wild Honey* album and commenced work on *Friends*. By the spring of 1968 the band's popularity seemed at an all-time low, having undertaken two costly and disastrous tours, one with the Maharishi, and the other a tour of the US South and Midwest that was forced to be curtailed due to the riots and curfews in the wake of the assassination of Martin Luther King in Memphis. It was estimated that these cost the band around half a million dollars.

"They are no longer the brilliant Beach Boys. They are grey and they are making sad little grey records"

Even the band's popularity in the UK seemed to show signs of weakening. Penny Valentine, a regular supporter of the band, wrote a scathing article in a May edition of *Disc & Music Echo*: "A carefully calculated warning to the Beach Boys - split up or get yourself together. There is something very stale in the Beach Boys camp. It is the smell of utter freedom run amok. It is the smell of staleness and inertia. It is not pleasant to reflect upon the Beach Boys and see what could have been and then face what it is. This fact has been brought home to me by the group's latest release. *Friends* is about the ultimate in sadness. Whither the progressive Beach Boys? Wither the same spine-tingling sensation one got with 'God Only Knows,' the Beach Boys' answer to the Four Tops' 'Reach Out'? Gone, gone, gone. It has been suffocated in the same boring, muffled voices, the same trivial words, the same droning, friendly-dull atmosphere. If the Beach Boys are as bored as they sound, they should stop bothering and retreat to the Californian foothills. If they're not, they should stop boring their public and insulting them with below-par performances…It is now time for them to stand still and take stock of themselves and the situation they are in today. They have been given too much freedom. Like greedy schoolboys in a sweetshop their sense has not prevailed - their control has snapped. They are no longer the brilliant Beach Boys. They are grey and they are making sad little grey records."[11]

Scathing indeed! But what could be done to fix it? Brian was beginning to distance himself from the band, only participating in recordings when the mood took him. But almost two weeks after Valentine's review, the band had gone into the studio to record "Do It Again," which would soon top the UK charts and reinstate, if only temporary, some of their lost prestige there. When Capitol released *Best of the Beach Boys Vol 3* around this time, in order to compensate for the failure of *Friends*, it peaked at an abysmal #153 on the Hot 200. Then came *Stack O Tracks* the following month, their first album not to chart at all. It was becoming a year the Beach Boys would rather forget.

At the end of July Brian had resumed tracking work on the experimental "Can't Wait Too Long" now as part of the sessions for their next album, *20/20*. But that was the last we would see of the still-unfinished song for 22 years, although in February 1980 overdubs were attempted on the original recordings for possible inclusion on the album *Keeping the Summer Alive,* and then abandoned.

In 1990 a number of takes of the song were edited to create a "complete" work and was finally released in sound collage form as a bonus track on the *Smiley Smile/Wild Honey* cd re-release. A shorter version followed with the *Good Vibrations* box set in 1993, with Brian heard instructing Carl on some of the lyrics which were never used. In 2001 a stunning 51-second a capella version was issued on *Hawthorne Ca* while a longer version was found on *I Can Hear Music: The 20/20 Sessions* in 2018. In 2008 Brian would record a new version of the song for his solo album *That Lucky Sun*.

So what are we left with? Three fragments, two of which are complex instrumental pieces with full vocal harmonies, while the third has simpler instrumentation in comparison. Brian sings what few lyrics there are, with a bass line resembling the *Smile* version of "Wind Chimes."[32] With several sections of chorus and a vocal middle section, the title phrase is repeated several dozen times, alternating with "*been away too long baby.*" In other places there is a simple couplet: "*I miss you darlin'/I miss you so hard*" which, as Brian is heard instructing other band members, intended to be followed with "*So come back baby/and don't break my heart.*" The final segment then segues into an R&B-inspired arrangement and a bass riff which was labelled for many years as being part of the "Heroes and Villains" suite.

David Leaf wrote: "[The song] gives us an indication of the production depth that *Smile* tracks would have had. A lot of the music that has come out has been fragmentary, and while 'Can't Wait Too Long' is unfinished, sections of it are complete enough to be a terrific example of how Brian, in Van Dyke Parks' words, used to "saturate the tape with music…In my opinion, it's the single best piece of unreleased music in the Beach Boys' archives."[261]

Andrew Doe and John Tobler called it "a shimmering example or repetition, elevated to an art form, that shows just what BW could still deliver, should he set his mind to it.[1] Rick Swan called it "An exquisite throwaway…a moving piece of music, rippling through with the melancholy emotions of its creator… It's all fantastic."[21]

84. It's About Time (*Sunflower* 1970)
(Dennis Wilson, Bob Burchman, Al Jardine, Carl Wilson)
Recording
06-07/70 Beach Boys Studio, LA (take #21 master)
Producer - The Beach Boys (Carl & Dennis)
Engineer - Stephen Desper
Band members

Carl Wilson (lead & backing vocals, lead guitar); Mike Love (lead vocals on bridge, backing vocals); Al Jardine (backing vocals, rhythm guitar); Dennis Wilson (backing vocals); Bruce Johnston (backing vocals)
Session musicians/guests
Jimmy Bond (double bass, electric bass); Earl Palmer (drums);Daryl Dragon (tack piano, maybe organ); Dennis Dragon (congas, cowbells, timbales)
Album released - 31/08/70
US single released - 12/10/70 b-side of "Tears in the Morning" Reprise 0957
UK single released - 11/70 b-side of "Tears in the Morning" Stateside SS 2181
Film/TV Performance
02/07/71 *Good Vibrations From Central Park* NBC (broadcast 19/08/71)

It was the time when the Beach Boys were at their nadir. After a spate of unsuccessful albums in terms of sales and low concert attendance (especially in the US), and also having recorded *20/20,* what would be their last studio album under contract with Capitol, they were in search of a new label. By late 1969 some of the major players in the business, like CBS, Polydor and MGM, had made the decision not to sign them, and only Warner Brothers showed genuine interest. But nobody wanted a band that was being dubbed by some music critics as "dated", "un-hip" and even, as far as *Rolling Stone* was concerned, "stiffs." Even band member Bruce had quipped to *NME* that their next album would be called *A Fading Rock Band Revival.*11 Brian's latest aversion to the music business was now gaining widespread knowledge within the industry and quickly eroding his "genius" status, although at the time his health issues were not being made public. Without him at the helm, the boys were finding it hard to come up with new material.

Despite recordings for a new album slowly under way, with the working title of *Add Some Music,* even Murry Wilson could see the writing on the wall and that the boys' days were now most likely numbered. With dollar signs clouding his vision, and being the sole owner of the band's music publishing company Sea of Tunes, he decided to cash in on the situation by selling the copyright to all Brian and Mike's songs to a publishing division of A&M Records for an estimated $700,000. It was alleged that he told Brian the songs would never "amount to much," although at the time of writing they are valued in the region of $100-200 million.

> **"If there wasn't the Beach Boys and there wasn't music, I would not even know them. I would not even talk to them. But through the music I fell in love with my brothers."**

In November 1969 the Beach Boys eventually signed what was an impressive deal with Warner/Reprise, whose boss Mo Ostin had tremendous faith that the boys could deliver, but only with the caveat that Brian got back in the studio for future recordings and the need for Dennis to contribute more. What followed over the next few months was a spate of new material and fresh input from new songwriting collaborators, with the band feeling invigorated to produce what they knew would be a make-or-break album. However, Ostin rejected two submissions, admitting they were not "contemporary" enough, before finally accepting the third, entitled *Sunflower,* in July 1970.

Among the new collaborators was 24-year-old, relatively unknown "hippie" poet (and future painter) Bob Burchman, an acquaintance of Dennis's, and an old school friend of his future wife Barbara Charren. One evening while the three of them were having dinner, Dennis gave him a tape of an instrumental track he had written that the band had just recorded and, after reading some of his poetry, asked him if he could write lyrics to it. Burchman recalled: "Dennis ran off a cassette tape copy for me, making me promise not to let anyone hear it. I took it home with me and listened to the track a few times to get a feel for what the music was saying to me. Then I drove to a shady spot in Benedict Canyon here in LA, parked my car and began writing, as I played and replayed the track over and over on my portable cassette player. The lyric literally took me 20 minutes to complete. It came in a flash. I don't think I've ever written a lyric that quickly since." Burchman gave Dennis the lyrics just before he staring filming for *Two Lane Backtop*.

Dennis called the song "It's About Time," an out-and-out rocker about the pitfalls of fame that was a deliberate attempt to update the band's profile. Not only was it the first song recorded after the rejection by Warner, but Burchman also became the first lyricist the band used. Engineer Steve Desper, who Mike Love dubbed a "mad genius," had worked with the likes of Jimi Hendrix and Frank Zappa, and was well-attuned to the music coming out during the summer of 1970. With a hypnotic bass, looping drums, guitars and congas, Desper was given free rein to experiment during the sessions, having the good fortune to work with legendary drummer Earl Palmer, and making full use of a spatializer (taking in mixed audio content to render a stereo stream to the audio) to work on a "centre channel quadrophonic sound."

During the session Dennis had to inform his friend that some of the lyrics had been changed. Burchman recalled: "Al Jardine added another whole other section to the lyric right there in the studio, without anyone advising me or getting my input." Carl also made some subtle changes. As for the song's title, which Carl chants in the chorus, Burchman admitted: "I didn't understand at the time where he was going with that," and later told *Rolling Stone*: "I felt a bit discounted and disrespected with how that went down, but it was The Beach Boys after all, and I was not about to make waves." In the end Brian split the wiring royalties four ways. "It's About Time" was one of four songs Dennis contributed to the album, more than enough to satisfy the label's conditions.

Although well-received by critics album sales once again failed to meet expectations. However, "It's About Time" was singled out for special praise. Biographer Timothy White wrote: "And undidactic commentary on rock indulgence and self-redemption, it was also a wishful scenario regarding both Brian and Dennis Wilson's sporadic personal troubles."[69]Dennis's biographer Jon Stebbins called the song an "epic jam", and saw him "pushing the Beach Boys into progressive territory,"[43] while Mathew Greenwald described it as a "total group effort," the band's "most contemporary piece of music" of the year, and "a solid, almost dark R&B/rock feel guides the melody with a sense of precision." Alexis Petridis of *The Guardian* wrote: "…a truly rare pleasure: Dennis's vocal is raw and powerful, the guitar solo stings, the Santana-inspired Latin percussion rattles along."[42]. Robert Christgau of *Village Voice* supplied probably the best review: "If you can feature the great candy-stripes grown up, then this is far more satisfying, I suspect, than *Smile* ever would have been. Maybe they weren't really surfers or hot rodders, but they were really Southern Californians, and that's what their music was about." 257

When *Sunflower* was finally released, the countercultural classic "It's About Time" would hold a special place as its only new composition. The song was later performed live during the documentary *Good Vibrations From Central Park*, filmed in June 1971 and televised on Aug 19th.

83. 4th of July (*Good Vibrations - Thirty Years of the Beach Boys* 1993)
(Dennis Wilson, Jack Rieley)
Recording
15/03/71 Beach Boys Studio, Bel Air (demo)
04/71 Beach Boys Studio, Bel Air
20/06/71 Beach Boys Studio, Bel Air (vocals)
07/71 Beach Boys Studio, Bel Air
Producer - Brian Wilson (or possibly Dennis)
Engineer - Stephen Desper
Band members inc.
Carl Wilson (lead vocal)
Session musicians - unknown
Album released - 29/07/93

One of two Dennis collaborations (along with the wonderful "(Wouldn't It Be Nice) To Live Again,") that should have graced 1971s *Surf's Up* instead of low-par tracks like "Take a Load of Your Feet" and "Student Demonstration Time." By doing so, it would have elevated a great album into a classic one. According to Dennis: "I had a belief in my music. And it sounds nothing like it should on the album - it should have a flow on it from one song to another - it didn't sound like the Beach Boys. They thought it did. I said 'bullshit' and pulled my songs off."

A number of biographers, as well as co-writer Jack Rieley, put it down to an alleged argument between Dennis and Carl over sequencing the album, while others opined that it was done to preserve harmony and cooperation within the band. With Brian's involvement becoming more infrequent since the collapse of *Smile*, it was left to the rest of the band members to step up. And they did so admirably, taking the reins and filling the void with both production and songwriting credits to their names.

But what about Dennis, looked on by some as immature, unable to take music seriously, and never having the drive to match that of his brothers? Well, things were about to change. With Brian now receding into the shadows, Dennis's star was in the ascendancy and this was his long-awaited chance to show the rest of the band and the music world just what a great talent for songwriting he really had. From this moment on, Beach Boys' albums would regularly have at least one Dennis composition included.

> *"Like a last waltz before the laying down of arms... an elegy for what we've lost, a wistful hymn for summers past"*

But while the three brothers (including Brian) wanted the band to progress and become more experimental, Mike, Al and Bruce felt that by sticking to "the formula" was the best and only way of regaining their popularity. And it was this schism within the band that led to the fallout over two of Dennis's compositions, the best of which is the highly-topical anti-war song "4th of July," with meaningful lyrics by the then co-manager Jack Rieley that were reportedly aimed at the Vietnam War and the government's censorship of the media over the infamous Pentagon Papers, symbolising the growing gulf between the hope and optimism of the 60's and the cynical and more darker feel at the dawn of the new decade.

With Carl's achingly beautiful voice in its prime, the song is full of iconic American imagery with little hints of patriotic anthems, marching drums, and a chilling piano/flute solo at the fade creating a sense of hopefulness in what after all was a dark and sombre time for a nation awash with profound disillusionment in its government. With no harmonies and seemingly unfinished, it still manages to create a sense of inconclusiveness and uncertainty. Alexis Petridis of the *Guardian* called it "an epic, deeply troubled meditation on Vietnam utterly at odds with the Beach Boys' old image as America's Band."42

Another critic described it perfectly as "sounding like a last waltz before the laying down of arms...an elegy for what we've lost, a wistful hymn for summers past, and a despondent memory of sitting on a blanket as a kid, watching fireworks and eating ice cream, when none of the rest of it f*****g mattered." Rick Swan referred to it as "a mature anti-war song that hints not only at Dennis's growth as a songwriter but also at what the Beach Boys were still capable of, even after their decline after *Smile*."21

Working on 2-inch 16-track the song was demoed as early as March 1971, along with Dennis's tender ballad "Barbara," and then recorded sporadically over the next four months, with the instrumental track and Carl's lead vocal on "4th of July" assembled from separate tapes. Both would remain shelved for over 20 years, with "4th of July" finally surfacing on 1993's *Good Vibrations* box set, and "Barbara" on *Endless Harmony* five years later.

82. Girls on the Beach (*All Summer Long* 1964)

(Brian Wilson, Mike Love)
Recording
10/04/64 Western Recorders, LA (tracking)
19/05/64 Western Recorders, LA (vocals -10 takes)
Producer - Brian Wilson
Engineer - Chuck Britz
Band members inc.
Brian Wilson, Dennis Wilson (bridge)
Album released - 13/07/64
Film/TV performance
05/65 *Girls on the Beach* movie

Voyeuristic, perhaps even lecherous, but this is Brian and Mike once again describing the type of girls "*all within reach*" with whom they would like to start a relationship, ones with "*tans of golden brown*" and "*the sun in her hair*". They had been there before in songs like drooling over a girl with a "*slit up her side*" in "The

Shift" on their debut album, and leering at a girl in a short skirt in "Pom Pom Play Girl" from *Shut Down Volume 2*.

Innocent romantic notions, maybe, but, as musicologist Philip Lambert points out, the difference lies in the fact that they sing *about* the girls to the *other* guys. Biographer Peter Carlin wrote: "Certainly, there is eroticism in 'The Girls on the Beach,' both in the lyrics and in the voices themselves, which fall, climb, and tangle languidly through a series of augmented chords with a loving intimacy that communicates all the passion beneath the words."32

Like the gorgeous "Hushabye" on the same album the song is heavily influenced by the Four Freshmen's harmonic style, with just a hint of pop thrown into the mix. Some commentators compare it favourably with the earlier ballad, "Surfer Girl," seeing it as a suitable follow-up. It actually begins with the same key that "Surfer Girl" ends with, but that's where the similarity ends. "Girls on the Beach" is noticeably much more complex in both its harmonies and key changes, with Brian "stepping up the gas a bit" by experimenting with chordal patterns and key mobility, and as already highlighted, lyrics that are a tad more semi-erotic.

"A loving intimacy that communicates all the passion beneath the words"

One of the highlights of the song is Dennis's sexy descant on the "*sun in her hair*" vocal bridge, which Brian simply described as "a nice job." Biographer Jon Stebbins called the block harmonies toward the end, "one of the group's finest moments," while also extolling Brian's "incredible vocal-arranging skill, with complex group blends and multiple key changes."43 David Leaf wrote: "It is in fact one of Brian's most astonishing compositions. It's almost impossible to find another rock song that changes keys as often and as smoothly as 'Girls On The Beach.'"44

Described by Brian in his 2016 memoir as the band's "last real surf-type song," the early sessions at Western were noted for interruptions caused by band members with their playful infectious laughter. It was also the last song to be recorded for the album.

Gary Usher and Nick Venet were given permission to use the song as the title track to the forthcoming beach movie of the same name, which was filmed over two days in April 1964 and released by Paramount on May 12th 1965. Directed by William N Witney and starring Noreen Corcoran and Martin West, it was a comedy about members of a college sorority house who try and raise funds for a supposed concert by non-other than the Beatles. With the film's music composed by Usher, the Beach Boys make cameo appearances as themselves, lip-singing the title song as well as "The Lonely Sea" and "Little Honda."

With the album now completed Brian was satisfied that he had produced something that would compete or even surpass that of his rivals, the Beatles, who several months ago had taken America by storm. But being Brian, there was still much room for improvement.

81. Disney Girls (1957) (*Surf's Up* 1971)
(Bruce Johnston)
Recording
03/06/71 Beach Boys Studio, Bel Air
23/07/71 Beach Boys Studio, Bel Air
Producer - The Beach Boys
Engineer – Stephen Desper
Band members
Bruce Johnston (lead & backing vocals, whistling, upright pianos, Hammond organ, Moog synthesiser, mandolins), Brian Wilson (backing vocals), Carl Wilson (backing vocals); Mike Love (backing vocals); Al Jardine (backing vocals)
Session musicians/guests
Ed Carter (electric guitar with wah-wah pedal; acoustic guitars); Dennis Dragon (drums); Kathy Dragon (flutes)
Album released - 30/08/71
Film/TV Performances
27/12/74 *The Old Grey Whistle Test* BBC-2 (Bruce solo, broadcast 24/01/75)

A flawless and quite haunting song which, despite seemingly out of touch with the album's main theme, is nevertheless one of the most enduring and much-covered compositions of Bruce's career. In an interview for BBC Radio 1 he recalled how it came about: "I came up with that song because I saw so many kids in our audiences being wiped out on drugs. I tried to think of a time when I was really young and what it was like being real naïve. I thought of 1957 and remembered what was going on in 1957 in my life, and I thought of a funny record called 'Old Cape Cod' by Patti Page. It was a big hit...I wrote a song about going back in time. I was 13 and I was afraid to go on to high school because I [might] get beaten up. Now 14 years later, I realise how tame those times were and I was thinking, 'Gee, how great it would be to go back there for a minute.' Because it's so hard these days, with everybody overdosing...and that is what that song is about. People being a little naïve but a little healthier." 11

As a slice of pop perfection it is beautifully sung by its composer, and admired by Brian for "the marvelous way he wrote the harmonies and chords." Jim Beviglia of *American Songwriter* called it one of the album's finest moments and identified with its message: "If you're not listening closely enough, you might read the title, hear some of the references in Johnston's opus, and think that it's easy nostalgia, something in which The Beach Boys have been known to trade. But what you come to realize, either by perusing the lyrics or listening to the subtle ache in those 'oohs and aahs,' is that the 'fantasy world' which the narrator fixates is just that, an idealized vision of happiness that he hasn't yet attained."45

> *"That's just the way I write. That wasn't anything other than a really nice song"*

The mandolin-driven dose of nostalgia is filled with iconic apple pie-images of America during the late Eisenhower years, with nods to tootsie rolls, church bingo, and "old time dances," and, of course, the titular Disney girls, a reference to the teenage "mouseketeers" of the tv show *The Mickey Mouse Club*, among whom was the soon-to-be teen idol Annette Funicello, later star of the movie *The Monkeys' Uncle.*

The song was later released as a single in Holland. backed with "Surf's Up," and went on to be covered by the likes of Doris Day, Art Garfunkel, Jack Jones and Captain & Tennille, as well as a version with Cass Elliott, Bruce and Carl. Bruce also performed the song on the UK's *Old Grey Whistle Test* in 1975, three years after leaving the band. In a 2011 interview, he modestly played down what was one of his finest songs: "That's just the way I write. That wasn't anything other than a really nice song. I was able to weave the voices into it, oohs and aahs. Not that it was ever a hit, but it sold millions of copies riding around other people's albums. People just loved the lyrical point of view. That's just one of those nice accidents."45

Sonny Baker, writing for *Mojo*, was more than impressed: "At times the whole production has a beautiful spectral atmosphere, as if pressing an ear up against the door of some long-abandoned dancehall to catch the echoes of a phantom Salvation Army band playing a waltz…It's a hallucination without the hallucinogens."46

80. Barbara Ann *(Beach Boys Party!* 1965*)*
(Fred Fassert)
Recording
23/09/65 Western Recorders, LA (tracking & vocals)
27/09/65 Mike Love's house, LA (sound effects)
Producer - Brian Wilson
Engineer - Chuck Britz
Band members
Brian Wilson (lead vocals); Carl Wilson (acoustic guitar), Al Jardine (bass guitar, backing vocals); Mike Love (backing vocals)
Session musicians/guests
Dean Torrance (lead vocals); Hal Blaine (bongos); Ray Avery (bongos); Steve Korthof (bongos); Ron Swallow (tambourine); Terry Melcher (tambourine); Marilyn Wilson (backing vocals)
Album released - 08/11/65
US single released - 20/12/65 b/w "Girl Don't Tell Me" Capitol 5561 #2
UK single released - 02/66 b/w "Girl Don't Tell Me" Capitol CL 15432 #3
Film/TV performances
23/10/65 *Jack Benny Hour* NBC Burbank (broadcast 03/11/65)
22/02/66 *Top of the Pops* BBC-1 London (exclusive film shot at Brian's house, broadcast 10/03/66)
15/12/67 *UNICEF Christmas For the Children of the World* TFI Paris (broadcast on BBC-1 London 27/12/67)
23/12/68 *Theater De Brakke Grond, Amsterdam* NCRV
16/06/69 Olympia Theater Paris TFI (filmed concert)
14/05/70 *The Tommy Leonetti Show* ATN-7 Sydney (broadcast 20/05/70)
21/06/80 Knebworth, England concert (later released on CD/DVD)
22/09/85 *Farm Aid*, Champaign Ill.

Following the release of *Summer Days (And Summer Nights!!)* in June 1965, the band's second album of the year, Brian began work on his next project *Pet Sounds*, with session work already begun the following month on the instrumental track for "Sloop John B." However, by early September, Capitol had made it clear to Brian that they needed a new Beach Boys album out in time for the Christmas market. From what they had already heard through the industry's grapevine, Brian was now heading in a new musical direction that they felt wasn't too reassuring to be successful in terms of sales, a view that was also shared by some of the band members. *Summer Days* had already seen a growing maturity in Brian's work, but as far as Capitol were concerned, more deep, meaningful songs didn't necessarily equate to bringing in more dollars.

Brian had neither the original material or the inclination to produce a new studio album in so short a space of time, so to appease both company and other detractors, a solution was found - make a "live-in-the-studio" album to simulate a genuine Beach Boys' party - simple and easy to produce, with minimal arrangements and, thankfully, no new material required.

For four days in September the boys got together at Western and recorded a collection of old favourites (including three Beatles songs) and a medley of two of their own hits, all accompanied by just acoustic guitar, bongos and a bass guitar. If vocals were messed up, what did it matter - this was a drink-infused party, after all. In order to give it the party ambiance, the boys gathered at Mike's house, along with wives and girlfriends, to tape laughter and background chatter to be overdubbed later in the studio.

On the last day of the Western sessions their friends Jan and Dean, recording in the next studio, heard the boys recording. 25-year-old Dean Torrance walked over to see what was going on and got talking to Brian. He suggested they have a crack at "Barbara Ann," a catchy song written by Fred Fassert for his Bronx group the Regents in 1961, which went on to be a #13 chart hit after the group broke up that same year. Fassert had written the song in 1958, naming it after his sister, and he gave it to the Regents, which, at the time, included his brother Charles.

Recording "Barbara Ann" would be one of the luckiest suggestions ever made to Brian and the band.

"If vocals were messed up, what did it matter - this was a drink-infused party, after all"

The result was basically a simple Brian-Dean duet, singing it with all the gusto of two friends meeting up in a karaoke bar and having a wail of a time. The acoustic guitar and bongo arrangement gave it the desired irresistible hootenanny campfire feel.

Due to contractual reasons Dean (who was signed to Liberty Records) could not receive any credit on the record or the album, but at the end of the song you can hear Carl saying, "Thank you, Dean."

And lucky it was. Capitol was thrilled with the concept of the album and rushed it out for a November release, eventually peaking at #6 on the Hot 200 album charts, and scoring an impressive #3 in the UK. Unprecedented radio play for "Barbara Ann" compelled Capitol's Al Coury to rush-release it as a single five days before Christmas, without even telling the band, and, by the end of January, it had leapt from #15 to #2 on the Hot 100, only beaten to the top spot by Petula Clark's "My Love." It also reached #3 in the UK, only their second Top 10 hit after "I Get Around", but now solidifying their status as serious chart rivals to the Beatles. The song was also included on the band's second EP *The Beach Boys Hits*, released in May 1966.

But what of Dean Torrance? Without any credit for it, he had just given away the idea for a song that his own duo Jan and Dean could have recorded for themselves, and no doubt would have scored a huge hit. But maybe in the back of his mind, he remembered that, two years before, Brian also giving him a song called "Surf City" that scored a #1 and made Jan and Dean household names (despite incurring Murry Wilson's wrath). So it made things pretty even after all.

The band members were apparently not too pleased to see that this throwaway track from the rushed *Party!* album was to become one of their defining sounds. Even Carl referred to it as "the bane of my existence."

However, with this makeshift album Brian had succeeded in buying himself time and the renewed inclination to produce what would become his magnus opus. Although *Beach Boys Party!* would be their last album to go top ten in the US for nearly eleven years, it should be fondly remembered as the lucky break that enabled the path to *Pet Sounds* that little bit smoother for Brian Wilson.

79. Be True To Your School (Single version 1963)
(Brian Wilson, Mike Love)
Recording
02/09/63 Western Recorders, LA (album version)
10/63 Western Recorders, LA (single version)
Producer - Brian Wilson
Engineer - Chuck Britz
Band members
Mike Love (lead vocals), Brian Wilson, Carl Wilson, Dennis Wilson, David Marks, Al Jardine? (backing vocals)
Session musicians - unknown
Album released - 07/10/63
US single released - 28/10/63 b/w "In My Room" Capitol 5069 #6
Film/TV performances
21/01/77 Capital Centre, Washington DC
21/06/80 Knebworth, England concert (later released on CD/DVD)
6/05/81 *National Cheerleading Championships*, Miami Beach

Brian and Mike's ode to having school loyalty and pride, a permanent fixture for American teens, but not so much in other parts of the world, especially the UK. The three Wilson brothers, Al Jardine, and David Marks had all attended Hawthorne High, while Mike had gone to Dorsey High in the View Park area of LA.

The song is full of high school vernacular, from the obligatory letterman sweaters, coloured window pennants, and cheerleader pom poms, almost alien to any other country outside of North America, and thus making the song just about as American is it can get.

After recording the song for the upcoming album, Brian felt that it had potential for a single, so he re-recorded it with added parts, with the biggest change being the inclusion of the female group The Honeys (Marilyn & Diane Rovell with Ginger Blake) to sing the cheerleader vocals inbetween the verses. Although Brian chose the melody of the University of Wisconsin's fight song "On Wisconsin," it just happened to have the same melody as that copied by Hawthorne High's "Onward Cougars." Not for the first time Brian went overboard with added sound effects, adding a booming bass drum, and snare cadences. Building up the tempo by mixing the saxophones down and guitars up, and adding different vocal and instrumental countermelodies, he injected a more vibrant feel to an otherwise average song by illuminating the song's themes.

"Just about as American is it can get"

With this song Brian and Mike successfully extol the virtues and appeal of high school, focusing on the pride of achieving sporting success at school, in this case football, with the cheerleaders yelling, *"get that ball and fight!"* It became an instant favourite with concert audiences who readily related to the pride shown in the powerful lyrics. Mike would be awarded co-writing credit after a successful lawsuit.

The single entered the Hot 100 top 40 on November 23rd 1963, the same day JFK was assassinated. It was the last charting song to include bass player David Marks, who soon left the band when Al Jardine returned to the fold. Even though it was before the album was released, it was too late to have him featured on the cover. Records show that David had officially left the band on August 30th 1963, three days before the first recording session, while Al had already returned to the band as a "temporary replacement" for Brian, who was already beginning to excuse himself from concerts. Not only that, he was said to be present at the recording of "Be True To Your School."11 In a 1981 interview, David claimed to have played on all five of the band's first albums, and that "Fun, Fun, Fun" was the last single recorded without him in January 1964.65

Many years later Mike did little to retain the song's innocent teenage charm by borrowing it to use as a beer commercial with the name changed to "Be True To Your Bud."

78. Vegetables *(Smiley Smile* 1967)
(Brian Wilson, Van Dyke Parks)
Recording - Smile
17/10/66 CBS Columbia, LA
04/11/66 Western Recorders, LA ("humorous" session with Parks, Danny Hutton and Michael Vosse)
11/11/66 Western Recorders, LA (chants)
16/11/66 Gold Star Studio, LA ("arguments" session with Michael Vosse and Hal Blaine)
03/03/67 CBS Columbia Studio, LA
04/04/67 Western Recorders, LA (vocals inc "Sleep a Lot")
05/04/67 Western Recorders, LA (vocals)
06/04/67 Western Recorders, LA (vocals)
07/04/67 CBS Columbia Studio, LA (tracking & vocals)
10/04/67 Western Recorders, LA(vocal & sound effects session inc Paul McCartney)
11/04/67 Western Recorders, LA(chorus 1&2 vocals)
12/04/67 Gold Star Studio/Western Recorders, LA (tracking)
13/04/67 Western Recorders, LA (finishing touches)
14/04/67 Western Recorders, LA (new lead vocal)
Recording - Smiley Smile
03/06/67 Wester Recorders, LA (vocals & organ overdub for new version)
05/06/67 Western Recorders, LA (tracking)
06/06/67 Western Recorders, LA (tracking)
07/06/67 Western Recorders, LA(tracking)

15/06/67 Beach Boys Studio, Bel Air (completion)
Producer - Brian Wilson
Engineer - Dave Hassinger (Columbia), Chuck Britz (Western), Jim Lockert (Bel Air)
Band members
Smiley Smile version - Al Jardine (lead, backing & harmony vocals, percussion, sound effects); Brian Wilson (backing & harmony vocals, grand piano, percussion, sound effects, electric harpsichord); Mike Love (backing & harmony vocals, sound effects); Carl Wilson (backing & harmony vocals, percussion, sound effects, Fender bass, ukulele); Dennis Wilson (backing & harmony vocals; percussion, sound effects, xylophone)
Session musicians
Chuck Berghofer (upright bass on verses); Jim Gordon (hi-hat, castanets, cups); Nick Pellico (vibraphone); Bill Pitman (tenor ukelele; Danelectro bass); Ray Pohlman (Fender bass on the fade); Lyle Ritz (upright bass on the fade); 2 violins, 2 cellos, 2 violas.
Smiley Smile album released - 18/09/67

After a month-long hiatus, Brian returned to the studio to carry on work for a track he called "Vega-Tables," and what would turn out to be one of the last, if not *the* last, tracks recorded for *Smile*. It also signalled the departure of co-writer Van Dyke Parks, following what would become the last session on April 14th 1967. Citing criticism over what was seen as his "absurdist" lyrics and pressure put on him by Brian, his departure literally spelt the death of the project, which was officially announced on May 5th.

The song itself was inspired by Brian's growing consciousness for health food, one that apparently began way back at high school and being exposed to the many fibre-building wheatgerm tv ads. Then came the well-publicised work of fitness guru Gypsy Boots, whose advocation of "alternative" lifestyles included eating healthier foods, especially vegetables.

While Brian was working on *Smile* he gave an interview for *Teen Set*: "I want to turn people on to vegetables, good natural food, organic food. Health is an important ingredient in spiritual enlightenment. But I do not want to be pompous about this, so we will engage in a satirical approach to the matter." In the late 60's he had taken it one step further when he and a friend opened a health food store in LA called the Radiant Radish. More inspiration had probably come when his assistant Michael Vosse (1941-2014) had mused of how taking marijuana could turn someone into a "vegetative" state.

It is generally believed that "Vega-tables," as it was originally called, was intended to be part of what was dubbed the "Elements," a four-song suite (orginally six) with "Vega-tables" covering the Earth segment. This, however, was put to the test when a December 1966 preliminary tracklist for the album was presented to Capitol, with "The Elements," "Wind Chimes," and "Vega-tables" down as three separate tracks.

It was plain and simply just a bit of fun

Al recalled one of the sessions: "I remember telling Brian, 'We've got to do something different on this thing.' What the hell, it was four in the morning. I filled some water bottles, tuned in to the key of the song and blew air into the bottles. What you hear sounds like an organ."[47]

Although it was widely rumoured that when Paul McCartney dropped in for one of the April sessions and was asked to contribute to the sound effects by chomping on a celery stick, there has since been no audio evidence unearthed to support it, although Marilyn Wilson recalled: "Brian had some fresh vegetables out, for the mood. He sprinkled salt all over the console table near the mixing board and started dipping celery into the salt and chomping it. Paul followed his lead and picked up the celery and did the same thing. It was priceless to see."48

McCartney also admitted in 2001 that he had no recollection of it happening, but in an interview 15 years later seemed to have a clearer memory and suggested he may have done it.

On April 29th it was announced by publicist Derek Taylor that "Vega-tables" would be the next single, backed with "Wonderful," and Al singing a "most vigorous lead." Apparently, Parks was dead against the idea and after arguments with Brian nothing came of it.

The song would undergo a number of changes during the later re-recordings for *Smiley Smile*. With Parks' original lyrics reworked and with a scaled-down arrangement, it was renamed "Vegetables." One critic described the revised version as sounding "like a skiffle or campfire song."5. Musical segments and lyrics of the *Smile* version would later resurface in other recordings, notably *Smiley Smile's* segment-rich "Heroes and Villains" and "Mama Says" on *Wild Honey*, where a re-recording of the unused "sleep a lot" segment closed the track.

In a 1968 interview for *Beat Instrumental* Mike Love probably shared the opinion of certain other band members that, with this album, they "were going too far" and "losing touch."49

With *Smile* and *Smiley Smile* now out of the way, it was becoming apparent that Brian had lost both his creative drive and control of the band. From this moment in time, he would be quite happy to take a back seat and let others handle the production. According to one reviewer, the album had been Brian's "abortive attempt to match the talents of Lennon and McCartney."50, while *Melody Maker* opined: "Undoubtedly the worst album ever released by the Beach Boys. Prestige has been *seriously* damaged."11 Others saw it as a new phase in Brian's musical development and a chance to chart new territory.

Described accurately by some critics as "psychedelic whimsy" and "endearingly daft," "Vegetables," in my opinion, should be remembered as that, and not as a serious, groundbreaking moment in Brian's career as some would see it. It was plain and simply just a bit of fun.

77. Let The Wind Blow (*Wild Honey* 1967)
(Brian Wilson, Mike Love)
Recording
29/10/67 Beach Boys Studio, Bel Air (possible date)
03/11/67 Beach Boys Studio, Bel Air
Producer - The Beach Boys
Engineer - Jim Lockert?
Band members
Mike Love (vocals), Brian Wilson (vocals, piano, organ); Carl Wilson (vocals, guitar, bass); Dennis Wilson (drums)
Session musicians - unknown

Album released - 18/12/67
US single released - 07/74 b-side of "I Can Hear Music" Reprise 1310

Dubbed by many as the hidden gem of *Wild Honey*, this simple, achingly beautiful song is one of Brian's most intimate, broken compositions. Reviewing it in 2016, Nathan Jolly wrote: "[Brian] is struck by the simple march of time, the impermanence of everything, the elemental beauty of nature. It's all quite nice until he realises if everything can and does change, then so might his lover's place in his life. So he begins praying for everything to simply be...needing assurance...Of course she won't - she can't."[51]

Recorded in the wake of Brian's abandoned *Smile* project, particularly the "fire" element, which led him to feel responsible for actual fires breaking out fire, his mental state could well have enhanced the song's veneer of fragility. With lyrics written mostly by Mike, and beautifully arranged by Brian, this piano-driven, waltz-style ballad was the first composition recorded by the group that is in 3/4 throughout. Although the song's lyrics are seen by some as simple, Mike delivers one of his finest vocals, leading to what is quite an unexpected climax with Brian's spellbinding falsetto.

"Swirls and throbs with a subtle psychedelia more hinted at than indulged in"

However, it did have its critics. Musicologist Rick Swan wrote: "The components haven't jelled, resembling sections of different song shoved together,"[21] but, on the whole, it was widely accepted to be the highlight of the album. Daniel Harrison saw it as "the most arresting and compositionally assured song on the album, and it echoed the formal and harmonic technique of "God Only Knows,"[52] while Jordan Blum of *Pop Matters* described it as "forlorn and urgent, with a gripping chorus and sombre production. It's fantastic."[53] *Stylus* magazine's Edwin Faust found it to be "a moody ballad that swirls and throbs with a subtle psychedelia more hinted at than indulged in."[54] Matthew Greenwald wrote: "Deeply heartfelt lyrics and an air of grace surrounding the melody make it easily one of the finest tunes on the *Wild Honey* album. Utilising the metaphor of nature to relate the essence of love, the song has a certain poetic feel surrounding it that is undeniable."[24]

The band later performed it on their 1973 album *The Beach Boys in Concert*, delivering a more polished version, and with Carl singing lead vocal. However, with its slower tempo, it didn't quite match the original's unique feel. A stereo mix of the song also appeared on the 2001 compilation *Hawthorne, Ca.*

76. Big Sur (*Feel Flows* 2021)
(Mike Love)
Recording
15/08/70 Beach Boys Studio, Bel Air
Producer - The Beach Boys
Engineer - Stephen Desper?
Band members

Mike Love (lead vocal); The Beach Boys (backing vocals)
Album released - 27/08/21
Promotional release (various formats) - 03/06/21

The Beach Boys' love letter to the rugged area of coastal central California that lies between Carmel and San Simeon, and long praised for its dramatic scenery. American novelist Henry Miller (1891-1980) described it as "the California that men dreamed of years ago, this is the Pacific that Balboa looked at from the Peak of Darien, this is the face of the Earth as the Creator intended it to look." The poetry of Robinson Jeffers (1887-1962) also helped popularise the romance of its wild, untamed nature.

It was allegedly written by Mike while retreating to the area following his recent divorce from Suzanne Belcher, his wife of three years, making it the first song in which he wrote both words and music. It would never be heard in its original form until the 2021 release of the wonderful compilation, *Feel Flows: The Sunflower & Surf's Up Sessions 1969-1971*. If Mike was indeed the sole author, and there's no reason to doubt him, then it has to be one of his finest moments and shows the band at their absolute height.

On September 1st 1970, just two weeks after the mastering of *Sunflower,* the band got together (probably at Artisan Sound Recorders) with the plan to make a new album out of existing recordings. Given the working title of *Landlocked*, thirteen tracks were chosen - Loop de Loop, Susie Cincinnati, San Miguel, H.E.L.P Is On the Way, Take a Load off Your Feet, Carnival (aka Over the Waves), I Just Got My Pay, Good Time, Big Sur, My Lady (aka Falling in Love), When Girls Get Together, Looking At Tomorrow, and How Deep Is Your Ocean (aka 'Til I Die).

"Emphatic proof that the Beach Boys never stopped making sublime, artful, spiritually invested music"

In an interview for *Rolling Stone* manager Jack Rieley revealed that he saw the proposed album title as "a departure...It was meant as a demarcation line, separating striped-shirt bullshit that had become irrelevant, an object of pure scorn, from artistry, new creativity and great new songs. We even had a cover designed, which featured stark bright white san-serif letters on a stark black field."11. However, Rieley couldn't hide his disappointment with the quality of the songs: "I heard the songs, among which were titles like 'Loop de Loop' and others which were even more forgettable. I was totally perplexed. No strategy was worth anything without the goods, and the goods were just not there. Embarrassed, I met with Mo Ostin, a true Beach Boys fan, at Warner Brothers, who listened to the songs, and he declared ,'No way.'"11.

So there would never be an album called *Landlocked,* although many of these songs would be included on *Surf's Up* and a number of subsequent albums. One of those songs, "Big Sur," was recorded at Brian's house in August 1970, two weeks before the release of *Sunflower*. Also recorded that day was "'Til I Die." Although little detail is known of the session and who played on it, "Big Sur" was chiefly the work of Mike, although it had Brian's stamp on it when it came to the *Pet Sounds*-inspired musicality and vocal harmonies. Although considered not good enough for the album in its original form, or, for that matter, anything else that came along in the next 40 years, it was, however, re-recorded as an acoustic number for the 1973 *Holland* album, re-titled "California Saga: Big Sur" as the opening song of a three-part suite. Rather than the 4/4 time signature of the original, Carl or Al decided it would sound better in 3/4 waltz time, and in doing so would make the original version if chosen look out of place on what is essentially a folksy, almost progressive sounding album.

In 2021 the world finally got to hear the original for the very first time, thanks to producer Mark Linett and archive manager Alan Boyd. The album, and particularly the lost gem that is "Big Sur," received universal praise. *Uncut* welcomed the "trove of hidden revelations," and said that this was "emphatic proof that the Beach Boys never stopped making sublime, artful, spiritually invested music, no matter how far they'd fallen in popular opinion."55

75. Wind Chimes (*Smile* version 1966)
(Brian Wilson, Van Dyke Parks)
Recording - Smile
03/08/66 Gold Star Studio LA (version 1 tracking - take # 9 master)
03/10/66 Gold Star Studio LA (version 2 vocals)
05/10/66 Western Recorders, LA (version 2 tracking, chorus vocals)
10/10/66 Western Recorders, LA (group vocal overdubs)
Recording - Smiley Smile
10/07/67 Beach Boys Studio, Bel Air (new instrumentation, vocal overdubs)
11/07/67 Beach Boys Studio, Bel Air (insert)
Producer - Brian Wilson
Engineer - Larry Levine (Gold Star); Chuck Britz (Western), Jim Lockert? (Bel Air)
Band members
Carl Wilson (lead vocal, Fender bass; 12-string electric guitar; finger snaps, wood blocks); Brian Wilson (overdubbed grand & tack pianos)
Session musicians
Hal Blaine (drums, sticks); Frank Capp (temple blocks); Al de Lory (electric harpsichord); Sam Glenn Jr (tenor sax); Billy Green (clarinet); Jim Horn (clarinet); Carol Kaye (Danelectro bass); Larry Knechtel (grand piano); Jay Migliori (flute, tenor sax); Don Randi (tack piano, celeste); Lyle Ritz (upright bass on chorus and tag); Charles Berghofer (upright bass on verses); Van Dyke Parks (marimbas)
Smiley Smile album released - 18/09/67
US single released - 23/10/67 b-side to "Wild Honey" Capitol 2028 #31
UK single released - 11/67 b-side to "Wild Honey" Capitol CL 15521 # 29

The first track recorded for the legendary unfinished *Smile,* the album which had been conceived during sessions for "Good Vibrations" and intended for an extension of the kind of music that Brian and new 23-year-old collaborator Van Dyke Parks were now composing.

Born in Mississippi in 1943, Parks was a former child actor before majoring in music at Carnegie Tech in Pittsburgh. Moving to California, he had formed a group with his older brother. Embracing the West Coast electric folk scene, he learned to play piano and write lyrics, heavily influenced by the Byrds' music and Bob Dylan's wordplay and sharp imagery. It was alleged that he first met Brian Wilson through David Crosby at his home in Dec 1965, and again in mid-July 1966 at the home of Terry Melcher. According to Parks, it was Brian who "sought him out" after learning that he experimented with psychedelic drugs.

Brian first asked Parks to re-write the lyrics to "Good Vibrations," having been unhappy with those written by Tony Asher. Luckily for us all, he declined. Then he took up the offer to write for the next album called *Smile*.

"All I can say is he found a new way to make musical changes in a song"

At the time Brian's state of mind was focused on the latest drug culture involving marijuana and LSD, and, referring to the first "trip" he had as "a very religious experience," he even claimed he had seen God. With Brian and Parks now sharing ideas as well as drugs, they got down to work on the new project. Marilyn Wilson recalled going shopping with Brian one day and buying some wind chimes which were hung outside the home, and watching them out the window gave him the inspiration to write a song. "I think that's how it happened. Simple. He does a lot of things that way."[56]

Anomalies surround most of the *Smile* tracks, finished or unfinished. It was widely believed that "Wind Chimes" would form the "air" segment of the four-part suite called "The Elements," with "Mrs O'Leary's Cow" being fire, "Love To Say Da Da" water, and "Vege-tables" earth, although hardly any documentation has been unearthed to support it. There was also a preliminary track list dated December 1966 that showed "Wind Chimes" and "The Elements" listed as separate tracks.

Thankfully what is considered by many to be one of the album's highlights, is one of just a few tracks that were considered complete, or close to being completed. Carl's stunning vocal and the haunting melody are unforgettable, while the contrapuntal "music box" tag is magical in its creation, with its multiple overdubbed pianos played in counterpoint from each other. Band associate Michael Vosse recalled in 1969: "Wilson in the control room, standing close to the center speaker, listens to the playback. He rushes to the board and supervises the throwing of switches and turning of knobs - more echo on the third track, a touch of reverb on the second honky-tonk overdub, this track dry and the other with more highs. Something happens to the sounds; they change, they move around and are transformed into a work of sheer beauty. Everyone in the booth has seen and heard the entire process."[57]

The vocal overdubbing was also unbelievable to watch, as Vosse explained: "Brian did something I've never heard anybody do: by recording everybody and doing the song straight through, and going back to the tape and eliminating voices, he had this little section where voices sounded like little percussion instruments - because he took everything out and would only let one little thing come in at a time, so suddenly there was this break and it was funny, but it worked so well that it built up the rhythm and made the change in such a way that all I can say is he found a new way to make musical changes in a song."[58]

Alexis Petridis of the *Guardian* noted that although the "dark side" of the psychedelic experience had been largely ignored in the past, it was quite evident in tracks like "Wind Chimes," with its "isolated, small-hours creepiness."[59] *Mojo* described it as being "not so much sloppy as fally-over, and wonderfully so…'Wind

Chimes' finds the languid lads slurring and sighing over said mystical/bloody annoying 'natural' instrument. Then sweet voices slip into screaky discord and 'mellow' goes Blair Witch Project until a long, distant fade restores choirboy innocence."25

After Parks left the project, partly due to friction with other band members, Brian abandoned the album altogether. The song was one of several tracks eventually re-recorded for the *Smiley Smile* album. Far inferior, in my opinion, and painfully slower, it was left to critics like Jamie Atkins of *Record Collector* to summarise: "'Wind Chimes,'" previously breezy and bucolic, became tense and claustrophobic; the usually angelic harmonies of the Beach Boys sound discordant, even malevolent."60

The original *Smile* recordings of the song appeared on the 1993 *Good Vibrations* box set, while the *Sunshine Tomorrow* compilation in 2017 features a short alternative tag that is simply spectacular in its brevity, but nevertheless still tops any of the previously unreleased material. According to musicologist Philip Lambert, who described the song as a "hallucinatory ode to the music of a back-porch breeze," pointed out that the *Smiley Smile* track "Can't Wait Too Long" (although not a *Smile* original) has a bass line very similar to that in "Wind Chimes."9

By listening to almost complete *Smile* originals like "Wind Chimes," we can fully appreciate and understand the profound sense of loss felt by both fans and music critics throughout the world for an album that, even in its non-existence, still manages to retain its legendary status to this very day.

74. Let's Go Away For Awhile (*Pet Sounds* 1966)
(Brian Wilson)
Recording
18/01/66 Western Recorders, LA (basic tracking - take #18 master)
19/01/66 Western Recorders, LA (flute overdubs)
Producer - Brian Wilson
Engineer - Chuck Britz
Session musicians
Hal Blaine (drums); Al Casey (12-string slide guitar); Roy Caton (trumpet); Steve Douglas (flute, tenor sax); Jim Horn (baritone sax); Jules Jacob (flute); Plas Johnson (tenor sax); Carol Kaye (electric bass); Barney Kessel (acoustic rhythm guitar); Al De Lory (piano); Jay Migliori (baritone sax); Lyle Ritz (upright bass); Julius Wechter (timpani, vibraphone); The Sid Sharp Strings (7 violins, 2 viola, 2 cellos)
Album released - 16/05/66
US single released - 10/10/66 b-side to "Good Vibrations" Capitol 5676 #1
UK single released - 28/10/66 b-side to "Good Vibrations" Capitol CL 15475 #1

One of Brian's finest ever instrumental compositions. This was the first track recorded specifically for *Pet Sounds,* and one of two instrumentals on the album, along with the title track. Although originally intended to be a vocal track, it was rumoured that Tony Asher had written lyrics for it, but both Brian and Tony have repeatedly confirmed there wasn't. Once Brian had heard how well the backing track played, it remained that way, recalling: "The track was supposed to be the backing for a vocal, but I decided to leave it alone. It stands up well alone."

It had a working title of "The Old Man and the Baby," and then as part of a running joke, "Let's Go Away For a While (And Then We'll Have World Peace)," the latter being a reference to the 1959 comedy album *How To Speak Hip*. Lyricist Tony Asher explained: "There was an album out called *How to Speak Hip*... a lampooning of the language instruction albums. I played it for Brian, and it destroyed him, killed him. Brian picked up a couple of references on the album. One of them was this hip character that said if everyone were 'laid back and cool, then we'd have world peace.' So Brian started going around saying, 'Hey, would somebody get me a candy bar, and then we'll have world peace.' [Brian] even made an acetate disc with a label on it with the title."61

Although some musicologists see the track may have influences with the 1959 *Exotica* album by Martin Denny, particularly the Les Baxter-penned track "Quiet Village, Brian pointed to the chord progression of some of Burt Bacharach's music, particularly Dionne Warwick's 1965 song "Are You There (With Another Girl)." In 1996 Brian actually described the song as "a great 'Burt Bacharach' type of thing."

"The track was supposed to be the backing for a vocal, but I decided to leave it alone"

During the sessions Brian would take special note of how the music was being played, and with any mishap, no matter how small, he would order a retake. He even went on to say that he "used dynamics like Beethoven. You know, Beethoven, the dynamic music maker." In an interview for *Melody Maker* in May 1966 he explained: "I applied a certain set of dynamics through the arrangement and the mixing and got a full musical extension of what I'd planned during the earliest stages of the theme. I think the chord changes are very special. I used a lot of musicians on the track; twelve violins, piano, four saxes, oboe, vibes, a guitar with a Coke bottle on the strings for a semi-steel guitar effect. Also, I used two basses and percussion. The total effect is 'Let's Go Away For Awhile,' which is something everyone in the world must have said at some time or another. Nice thought; most of us don't go away, but it's still a nice thought."62

Musicologist James Perone gave his description: "There are melodic features but no tune to speak of. As an instrumental composition, this gives the piece an atmospheric feel; however, the exact mood is difficult to define ...to the extent that the listener hears 'Let's Go Away For Awhile' as an incomplete piece, it is possible to understand it as a reflection of the alienation - the sense of not quite fitting in - of the bulk of Tony Asher's lyrics in the songs on *Pet Sounds*." Jim Fusilli pointed out that the song didn't require lyrics to clarify its message, but nevertheless pondered over what it would have sounded like with voices added: "It's a wistful tune and, despite the pounding drums, it conveys a sense of contentment. Exactly the feeling you'd get if you created a wonderful fantasyland in your mind and lingered there for a long time."130

The moody and complex track has gentle Bacharach touches, beginning with just guitar, bass and vibes, before Brian brings in horns and violins, until it sounds like a full-blown orchestra, before concluding with the memorable face-off between drums and timpani. Simply superb. When one of Brian's friends asked him how the track came about and how it pulled it off, he replied to her, "Here's a good way to describe it. Try to hum it. Good luck."

A rather pointless version without strings appears on 1997's *The Pet Sounds Sessions*.

73. You're So Good To Me (*Summer Days(And Summer Nights!!)* 1965)
(Brian Wilson, Mike Love)
Recording
05/65 Western Recorders, LA (tracking - take #24 master)
24/05/65 CBS Columbia Studio, LA (vocal overdubs)
Producer - Brian Wilson
Engineers - Chuck Britz (*Western*); Ralph Valentin? (*Columbia*)
Band members
Brian Wilson (lead & backing vocals, piano, handclaps); Mike Love (backing vocals); Carl Wilson (backing vocals, electric lead & rhythm guitars); Al Jardine (backing vocals, electric rhythm guitar, bass guitar); Dennis Wilson (drums); Bruce Johnston (backing vocals, Hammond organ)
Guests
Ron Swallow (tambourine); Marilyn Wilson (possibly backing vocals)
Album released - 05/07/65
US single released - 21/03/66 b-side to "Sloop John B" Capitol 5602 #3
UK single released - 04/66 b-side to "Sloop John B" Capitol CL 15441 #2

Apparently composed while on vacation in Hawaii, Brian later recalled: "I wanted to write something different," and indeed it was. This thumping ball of energy is a perfect example of how at times he makes the conscious decision to keep things simple. With the backing of an exceedingly catchy but unconventional six-note riff provided by Carl's vibrato guitar, coupled with Dennis's pounding drums, Brian's lead vocal has all the markings of his soulful R&B influences. He later revealed that the song was "spearheaded by a guitar sent through a Leslie speaker, giving it "an eerie effect."[64]

According to *Mojo* the song was "a four-to-the-floor, Motown-infected stomper - the closest they got to Northern Soul." [25] In an interview for *American Songwriter*, Brian recalled: "The ones that aren't the hardest, right, they're the best... 'You're So Good To Me' was written in 20 minutes. I knew it was special. The songs that come the fastest are the ones I like most."[63]. He even dubbed it a "tongue song", referring to the repeated "la, la, la" backing vocals in the chorus.

> *"I knew it was special. The songs that come the fastest are the ones I like most"*

Mike's romantic lyrics about the faithfulness of a loving partner may sound incongruous to the vibrant melody, but, nevertheless, Brian has pulled out of his hat another memorable song that should have been a stand-alone single and not confined as a flip-side to what was a Beach Boys' classic.

None of Brian's rocking melodies plant themselves firmly inside the brain like this one does, and the foot-stomping percussion reinforces the desire for what is possibly Brian's apologetic love letter to wife Marilyn for having to live and deal with his unpredictable mood swings.

72. Lonely Sea *(Surfin' Safari* 1962)*
(Brian Wilson, Gary Usher)
Recording
19/04/62 Western Recorders, LA (demo tape)
Producer - Nick Venet
Engineer - Chuck Britz
Band members
Brian Wilson (lead vocal), Carl, Mike, Dennis, Al (backing vocals)
Album released - 01/10/62
Film/TV performance
05/65 *Girls on the Beach* movie

In January 1962 Gary Lee Usher (1938-1990), a bank teller in Beverly Hills who lived with his grandmother in Hawthorne, just happened to be visiting his uncle at his home on 119th Street, right across the street from the Wilson home. As a night student at El Camino Junior College, he was an aspiring songwriter and fledgling recording artist who had several single releases already to his name. His uncle suggested he go over the road and introduce himself to Brian, who at the time were heard rehearsing with Mike and Al in their garage music room.

In one of those many milestone moments of Brian's life, he not only welcomed Usher into the fold, but in no time at all had handed him a guitar and asked him to play while he tinkered on the organ. 23-year-old Usher was already well experienced in the music business, much more so than Murry Wilson, whose own concepts belonged to another age, but he had to admit that here was an opportunity to further the boys' career. The demos they had made for Hite and Dorinda Morgan, which included "Surfin' Safari," were being passed around labels with little success, and Candix, the little label that had issued the band's debut single, "Surfin,'" was about to fold.

"Brian was like a piece of clay waiting to be molded. He looked for leadership, for someone to share ideas"

As the story goes, within hours of their first meeting Brian and Usher had written "Lonely Sea" in its entirety in just "a few minutes." After discussing with Brian his current interests, which included hot-rods, Usher played him what he called "Teddy-Bears-type chord patterns" and by doing so it struck a creative nerve with Brian. According to Usher, "it was Brian's melody on a new chord progression I was working on, and I think we wrote the words together."65.

Usher described his first impressions of Brian: "He had incredible pitch and refreshing musical concepts, but they weren't top 40 oriented. Brian was attuned with the pure, creative soul aspect of his music. I was able to introduce him to the business aspect of music...Brian was like a piece of clay waiting to be molded. He looked for leadership, for someone to share ideas with and for someone he could relate to. And he was looking for a friend. He wasn't that close to any of his brothers on a social level and, to my knowledge, did not have any close personal friends except his girlfriend, Judy Bowles."66. In return, Brian related his impression of Usher: "He kind of showed me the spirit of competition, how to write songs."

Just three months after meeting Usher Brian and the band were invited by him to go to Western Recorders at 6000 Sunset Boulevard, Hollywood to meet 34-year-old engineer Charles "Chuck" Britz and record demos of two of their earliest collaborations - "One Way Road to Love" and My Only Alibi" (aka "Human"), as well as Usher's own "Beginning of the End." While Brian provided lead vocals for "Beginning of the End" and "Visions," the boys provided all the instrumentation.

Three days later on April 19th 1962 they returned to the studio to do another session, this time for two of the Wilson/Usher collaborations, "Lonely Sea" and the hot-rod song "409," as well as a re-recording of "Surfin' Safari." Apparently, Brian, with his perfectionist head on, insisted that they needed a realistic ocean sound for the recording, so the two of them drove to the beach in Usher's car, along with a Wollensak electric reel-to-reel tape recorder and a 100-foot long extension cord. Usher recalled having to knock on a door in the early hours to ask permission to plug the recorder into an outlet and remembered telling Brian, "This isn't music…it's madness!"

According to historian James B Murphy, there is no documentation to support sessions taking place on April 19th, but were probably held earlier in the month.3

The hauntingly beautiful "Lonely Sea" was by far their most sophisticated collaboration up to this time, employing to great effect the well-used metaphor of the sea to describe the anguish and pain felt by the narrator over a lost love, and probably referring to Brian's relationship with then-girlfriend Judy Bowles who, as Usher surmised, was because he had bought her an engagement ring but hadn't actually proposed. It raised the possibility that their relationship was coming to an end (which it did two months later). David Marks recalled the session: "What most people don't know is that Gary wrote the music including the guitar intro…Brian helped with the melody, but his main contribution was the great lyrics. Carl and I helped them work out the arrangements on our guitars." Some musicologists think that Brian's spoken voice on the bridge is an embarrassment, but this is actually a prime example of reflecting teenage angst, which, after all, is the whole point of the song.

Brian struck an instant rapport with the thoughtful Britz, who became the necessary buffer between the sensitive and fragile singer and the in-the-face, blunt directions of his father Murry Wilson. More than anybody, he got to know Brian's strengths and weaknesses and became his moral compass in the studio for the next half a dozen or so years. He recalled: "Brian was the guiding light, producing everything even at that early stage. He knew what he wanted and was the only guy who could put all the parts together."

Although inexplicably left off the debut album, "Lonely Sea" was one of the songs included on the band's following album *Surfin' USA*. As a result Brian made some subtle changes to the track. A stereo mix was created by placing the original mono instrumental and Brian's lead vocal on the left channel of a new two-track recording, and new background vocals recorded on the right channel, that now included the voice of Al Jardine, who had recently returned to the fold.

Brian and Usher would write four more songs together for the Beach Boys - "409," "Ten Little Indians," "In My Room," and "We'll Run Away." In time, Usher would find himself bonding more with Dennis, with both sharing a loathing for Murry Wilson. In 1988 he would return to work with Brian one more time on his debut solo album, before passing away two years later.

71. Our Sweet Love (*Sunflower* 1970)
(Brian Wilson, Carl Wilson, Al Jardine)
Recording
19/03/68 Beach Boys Studio, Bel Air (tracking for "Our New Home" - take #5 master)
06/11/69 Beach Boys Studio, Bel Air (2-inch 16-track tape started on "Our Sweet Love")
26/01/70 Beach Boys Studio, Bel Air (strings overdubbed)
Producer - The Beach Boys
Engineer - Stephen Desper
Band members inc.
Carl Wilson (lead & backing vocals, electric guitar, clavinet, sleigh bells); Brian Wilson (backing vocals, piano)
Session musicians
Hal Blaine (drums, castanet); Abe Luboff (arco double bass); Michel Colombier (string arrangement); 8 violins; 4 viola; 2 cellos
Album released - 3108/70

Although considered to be one of the highlights of *Sunflower*, the song has a chequered history, having first been recorded during the sessions for *Friends* in March 1968 under the title "Our New Home" (aka "Our Happy Home"), then left unfinished and subsequently unreleased until its appearance on the 2018 compilation *Wake the World: The Friends Sessions*. Music journalist Brian Chidester described it as a "short, bouncy riff that maintains the gentle air of the *Friends* sessions."67

Friends was like a harbinger of trouble to come, and over the next two years the band were stymied by a series of misfortunes. To begin with, *Friends* was a huge disappointment in terms of sales and chart success and the mixed reviews it received were more or less a reflection of Brian's state of mind. Then there was the car crash that was their association with the Maharishi Mahesh Yogi, a self-styled master of transcendental meditation, that brought with it the aggravating chant-like mantras. Although other artists doubted the Maharishi's sincerity, Mike became a devoted disciple and as a result missed many of the *Friends* sessions. Not only that, he planned with Brian to have the band tour the country with the Maharishi as their opening act, but the whole thing turned into a disaster, with dwindling audiences preferring music to mantras, and after a few dates the tour was cancelled, costing the band thousands of dollars. In the age of Woodstock, Vietnam, high-profile assassinations, and the dawn of Women's Lib, the Beach Boys had seemingly become irrelevant.

> ***"It may be one of the best Beach Boys love ballads.***
> ***Exquisitely arranged and performed"***

Then came *20/20*, an album with little input from Brian, who was still suffering with his mental state and the lawsuit over questionable accounts against Capitol, which would result in the termination of their seven-year relationship. With royalties suspended for all their pre-*Pet Sounds* albums, the money was quickly drying up. More controversy surrounding the band emerged in early 1970 with Carl's refusing his military draft and Dennis's continuing involvement with Charles Manson. When Mo Ostin of Warner came to the rescue with an offer of a deal with his Reprise division, it was dependent on Brian becoming more involved in future recordings - a make-or-break situation that called for a quick solution.

Apart from old unreleased songs like "Our New Home," the last twelve months had seen the band record nearly 50 new tracks for their proposed next album, which originally had the working title of *Sun Flower,* before being changed to *Add Some Music - An Album Offering From the Beach Boys*. Warner rejected two album submissions for their lack of strong tracks before finally settling on a third, which by then had reverted back to the slightly revised name, *Sunflower*.

The rejigged "Our Sweet Love" certainly fit the bill when it came to a strong track. Interviewed for *Record Collector,* Brian recalled working with Carl on the song, saying, "Carl was a very, very sensitive writer, he was a sensitive person, he was a very good artist."68. But, as we have come to know him, Brian would often contradict what had already been said, and in another interview recalled: "I wrote that for Carl. After I wrote it I said, 'Hey, he could sing this good' so I gave it to Carl."69. To add even more confusion Al recalled that Brian had given up on the song and that it was left for the rest of the band to complete it, saying the song, "was one we finished with Brian. He just didn't want to finish it. So we kind of helped. We became completers of ideas. We all worked on his songs from time to time, and then we'd put them on the shelf. You start a song and put it away, start a song and put it away."47. Al's comment was good enough for him to be given co-writing credit.

High praise for the song came from *Rolling Stone's* Jim Miller, who described it as being "most reminiscent of the mood of *Pet Sounds.*"70. *AllMusic's* Matthew Greenwald was in agreement, calling it "a song that defines *Sunflower's* elegant charms and artistry…celebrating the simple pleasures of pure love and tranquillity, it may be one of the best Beach Boys love ballads. Exquisitely arranged and performed."71

The song was later featured on the *Feel Flows* compilation in 2021, with track-only and vocal-only versions, together with strings-only part.

70. Surfin' USA (*Surfin' USA* 1963)
(Chuck Berry, Brian Wilson)
Recording
05/01/63 Western Recorders, LA (tracking & vocals)
31/01/63 Western Recorders, LA (vocal overdubbing, mixing)
Producer - Nick Venet (mainly Brian)
Engineer - Chuck Britz
Band members
Mike Love (lead vocal); Brian Wilson (backing vocal, bass guitar, organ); Carl Wilson (backing vocal, lead guitar); David Marks (backing vocal, rhythm guitar)
Session musician
Frank DeVito (drums)
Album released - 25/03/63
US single released - 04/03/63 b/w "Shut Down" Capitol 4932 #3
UK single released - 06/63 b/w "Shut Down" Capitol CL 15305 #34

US single re-released - 07/74 b/w "The Warmth of the Sun" Capitol 3924 #36
Film/TV performances
02/03/63 *The Steve Allen Show* KFMB San Diego
28/10/64 *The TAMI Show* (recorded at the Civic Auditorium Santa Monica, for cinema release)
03/06/69 *Beat Club* Radio Bremen TV, Bremen West Germany (broadcast 02/08/69)
21/01/77 Capital Centre, Washington DC
13/07/85 *Live Aid*, Philadelphia Pa.

In an interview for *Billboard* magazine Brian spoke about his music influences: "As a writer, I've had a few influences, and Chuck (Berry) is primary. As a producer, he also informed my sense of how a record should feel. There were only two other producers I studied closely. The first was Phil Spector, who taught me how to make tracks and craft what some might call 'baroque' backgrounds. The second was Bob Crewe, famous for his work with Frankie Valli & The Four Seasons, who showed me how to utilize horns to sharpen and sculpt an overall sound."

The sessions for the Beach Boys' second album *Surfin' USA* proved to be an important step in Brian's development as a producer, with the tracks recorded on a three-track tape machine that could produce a true stereo mix and allow Brian to double-track vocals, thus creating a more sophisticated and fuller sound. Brian, appearing like a boy with a new toy, recalled how it worked on the title track, "Surfin' USA": "It was the first time we had ever sung out voices twice on one record. It strengthens the sound. Sing it once, then sing it again over that, so both sounds are perfectly synchronised. This makes it much brighter and gives it a rather shrill and magical sound without using echo chambers. It makes it sound spectacular, so much power."3

"It was the first time we had ever sung out voices twice on one record. It strengthens the sound"

As for the song's inspiration Brian recalled in a radio interview: "I started humming 'Sweet Little Sixteen,' and I got fascinated with the fact of doing it. And I thought to myself, 'God, what about trying to put surf lyrics to…the melody.' The concept was about, *"They're doing this in this city, they're doing that in that city,"* the Chubby Checker 'Twistin' USA' concept. So I thought of calling it 'Surfin' USA.' I was going with a girl named Judy Bowles at the time and her brother Jimmy was a surfer and he knew all the surfing spots. I said to Jimmy, 'I want to do a song mentioning all the surf spots.' So he made a list and, by God, he didn't leave one out."3, 32

Brian's idea was to use the song to drive the stereotypical images of California to the rest of the country, with the opening line, *"If everybody had an ocean across the USA,"* theorising that if everyone was privileged enough to live by a beach, then everyone could enjoy the sport.

With Jimmy Bowles' surfing travelogue in his back pocket, Brian sat down and came up with some clever lyrics, with a chorus namechecking 15 surfing beaches, mainly Californian - Del Mar, Ventura County Line, Santa Cruz, Trestles, Narrabeen (Australia), Manhattan, Doheny, Haggerty's, Swami's, Pacific

Palisades, San Onofre, Sunset (Hawaii), Redondo, La Jolla, and Waimea Bay (Hawaii).

Of course, the song didn't come without its share of controversies. On its release as a single, Brian was listed as the sole composer, despite it being published by Berry's Arc Music. Under the threat of legal action this was changed to Berry's name, beginning with its appearance on the 1966 album *Best of the Beach Boys*. Apparently, due to pressure from Arc Music, Murry Wilson had given the full copyright, including Brian's lyrics, to Berry's publisher prior to the single's release. But even though the melodies are similar, there was no denying the lyrics were solely Brian's, and eventually later releases list both writers.

Randy Nauert, bass player of the surfing band the Challengers, claimed: "I had written surfing lyrics to 'Monster Mash' and 'Sweet Little Sixteen', but were never recorded.3

Then there was Mike's claim to writing the lyrics, but as the copyright belonged to Arc Music he was unable to gain any credit. However, in a 1974 radio interview, Brian admitted: "When we first got going, Mike was a Chuck Berry fan, so…he and I turned the lyrics into a surfing song."262

On its release in March 1963 the song peaked at #3 on the Hot 100, becoming their first top ten hit, and, according to *Billboard*, going on to be the "best-selling record of the year." *Cash Box* described it as "a pounding 'Sweet Little Sixteen' - flavoured rocker…that the Beach Boys belt out coin-catching enthusiasm…[a] terrific instrumental show case,"263 while, more recently, *Paste* magazine wrote: "With a lyrical cache of about two-dozen surf spots, the Beach Boys made the world of Southern California seem like an oasis folks from all over the world could migrate to…a picturesque daydream we're all chasing 60 years later."264

Rick Swan wallowed in the song's perfection: "No one before had done it more impressively than BW…Then there is the thrilling falsetto hook, courtesy of BW at the end of the chorus. The choir comes next, strong multi-tracked harmonies hinted at in Surfin Safari but polished to perfection here. Again, credit goes to BW and his ever-expanding bag of studio tricks. The vocalists are stacked in a specific combination - Brian on top, Mike on the bottom, Carl and Dennis in the middle - with vibrato stickly forbidden and everything double-tracked. The result - a light blending of confident voices, otherworldly and gorgeous.21

A demo version of the song with Brian singing and playing piano was featured on the *Good Vibrations* box set in 1993, while a different version with drums added was included on *Hawthorne Ca* in 2001. Both had minor lyrical differences.

69. I'm So Young (*The Beach Boys Today!* 1965)
(William H "Prez" Tyus Jr)
Recording
09/09/64 Western Recorders, LA (arrangements, vocal overdubs, mono mixes)
18/01/65 Western Recorders, LA (tracking on new version)
19/01/65 Western Recorders, LA (guitar & vocal overdubs)
Producer - Brian Wilson
Engineer - Chuck Britz
Band members
Brian Wilson (lead vocal, 6-string electric bass guitar, Hammond B3 organ); Carl Wilson (backing & harmony vocals, electric rhythm/lead guitar on intro; 12-string rhythm guitar; 6-string electric bass

guitar); Mike Love (backing & harmony vocals); Dennis Wilson (backing & harmony vocals, drums); Al Jardine (backing & harmony vocals; electric bass guitar)
Session musician
Ron Swallow (tambourine)
Album released - 08/03/65

Originally recorded during the first session for the *Today!* album, this was another stab at copying a Phil Spector production, following on from "Frosty the Snowman" on the previous year's *Christmas Album*. It is highly probable that Brian preferred this to the original version recorded by the doo-wop group the Students, a #26 Hot 100 hit in 1961. Spector recorded it as "So Young" in March 1964 for Veronica (aka Veronica Bennett, his future wife). Without deviating much from the original, Brian produced a song with a competent instrumental backing together with his own understated lead vocal. The initial session in September 1964, with Brian, Carl and Al in attendance, features a flute (played by Jay Migliori), a more prominent bassline from Brian or Al, and drums reportedly played in Dennis's absence by sessionist Maurice Miller. This version was different from that which later appears on the album, and remained unreleased until appearing on the *Today/Summer Days* cd reissue in 1990.

Work on the song resumed in January 1965, with Brian discarding the flute-based doo-wop sound of the original, and producing a new backing track and vocals. Studio chatter has Brian in the control room coaching Carl on his guitar playing: "Carl, give me a good, smooth, uh, pattern of it once.." To which Carl replied: "I can't do - it's sorta high, Brian." "You can't play it?" replied Brian, to which his brother said: "That's high!...I can't reach for it." Brian then replied: "Just play your top strings, Carl...your top strings!...A little faster, huh?" This was typical of the interaction often heard in the studio between Brian and the band, with the producer steadily learning his craft while others did their best to take things a little more seriously and be guided by his instructions.

"Brian had shown the world how he could both emulate and even outdo his great idol with great ease"

These last sessions also indicated that Brian was racing against the clock to get the new album completed, and it served as an example of how, even when under that sort of pressure, he could pull it out of the hat and deliver a solid piece of work all by himself. The resulting song features on side two of *Today!* among some of the finest teen love ballads of Brian's career, and seen by many as a precursor to *Pet Sounds*. With it's tale of two lovers finding no solution to their plight but nevertheless not agonising about growing up, it's easy to compare it to side one's "When I Grow Up (To Be a Man"). The theme of being "too young" to get married will later be repeated on the classic "Wouldn't It Be Nice."

A highlight of the album version of "I'm So Young" is the extended contrapuntal ending, with its mixture of Brian's gorgeous falsetto, voices overlapping the phrase *"can't marry no one,"* and Mike's deep deep-down pitch on the word "no." In songs like this and "Don't Worry Baby" Brian had shown the world how he could both emulate and even outdo his great idol with great ease, and, as we all have discovered, would now lead to greater things to come…

68. Sail on Sailor (*Holland* 1973)
(Brian Wilson, Van Dyke Parks, Tandyn Almer, Ray Kennedy (*lyrics*), Jack Rieley (*lyrics*)

Recording
28/11/72 Village Recorders, LA (backing tracks by Carl, Blondie & Ricky)
29/11/72 Village Recorders, LA (backing tracks by Carl, Blondie & Ricky)
29/11/73 Village Recorders, LA (backing vocals)
30/11/73 Brother Studio, Santa Monica (final lead vocal by Blondie)
Producer - The Beach Boys (Carl Wilson)
Engineers - Stephen Moffitt, Rob Fraboni
Band members
Blondie Chaplin (lead & backing vocals, bass guitar); Carl Wilson (backing vocals, grand pianos, Wurlitzer electric piano, electric guitar, Hammond organ; ARP Odyssey synthesisers); Mike Love (backing vocals); Ricky Fataar (backing vocals, drums)
Session musicians/Guests
Gerry Beckley (backing vocals); Kevin Michaels (tambourine); Tony Martin (backing vocals); Billy Hinsche (backing vocals)
Album released - 08/03/73
US single released - 02/73 b/w "Only With You" Brother/Reprise 1138 US #79
US single re-released - 10/03/75 b/w "Only With You" Brother/Reprise 1325 #49
UK single released -06/75 b/w "Only With You" Reprise K 14394
Film/TV Performances
21/01/77 Capital Centre, Washington DC
12/86 *The Beach Boys: 25 Years Together* Hawaii

The genesis of this great song began with a meeting around May 15th 1972 between Brian and his old *Smile* collaborator Van Dyke Parks, the same day that the band's latest album *Carl and the Passions - So Tough!* was released. At the time, Parks was director of audio-visual services at Warner. He explained in a radio interview how on a whim he showed up at Brian's house: "Once upon a time, I visited him there one day, with a trusty Sony tape recorder in my hand. I went to Bellagio Drive to work on a song with Brian. The entire group [had been] working on a record for delivery to the Warner Brothers label. Mo Ostin [of Warner] held great expectations for that record and suggested that my working with Brian again might goad him to similar creative heights we had reached with *Smile*. Ostin was astonished that Brian wasn't participating in the album, and feeling somewhat deceived, I thought I should step forward, as I was in large part the reason for their commitment to the group. Having only got a partial song out of the one meeting with Brian [a song that would later become "Sail on Sailor"], I put the tape away and lay low. I wanted to avoid getting involved with the internecine group dilemmas once again."[11]

> *"You could say I did the Beach Boys a nice turn there.*
> *It was just a nice thing to do"*

In another interview, Parks told a slightly different version: "I called [Brian] up out of the clear blue sky and at some point he said, 'Let's write a tune.' It was better than having him stare at the angels on his headboard and write tunes about them."123. He also claimed credit for being the main composer of the song: "I went over to Brian's with my [new tape recorder] and told him the name of the tune and sang those intervals, and he pumped out the rest of the song,"8 while Brian asserted in 2002: "Van Dyke really inspired this one. We worked on it originally; then, the other collaborators contributed some different lyrics. By the time the Beach Boys recorded it, the lyrics were all over the place…"107

According to biographer Peter Carlin, the original song dated back to 1971 when Brian and Parks had first recorded the music with engineer Steve Desper and aired it out in an impromtu session at their friend Danny Hutton's house. Brian recalled in 2007: "I was at Danny Hutton's one time. Tandyn Almer and I wrote a song, "Sail on Sailor"…on a Wurlitzer electric piano and Ray Kennedy was there and started writing some lyrics…We wrote the thing in about an hour and a half or two hours. Later, Van Dyke Parks tweaked it a little bit."32.

Songwriter Kennedy claimed the song was originally intended for Hutton's band Three Dog Night, and that he and Brian had actually written the song in three days in 1970: "We went in and cut the basic tracks with Three Dog Night; we hadn't slept in about a week. Then Brian got up with a razor blade and cut the tapes, and said, 'Only Ray Kennedy or Van Dyke Parks can do this song,' and he left. We all stood there looking at each other going, 'What?' He called me every day after that, and I wouldn't talk to him…"177. Kennedy would later sue Brian for recognition as co-writer.

On October 10th 1972 the band submitted the completed *Holland* album to Warner, hoping it would be accepted after their disappointment with *Carl and the Passions - So Tough!* However, it was rejected as "un-releasable" by their executives on the basis they could not see a hit single, and they needed one to promote the album. On hearing this, Parks stepped in to save the day. Fortunately, he still had the cassette tape of the original song which he now presented to Warner's David Berson: "Knowing the company's enormous investment, and the high stakes involved, I got out the tape cassette…gave it a listen, and delivered it to the company with my assurance that it would solve all their problems."11 Warner liked the song and suggested it take the place of "We Got Love," the Chaplin/Fataar/Love song what they considered the weakest track, despite it having been earmarked by the band as the next single.

According to Rieley: "We delivered *Holland* to Warner Bros and I was still in Holland. Brian was in transit back to the States when David Berson from Warners said, 'Jack, there's some gorgeous music on this album but Van Dyke Parks is telling us that you're holding back a song.' Parks had heard an early skeletal version of what later became 'Sail On, Sailor' and raved about it to Warners. He told Mo Ostin and David Berson that I was holding back a great song. I didn't have a clue what he was talking about so I called Brian, and at first he didn't have an idea either."99

Rieley flew back from Holland to LA and wrote new lyrics for the bridge that "reflected how I felt 'lost like a sewer rat,' Parks told Scott Keller: "*Holland* arrived at the Burbank offices and it was the consensus of everyone in A&R promotion, and distribution, that the album was "un-releasable." Knowing the company's enormous investment, and the high stakes involved, I got out the tape cassette from [the May] session with Brian…gave it a listen, and delivered it to the company with my assurance that it would solve all their problems. I came up with that lyric when I was working with Brian, as well as the music pitches those words reside on. I did nothing with that tape until I saw the Beach Boys' crisis at the company where I was working, earning $350 a week."

On their return from Holland, the Beach Boys began recording the song on November 28th, with Brian admitting that he was being "grossly incompetent," even failing to turn up for some sessions. When he did turn up he kept tinkering with the song to make everything sound perfect. Eventually, the rest of the band refused to allow him back into the studio and it was left once again for Carl to step up and produce. With Rieley appending new lyrics, both Dennis and Carl tried out the lead vocal. On the day Dennis was supposed to record his, he had just purchased a new surf board and left the session to go surfing with only a part-recording. At Carl's suggestion, the lead was finally given to Blondie Chaplin, resulting in a soulful rendition and arguably his best work for the band.

Parks continued: "Well, they recorded the song, and it was a hit. And I'm glad that everyone came out of their little rooms to claim co-writing credit on that song…On the tape its clear from the contents that I authored the words and the musical intervals…It's also clear that I composed the chords to the bridge, played them, and taught them to Brian. You could say I did the Beach Boys a nice turn there. It was just a nice thing to do."

Steve Desper later contended that the *Holland* version "sounds awfully like the one I recorded" back in 1971. Tony Asher, despite admitting his dislike for most of the band's post-*Pet Sounds* material, called the song "just dandy."[178]

Released as the lead single from *Holland* it peaked at a disappointing #79 on the Hot 100, but did slightly better when re-released in March 1975, reaching #49.

67. Good To My Baby (*The Beach Boys Today!* 1965)
(Brian Wilson, Mike Love)
Recording
13/01/65 Western Recorders, LA (tracking - take #19 master)
19/01/65 Western Recorders, LA (guitar, vocals overdubs - take #4 master)
Producer - Brian Wilson
Engineer - Chuck Britz
Band members
Brian Wilson (lead & backing vocals, grand piano); Mike Love (lead & backing vocals); Carl Wilson (lead & rhythm guitars, backing vocals); Al Jardine (backing vocals); Dennis Wilson (backing vocals)
Session musicians
Hal Blaine (drums); Steve Douglas (tenor sax); Plas Johnson (tenor sax); Carol Kaye (bass guitar); Jay Migliori (baritone sax); Bill Pitman (electric & acoustic rhythm guitar); Don Randi (tack upright piano on verses, Hammond B3 organ on chorus); Billy Strange (lead guitar); Ron Swallow (tambourine); Tommy Tedesco (rhythm guitar, autoharp); Julius Wechter (conga drums)
Album released - 08/03/65

Just one of the Beach Boys' great feel-good songs of the mid-60's with all the necessary ingredients - a memorable guitar riff, superb alternating lead vocals from Brian and Mike, and a stunning a capella intro kicking off with Mike's great bass voice, followed by Brian (with Dennis and Al harmonising), Carl, and then Mike again - altogether one of Brian's most complex arrangements prior to *Pet Sounds*.

With its message about monogamy, this is a perfect example of Brian now shedding the restraints of touring with the band and focusing more on producing masterful works of art. The song forms a suitable artistic divide between the writing style "Do You Wanna Dance?" and "Dance, Dance, Dance," the two tracks that bookend side one, and the mind-blowing ballads of side two that indicate both a more sophisticated approach to his writing and clear signs he is heading in a completely new musical direction. Apparently, throughout the chorus, Dennis can be heard singing in his rich baritone what is an undecipherable lyric that's different to the others.

"A straightforward message about the rewards and benefits of monogamy"

This was another song originally credited solely to Brian, where Mike was later given co-writing credit after filing a lawsuit against his cousin and the publishers. In fact he went on to claim that he wrote *all* the lyrics.

Philip Lambert wrote: "It has all the earmarks of a classic feel-good Beach Boys song: powerful, catchy vocals, including back-and-forth leads between Brian and Mike, a clean, tight instrumental track, and a straightforward message about the rewards and benefits of monogamy."[9] Biographer Peter Carlin interpreted it as presenting "one oddly defensive man's arguments against unnamed critics,"[32] while Scott Interrante wrote more recently: "It's not that 'Good to My Baby' isn't musically exciting or complex, but of all the tracks on *Today* it's the most similar to the Beach Boys' early music. So, just like covering a popular song provides a reference point to see their creative arrangements, the familiar songwriting on 'Good to My Baby' acts as a reference point to compare the more innovative songs on the album against."[37]

The website *Rocksucker* pointed out that the song "establishes a formula - that of simple verses followed by deceptively complex bridges and choruses - and throws down its credentials, as if challenging ensuing songs to beat it for sheer craft and joyous enthusiasm....when pumped into your brain via your ears, its soul-strikingly beautiful and drops you off at a chorus that could be deemed 'unusual' were it not so damn catchy."[301]

Often regarded as just an album 'filler,' "Good To My Baby" has since been re-evaluated and is now seen as a fine example of how Brian's incredible creative processes displayed here would lead the way to *Pet Sounds*, and even more remarkable that it was recorded barely two weeks after his nervous breakdown while on a flight to Houston at the start of the band's US tour.

66. Add Some Music To Your Day (*Sunflower* 1970)
(Brian Wilson, Joe Knott, Mike Love)
Recording
28/10/69 Beach Boys Studio, Bel Air (basic track)
19/12/69 Wally Heider Studio, Hollywood (stereo mixes)
12/69 Beach Boys Studio, Bel Air
01/70 Beach Boys Studio Bel Air
18/02/70 Beach Boys Studio, Bel Air (mastering)

Producer - Brian Wilson
Engineer - Stephen Desper
Band members
Brian Wilson (lead vocals, harmony & backing vocals, Rocksichord); Mike Love (lead vocals, harmony & backing vocals); Carl Wilson (lead vocals, harmony & backing vocals, 12-string acoustic guitars, Chamberlin); Dennis Wilson (harmony & backing vocals, drums, percussion); Al Jardine (lead vocals, harmony & backing vocals); Bruce Johnston (lead vocals, harmony & backing vocals, bass guitar)
Album released - 31/08/70
US Single released - 23/02/70 b/w "Susie Cincinnati" Brother/Reprise 0894 #64
Film/TV performance
09/03/70 *Get It Together* ABC New York (broadcast 14/03/70)

Originally the title track of the eponymous album *Add Some Music*, which eventually became the critically acclaimed *Sunflower*, although remembered by some for the two dozen or so songs written that didn't make the final cut. These included "Loop de Loop," Got To Know the Woman," "When Girls Get Together," "Break Away," San Miguel," "I Just Got My Pay," "Susie Cincinnati," "Games Two Can Play," "Lady," "Good Time," and "Take A Load Off Your Feet", all of which in time would resurface on later studio albums or compilations.

"Add Some Music To Your Day" is their celebration of the healing power of music and how, in any form, it helps enrich our daily lives. It was the perfect track to beckon in a new chapter in the band's faltering career, with its blend of breathtaking group harmonies and meaningful lyrics, sadly missing from some of their previous albums. The song also features a unique lead vocal relay with all band member apart from Dennis taking their turn. Brian recalled: "I think we wrote it at my house in Bel Air. It was written by me and Mike and Joe Knott, who was a friend of mine who wasn't a songwriter but he contributed a couple of lines. But I can't remember which ones! The lyrics are wonderful"69

The song, although initially being one of the tracks rejected by Reprise, later had the label show enough interest to have it released as the band's debut single, some six months prior to the album's eventual release. Like the album, it would receive mixed reviews and have little impact on the charts. As good as it was, some radio stations simply refused to have it on their playlists. Band promotor Fred Vail was tirelessly out there promoting the song and getting the top radio stations to put it on their playlists. Jay Cook, the program director at Philadelphia's WFIL, had championed the band ever since their "Surfin' Safari" days, but now told Vail that he couldn't play the song, as the band just weren't "hip anymore."

> *"Even at their lowest points, the Beach Boys had the ability to sound happy they were alive, and delighted to be sharing that happiness"*

Despite this commercial setback many music critics were impressed with its pristine production. *Record World* saw it as having "the same magic sounds that made them famous,"77 while *Billboard* identified that, with the song, the band "has a strong commercial item in this original, easy-beat rhythm number. Will prove a big chart winner." 78 *Cash Box* also praised the song and how the band "strike up a whole new brand of teen excitement tinged with a trace of their old 'Good

Vibrations' work sparked with vitality. The sound and initial sales portend a bright top 40/FM return and BB era beginning once more."[79] Peter Carlin wrote that the song "seemed like a perfect statement of purpose to lead off the band's second decade, given the tune's shared, round-robin style lead vocal, full background harmonies, and plainspoken lyric."[32]

Michael Hann of the *Guardian* wrote: "What makes the song, of course, is the singing: for all the facility of the instrumental arrangement, there's barely a song at the heart of this - it's a custom-built vehicle for the voices…and the richness of their harmonies is almost ambrosial, the sense of security compounded by percussion that's more heartbeat than drumbeat. Even at their lowest points, the Beach Boys had the ability to sound happy they were alive, and delighted to be sharing that happiness."[80]

One of the finest compliments came from musicologist Philip Lambert: "Choral cushions and weaving countermelodies come at us from all directions, giving us a very real sense of how music can control and transform our consciousness…we're thoroughly convinced, not to mention a little breathless with wonder. Brian's lifelong musical message has never been more powerfully or poignantly conveyed."[9]

A bona fide highlight in an album brimming with highlights. A vocals-only track appears on the 2001 *Hawthorne Ca* compilation.

65. Hushabye *(All Summer Long* 1964)
(Doc Pomus, Mort Shuman)
Recording
29/04/64 Western Recorders, LA (tracking & vocals)
30/04/64 Western Recorders, LA (possible extra date)
Producer - Brian Wilson
Engineer - Chuck Britz
Band members
Brian Wilson (lead & backing vocals, piano); Mike Love (lead & backing vocals); Carl Wilson (backing vocals, electric guitar); Dennis Wilson (backing vocals, drums); Al Jardine (backing vocals, bass guitar)
Session musicians
Glen Campbell (possibly 6-string bass guitar); Ray Pohlman (possibly 6-string bass guitar)
Album released - 13/07/64
US EP Four by the Beach Boys released - 21/09/64 Capitol R-5267 #44
UK EP Four by the Beach Boys released - 11/64 EAPI #11

Seemingly out of place on an album full of Beach Boy originals, this beautiful cover of the Mystics' 1959 doo-wop hit, which itself was inspired by the Elegants' #1 hit "Little Star" recorded the previous year. As the story goes, writers Pomus and Shuman had written "Teenager in Love" intended for the Mystics to record, but their record label decided to give it to the more popular Dion and the Belmonts, who scored a #5 with it on the Hot 100 chart. By way of a sort of apology the label asked the writing pair to compose a song for the Mystics in the style of "Little Star," which was basically a doo-wop version of the 1806 English lullaby "Twinkle, Twinkle, Little Star". The result was "Hushabye," based on the old American children's lullaby "All the Pretty Little Horses," and it went on to give the group a #20 hit on the Hot 100.

Brian must have had a strong affinity with the Mystics' ultra-smooth doo-wop vocal arrangement and conjured up a version that knocked the original out of the park. The exquisite 15-second near - a capella introduction is by itself enough reason for its inclusion here. In a different style to the original, Brian uses his magnificent falsetto to sing "oohs" and "aahs" before Mike joins him in perfect harmony on the verse, with backing vocals from the other band members adding to what is a sonic tapestry. The introduction is then repeated at the end but slowed down almost like a loving whisper, thus bookending what is certainly one of Brian's greatest vocal arrangements in terms of depth and complexity. Also worth mentioning is Dennis's simple but effective drumming.

> *"To listen to a band best remembered for their vocal arrangements, there's no better place to start than here"*

A live version and a stunning vocal split mix appeared later on the 1993 *Good Vibrations* box set.

The track was one of four released on *Four By the Beach Boys*, that also included "Wendy," "Little Honda," and "Don't Back Down." *Billboard* described the label's idea that had been prompted by the recently-released *Four by the Beatles*" EP: "Capitol have developed a space age, super single concept which debuts later this month. Tagged the '4-By' series, the new product is four singles by one artist, principally in the teen-age field, which will be merchandised and sold as a single, not an EP…The series will be restricted to acts with immediate market success, with no set release pattern. The four singles will be offered in a soft paper colour sleeve, to get away from the hard carboard EP concept, which, generally speaking, has not been that successful for the industry."[258] Although airplay was sufficient to get "Wendy" and "Little Honda" charted, the other two tracks were not so lucky.

To listen to a band best remembered for their vocal arrangements, there's no better place to start than here.

64. Dance, Dance, Dance *(The Beach Boys Today!* 1965)
(Brian Wilson, Mike Love, Carl Wilson)
Recording
22/09/64 CBS Columbia Studio, Nashville (first tracking & vocal overdubs)
09/10/64 RCA Victor Studio, LA (new tracking - 17 takes; vocal overdubs - 14 takes)
10/64 Western Recorders, LA (mixing)
Producer - Brian Wilson
Engineer - David Hassinger (22/09), Chuck Britz (10/64)
Band members
Brian Wilson (lead, backing & harmony vocals, bass guitar); Mike Love (lead, backing & harmony vocals); Carl Wilson (backing & harmony vocals, 12-string lead guitar); Al Jardine (backing & harmony vocals, rhythm guitar); Dennis Wilson (backing & harmony vocals, drums)
Session musicians
Hal Blaine (sleigh bells, triangle, tambourine, castanets); Glen Campbell (acoustic rhythm/lead guitar); Steve Douglas (tenor sax); Carl Fortina (accordion); Jay Migliori (baritone sax); Ray Pohlman (Danelectro 6-string bass guitar)
Album released - 08/03/64

US single released - 26/10/64 b/w "The Warmth of the Sun" Capitol 5306 #8
UK single released - 10/65 b/w "The Warmth of the Sun" Capitol CL 15370 #24
Film/TV Performances
28/10/64 *The TAMI Show* (recorded at the Civic Auditorium Santa Monica, for cinema release)
18/12/64 *The Bob Hope Comedy Special* NBC
23/12/64 *Shindig!* ABC

The day after appearing at Knoxville's Civic Auditorium on Sept 21st 1964, Brian and the band took a short break and went to what was the nearest available studio to record a version of a new song, "Dance, Dance, Dance," with music by Brian and Carl, and lyrics by Brian and Mike. Seventeen days later they re-recorded it at Western with very little changes.

This energetic rocker about shaking off the blues by just dancing them away originated from a simple guitar riff by Carl (hence his writing credit), thus giving him his first writing contribution to one of the band's singles. According to Mike in his interview for *Goldmine* in 1992: "I asked Carl if he wrote any lyrics for the song and he said no. He just came up with the guitar line...It is a cool line. Brian Wilson and Mike Love split 50-50 on that. I was the one who wrote the Chuck Berry-styled alliteration lyrics. That's my scene."93 (Mike, of course, would go on to win a lawsuit and be awarded a third of the co-writing credit and royalties).

The song begins with the memorable riff supplied by sessionist Ray Pohlman with his Danelectro electric bass guitar, soon accompanied by Carl and Glen Campbell, the latter soon to become a touring Beach Boy himself.

Carl in fact played his guitar "live" on the recording rather than overdubbing it later as usual. Studio chatter at the time shows the boys messing around and engaged in conversation about their forthcoming European tour rather than focusing on the double-tracked vocals.

Billboard wrote in its review: "A smash entry. Expected outdoor sound featuring a tremendous rock-surfin' beat and groovy lyrics. Boys have never sounded better,."81 while *Cash Box* offered: "The Beach Boys amazing string should soon see the addition of this two-sided follow-up...that zips along with monkey-making glee...Look like a big double-header."82. In its retrospective review, the *Guardian's* Alexis Petridis wrote: "It says something about the company it kept that 'Dance, Dance, Dance,' feels undervalued among the Beach Boys' run of classic singles. Carl's riff is great, its 12-string guitar and frantic solo bear the influence of the Beatles' 'A Hard Day's Night,' but the sudden key change midway through the third verse is pure Brian."83 The instrumental track was later included on the 1993 *Good Vibrations* box set.

"I was getting far out, coming undone, having a breakdown, and I just let myself go completely"

With this, their 16th single heading for the Hot 100 Top Ten, the Beach Boys were on the crest of the proverbial wave, and Capitol continued to put pressure on Brian to deliver much of the same. But things were about to change, as Brian recalled: "I was run-down mentally and emotionally because I was running around, jumping on jets from one city to another, on one-night stands, also producing, writing, arranging, singing, planning, teaching - to the point where I had no peace of mind and no chance to actually sit down and think or even rest. I was so mixed up and so overworked."11

Just two months after the release of "Dance, Dance, Dance," the Beach Boys set off on their two-week South/Midwest US tour. On the flight to Houston, Brian had a nervous breakdown. Speaking to David Leaf for *Teen Beat* he recalled: "I was getting far out, coming undone, having a breakdown, and I just let myself go completely. I dumped myself out of the seat and all over the plane. I let myself go emotionally…They knew what was happening and I was coming apart. The rubber band had stretched as far as it would go."11

After doing the show that night, Brian flew back to LA with his road manager the next morning. It would be his last concert with the band for nearly 12 years. It may not have been apparent at the time but this would be a pivotal and historic moment in the story of The Beach Boys.

Jonny Abrams of *Rocksucker* wrote: "The transition from 'Dance, Dance, Dance' to 'Please Let Me Wonder' mirrors the transition of the Beach Boys from surf-rocking youth culture phenomenon to stately, soulful visionaries responsible for some of the most awe-inspiring music ever written and recorded."301

63. Little Deuce Coupe (*Surfer Girl* 1963)
(Brian Wilson, Roger Christian)
Recording
12/06/63 Western Recorders, LA (tracking & vocals)
Producer - Brian Wilson
Engineer - Chuck Britz
Band members
Mike Love (lead vocal); Brian Wilson (piano, vocals); Carl Wilson (bass guitar, vocals); Dennis Wilson (vocals), David Marks (lead guitar)
Session musician
Hal Blaine (drums)
Album released - 16/09/63
US single released - 22/07/63 b-side to "Surfer Girl" Capitol 5009 #5
Film/TV performances
24/01/64 *Surf Sound* ATN-7 Sydney (broadcast 08/02/64)
14/03/64 NBC Television Studios, Burbank (part of concert for screening in selected US cinemas; later released in 1998 as *The Lost Concert*
21/01/77 Capital Centre, Washington DC
21/06/80 Knebworth, England concert (later released on CD/DVD)

This was the first car-related collaboration between Brian and Buffalo-born radio personality Roger Christian (1934-1991), although their second, "Shut Down," was actually recorded first for the album *Surfin' USA*. Both would eventually be paired together on *Little Deuce Coupe*.

The car in question was the Ford Model 18, with the 1932 coupe model known as the "deuce coupe," and it was Christian's dream of having one that led him to California in 1959. He recalled in an interview with Bob Shannon: "Everyone wanted one because deuce coupes had great lines, and you could make street rods out of them that looked so pretty." Where such cars in his hometown were susceptible to rust due to salt on the roads in winter, Christian headed to the coast to fulfil his dream. After finding a job and saving enough money he bought a cherry deuce coupe.

After his meeting with Brian, arranged by Murry after hearing him talking about "409" on his radio show, Christian wrote the lyrics to "Shut Down," based on one of his car-related poems. According to Christian: "Mike Love brought up

"It's a legend of empowerment, an idealisation of teenage nirvana"

the subject of deuce coupes because he owned one. Mike told Brian that he thought it would be great to a do a song about it. So Brian came back and said, 'You still got that song about the deuce coupe?' I said, sure, and gave it to him." Apparently, Brian made one significant change to the lyrics, adding the line "*and one more thing I got the pink slip, daddy*," (referring to the certificate of ownership). Brian later commented on the song: "We loved doing 'Little Deuce Coupe.' It was a good 'shuffle' rhythm, which was not like most of the rhythms of the records on the radio in those days. It had a bouncy feel to it. Like most of our records, it had a competitive lyric. This record was my favourite Beach Boys car song."44

Christian felt that Brian liked working with a collaborator as he needed "a sounding board, almost like a competition thing." He continued: "Two creative people get together and they bring out the best in each other. [But] he did a lot of things by himself. Brian was the most talented creator I've ever worked with. Brian would do it all. He would write the words, write the music, teach the guys the harmony, produce the record [but] as confident as he was, or as he should have been because he was a master, he still needed someone to encourage him and give him confidence. Brian was up and down. One day he knew he had it made, and the world was digging what he did. And the next day one little thing would happen and put him on a downer. When he was happy, he produced great stuff. It was easy for me to see that and encourage him."44

The vibrant, sing-along track introduced the familiar basic backbeat that would be a feature of many of their records over the next few years. It was cut on three-track in the same session as a re-recording of "Surfer Girl." Engineer Chuck Britz recalled how Brian and the boys worked in the studio during those early days: "We did everything live. After we did the instrumental track, I just set three mikes out there, and i'd put Carl, Dennis and Al on one, and I'd put Brian on one. And Brian would either sing into the lead mike when it was his lead, or into the background when Mike sang lead. Mike was always on a separate mike. Brian always doubled the lead; there were times he would sing it so right on, that it was hard to figure out whether there was a delay or not."

This was also the first session that had Brian as official producer, and one of the last sessions before the return of Al Jardine and the departure of David Marks. According to Christian, Brian had to replace Dennis with session drummer Hal Blaine.

Both "Little Deuce Coupe" and "Shut Down" have similar melodic lines, although on a demo of "Little Deuce Coupe" (found on 2001's *Hawthorne Ca.*) they sound different, more like those of Chuck Berry's "Johnny B Goode."

Musicologist Philip Lambert suggests that the similarity may have been behind the delay in putting "Little Deuce Coupe" on an album in light of the recent authorship problems caused by similarities between "Surfin' USA" and Berry's "Sweet Little Sixteen."[9] *Mojo's* Bill Holdship wrote: "In crafting one of the most durable car songs ever, that "surf" band had turned his vehicle into a legend of empowerment, an idealisation of teenage nirvana."[25]

"Little Deuce Coupe" is also one of the songs performed on *The Lost Concert* video, with Mike introducing the song with short instrumental segments, starting with Dennis on drums, Al on rhythm guitar, Carl on lead, and Brian on bass, before they all launch into the full song. The idea had apparently come to Mike while on tour in July 1963.

Mike recalled: "Here's how impulsive Brian was. 'Little Deuce Coupe' was finished in the studio and we'd drive a couple of blocks down the street to the radio station and have them play it, much to the chagrin of the record company who would like to press it up and have it available for sale. But he wanted to hear it on the radio that night. So it played at like 1:00am for the first time on the radio."[3]

In Spielberg's 2005 movie *War of the Worlds,* Tom Cruise sings the song to Dakota Fanning as a lullaby.

62. Be With Me (*20/20* 1969)
(Dennis Wilson)
Recording
02/11/68 Capitol Studio, Hollywood (tracking & vocals - 14 takes)
11/11/68 Capitol Studio, Hollywood (mixing)
Producer - Dennis Wilson
Engineer -Stephen Desper
Band members inc.
Dennis Wilson (lead vocal)
Session musician
Van McCoy (strings arrangement)
Album released - 10/02/69

Dennis Wilson had once told the world: "Brian is the Beach Boys. He is the band. We're his f*****g messengers. He is all of it. Period. We're nothing. He's everything." There's no doubt that up until mid-1968 that statement may appear to carry weight but at the same it disparages what contributions other band members made, especially Mike and Carl. Dennis would probably agree that his role in that period was rather insignificant. The *Friends* album saw him stepping from the shadows and emerging as quite a creative talent with two songs, "Little Bird" and "Be Still," co-written with friend and poet Steve Kalinich, and both showing maturity and depth.

Then came his fated association with ex-con and soon-to-be murderer Charles Manson. Within a few months, any fascination he had for Manson and his followers evaporated as it turned to death threats once the "evil wizard" had shown his true colours. The very same month that the Beach Boys' new album would be released, Manson would go on trial and be charged for the infamous Tate-La Bianca murders.

The new album *20/20* would see Carl and Bruce rising to the occasion with both writing and production credits, and although the inclusion of two near-intact

Smile songs would be the surprising highlight for many, it served as another platform for Dennis to show just how sophisticated a writer he had become with two outstanding tracks. At least one (maybe both) would have a connection with Manson.

> *"Brian is the Beach Boys. We're his f*****g messengers. He is all of it. Period. We're nothing. He's everything"*

In "Be With Me," a solo effort in both writing and accompaniment, Dennis employs his own artistic sensibility to create a wonderful ballad that is both lush and darkly haunting in its complexity. With its descending horns, dynamic drumming (Dennis?), lavish string arrangement (by Van McCoy), and the unexpected, exploding chorus, this is as momentous as it can get. With his arousing voice still in its prime, and no apparent contributions from other band members, this is Dennis announcing to the world he has truly arrived as an accomplished writer and producer.

With the song's eerie, ominous overtones, there are strong rumours that Manson may have had a hand in the writing, but there is no evidence to support it. David Leaf described it as being "dark and eerie...perfectly capturing the emotions of the era."[26]

Another of Dennis's songs recorded at the time was the gorgeous ballad "A Time To Live in Dreams," co-written with Kalinich, and later included on 2001's *Hawthorne Ca.* compilation. A missed opportunity by the band or label, as it should have made the album instead of the other Wilson-Kalinich track, the less impressive "All I Want To Do."

One of the finest reviews of the song came from Peter Doggett: "While Brian painted with delicate brush strokes, Dennis's approach was a splash of technicolour, emotionally overpowering. Its dramatic flourish added psychic dimension to a lyric that was a little more than mundane."[19]

The sheer beauty of the backing track for "Be With Me" can be found on 2001's *Hawthorne Ca.,* while Dennis's sensuous original demo with just piano accompaniment can be savoured on 2013's *Made in California.*

61. The Night Was So Young (*The Beach Boys Love You* 1977)
(Brian Wilson)
Recording
10/76-11/76 Brother Studios, Santa Monica
Producer - Brian Wilson
Engineers - Stephen Moffitt, Earle Mankey
Band members
Carl Wilson (lead vocal); The Beach Boys (backing vocals, instruments unknown)
Album released - 11/04/77

A song apparently written about Brian's tangled affair with 19-year-old telephone operator Debbie Keil, who, according to Brian's biographer Steven Gaines, moved from her home in Kansas with the sole intention of getting close to the singer. Working as the band's non-paid fan mail sorter from 1969-70, Brian allowed her to make nightly visits to his home, much to the chagrin of his wife Marilyn.

Brian once referred to Keil as a "golden-haired angel coming in at night."[123] She had first met the band after travelling from Kansas to Atlantic City to see them in concert. Even after Marilyn fired her after hearing that Brian had driven her home from the office one day, she still found it almost impossible to keep her away, with Brian inviting her over whenever he felt lonely. Carlin described how the song revelled "in traditional shades of self-pity, jealousy, and loneliness."[32]

"A stark image of an abandoned man contemplating an empty future while sipping milk at three in the morning"

Despite the alleged infidelity, the song is still a powerful and romantic ballad with Carl once again handling Brian's heartfelt lyrics about a girl who "*has to hide*" and "*won't even try*" to fulfil his desires. Rick Swan revelled in the song's "stark image of an abandoned man contemplating an empty future while sipping milk at three in the morning. Immersed in sorrow while entertaining an illusion (he really thinks his beloved would welcome a visit in the middle of the night)"[21] Al called it one of his favourite songs by the band: "Oh God, isn't that a remarkable bridge? With that little tempo change, its beautiful. It is Brian and Carl at their best."[47]

Brian claimed that the song was one of his favourites and one of the most underrated,[63] and in his 2016 memoir added his praise for the "beautiful ballad" and its "great harmonies."[35] In 2021 he would re-record the song for the documentary, *Brian Wilson: Long Promised Road*. Erik Kempke, writing for *Pitchfork,* highlighted the song's "beautiful harmonies," adding that it sounded "like it could have been a *Pet Sounds* outtake, were it not for the beautiful synths."[124] Musician Dennis Diken of the Smithereens described it as his favourite track on the album and the "most realised" in terms of its instrumental arrangement.[125]

60. Never Learn Not To Love (*20/20* 1968)
(Dennis Wilson)
Recording
11/09/68 Beach Boys Studio, Bel Air (tracking)
16/09/68 Beach Boys Studio, Bel Air
17/09/68 Beach Boys Studio, Bel Air
18/11/68 Beach Boys Studio, Bel Air (strings)
09/68 Beach Boys Studio, Bel Air (vocals)
14/10/68 Capitol Studios, NY
15/10/68 Capitol Studios, NY (mastering)
Producer – Dennis Wilson
Engineer – Stephen Desper
Band members
Dennis Wilson (lead & backing vocals, piano); Brian Wilson (backing vocals); Carl Wilson (backing vocals, bass, guitar); Mike Love (backing vocals); Al Jardine (backing vocals); Bruce Johnston (backing vocals)
Session musicians
John Guerin (drums, percussion, sleigh bells); Don Randi (piano, organ); Lyle Ritz (upright bass).
Album released - 10/02/69
US single released - 02/12/68 b-side to "Bluebirds Over the Mountain" Capitol 2360 #61

UK single released - 29/11/68 b-side to "Bluebirds Over the Mountain" Capitol CL 15572#33
Film/TV performance
01/04/69 *The Mike Douglas Show* Westinghouse, Philadelphia (broadcast 09/04/69)

33-year-old Charles Milles Manson was not just an ex-con when he met Dennis in April 1968 but also an amateur songwriter with limited talent, yet still good enough for one Beach Boy to be convinced and form a kind of "musical kinship" with him. It was a time when Dennis, maybe feeling guilty about his wealthy status, had no qualms about giving away money to total strangers, and Manson took full advantage of his generosity, eventually moving into his Sunset Boulevard home with his "Family" of disciples. Dennis, as well as his friends Gregg Jakobson and Terry Melcher, were stimulated by the "wizard's" lifestyle and spiritual philosophising.

Showing an interest in some of Manson's songwriting, Dennis was keen to have him signed to the Brother label, although later claiming "he didn't have a musical bone in his whole body." Introducing him to engineer Steve Desper at the Beach Boys' newly-built studio, they agreed to cut a demo for Manson, who insisted on one caveat - "I don't care what you do with the music. Just don't let anybody change any of the lyrics." Some six to eight songs were allegedly recorded, some of them not demos at all but actually well-produced, polished songs, with some overseen by Carl and possibly a couple by Dennis. A short while later, Beach Boy manager Nick Grillo stepped in and put a stop to any more recordings.

"Dennis took Manson's original concept and made something of it - something Manson could never have done"

One of those songs was called "Cease To Exist," which Manson had intended for the band to record on acoustic guitar, and allegedly inspired by the current in-fighting among the band members, especially the brothers. He explained later: "[They] were fighting amongst themselves, so I wrote that song to bring them together. 'Submission is a gift, give it to your brother.' Dennis has true soul, but his brothers couldn't accept it."89

One of Manson's followers, the infamous Lynette "Squeaky" Frome, recalled: "Charlie made up a song for Dennis, and we wrote down the words. Part of it was from a man to a woman, and part from a man to his brothers...Dennis would later talk the Beach Boys into recording the song, but someone would talk him into changing the rhythm and words, and failing to even mention Charlie."90

During the summer it was reported that Manson and his family spent over $100,000 of Dennis's generosity on food, clothing, studio time, drugs, and doctors' bills. But Manson's true colours were beginning to show with head-on clashes with Dennis, even putting a knife to his throat and threatening to kill him. Melcher's offer to get him a record deal with a major label also never materialised.

In September, Manson got to hear that his song "Cease To Exist" was to be included on the band's next album *20/20*, but with its new title "Never Learn Not to Love" and the opening line changed to *"cease to resist."* Also revised was the line "*Submission is a gift, go on give it to your brother.*" By simply changing "brother" to "lover" the message was sterilised into a line of romantic seduction.76.

Manson was furious that his lyrics had been changed, and even more so when it was released in December as the flip-side to the single "Bluebirds Over the Mountain," and only reaching #61 on the charts.

As well as the lyric change Dennis and Desper had together completely reworked the original blues-inspired song, with a new vocal arrangement, a forbidding-sounding backward cymbal intro, and an additional bridge. The eerie opening sound to the song was achieved by simply playing a cymbal backwards.

According to Desper: "Manson only had a song with basic chords on the guitar and a melody lead line. It was the Boys who took the basic concept and turned it into a real commercial tune...Dennis took Manson's original concept and made something of it - something Manson could never have done."91 Desper even went on to confirm that all the added vocal arrangement was the work of Brian and Carl. Al recalled: "It was just a melody...but there was a mantra behind it. Then Dennis wanted to put in everything. I thought, 'Oh Boy, this is getting to be too much.'47. Mike went on record to admit that, at the time, he wasn't aware that Manson had written the lyrics, believing it to be Dennis. Even fans of the band had to wait many years to discover the truth.

With Manson's ever-growing erratic and threatening behaviour for changing the lyrics, Dennis soon put an end to their friendship. As for the expected royalties to come his way Manson was never actually given writing credit by the band, although, according to Dennis, he had agreed to exchange his credit for cash and a motorbike. Desper called it "retribution" for gleaning so much money from Dennis, going on to say that Manson only spent one evening in the studio with his "silent girls" and "never conferred or worked in any way with the group... Manson was a thief and did not play by civil rules. By those rules, he was compensated as far as they were concerned."91

On April 1st 1969 the band performed "Never Learn Not To Love" on the *Mike Douglas Show* (broadcast eight days later), with live vocals over a taped backing track, and Carl replacing Dennis on drums. Four months later, Manson and his cult committed the infamous Tate/La Bianca murders, and in the trial that followed nearly a year later Manson was given a life sentence.

Mark Dillon believed that the Manson episode pushed Dennis over the edge into a spiral of self-destruction, consuming him with guilt for both his association with Manson and the murders that followed.10 During the trial, and with a sad touch of irony, Manson's debut album *Lie: The Love and Terror Cult* was released, including his version of "Cease to Exist."

Michael Little believes Manson's version to be far superior to the Beach Boys, especially the vocals: "You expect a tattered, raw, and raggedy voice, with a touch of lunatic rage, but what you get is a smooth-voiced folk singer...[and one that] gives the song an impressive lo-fi immediacy that is a million miles away from the Beach Boys' treatment."88

I would rather avoid it like the plague...

59. Wild Honey (*Wild Honey* 1967)
(Brian Wilson, Mike Love)
Recording
26/09/67 Beach Boys Studio, Bel Air (tracking & vocals)
27/09/67 Beach Boys Studio, Bel Air (Electro theremin overdub)
Producer - The Beach Boys
Engineer - Jim Lockert
Band members
Carl Wilson (lead & backing vocals, guitar, tambourine); Brian Wilson (backing vocals, piano); Mike Love (backing vocals); Dennis Wilson (backing vocals, drums, bongos); Al Jardine (backing vocals); Bruce Johnston (backing vocals, Farfisa organs, bass guitar)
Session musician
Paul Tanner (Electro-theremin)
Album released - 18/12/67
US single released - 23/10/67 b/w "Wind Chimes" #31
UK single released -11/67 b/w "Wind Chimes" #29

In recent years Mike Love gave his opinion on *Wild Honey*: "That was an underground album, I figure, for us. It was completely out of the mainstream for what was going on at that time, which was all hard rock/psychedelic music. It just didn't have anything to do with what was going on, and that was the idea."[92] The title track for the album, the band's first foray into R&B, was a light-hearted take-off of Brian's health food craze.

"One more gift of music from probably the greatest musician alive"

In an interview for *Goldmine* in 1992, Mike revealed how he got the idea for the song while at Brian's house: "So there's this can of wild honey and we're making some tea. So I said, I'll write the lyrics about this girl who was a wild little honey. And I wrote it from the perspective that that album was Brian's R&B-influenced album, in his mind. It may not sound like it to a Motown executive, but that was where he was coming from on that record. In that particular instance, I wrote it from the perspective of Stevie Wonder singing it."[93].

In a 2012 interview for *Billboard*, Mike had a similar recollection: "What would Stevie Wonder say to his mother about a girl that maybe she didn't want him to get involved with, but then says, 'Screw it' - he really digs the chick. This was the premise of the song."

Apparently recorded in just one day at Brian's home studio on September 26th 1967 the song begins with Bruce's organ and bass guitar, followed by percussion, tambourine, and Brian's piano, and then Carl's lead guitar overdubbed. Instrumental inserts followed, including Dennis playing his bass drum out in the hallway. Rounding off the session were more vocal overdubs and an organ solo by Bruce. The Electro-theremin played by sessionist Paul Tanner produced the catchy riff that was easily the song's highlight and unique selling point, and was the third time the band had utilised the instrument (after "I Just Wasn't Made For These Times" and "Good Vibrations."). Only Carl's gritty but stretched lead vocal had cause for criticism.

The beauty of the song, and the album as a whole, is in what Paul Williams, founder of *Crawdaddy*, described as being "new and fresh and raw and beautiful, and the first step in the direction of even greater things than what was once to be...a work of joy, and one more gift of music from probably the greatest musician alive."[94] *Billboard* called it "an easy rocker with a steady and solid dance beat,"[95] while *Cash Box's* review predicted "a sweet ride to the upper reaches of the charts...with a thumping, pulsing ditty."[96]. *Rolling Stone* was not so impressed: "The title track is one of the nicest: theremin, heavily chorded piano and a repetitious melody line. The sexual associations are a touch too obvious, and the sock-it-to me line really out of place."[97] *Mojo* described it as a "guileless romp of a song," but couldn't help passing a comment about the lyrics: "The love-tasting-of-honey lyrics are all faintly suggestive...but since the whole thing is posed as a plea for understanding from his mama, we must believe the homebound Brian's explanation that the song came from a tin of honey sat on his kitchen shelf."[25]

Wild Honey became the last Beach Boys album to have Brian as primary composer until *Love You* in 1977, and only the second album not to list him as producer. His reluctance to steer the ship this time maybe have been down to his state of mind and demoralisation for the abandonment of *Smile,* and the commercial failures that followed with *Pet Sounds* and *Smiley Smile.* But with *Wild Honey* the band were going "back to their roots", playing their own instruments and no longer "ball-less choir boys" as one critic described them.

With Brian taking a back seat when it came to production, it gave some other band members a chance to shine. But this was 1967 when most rock groups were turning to psychedelia. Instead of jumping on the bandwagon, the boys, with or without Brian, were deliberately aiming to go back to basics, heading in a completely different music direction with hithero unexplored acoustic pop and white soul. Commenting on the album, Mike Love confirmed it had been a conscious decision: "That was an underground album, I figure, for us. It was completely out of the mainstream for what was going on at that time, which was all hard rock/psychedelic music. It just didn't have anything to do with what was going on, and that was the idea"[92]. *Rolling Stone* were quick to spot the irony: "It's kind of amusing that the Beach Boys are suddenly re-discovering rhythm and blues five years after the Beatles and Stones had brought it all back home."[97]

Only time would tell if the decision had been the right one...

58. Pet Sounds (*Pet Sounds* 1966)
(Brian Wilson)
Recording
17/11/65 Western Recorders LA (take #3 master)
Producer - Brian Wilson
Engineer - Chuck Britz
Band members
Brian Wilson (grand piano)
Session musicians
Roy Caton (trumpet); Bill Green (alto sax, guiro); Jerry Cole (electric lead guitar); Ritchie Frost (drums, bongos, Coca-Cola cans with sticks); Jim Horn (bass sax); Plas Johnson (tenor sax, tambourine); Carol Kaye (electric bass); Jay Migliori (baritone sax); Lyle Ritz (upright bass); Billy Strange (guitar with Leslie effect); Tommy Tedesco (archtop acoustic rhythm guitar)
Album released - 16/05/66

With the original title of "Run James Run," this instrumental (one of two on *Pet Sounds*) was apparently intended for a James Bond movie. According to Brian in 1996: "'Pet Sounds' was supposed to be a James Bond type of song. We were gonna try to get it to the James Bond people. But we thought it would never happen, so we put it on the album."[85]

The movie Brian was referring to was *Thunderball*, the fourth in the franchise, and released in December 1965. In his 2016 memoir, he recalled: "I loved Thunderball, which had come out the year before [the album *Pet Sounds*], and I loved listening to composers like Henry Mancini, who did these cool things for shows like Peter Gunn, and Les Baxter, who did all these big productions that sounded sort of like Phil Spector productions."[35]

Recorded at Western, with no other band members present, the session sheet had the notation, "This is a working title only." The unique percussion sound, which was Brian's idea, comes from session drummer Ritchie Frost playing two empty Coca-Cola cans with sticks. Other percussion is provided by reverberated bongos and a güiro (an open-ended hollow gourd with notches cut in one side and played by rubbing a stick along the notches to produce a ratchet sound).

"We were gonna try to get it to the James Bond people. But we thought it would never happen, so we put it on the album"

With the decision to place "Run, James, Run" on the new album, the name was changed. and it became the title track. On March 3rd 1966 Capitol issued an update to a previous memo that listed intended songs for the *Pet Sounds* album, and now omitted "Good, Good, Good Vibrations" in favour of "Pet Sounds."

Like "Sloop John B," it's inclusion has been criticised for not fitting in with the album's theme. Noted Beach Boy historian Charles Granata wrote: "Of the album's two instrumentals, 'Pet Sounds' is the least fitting. Curiously sandwiched between a pair of sumptuous ballads ...the stylised tempo arrangement is jarringly out of place...like 'Sloop John B' it bears no thematic relevance to the balance of songs."[74] However, he admitted that "[it] neatly ties together all the instrumental elements that make the album a marvel. From its sensual Latin percussion...to the steely edginess of a heavily reverbed electric guitar, the tune is texture personified: a two-and-a-half minute rendezvous to a tropical paradise"[85]

Christian Matijas-Mecca wrote: "This instrumental is easily overlooked and often is dismissed for its unstructured "lounge" groove. It is a fun and quirky piece and a reflection of Brian's grand sense of humour while it also provides an emotional release prior to the album's concluding, and heartbreaking final track, 'Caroline, No.'"[5] According to Jim Fusilli, "The inventiveness of the arrangement makes it worthy [to be on the album]. Though its overly busy and lacks a focus...it links to the theme of the rest of the album."[130] *Mojo* saw it as "an ambiguous, jet-age update of Martin Denny-style 1950s exotica."[25]

In his fine study of *Pet Sounds*, Kingsley Abott called it "a great collage of sound that balances the relaxed feel of 'Let's Go Away For Awhile.' It also vividly illustrates Brian's explorations of new guitar and percussion sounds. Woodblocks and a soda can being struck combine with the guiro and sleigh bells, while a winding, hypnotic guitar figure provides the song with a weepy sound."75

Once again, Rick Swan provides a more light-hearted review: "The arrangement glistens with clever touches, including a phalanx of saxes, heavily echoed tambourines and something that sounds like a croaking frog."21

57. Tears In the Morning *(Sunflower* 1970)
(Bruce Johnston)
Recording
18/11/69 Beach Boys Studio, Bel Air (tracking)
26/01/70 Valentine Studio, Studio City CA (strings?)
28/01/70 Valentine Studio, Studio City CA (different lyrics, vocals, solo piano tag)
18/02/70 Beach Boys Studio, Bel Air (mastering)
Producer - The Beach Boys (Bruce Johnston)
Engineer - Stephen Desper
Band members
Bruce Johnston (lead vocals, harmony & backing vocals, Rocksichord, grand piano on coda); Brian Wilson (harmony & backing vocals); Carl Wilson (harmony & backing vocals, guitar); Mike Love (harmony & backing vocals); Al Jardine (harmony & backing vocals)
Session musicians
Hal Blaine (drums); Ronald Benson (guitar, mandolin); Ray Pohlman (bass); Daryl Dragon (vibraphone); Carl Fortina (French concertina); Abe Luboff (arco double bass); unknown (trumpet); Michael Colombier (string arrangement); 8 violins, 2 cellos, 4 viola
Album released - 31/08/70
US single released - 12/10/70 b/w "It's About Time" Brother/Reprise 0957
UK single released - 11/70 b/w "It's About Time" Stateside SS 2181
Film/TV performance
18/11/70 *Top of the Pops* BBC-1 London (broadcast 19/11/70)

Another slightly remixed *Add Some Music* original, this was Bruce's other contribution to *Sunflower* following on from the slightly less impressive "Deirdre." Both songs relate to the singer's past relationships, but this one finds him in full melodramatic, heartbreaking flow about a girl who leaves him and then goes off to Europe with his unborn child. Of course, this was stretching the truth a little. According to Bruce: "I had a girlfriend that broke up with me, so I let my mind run away with itself. It's a waltz, like 'Disney Girls' ...Mike calls me the Waltz King. It was never supposed to be a single."11

Although both songs were considered slightly at odds with the tenor of the album, this beautiful ballad of lost love brings a marked change of pace and an injection of straightforward old-fashioned "pop" into an otherwise innovative album, arguably their best since *Pet Sounds*. *Record World* suggested that the band "should smile at the projected success of this excellent Bruce Johnston composition...It will happen,"100 while Timothy White wrote: "The unusual approach for modern rock-pop is redeemed by the track's production clarity."69

> *"At least it can be said that they got one last good record in there before they really started sucking"*

Swamped by gratuitous strings, once again arranged by "funky Frenchman" Michael Colombier, and with even a Parisian accordion thrown in for good measure, this and Bruce's "Deirdre" were a much-welcomed addition to the band's first album for their new label, with "Tears in the Morning" chosen as its second single. Although dropping like a stone on the US and UK charts, it nevertheless scored a surprising #4 hit in Holland. When Bruce performed it live with just piano and no accompaniment, it lead Michael Ledgerwood of British magazine *Disc & Music Echo* to write an interesting review: "I must admit, it went down a storm, as the song benefited from the simple piano-voice presentation. But if you'd seen the expressions and heard the mutterings of the others in the group as they were ordered off stage, it looked decidedly as though Bruce could find himself in the doghouse."[102]

On November 18th 1970 the band performed the song on BBC's *Top of the Pops*. Unfortunately, like a number of their performances around this time, there is no surviving footage.

Although sales of the album were once again disappointing, the band could not have asked for better reviews from their erstwhile critics. In more recent years that appreciation has never been more widely felt. *Pitchfork* wrote: "The group dynamic (no longer as Brian Wilson-focused) reinvigorated the production and songwriting remarkably. The thematic and lyrical content is suitably eccentric and cheesy at times, but that element is as much a part of the work of the Beach Boys as musical invention...Some say out of strife and tension comes the best music, and while this doesn't apply to the band's follow up, *Surf's Up*, at least it can be said that they got one last good record in there before they really started sucking."[101]. *Mojo* described it as "a harrowing rumination on the 'cancelled future' of a man and his wife...[confirming] that the Beach Boys were ready to match the singer-songwriters they heard at the dawn of a less innocent decade."[25]

56. I Bet He's Nice *(The Beach Boys Love You 1977)*
(Brian Wilson)
Recording
10/76-01/77 Brother Studios, Santa Monica (demos, tracking, vocals, overdubbing)
Producer - Brian Wilson
Engineer - Earle Mankey
Band members
Brian Wilson (lead vocals, keyboards, synthesisers, drums); Carl Wilson (lead vocals, certain instruments); Dennis Wilson (lead vocals, certain instruments); Mike Love (backing vocals); Al Jardine (backing vocals)
Album released - 11/04/77

By the mid-70's the "Brian is Back" campaign was in full flow when it came to concert and album promotions, beginning with the largely indifferent album *15 Big Ones*, released in July 1976, but the public's visual perception of the "new" Brian was somewhat overshadowed by the intense, unconventional round-the-clock therapy he was receiving at the hands of unscrupulous psychologist Dr Eugene Landy (1934-2006). But three months later came *Love You,* at first glance a semi-autobiographical nod to Brian's boyhood, with songs brimming with almost fragile, childlike simplicity.

With most of the other band members feeling less enthusiastic about recording another album, it was left to an invigorated Brian to create what turned out to be an almost solo effort, apart from a few added vocals by the other band members. While Brian spent some three months at work in studio, Dennis was producing his own masterpiece, *Pacific Ocean Blue*; Al was apparently taking time out with his family on the farm; Carl was producing the album *Beached* for Ricci Martin's band the Pack; and Mike?... well, he was quite happy preaching TM to those who would listen.

The first time since Smile that Brian was given full control on a Beach Boy recording

With *15 Big Ones* being another disappointment as far as fans and critics were concerned, Brian had made a promise that the next album, their penultimate one with Warner, would be a "masterpiece." In December 1976 not only was Dr Landy dismissed for what were seen as his controversial methods of treatment, but Brian revealed his notion of having the freedom to do a solo album.103. Fearing how this would affect the band members made him change his mind. Prior to recording, Brian previewed them some of the songs he had written, but for most of the time it was he alone in the studio with his engineer.

Not only was this the first time since *Smile* that Brian was given full control on a Beach Boy recording, it was also an album that some considered to be about a man hoping to regain his shattered personality, with the type of lyrics that Brian was hoping his fans were looking for from the band. Like Bruce had revealed with "Tears in the Morning," the song "I Bet He's Nice" is another potential heartbreaker, where the narrator clings to the soothing but bittersweet memories of a love lost. Painfully honest, it features Brian and Dennis trading their gruff vocals on the verses, a wonderful bridge by Carl, and a coda not too dissimilar (although not near as good) to that of "God Only Knows."

This song, along with "The Night Was So Young" and its similar tale of loneliness and abandonment, are the highlights of what turned out to be quite an improvement on *15 Big Ones,* and a much more convincing advert for the "Brian is Back" campaign. No masterpiece, that's for sure; not even comparable to *Pet Sounds* or *Sunflower* for certain, but with superlative tracks like these, it's not hard to realise that, even with what turned out at the time to be a short-lived creative rejuvenation, Brian Wilson was still a major force to be reckoned with.

55. Then I Kissed Her (*Summer Days (And Summer Nights!!)*
1965
(Phil Spector, Ellie Greenwich, Jeff Barry)
Recording
03/05/65 Western Recorders, LA (tracking - 16 takes; instrumental inserts, vocal overdubs)
Producer - Brian Wilson
Engineer - Chuck Britz
Band members
Al Jardine (lead vocals); Brian Wilson (harmony & backing vocals, bass guitar, grand piano, timpani); Carl Wilson (harmony & backing vocals, electric & 12-string acoustic guitars); Mike Love (harmony & backing vocals); Dennis Wilson (drums); Bruce Johnston (Hammond B3 organ, castanets)
Session musicians/Guests
Ron Swallow (tambourine); unknown (castanets)

Album released - 05/07/65
UK single released - 28/04/67 b/w "Mountain of Love" Capitol CL 15502 #4
Film/TV Performances
28/04//67 *Top of the Pops* BBC-1 London (broadcast 18/05/67) (promo film)
25/12/67 *Best of TOTP Pt 1* BBC-1 London (repeat showing)

Brian's on-going homage to his great idol Phil Spector continued with this Crystals' classic from 1963. What had started with "Don't Worry Baby" being his direct answer to "Be My Baby," was then followed in succession by his Spector-influenced *Christmas Album*; writing "Don't Hurt My Little Sister" for him to record, and then doing his own covers of the Crystals' "There's No Other (Like My Baby)" for the *Party* album; and finally "I'm So Young" by Spector's wife-to-be Veronica for *Today!* It was only a matter of time before he gave one of Spector's more familiar hits the Beach Boys treatment.

Originally titled "Then He Kissed Me," the Crystals had scored a #6 Hot 100 hit with it in July 1963. Recorded at Gold Star, the lead vocal belonged to 15-year-old Dolores "La La" Brooks. For the Beach Boys' version, the story of a young girl's romantic encounter and eventual engagement to a young man had to undergo a gender swap and slightly revised lyrics to see it from the male point of view with "Then I Kissed Her."

> **"It was only a matter of time before [Brian] gave one of Spector's more familiar hits the Beach Boys treatment"**

Instead of doing a reinterpretation, Brian opted to remain faithful to the original without trying to emulate Spector's iconic "wall of sound" (despite being able to do it at the drop of a hat, and by using the same "Wrecking Crew" musicians if he had desired). The only distinct changes were its shortened length created by omitting the instrumental break and having no verse repetition at the end. Brian praised Al's lead vocal, his second after "Help Me Ronda" on *Today!*: "The opening riff is my favourite riff ever written. On the record I wanted to feature Al and give him a chance to stand up and sing. It's hard to describe Al's vocals, but he can get up there and get pretty high."

Ironically, Al was conspicuous by his absence on the cover of the *Summer Days* album, which features other band members, including newcomer Bruce Johnston, on a yacht. He admitted later: "Sorry I missed the boat on this album cover. That very day the pictures were taken I had to spend in bed with a flu bug instead of on a yacht with the photographer."

Almost two years after the album was recorded, Capitol, always hungry for another hit, decided to rush-release the song as a single in the UK to satisfy their British fans and plug the gap between "Good Vibrations" and "Heroes and Villains." Apparently, it was done against the band's wishes, and they felt it had seriously dented their image as the "world's number one vocal group." In an interview for *NME*, Mike explained: "The record company didn't even have the decency to put out one of Brian's own compositions. The reason for the hold up with a new single has simply been that we wanted to give our public the best and the best isn't ready yet."104.

Bruce was of the same opinion during an interview with *NME's* reporter Keith Altham: "It's really ridiculous. The record is no way representative of the things we are doing now, or were doing even a year ago. This is not the music that won us *NME* award for the World's Top Vocal Group. I've got some tapes at home of the new tracks to be on the *Smile* LP which would blow your mind. All the ideas are new and Brian is coming up with fantastic ideas all the time."11.

Even the British press were critical of the band for releasing a two-year-old track as the follow-up to "Good Vibrations." *NME* made the point: "This is a complete puzzlement...Well, if Mr Wilson can't get the new single ready, and they've got to release an old one, why *this* one, which reverts the group to a sound ages old. Why not something from *Pet Sounds*? Oh well, it will succeed, of course, because they have such power. But their version of this old Crystals number is so well known, it's a bore!"11

Despite the band's concerns, the single peaked at #4 on the UK charts, the band's fifth consecutive single to make the Top Five in as little as 18 months.

Brian recalled a meeting with Spector in 1963 where he heaped praise on him for the classic song "Be My Baby," to which the response came, "I think 'Then He Kissed Me' is better. Brian most probably kept that thought in his pocket for future reference.

So which is the best version - Brian's or Phil's? The answer has to be the latter, but to hear the Beach Boys' laid-bare cover is to appreciate the fact that Brian had no reason at all to emulate his idol's production, and the result is something much more warm and personal. Carl's distinctive acoustic guitar, with castanets and tambourine thrown into the mix and stirred together with lush backing harmonies, is all that was needed.

54. Wendy (*All Summer Long* 1964)
(Brian Wilson, Mike Love)
Recording
29/04/64 Western Recorders, LA
Producer - Brian Wilson
Engineer - Chuck Britz
Band members
Brian Wilson (chorus falsetto lead vocals, harmony & backing vocals, upright or grand piano, Hammond B3 organ); Mike Love (lead & backing vocals); Carl Wilson (harmony & backing vocals, electric lead guitars); Dennis Wilson (harmony & backing vocals, drums); Al Jardine (harmony & backing vocals, electric rhythm guitars, bass guitar)
Album released - 13/07/64
US EP Four by the Beach Boys released - 21/09/64 Capitol R 5267 #44
UK EP Four by the Beach Boys released - 11/64 EAPI 5267
Film/TV Performance
27/09/64 *The Ed Sullivan Show* CBS

Brian's intention here was to pay some kind of homage to the harmonising style of their East coast competitors, the Four Seasons. The so-called East/West Coast rivalry had been simmering for a year, ever since the Beach Boys had recorded "Surfers Rule" for the *Surfer Girl* album, a tongue-in-cheek dig at the Newark doo-wop group. With the closing lines, "*Surfers rule (Four Seasons you better believe it")*, Brian mimicked Franke Valli's falsetto on "Walk Like A Man."

Responding in kind the following year, the Four Seasons recorded "No Surfin' Today" for their *Born to Wander* album, also releasing it as the flip-side to their #3 hit "Dawn (Go Away)." Emphasising the dangers of the sport, the line "*angry sea took my love from me*" was an obvious nudge at Brian's "Lonely Sea."

"I wanted to try and imitate the Four Seasons a way they would like to hear it"

Although comparing the harmonic qualities of the two groups is rather pointless, the rivalry should be seen as for what it probably was - just a marketing ploy. But we should also bear in mind that Murry Wilson was aware at the time that the Beach Boys had yet to have a chart-topping single, while their East Coast counterparts had already had three. There's little doubt that it probably stuck in his craw and goaded Brian to write "Surfers Rule."

The story of "Wendy" reveals two things. Firstly, it was not written about Brian's daughter, as she was born much later. Secondly, the unique 15-second stammering guitar/drums intro, was in fact quite intentional, reflecting musically how the narrator is fumbling for the right words to convey his feelings for losing the love of his girl.

The girl in the title is leaving him for another guy, one he assures her cannot be trusted and whose future "*looks awful dim*," but she goes anyway, leaving him to wallow in self-pity with the final words to her, "*you're so bad*."

Brian recalled: "It started with a bass slowed down with a guitar. It was an attempt to flatter the Four Seasons. I wanted to try and imitate the Four Seasons a way they would like to hear it. Cause I like …the way they do their vocals."105. Al remembered: "We did 'Wendy' in 10 minutes, and it was like 'Boom!' That was a big song. [Brian] stopped doing one thing and went right to that and it was like, 'Bang!' Come to think of it, maybe the track took 10 minutes to do and then the vocal track didn't take much longer. We laughed a lot in the studio. They were great times."47

The *Guardian's* Alex Petridis wrote: "The Four Seasons' overcast Newark toughness is replaced by dreamy melancholy that feels sunlit even as it ponders a future that looks "awful dim."42 One web critic opined: "'Wendy' is a fiendishly catchy yet emotionally delicate breakup song that sits alongside 'We'll Run Away' as a song that gradually marks its territory on your consciousness."

In September 1984 the song "East Meets West" was released as the flip side to the Four Seasons' "Rhapsody" and credited to both groups, with Brian singing on the outro: "*Two different drummers, playing side by side…You know the best of them will survive…*" When asked to comment on the song, Bruce didn't hold back: "I hated it. Those guys know nothing about harmony."

This is another song that Mike Love would later receive co-writing credit. Although recorded in mono a stereo version of "Wendy" is featured on the 1993 *Good Vibrations* box set and a distinct "cough" is audible during the organ solo at around 1:18.

When *All Summer Long* was released in the summer of 1964 the rear cover had personal messages from each band member (surely a first for a rock group), all thanking their fans for their support. But it was 19-year-old Dennis who provided a few lines which turned out to be both moving and prophetic: "They say I live a fast life. Maybe I just like a fast life driving my Stingray and XKE, playing my drums, and meeting so many girls and guys (especially girls). I wouldn't give up this life for anything in the world. It won't last forever, either, but the memories will."

53. Marcella *(Carl and the Passions - So Tough 1972)*
(Brian Wilson, Tandyn Almer, Jack Rieley)
Recording
12/71 Beach Boys Studio, Bel Air
17/02/72 Beach Boys Studio, Bel Air (tracking & vocals)
Producer - Carl Wilson
Engineers - Stephen Desper (Dec); Steve Moffitt (Feb)
Band members
Carl Wilson (lead & backing vocals, electric & acoustic guitars); Brian Wilson (backing vocals, grand piano, Wurlitzer electric piano, Hammond organ, Moog synthesiser (bass), vibraphone); Mie Love (tag lead vocal & backing vocals); Dennis Wilson (drums); Al Jardine (backing vocals); Bruce Johnston (backing vocals on verses); Ricky Fataar (drums, castanets)
Session musicians/Guests
Tandyn Almer (autoharps); Billy Hinsche (backing vocals); Tony Martin Jr (pedal steel guitars); Jack Rieley (backing vocals); Unknown (2 trumpets, trombone, bass trombone, sleigh bells, cabasa, bongos)
Album released - 15/05/72
US single released - 26/06/72 b/w "Hold On Dear Brother" Brother/Reprise REP 1101 #110
Film/TV performance
24/02/72 *Toppop* NOS Studios Hilversum, Holland (broadcast 02/05/72)

A song about Brian Wilson lusting after his favourite massage therapist would not at first be seen as a suitable subject for a Beach Boys' album track, let alone a single, but the result was a gem, despite what some critics called Jack Rieley's usual "gibberish" lyrics. According to musicologist Nick Kent, the Spanish masseuse in question had a parlour in West Hollywood called Circus Maximus, and allowed Brian to stay and chat with her after each session, even though what he had to say was, in her mind, just "crazy bullshit."

Rieley recalled: "At first he spoke only of going there for massages. Some days later he began going on and on about the masseuse who he said was turning him on…The only thing I could think of to quell Brian's fixation was to channel it. Thus it was I who suggested 'Marcella' as the title for a tune Brian had been working on. With my promise to write the 'Marcella' lyric, he jumped into the project with immense enthusiasm." As for the "gibberish" lyric, Rieley admitted it "was minor…efficient at best."[106]

> *"The only thing I could think of to quell Brian's fixation was to channel it"*

With a working title of "One Arm Over My Shoulder," Brian for once put every ounce of effort into the recording, with help from Carl and engineer Desper. The song uses a verse melodic sequence that harks back to the *Today!* out-take, "All Dressed Up For School," and more recently the similar *Sunflower* cast-off "I

Just Got My Pay." Although seemingly a little under-produced, the song highlights Carl's punchy lead vocal and the syncopated voices careening off each other in the chorus, some of the best since *Pet Sounds*. According to Brian, one of the guitar parts played through a Leslie speaker was inspired by George Harrison's solo on 1970's "Let It Be." Another time he claimed: "It represents one of the first times we tried to emulate the Rolling Stones. In my mind, it was dedicated to the Stones, but I never told them that. It's one of the rockingest songs I ever wrote."[107]

Songwriter Tandyn Almer, who had an ear for smooth, glossy pop, was brought in to help with the lyrics after his success with writing "Along Comes Mary," the #7 Hot 100 hit for the Association in 1966.

Musician Joseph Deaguero had introduced 20-year-old Almer to Brian, and recalled in the *Washington Post*: "Everyone thought he was going to be the next Dylan or Elton John…he was totally an eccentric, but he was in a league of his own…this guy was really good."[108] Although Almer and Brian would collaborate on several other projects, including co-writing "Sail on Sailor" on the next album, their friendship was put to the test after Almer allegedly had an affair with his wife Marilyn and was also accused of stealing recording equipment.

Despite "Marcella" faring badly in the charts it became a concert favourite over the next few years. *Record World* described it as "the Beach Boys at their very best."[109]

Although the album would see the departure of Bruce Johnston, who now embarked on a solo career (he would return for the *L.A Light Album* in 1978), it also saw the arrival in the recording studio of drummer Ricky Fataar and guitarist Terence "Blondie" Chaplin, ex-members of the South African band Flame. After seeing the band perform live in London the previous year, Carl signed them to the Brother label, produced their first album, *The Flame,* and eventually recruited them as fully-fledged Beach Boys.

Although Blondie didn't get to play on "Marcella," the two of them contributed two songs for the album, including the impressive "Hold On Dear Brother," which was chosen as the flip-side to the single.

52. Steamboat *(Holland 1973)*
(Dennis Wilson, Jack Rieley)
Recording
06/72-08/72 Baambrugge Centraal 2 Studio, Baambrugge, Utrecht, Holland (tracking & vocals)
19/07/72? Baambrugge Centraal 2 Studio, Baambrugge, Utrecht, Holland
09/72-10/72 Village Recorders, LA (overdubs)
19/09/72 Village Recorders, LA (overdub?)
Producers - Dennis & Carl Wilson
Engineers - Steve Moffitt (Holland); Steve Moffitt, Rob Fraboni (LA)
Band members
Carl Wilson (lead vocal, backing & harmony vocals, upright piano, acoustic guitar, jaw harp);
Dennis Wilson (backing & harmony vocals, bridge cameo vocal, Hohner clavinet, Wurlitzer electric piano, celeste, Moog synthesisers (bass, white noise percussion); Ricky Fataar (backing & harmony vocals, drums); Carl or Dennis (Hammond organ, ARP Odyssey synthesiser, water chimes)
Session musicians/Guests
Jack Rieley (backing & harmony vocals); Tony Martin Jr (pedal steel slide guitar)
Album released - 08/01/73

Arguably one of Dennis Wilson's most underrated and misunderstood compositions, possibly due once again to Jack Rieley's impenetrable, head-scratching lyrics. But its Dennis's cerebral arrangement that knocks this straight out of the park. With a working title of "The River" the song references American inventor Robert Fulton (1765-1815), widely credited for developing the world's first commercial steamboat.

This is Dennis playing a wild card by creating something entirely different to anything he had done before and he does it with something quite extraordinary. Yes, he could have written lyrics himself given his usual inclinations, but with Rieley's penchant for baffling phrases, Dennis's moving arrangement perfectly captures the mood of the evocative lyrics. Carl's ethereal laid-back lead vocal, the breathtaking backing voices, and the jarring slide guitar solo, all conspire to make this an incredible, unforgettable song.

Dennis will write better songs, but none as evocative as this

With its textured, layered atmosphere, Peter Carlin called it "a dreamlike journey back to the mythical heart of Mark Twain's America, borne by the insistent chug of an actual steam engine, hurtling keyboard glissandos, and a wonderfully bluesly slide guitar break."[32]

Another reviewer wrote: "Shrouded in hazy waters…[it] feels like something of a prologue to Carl Wilson and Reiley's episodic 'The Trader.' As a piece, the song's eerie fade-in and moody off-kilter rhythm conjure a haunted past of wicked deeds exacted by greedy men - rich, pioneering explorers entering the promise of a paradise in an exchange for a guarantee of their own: to be true and right and good to the earth they were expanding upon. The exchange, an eternity of deception."[110]

Writing for *Rocksucker.co.uk,* Jonny Abrams opined that the song "lives up to the high standard already set, conjuring with its sleepily isolated feel an atmosphere that could well trick you into thinking you were actually on a steamboat making its way back to a Dutch harbour…[It] flaunts some ridiculously pleasing barbershop-baritone *do do dos*, and at its apex (the '*we'll get your steamboat going*' section) vaguely echoes 'Til I Die' from *Surf's Up.* That big, echo-y guitar solo seems to ring out to sea, casting forth its light to guide wearily travellers safely back to port. It's magical, basically."[111]

Not everyone was impressed. Rick Swan described it as "a lazy venture into Dennis's version of rock and roll, close to but not quite the real thing."[21]

Dennis will write better songs, but none as evocative as this.

51. All Summer Long (*All Summer Long* 1964)
(Brian Wilson, Mike Love)
Recording
06/05/64 Western Recorders, LA (tracking - take #43 master)
07/05/64 Western Recorders, LA (vocals)
Producer - Brian Wilson
Engineer - Chuck Britz
Band members

Mike Love (lead & bass vocals); Brian Wilson (harmony & backing vocals, marimba); Carl Wilson (harmony & backing vocals, electric rhythm guitars); Dennis Wilson (harmony & backing vocals, drums); Al Jardine (harmony & backing vocals, electric bass guitar)
Session musicians
Steve Douglas (tenor sax); Jay Migliori (piccolo or fife)
Album released - 13/07/64
UK single released - 03/65 b/w "Do You Wanna Dance?" Capitol CL 15384

The title song to what has been described as the band's first conceptional album, and one that takes a semi-autobiographical look at the experiences of a sun-kissed California teenager. The album also finds Brian writing more refined and sophisticated melodies and vocal arrangements and seen as one more stepping stone toward *Pet Sounds*. What is most surprising is the fact that this great title track was not considered good enough by the label to be released as a single in America.

With its memorable intro, courtesy of Brian's marimba (not xylophone, as sometimes listed), this is a joyous, energetic ode to long hot summers and fleeting innocence, with a guy and his girl reminiscing about all the customary things associated with it - Hondas and miniature golf, t-shirt cut-outs and thongs (yes, thongs), all encapsulated by the bouncy music backdrop that just oozes with blissful sunshine. Behind all the sun-drenched nostalgia lies Brian's unforgettable arrangement with some subtle chord changes, going almost unnoticed, that perfectly highlight his on-going mastery of songcraft.

One reviewer wrote: "[It] represents perhaps the Beach Boys most successful infusion of introspection into an ostensibly up-tempo song pre-*Pet Sounds*. This emotional duality is evidence of Brian's progression from prodigious young talent to unrivalled master of the game, with his distinctive falsetto completing those ever-present harmonies with almost supernatural ingenuity…"

In 1992 Mike revealed that he wrote about half of the song's lyrics, including the line, *"Remember when you spilled Coke all over your blouse."*[93] However, Brian claimed he wrote the line in reference to meeting singer and future girlfriend Marilyn Rovell (although it was actually hot chocolate). In his 2016 memoir, he stated: "I changed this around a little. I changed hot chocolate to Coke because it fit the lyrics better, and I changed it so that she spilled it on herself because that seemed funnier."[35]

Brian commented on the album in his discredited memoir: "I finally felt the Beach Boys had put out an LP that was competitive with Spector and the Beatles. The vocals were tight, the production was sharper and more inventive than anything we'd done previously. We were in a higher harmonic place and generally more exciting musically."[28] 25 years later he hadn't changed his mind, calling it "a turning point for me and for the band - or maybe it makes sense to say it's a turning point for how I understood how to write for the band."[35]

> *"Brian almost had to create a backing track on top of which would sit the most sumptuous harmonies in American popular music"*

Lyrically engaging and with Mike's exuberant lead vocal, the song is propelled along by Brian's marimba and Jay Migliori's piccolo (or is it a fife?), and is noted for Dennis yelping "*Not for us now*" in answer to the line, "*won't be long til summer time is through.*" With that, maybe Dennis is indicating that the band has a lot more to follow.

Jim Fusilli summed up the album: "But this isn't Brian and the group at its best. They weren't kids anymore. They weren't *Beach Boys*. 23-year-old Mike had a two-year-old daughter; and though Carl was only seventeen, Audree once said that he was born thirty, and he was serious about his music and the group. And yet, they were still singing about school and drive-ins. Looking back, it seems they were resisting the transition."130

For a long time the song was not performed live in concert, perhaps because it was found difficult to integrate the marimba intro with the standard instruments or even to recreate the dense vocal-harmonic wall of the recording. Criticism was also aimed at Mike for his occasional mumbling of words and struggle to hit the high notes. Despite its short length (2:06 minutes) George Lucas chose the song to be played over the end credits for his 1973 cult movie *American Graffiti* about a group of teens enjoying their last summer together after graduating from high school. The only flaw was that the movie was set in 1962, two years before the song came out.

At the time of writing, no true stereo mix has yet to surface, although a vocal spit was included on 1993's *Good Vibrations* box set.

50. We'll Run Away (*All Summer Long* 1964)
(Brian Wilson, Gary Usher)
Recording
c29/04/64 Western Recorders, LA (tracking)
18/05/64 Western Recorders, LA (vocals)
Producer - Brian Wilson
Engineer - Chuck Britz
Band members
Brian Wilson (double-tracked lead vocal, harmony & backing vocals, upright or grand piano, Hammond B3 organ); Mike Love (backing vocals); Carl Wilson (harmony & backing vocals, electric lead guitars); Dennis Wilson (harmony & backing vocals, drums); Al Jardine (harmony & backing vocals, electric rhythm guitars, bass guitar)
Session musicians
Hal Blaine (timbales with brush); Ray Pohlman (6-string electric bass guitar)
Album released - 13/07/64

Brian's last collaboration with Gary Usher until "Let's Go To Heaven In My Car," written for the 1987 movie *Police Academy 4: Citizens on Patrol*. Perhaps dating from two years earlier, it relates the story of a young couple hoping to elope against the wishes of their respective parents. Music journalist Nick Kent described it as having "zeroed in" on the kind of teen trepidation that would resurface again two years later with the classic "Wouldn't It Be Nice."73 Inspiration for the song may have been found in two of Phil Spector's recent hit records - "Not Too Young To Get Married" by Bob B. Soxx and the Blue Jeans, and "So Young" by Veronica of the Ronettes.

Brian's beautiful double-tracked falsetto and the heartfelt, wistful lyrics make this an undeniable gem, on a par with the pair's previous ballad, "Lonely Sea" on

Surfin Safari. So good in fact that it could have been saved for the *Today!* album and still not have looked out of place. David Leaf commented on the unusual "church-like" organ sound, heard prominently at the end, describing it as "an unorthodox application of the instrument on a rock record."44

Usher described working with Brian on the song: "We always liked to get involved in sensitive issues, because we rarely had the opportunity, and so I said, 'Let's write a song about a young boy and girl'...anyway, we decided to write a sensitive song about a young boy and girl who no one believes are old enough to get married or have a relationship. They have no choice but to leave that world and run away into their own world. We wrote that song in about half an hour. We never did spend much time writing a song. They just seemed to come through us. If memory serves me correctly, the song was a total collaboration, and Brian liked the end result so much that he told me he was going to record it with the guys the following week. He asked me if I cared and I replied, 'No, I'd be thrilled.' Sure enough, he went into the studio shortly thereafter and cut it. A few weeks later, I got a phone call from him to say that it came out great, and it was going to be on their next album."65

> *"We wrote that song in about half an hour. We never did spend much time writing a song. They just seemed to come through us"*

Jonny Abrams, writing for *Rocksucker*, praised the song as being such a "languid, pretty little thing that it's easy to overlook, but repeated listens reveal it to be the kind of innocently romantic pop marvel that so frequently punctuated the Beach Boys' early output," while Rick Swan called it "a homage to Brian's affection for juvenile ballads...Singing like a heartsick middle schooler, Brian stumbles over the double tracking, sounds insincere throughout, and bungles the ending like he's choking on his bubble gum."21

All Summer Long was an album that saw a marked change in course for the band. Despite the inclusion of one last car song and several unnecessary 'fillers,' this was Brian distancing him away from the surf boards and hot rods of their previous output to create what many see as their first true concept album and one celebrating typical teenage experiences in the California sunshine. Brian later went on record to call it a "turning point" for the band and an album that he felt could now compete against the Beatles.

Knowing that they could never match their rivals when it came to public image, at least he could now focus on the music and try to outdo them in the recording studio. With that, he certainly stepped up to the mark.

49. Darlin' (*Wild Honey* 1967)
(Brian Wilson, Mike Love)
Recording
10/10/67 Wally Heider Studio, Hollywood
11/10/67 Wally Heider Studio, Hollywood (instrumental session for Redwood; guide vocal by Hutton)
27/10/67 Wally Heider Studio, Hollywood (tracking & vocals)
Producer - The Beach Boys

Engineer - Jim Lockert or Bill Halverson
Band members
Carl Wilson (lead vocals, drums?); Brian Wilson (piano); The Beach Boys (backing vocals, tambourine, other percussion); Ron Brown (bass)
Session musicians
Hal Blaine (overdubbed drums); Lew McCreary (bass trombone); Jay Migliori (baritone sax); Ollie Mitchell (trumpet), Harold Billings (trumpet); Virgil Evans (trumpet)
Album released - 18/12/67
US single released - 18/12/67 b/w "Here Today" Capitol 2068 #19
UK single released - 01/68 b/w "Country Air" Capitol CL 15527 #11
Film/TV performances
15/12/67 *UNICEF Christmas For the Children of the World* TFI Paris (broadcast on BBC-1 London 27/12/67)
05/01/68 *All Systems Freeman* BBC-1 London (miscellaneous film footage)
08/02/68 *Top of the Pops* BBC-1 London ((miscellaneous film footage)
29/02/68 *Top of the Pops* BBC-1 London ((miscellaneous film footage)
14/12/68 *Twien*, Theater De Brakke Grond, Amsterdam (broadcast 23/12/68)
16/06/69 Olympia Theater Paris TFI (filmed concert)
01/11/74 *Chicago's New Year's Rockin Eve* ABC New York (broadcast 31/12/74)
21/01/77 Capital Centre, Washington DC
21/06/80 Knebworth, England concert (later released on CD/DVD)

According to Keith Badman, Mike had met 20-year-old wannabe singer Sharon Marie (Esparaza) at a Beach Boys concert in Rio Nido, Sonoma County, on June 1st 1963 and then helped her to get a recording contract with Capitol. She had informally auditioned for Brian and Mike by singing opera standards stage-side at the concert.11

Two weeks later she was at Gold Star studio with Brian and Mike to record their song as her first single, "Run-Around Lover." Brian had composed the instrumental track with a working title of "Black Wednesday" and brought in the Honeys (Darlene Love and Ginger Blake) to provide backing vocals, along with a group of Spector's session musicians. Produced by Brian, the single was released on October 21st but failed to chart.

"Brian's mental health had collapsed, tastemakers were deriding them as unhip. You wouldn't know from 'Darlin'"

Undaunted, Brian brought her back into the studio in April 1964 to record another Wilson-Love song called "Thinkin' Bout You Baby," with their "Story of My Life" on the flip-side. With the Honeys again in support, the record was released on June 1st 1964 but, once again, despite its credentials and a superb lead vocal, it met with little success, signalling the end of Sharon's short career, at least for the time being.

Three years later during the *Wild Honey* sessions, Brian returned to "Thinkin' Bout My Baby" and reworked the song into "Darlin,'" with new, though less-sophisticated, lyrics than the original. When the band had formed Brother Records in 1967, the plan had been that everybody would produce outside artists. Brian's first signing was Redwood, a band formed by his friend Danny Hutton, who, up to that time, was probably best known for his 1965 hit "Roses and Rainbows." Brian intended to give "Darlin'" to Redwood, but Hutton only got as far as recording a guide vocal before Mike and Carl stepped in and voiced their disapproval of Brian giving away quality songs to anyone other than the Beach Boys. With pressure put on him, the Redwood project was abandoned and as a result he decided to record it for *Wild Honey*, using the original instrumental track and adding Carl's lead vocal. Redwood, of course, would later evolve into the hugely successful Three Dog Night.

Referring to the song Brian explained: "I was writing more in a soul/R&B bag. The horns were conceived as a Phil Spector kind of horn thing...That song took about a week to write," and in relation to Redwood he said, "They recorded it and said, 'No, you can have it,' so I gave it to Carl to sing."[63] Brian also praised Carl for his "amazing" lead vocal, and, in a 2015 interview, actually stated that "Darlin'" was the best song he had ever written.[165]

Cash Box described it as "a shift in sound from the Beach Boys into a less elaborate but extra-commercial teen beat right between mid-and-up tempo. The deck's hard-throb rhythm and very fine group sound is complemented by a good set of teen-oriented lyrics to catch a maximum of exposure on the top pop programs Instant breakout selection."[166] *Rolling Stone* opined that the band "really take R&B styling and make it work in an original way,"[167] while on reflection the *Guardian* wrote: "Brian's mental health had collapsed, tastemakers were deriding them as unhip. You wouldn't know from 'Darlin,' a heart-swelling triumph with a great Carl vocal: in its own way, its pared-back R&B-infused sound fitted the rootsy post-psychedelic mood."[83]

In 1972 Brian would produce the original "Thinkin Bout You Baby" for Spring's eponymous debut album, featuring sisters Marilyn Wilson and Diane Rovell. Three years later, teen idol David Cassidy recorded "Darlin'" for his album *The Highter They Climb*. Produced by Bruce Johnston, the single reached #16 on the UK chart.

48. Friends (*Friends* 1968)
(Brian Wilson, Carl Wilson, Dennis Wilson, Al Jardine)
Recording
13/03/68 Beach Boys Studio, Bel Air (tracking - take #6 master; lead & backing vocals;guitar & strings)
14/03/68 I.D Sound Studio, Hollywood (vocals & original mono mix)
15/03/68 I.D Sound Studio, Hollywood (vocals & revised mono mix)
Producer - The Beach Boys
Engineer - Jim Lockert (Bel Air)
Band members
Brian Wilson (lead & backing vocals); Carl Wilson (lead & backing vocals, guitar); Dennis Wilson (backing vocals); Al Jardine (backing vocals); Bruce Johnston (backing vocals)
Session musicians
Jim Ackley (keyboard); Jimmy Bond (upright bass); Norm Jeffries (drums); Alan Estes (vibes); Tommy Morgan (standard & bass harmonicas); Jim Horn (sax & clarinet); Jay Migliori (sax & clarinet); 3 violins, 1 viola
Album released - 24/06/68
US single released - 08/04/68 b/w "Little Bird" Capitol 2160 #47
UK single released - 05/68 b/w "Little Bird" Capitol CL 15545 #25
Film/TV performances
09/05/68 *The Mike Douglas Show* Westinghouse, Philadelphia (broadcast 15/05/68)
12/08/68 *Happening* ABC, LA (broadcast 17/08/68)
13/08/68 *The Dick Cavett Show* ABC New York
14/12/68 *Twien* NCRV Theater De Brakke Grond, Amsterdam (broadcast 23/12/68)

Back in the late 60's, some fans would buy a Beach Boys album without even listening to it first, expecting it would be even better than the one before (like *Today!* and *Pet Sounds* proved to be*)*, but there were times when, hold on, the voices sound the same, but what is this they're singing? It happened with *Smiley Smile* and *Wild Honey,* polar opposite of *Pet Sounds* when it came to sophisticated production. Either you were in the Mike Love "don't f**k with the formula" camp or you welcomed the band's new direction like a breath of fresh air. But this certainly wasn't messing with the formula - this was fuelled by both the country's socio-political ruptures of the time and the counterculture focus on anything that was absurd and crazy, manifesting itself in the music of bands like the Beatles, the Byrds and the Stones with their psychedelic sounds and drugs-inspired lyrics. It all sounded pretty good, and the Beach Boys were not going to be left behind. Despite what Brian's motivations may have been, the seismic cultural shift that was underway in the late 60's could not be ignored.

In hindsight, their next album *Friends* could not have been released at a worse time for the band. To begin with, Brian's participation in the recording was only half-hearted, leaving Carl once again to step up to the mark. Then there was the band's controversial and costly involvement with the Maharishi Mahesh Yogi, the self-styled master of "transcendental meditation," and the new spiritual guru to the Beatles. With its philosophy of spiritual growth rooted in Hinduism, it was practiced by simply sitting comfortably for a few minutes and uttering mantras. Mike and the band had been introduced to him during rehearsals for a Paris concert in December 1967 and after practicing the techniques were intrigued, especially Mike. Two months later, just as the sessions for *Friends* had gotten underway, Mike had flown out to India to join the Beatles and other stars at the Maharishi's Academy, staying there for over two weeks.

During that time, it began to emerge that they were being hustled by what allegedly turned out to be a conman. The Beatles quickly cut their ties with him, but Mike, now fully obsessed by the practice, had other ideas, and on his return suggested to the other band members that they organise a short US tour the following spring with the Maharishi along to give lectures on TM. Two poorly-attended US tours followed, the first overshadowed by the assassination of Martin Luther King and the riots that followed, and the second, with the Maharishi, an ill-conceived financial disaster right from the start, with many dates cancelled.

> ### *"Brian was tired of dealing with the demands of artistic leadership. Now, he was going to make records that reflected his lifestyle"*

Hardly wasting time after *Wild Honey* the band had returned to the studio in February 1968 to begin recordings for what would hopefully be seen as a more friendly and upbeat album. Unlike the previous two albums, there would be no *Smile* remnants, but tracks that had writing input from all band members apart from Bruce, and songs reflecting external aspects of everyday life rather than emotional inner feelings.

Top biographer David Leaf, who cited *Friends* as being his favourite Beach Boys album, wrote: "Brian had begun to ignore the outside world and was writing songs because it was his job, not out of any sense of artistry. Brian was tired of dealing with the demands of artistic leadership. Now, he was going to make records that reflected his lifestyle."26

The title track was recorded in 4/4 time for its first take. Brian then rearranged the song after realising that the radio were not playing many waltzes, and remarked: "'Friends' was, in my opinion, a good way to keep waltzes alive." In fact, according to Peter Raum, the song had since been used at Berklee College of Music for teaching students how to write in 3/4 time.26

Highlighted by a sterling lead vocal by Carl, outstanding group harmonies, and Tommy Morgan's bass harmonica, this most autobiographical of their songs is both simple and comforting, with a sparkling melody that has so many twists and turns that it is now considered one of Brian's best. Brian explained the choice of Carl to sing lead: "'Carl had sung 'Darlin' and some others before and now he spearheaded this cut with a heavy vocal performance."26

Brian later called the song his favourite from the album: "'Friends' is great. I thought there was a lot of humour in it and I thought, y'know, songs usually don't have that much kinda humour, but 'Friends' had a lot of humour in it. So that'd why I like it."265. Bruce, despite calling the album "weak" and "wimpy," described the song as being "fabulous, especially the bassline, but still remarked: "I don't think we were doing anything where Brian was at full strength."38 In an interview for *Mojo* in 2007, Bruce looked back on the album: "*Friends* came out just after Hendrix and Cream. The whole country had discovered drugs, discovered words, discovered Marshall amplifiers, and here comes this feather floating through a wall of noise."

On its release as a single, "Friends" only managed to reach a disappointing #47 on the Hot 100, maybe due to its simplicity and gentle arrangement which looked out of step with current commercial trends. However, this didn't alter Brian's fondness for the album: "It seems to fit the way I live better - it's simple and I can hear it anytime without having to get into some mood. *Pet Sounds* carries a lot more emotion, at least for me...*Pet Sounds* is by far my very best album. Still, though, my favourite is *Friends*."26

Cash Box wrote: "Barbershop harmonies to a soft rock backdrop provides the Beach Boys with a departure from their 'Wild Honey/Good Vibrations' style. Easy-throbbing waltz tempo and a unique vocal sound cast a new type of magical spell for the team, one that should have them rising rapidly on the best seller charts. Outstanding track." 266

Rolling Stone singled out the title track as an album highlight: "[It is] a more mature (in that it lacks their usual immediacy) evocation of the surfer 'pack' or 'club' vision - why go out with a girl when you can go cruising with the guys on Saturday nights? It's really warm, simple, touching, saying in not so many words that friendship isn't about words."267 More recently, *AllMusic* commented: "This mellow, lovely track is a good example of the Beach Boys' late-60's output: it is far less musically complex than 'California Girls' or 'Wouldn't It Be Nice,' but possesses a homespun charm all of its own."268 Rick Swan wrote: "The melody, with all its twists and turns, remains one of Brian's best, an exquisite charmer that not only serves as a template for the rest of the album: deceptively simple, comforting, and beneath the surface, a little sad, as if *Pet Sounds* hadn't worn off yet."21

More than anything else, *Friends,* according to the great David Leaf, sounded and felt like a true Beach Boys album, and that the vocal arrangement on the title song "let the world know that Brian was back mixing his magical harmonic brew."26

47. Cool, Cool, Water *(Sunflower* 1970)
(Brian Wilson, Mike Love)
Recording (Smiley Smile sessions)
07/06/67 Western Recorders, LA (version 1 of "Cool, Cool, Water")
Recording (Wild Honey sessions)
26/10/67 Beach Boys Studio, Bel Air (version 2 - basic tracking, inserts, vocal work, mixdown)
29/10/67 Wally Heider Studio, Hollywood (double-tracked vocals)
Recording (Add Some Music/Sunflower)
01/70 Beach Boys Studio, Bel Air (vocals)
07/07/70 Beach Boys Studio, Bel Air
08/07/70 Beach Boys Studio, Bel Air (mixdown)
21/07/70 Beach Boys Studio, Bel Air (possible Moog synth overdub)
Producer - The Beach Boys
Engineers - Jim Lockert, Bill Halverson, Stephen Desper
Band members
Brian Wilson (lead vocals, harmony & backing vocals, group vocals, guitar, finger snaps); Mike Love (lead vocal, harmony & backing vocals, group vocals, finger snaps); Carl Wilson (harmony & backing vocals, group vocals, guitar, bass, finger snaps); Dennis Wilson (group vocals, tom-tom, bongos, finger snaps); Al Jardine (harmony & backing vocals, group vocals, guitar, finger snaps); Bruce Johnston (harmony& backing vocals, group vocals, finger snaps)
Guests
Stephen Desper (Moog bass, wave effects & programming); Paul Beaver (Moog programming); Bernard Krause (Moog programming)
Album released - Aug 31 1970
US single released -03/71 b/w "Forever" Brother/Reprise 0998
Film/TV performance
07/05/71 *The David Frost Show* Westinghouse, Philadelphia (broadcast 28/05/71)

Another song inspired by a snippet of a *Smile* track, and one that Brian later called "one of my very, very favourite songs that we ever did."120 "Love To Say Da Da" was an unfinished song recorded at both Columbia and Gold Star studios between December 1966 and May 1967, becoming the final session for the soon-to-be aborted album. Marilyn Wilson recalled: "When he was writing [the song] he had me buy him a baby bottle and fill it with chocolate milk, and he would sit and write and drink from it. It was hilarious, I thought."48 The song was included on an initial tracklist for the *Wild Honey* album in October 1967 but failed to make the final cut. The initials - LSD - and its alleged drug reference did not go unnoticed.

According to biographer Byron Preiss the song was "planned as an ode to water, reflecting not only the element but the pleasure people experienced with it," and was "briefly considered" to be coupled with "Surf's Up" to form part of the water-themed section of "The Elements Suite."56 Engineer Steve Desper later admitted that Brian had been obsessed for years with the riff that later developed into "Cool, Cool Water," although Brian recalled for *Rolling Stone* that "there was a chant I wish we hadn't used. It fits all right, but there's just something I don't think is quite right with it. But, all in all, with some good airplay, the record should do very well."11

"[The Beach Boys]...*crafted what turned out to be one of the most inviting stiff albums ever released*"

Three years later, the Beach Boys were in the process of putting together *Sunflower*, their first album for their new label Warner. After hearing the unfinished tape of the song, including Carl's double-tracked lead vocal recorded in October 1967, the label's A&R executive Lenny Waronker convinced Brian to complete it, insisting that it should be added to the album (Warner having already rejected two album submissions). Hugely impressed with the song, Waronker went on to say: "If I ever get the opportunity to produce Brian, I'd encourage him to do something that combined the vividness of 'Good Vibrations' with the non-commercial gentleness of 'Cool, Cool, Water.'"

With a new arrangement written by Brian and new lyrics by Mike, developing the song was mainly down to Carl as Desper explained in 2012: "There was no final version. When Brian became ill, Carl took over and salvaged a few tracks...almost all of 'Cool, Cool, Water,' the *Sunflower* version, was by Carl's production...Carl and the entire group was under a lot of pressure to record. Carl took what Brian had done (which was very little) and made it into the *Sunflower* CCW. That production was almost entirely original."121

The song was released as a single seven months after the album, although as an edited 3:20-minute version (compared with the album's 5:03) it failed to chart. In his description of the album track, musicologist Rick Swan celebrated the mini-symphony: "It opens with the gentle counterpoint of the Beach Boys taken from the post-*Smile* experiments. Voices are added to the original to create the sound of a stream or dripping faucet. After repeating once, the segment eases into a pure electronic section, creating this roaring waves that consumes the landscape. Then more voices, intimate and ominous, repeating the word Water and gradually settling down like a rainstorm giving way to the dawn."21

In a later interview, Brian described how the song came about through divine inspiration: "I had just moved into a new house on Bellagio Road in Bel Air...and the first day I moved in, there was a piano there, and I went to the piano and wrote "Cool, Cool Water". I sat and wrote the gist of it, the basic song. It was finished much later of course."69

Despite becoming the band's lowest-charting album in the US at that point, it remains one of their finest post-*Pet Sounds* recordings. *Uncut's* Bud Scoppa wrote: "Working as a fully functioning interactive unit for the first time, they'd crafted what turned out to be one of the most inviting stiff albums ever released."308

46. Busy Doin' Nothin' (*Friends* 1968)
(Brian Wilson)
Recording
26/03/68 Beach Boys Studio, Bel Air (tracking for "Even Steven"/ "Even Time")
01/04/68 I.D Sound Studio, Hollywood (vocals for "Even Steven")

11/04/68 I.D Sound Studio, Hollywood (vocals for "Busy Doin' Nothin' - 27 takes)
Producer - Brian Wilson
Engineer - Jim Lockert
Band members
Brian Wilson (lead & backing vocals)
Session musicians/Guests
Marilyn Wilson (lead on second bridge & backing vocals); Jim Ackley (keyboard); Al Vescovo (guitar); Lyle Ritz (upright basses); Alan Estes (vibes & blocks); Gene Pello (drums); David Sherr (oboe); Tom Scott (bass flute); Don Englert (clarinet); Jay Migliori (bass clarinet)
Album released - 24/06/68

One of the most intimate of Brian's autobiographical songs written around this time, and one of only two self-penned tracks on an album that he later cites as his favourite. With working titles of "Even Steven" or "Even Time," the sweet and breezy bossa nova "travelog" describes an average day in Brian's life at his new Bellagio Road home in Bel Air, complete with step-by-step directions how to find it (as long as you know where to start from). The song is one of several of Brian's "slice of life" compositions written during this period, together with "I'd Love Just Once To See You" on *Wild Honey* and "I Went To Sleep" on *20/20*. This is also the only track on the album where session musicians were used exclusively.

The minutiae detail of a day in his life is extraordinary, talking about the temperature, writing down thoughts, and taking three verses just to describe the act of trying to phone a "good friend" who is not at home. Rick Swan described it as "too middle of the road to be memorable, it remains an anthem for introverts of all persuasions."[21]

"...the eccentric genius of dreams, entirely weird, but happily and productively so, nursing whatever psychic wounds he might carry in the balm of his own brilliance"

But memorable it definitely was, as biographer Peter Carlin eloquently pointed out: "In 'Busy Doin' Nothin' [Brian] is the eccentric genius of dreams, entirely weird, but happily and productively so, nursing whatever psychic wounds he might carry in the balm of his own brilliance."[32] As for the intimacy of the lyrics, Carlin writes: "None of these things matter, except for the fact that these tiny moments make up the essential fabric of existence, and this elegant recognition of their innate beauty is a small triumph not just in the career of Brian Wilson, but in the entire scope of popular music."[32]

David Leaf wrote in his celebrated biography: "Backed by a bosa nova beat, Brian's solo vocal describes a very mundane existence. Brian had mellowed in his retreat, and he's found a certain peace away from the hectic demands of creation."[122]

The night after the April 11th session, which had seen all the boys in attendance, Dennis pulled into his driveway on Sunset Boulevard at around 3am and was approached by a small, shadowy figure. A nervous Dennis said: "Are you going to hurt me?" The man replied, "Do I look like I'm going to hurt you, brother?" then got on his knees and kissed Dennis's trainers, saying he was "a philosopher, a god, and a musician." His name was Charlie Manson...

45. That's Not Me (*Pet Sounds* 1966)
(Brian Wilson, Tony Asher)
Recording
15/02/66 Western Recorders, LA (tracking - take #15 master, vocals)
02/66 Western Recorders, LA (percussion overdubs, vocals)
Producer - Brian Wilson
Engineer - Chuck Britz
Band members
Brian Wilson (lead vocal on chorus, backing vocals, Hammond B3 organ, overdubbed bass guitar, Danelectro bass); Mike Love (lead vocal on verses & chorus, backing vocals); Carl Wilson (backing vocals, lead guitar, overdubbed 12-string lead guitar); Al Jardine (backing vocals); Dennis Wilson(drums); Bruce Johnston (backing vocals)
Session musicians/Guests
Hal Blaine (probably temple blocks), Steve Korthof (tambourine); Terry Melcher (tambourine).
Album released – 16/05/66

One of the more modest productions on what is considered to be Brian's masterpiece, but still as spellbinding as *Pet Sounds'* two previous tracks, "Wouldn't It Be Nice" and "You Still Believe In Me." It serves as a prime example of the musical twist and turns that should be studied by every would-be composer in music class.

The narrator is no longer the super-cool, fun-loving guy of the earlier hits, but a sensitive soul with deep-seated self-doubts over his aspirations and relationships. In his excellent profile of Brian, Kirk Curnutt described the song: "The young man in 'That's Not Me' strikes off for the city to prove his independence. Leaving behind both his girl and his parents, he quickly finds himself overwhelmed by loneliness. Realising the selfishness of his behaviour, he begs forgiveness for abandoning his lover "at the wrong time" and assures her that he now understands the importance of commitments."[84]

Brian admitted to Peter Fornatale in 1976: "I think 'That's Not Me' reveals a lot about myself, just the idea that you're going to look at yourself and say, ' Hey, now look, that's not me, kind of square off with yourself and say, "this is me, that's not me."'[61] Biographer Timothy White surmised that the lyrics were more likely a metaphor for Brian's decision to withdraw from the touring line-up,[29] while Philip Lambert offered that "the song does say a little about his thoughts and concerns relating to his professional aspirations and relationships with, and devotion to, his group, especially his brothers."[9] Others suggested that it was psychedelic drugs that made him turn his attention inwards. According to Jim Fusilli, the song might be about Brian's wife-to-be, Marilyn Rovell, with the lyric "*I miss my pad*" seeming to refer to a house in Beverly Hills.[130]

> ***"A largely underappreciated gem - overshadowed by the even better tracks that surround it on side one of Pet Sounds"***

The song features Mike's first lead vocal on the album, and his questions are countered by Brian's plaintive vocal on the bridge. In a 1997 interview Brian recalled: "[Mike] just really nailed it, real powerful voice, very souped-up kind of a sound," and that "this showcased Mike Love's voice pretty good."72 Brian also praised Carl's restrained guitar playing: "Listen to his 12-string guitar right after the lyric '*I'm a little bit scared cause I haven't been home in a long time.*'"

In an interview with David Leaf, Carl commented on his playing, reminiscent of the sound on "Don't Worry Baby": "I remember playing 12-string direct, right through the board. My playing wasn't as consequential as it had been before, and would later become, because everything had become more of an orchestra, part of a whole. It really wasn't appropriate for us to play on those dates - the tracking just got beyond us."85 Bruce remembered how the backing vocals gently build: "That's just an 'ooh and aah' song vocally. That was easy; a gymnastic experience. I'm pretty rangy in my voice. But that was really a song for a lead vocal."72

"That's Not Me" is the only track on the album where most of the instruments are played by the band members themselves instead of using session musicians. Brian's cousin Steve Korthof and friend Terry Melcher were also invited to play on the record.

Lyric writer Tony Asher, admitting that he contributed music ideas to a number of songs on the album: "It felt like we were writing autobiography, but oddly enough, I wouldn't limit it to Brian's autobiography. We talked about our experiences and feelings about women and the various stages of relationships."130 He described how the lyric to "That's Not Me" illustrates a "young man on his path toward self-discovery and independence.

Jim Fusilli wrote: "Reflecting on his past, the narrator realises that when it comes to his personal development he has not achieved his full potential, and then decides to leave both his home and his lover. He then comes to realise he would be better off staying in a relationship rather than pursuing a solitary life to fulfil a dream. Pleading forgiveness for abandoning his lover, he nevertheless feels grateful that he did, and now feels more certain that home is where he belongs and is ready to carry on."130

Asher also criticised his own lyrics: "I've always felt like I'd like a shot at rewriting that song…It's a very interesting series of chord changes. It goes in wonderful places that you don't expect it to. But for some reason, I found it very difficult to write to. I've never been quite as satisfied lyrically with it as I would like. It feels, to me, slightly artless. I have a feeling when I listen to the lyric that it still feels and sounds laboured like it was not easy and it wasn't…"72

Jim Fusilli continued: "It's a well-crafted and eminently logical expression of a man returning to what's familiar, to his girl and the comforts of home. And there is ambiguity - why did he leave? Brian and Asher seem to suggest that it might have been, at least in part, because of her."130

Although lacking the full orchestration found in many of the album's tracks, it's sophisticated harmonic structure and unexpected shifts in mood make this song stand out, as noted by Charles Granata: "The uncluttered arrangement (featuring guitar, organ, bass and percussion) allows each instrument to breathe, making the tune a study in contrast and texture. Here, the vibrancy of the bass stands out front and centre."85

Norman Jopling of the *Record Mirror* gave his "unbiased" opinion of the song, calling it a "quizzical sort of beat ballad [with a] self-obsessed sort of lyric which is clever without being in the least appealing...Spectorish at times,"[86] while, more recently, *AllMusic's* Stewart Mason probably hit the nail on the head by describing it as "the closest thing to a conventional rocker...a largely underappreciated gem...overshadowed by the even better tracks that surround it on side one of *Pet Sounds.*" He goes on to write: "The start-stop quality of the tune - a trick that Brian Wilson used quite a bit during this period of his career - gives the song a sense of nervous tension that's exacerbated by the beaten-down, anxious quality of Tony Asher's lyrics."[87] *Mojo* described it as "a nostalgic, two minute 22-second paean to rueful self-awareness."[25]

44. Cottonfields (single version 1970)
(Huddie Leadbetter)
Recording (20/20 version)
18/11/68 I.D Sound Studio, LA (tracking for "Cotton Fields (The Cotton Song")
19/11/68 I.D Sound Studio, LA(vocals)
20/11/68 Capitol Studio, Hollywood (mono mix)
21/11/68 Beach Boys Studio, Bel Air (stereo mix)
Recording (Single version)
08/08/69 Sunset Sound LA (tracking for "Cottonfields")
15/08/69 Sunset Sound LA (vocals)
Producers - Brian Wilson & Al Jardine (*20/20*); The Beach Boys (single)
Engineer - Bruce Botnick? (Sunset)
Band members
Alan Jardine (lead vocal, guitar, arranger); Brian Wilson (vocals); Mike Love (vocals); Carl Wilson (guitar); Dennis Wilson (drums); Bruce Johnston (keyboards)
Session musicians (single version)
Frank Capp (percussion); Ed Carter (bass); Daryl Dragon (keyboards); Orville "Red" Rhodes (pedal steel guitar); Bill Peterson (horns); Fred Koyen (horns); David Edwards (horns); Ernie Small (horns)
US single released - 20/04/70 b/w "The Nearest Faraway Place" Capitol 2765 #103
UK single released - 05/70b/w "The Nearest Faraway Place" Capitol CL15640 #5 (Melody Maker #2)
Film/TV performances
16/06/69 Olympia Theater Paris TFI (filmed concert)
30/06/69 *De Raiders En De Beach Boys* NCRV Amsterdam (broadcast 03/07/69)
19/09/69 *Happening* ABC Los Angeles (broadcast 20/09/69)
70   Promo
28/05/70 *Something Else* New Orleans (syndicated 04/04/70)
21/06/80 Knebworth. England concert (later released on CD/DVD)

Al Jardine had an affinity for old folk songs and had been urging Brian to do some folk covers even before joining the band, and it was at his suggestion that they eventually recorded their splendid version of "Sloop John B," a top five Hot 100 hit in 1966. That was the time when the Beach Boys were being dubbed the "best vocal group in the world," but two years later their popularity was in a downward spiral, due to following a change in their musical direction and the lukewarm response to three successive albums. In a scathing review, *Rolling Stone* summed them up as "just one prominent example of a group that has gotten hung up on trying to catch the Beatles. It's a pointless pursuit." The only respite came with the release of the stand-alone single "Do It Again" which gave them their second chart topper in the UK.

***"I was determined to record a new version for the Beach Boys
at a time when we were going off in quite a few
different musical directions"***

Sometime in May 1968, Al had suggested to Brian that they do a cover of the folk standard "Cotton Fields (The Cotton Song")", originally written and recorded in 1940 by blues musician Huddie William Ledbetter (aka Lead Belly) but made famous by its inclusion in the 1954 album *Odetta & Larry* (Odetta Holmes and Lawrence Mohr), when it was titled "Old Cotton Fields At Home", arguably the definitive version. Harry Belafonte and Lonnie Donegan also had success with versions in their respective countries.

Al recalled: "I first heard it in the mid-50's. I loved Lead Belly's vocals and of course his 12-string guitar sound but it was really his heartfelt emotional lyrics written during the Great Depression that affected me. I was determined to record a new version for the Beach Boys at a time when we were going off in quite a few different musical directions."[126]

However, it would be another 18 months before he finally convinced Brian to record it and that was only due to Brian struggling to find new material for the next album. The first two sessions took place at I.D Sound Studio in LA with the intention of making it a single release. Although further mixing was done for possible use in future television performances, no single materialised, and this first version of the song went on to be included on *20/20* the following year, with Brian calling the song, "one of the best [records] we've ever made." Despite some imaginative and interesting flourishes, the song seemed under-produced, with the suggestion that Brian may have lost interest in completing the project, leaving it to others like Al and Dennis to see it through in whatever way they saw fit.

In August 1969 Brian looked again at "Cotton Fields." Unhappy with the first "baroque-pop" version, Al once again suggested to him that it should be re-recorded with a more country-rock flavour, as that type of music was in vogue at the time, especially in the US. Brian liked the idea and said it would be released as their next single (and final one for Capitol), with the slightly amended title of "Cottonfields." He also brought in the legendary Orville "Red" Rhodes to play pedal steel guitar.

Al recalled: "I wanted another 'Sloop John B.' I tried to introduce a country influence, and I don't think that it worked cause people weren't into country at the time - steel guitars, Red Rhodes on steel guitar. I think it sent the wrong message to people. I wanted to use the live band, which I did, which I think worked kind of good. Dennis agreed. He thought it was a good idea. So he went in there and played for me, and the guys went along to Sunset Sound and we all set up and played it live. It was really good. But again, sonically, it didn't come out crisp or sharp. And it's undefinable. I don't know how Brian got those sounds."[33]

In another interview Al revealed: "Well, I thought Brian was going to give me another 'Sloop John B.' We went into the studio, and it just didn't happen. It was quite flat, I thought, and very un-Beach Boy-like. It sounded more like a country thing. Not even that, it just sounded like a demo. So, I picked up the gauntlet and took the appearance band into the studio, and we re-recorded it with my band, which is much more powerful than the studio guys we were using at the time. And I thought it was great. And Dennis Wilson kind of helped me out. He was, you might say, our spark plug guy; he was our energy guy, and he really believed in it…It was just a good live band recording."76

Unfortunately, the single just failed to break into the Hot 100, becoming the only cover single by the band not to do so (until their 1996 version of "I Can Hear Music" with Kathy Troccoli). However, and not too surprising for the band, it was a big success abroad, topping the charts in Australia and Norway, and peaking at #5 on the UK official chart and #2 on *Melody Maker's* hit list. The song was also included as the opening track on the international release of *Sunflower*.

At the Big Sur Festival in October 1970, Mike introduced "Cottonfields" by saying that, despite it being a huge hit abroad, it was being largely ignored on US radio, and then sarcastically snapping, "A lot of people thought it was too trite, so we all missed it that time, folks."

The first publicity shot for Capitol in 1962 with David Marks on the right

Taft High School Nov 22 1962

Publicity shot 1962

With Capitol executives 1964

Publicity shot 1964

Performing "Dance, Dance, Dance" on the Bob Hope Comedy Special, December 18 1964

Performing "I Get Around" on the Ed Sullivan Show, September 27 1964

Publicity shot c1964

Publicity shot to promote "I Get Around" 1964

Publicity shot, September 11 1965

Philadelphia Convention Hall, February 13 1965

Brian Wilson at home 1966

Brian making *Pet Sounds*, Cash Box ad May 7 1966

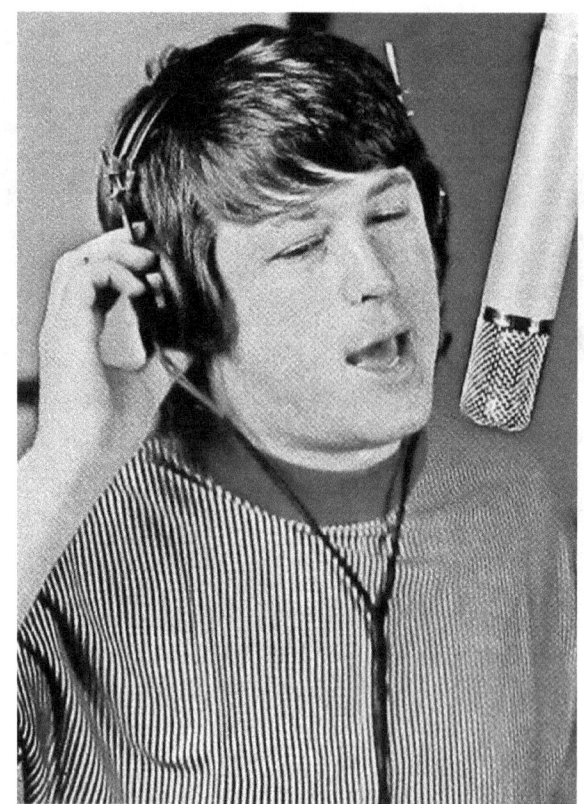
Brian in the studio, Cash Box ad May 7 1966

Brian with Carl and Chuck Britz in the studio, Cash Box ad May 7 1966

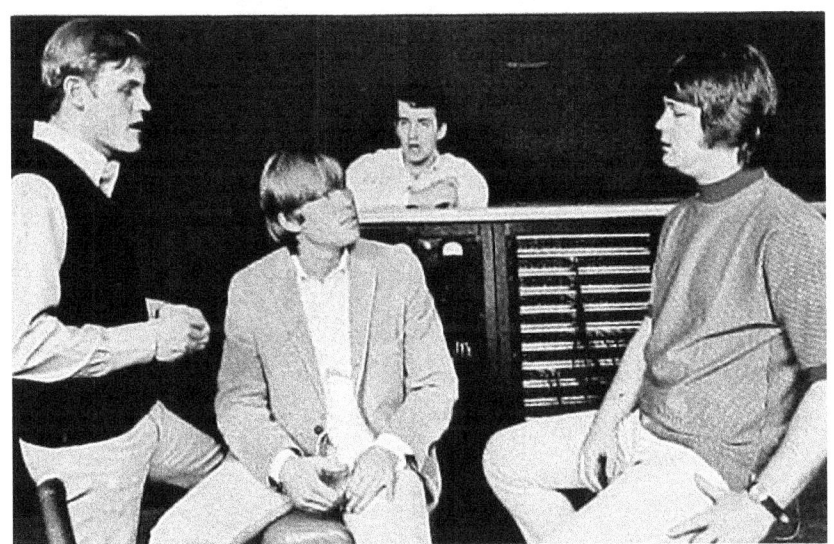
Brian with Bruce Johnston, Terry Melcher and Tony Asher, Cash Box ad May 7 1966

Billboard award, December 21 1966

Carl, Cash Box ad May 7 1966

Mike, Cash Box ad, May 7 1966

Al, Cash Box ad, May 7 1966

Dennis, Cash Box ad, May 7 1966

Bruce, Cash Box ad, May 7 1966

Hawaii August 67

Publicity shot 1968

Dennis in promo for movie *Two-Lane, Blacktop*, 1971

Central Park, New York July 2 1971

Billboard ad Nov 6 1971

Brian behind the mixing desk c1976

August 11 1976

Publicity shot c1979

Brian February 13 1990

New Orleans Jazz & Heritage Festival April 27 2012

Reunited - May 2012

43. I Know There's An Answer (*Pet Sounds* 1966)
(Brian Wilson, Terry Sachen, Mike Love)
Recording
07/02/66 Western Recorders, LA (tracking - take #12 master, Brian's lead vocal, two mono mixes)
09/02/66 Western Recorders, LA ("Let Go of Your Ego" vocal inserts by Mike & Al)
16/02/66 Western Recorders, LA ("Hang On to Your Ego" Al's lead vocal - 18 takes, vocal overdubs)
03/03/66 Western Recorders, LA (mono mix with incomplete vocals)
17/04/66 Western Recorders, LA ("I Know There's An Answer" vocals)
Producer - Brian Wilson
Engineer - Chuck Britz
Band members
Mike Love (lead vocal on verse opening line; backing bass vocal); Brian Wilson (lead vocal on chorus, backing vocals, keyboard overdub); Carl Wilson (backing vocals); Al Jardine (lead vocalon verse; harmony vocal)
Session musicians
Hal Blaine (tambourine); Glen Campbell (12-string electric guitar, overdubbed banjo); Al De Lory (tack upright piano); Steve Douglas (clarinet); Jim Horn (alto flute); Paul Horn (alto flute); Bobby Klein (clarinet); Barney Kessel (12-string electric mando-guitar); Larry Knechtel (Hammond B3 organ); Jay Migliori (bass clarinet); Tommy Morgan (bass harmonica); Ray Pohlman (electric bass guitar); Lyle Ritz (upright bass); Julius Wechter (timpani).
Album released - 16/05/66

Originally written by Brian with the band's road manager Terry Sachen as "Hang On To Your Ego," it was inspired by an experience he had with LSD that resulted in what was known as a "full-on ego death" (a complete loss of subjective self-identity, or a fundamental transformation of the psyche). Looking back on the song in his 2016 memoir, Brian commented: "People took [LSD] to get away from themselves, but that wasn't the right way to take it. It was supposed to make you go deeper into yourself. I wanted to remind people that they could survive everything best if they remembered who they were."35.

Talent agent Loren Darro Schwartz (1937-2017) was employed by the William Morris Agency, who represented the band, and allegedly first met Brian at a Hollywood studio in the early 60's and soon became close friends. Another account has Tony Asher introducing him to Brian in 1963, although the singer would later refute that claim. Schwartz later revealed that Brian chose Asher as his collaborator because he assumed that "anybody that hung out with Loren Schwartz was a very brainy guy, a real verbal type person."127

> ***"I just didn't want to have anything to do with it, therefore I didn't go down that road of acid and the things that destroyed Brian's brain"***

What we do know, however, is that Schwarz was the one who introduced Brian to marijuana and LSD in late 1964, although he stated the latter drug was just a one-off and went on to claim that it was road manager Terry Sachen who supplied Brian "with marijuana, hashish and tempting him with other substances."127 Although Brian remembered how taking LSD gave him a "religious experience," he never became addicted to it. When asked if the song related to his struggle in maintaining his ego, he replied: "Yeah. I had taken a few drugs, and I had gotten into that kind of thing. I guess it came up naturally."72

The band had just returned from a tour of Japan when they joined Brian in the studio on February 9th. Al recalled the tension it caused during the session: "We had this discussion about the lyrics. Brian was very concerned. He wanted to know what we thought about it. To be honest, I don't think we even knew what an ego was. It wasn't as if we were prepared for what was to come. But that was the first discussion. Finally, Brian decided, 'Forget it. I'm changing the lyrics. There's too much controversy.' It's funny...Now it seems like no big deal; it just seemed like it at the time."72

Brian later admitted it had been "an inappropriate lyric," saying that it was "an ego statement in and of itself, which I wasn't going for, so I changed it. I gave it a lot of thought."128 It was Mike who strongly objected to the lyrics, saying they needed to be rewritten: "I changed the lyrics because I thought it was too acid to me. That was those guys doing acid, Van Dyke Parks, and Brian and Tony Asher...Some of the words were so totally offensive to me that I wouldn't even sing 'em because I thought it was too nauseating...That was too much of a doper song to me. I just didn't want to have anything to do with it, therefore I didn't go down that road of acid and the things that destroyed Brian's brain. I didn't want to go that route...I just didn't think the psychedelic route was the way to go."129. In another interview he said: "I wasn't interested in taking acid or getting rid of my ego. The people that I'd seen indulge in those things exhibited behaviours and mannerisms that left much to be desired."74

After listening to Mike's objections, Brian allowed him to revise the lyrics to make it be more about "finding meaning within oneself and allowing others to live as they wish." This offset any danger of a rift that was threatening to develop between the Mike-Al camp, which feared a public backlash to Brian's downbeat direction, and the Carl-Dennis-Bruce camp which supported Brian's new music direction. Apart from the title change, the line *"hang on to your ego/hang on but I know that you're going to lose the fight"* was changed to *"I know there's an answer/I know now but I have to find it by myself,"* but, surprisingly, the line *"they trip through the day and waste all their thoughts at night"* remained unchanged. According to Mike, Brian "didn't balk" at the lyric changes, saying, "Maybe he cared, maybe he didn't. He never said anything to me directly,"130 but in 2007 Brian confirmed that he didn't mind the changes, but went on to say, "You know what? The ego of the band was Mike. He was the ego guy."131

Marilyn Wilson saw the song as autobiographical: "When I heard that, I thought this is Brian and how he is really thinking about how he cannot relate to life and how people think, and there's gotta be something else. Basically, I thought that most of *Pet Sounds* was just him saying how frustrated he was in this life. Frustrated that nobody could relate to him musically or intellectually or whatever."72

"I Know There's An Answer" was one of two songs on *Pet Sounds* that pre-dates Tony Asher's involvement, and one of five that he and Brian did not write together. Asked later about his reaction, Asher recalled: "Brian startled me one afternoon by saying 'Oh listen - I just wrote a song with Terry.' I listened to it and said to myself, 'You mean I'm not writing all the songs for the album?' I was kind of surprised - I didn't know he was writing with anyone else. Then I got a grip on reality and thought, 'He doesn't have any obligation to write anything with me, let alone the whole album.' I didn't feel betrayed - I was just surprised."74

Brian neglected to give Mike official writing credit for both versions of the song when it was published, leading his cousin to successfully sue him in 1994 and be granted co-writing credit for these and 35 other Beach Boys songs, with a settlement of around $10 million.

D Strauss of the *New York Observer* believed the song "demonstrated how *Pet Sounds* made the Beach Boys the first major rock group to look music trends firmly in the eye and declare that rock really didn't matter."132 *Mojo* meanwhile described it as "a fried treatise on how LSD separates the turned on 'us' from the uptight 'them'…and strong lyrical echoes of John Lennon's similarly-themed 'Rain.'"25

42. Please Let Me Wonder (*The Beach Boys Today!* 1965)
(Brian Wilson, Mike Love)
Recording
07/01/65 Western Recorders, LA (tracking - take #23 master)
09/01/65 Western Recorders, LA (lead vocal overdub; backing vocal overdubs - 9 takes)
Producer - Brian Wilson
Engineer - Chuck Britz
Band members
Brian Wilson (lead vocal, harmony & backing vocals, upright piano, Farfisa organ); Carl Wilson (harmony & backing vocals, 12-string lead guitar); Mike Love (harmony & backing vocals); Dennis Wilson (harmony & backing vocals, percussion, tambourine, tom-tom); Al Jardine (harmony & backing vocals)
Session musicians/Guests
Glen Campbell (12-string acoustic guitar); Steve Douglas (tenor sax); Plas Johnson (tenor sax); Carol Kaye (bass guitar); Barney Kessel (classical guitar); Jack Nimitz (baritone sax); Earl Palmer (drums, timbales); Don Randi (grand piano, Hammond B3 organ); Billy Lee Riley (double-reed harmonica); Billy Strange (acoustic guitar); Jerry Williams (vibraphone, woodblock); Ron Swallow (tambourine, woodblock)
Album released - 08/03/65
US single released - 15/02/65 b-side to "Do You Wanna Dance?" Capitol 5372 #12
Film/TV performances
21/04/65 *Shindig!* ABC New York
16/06/69 Olympia Theater Paris TF1 (filmed concert)

A song written and recorded just two weeks after Brian had his nervous breakdown on a flight from LA to Houston on December 23rd 1964. While returning home to recover, the band continued their tour with sessionist Glen Travis Campbell (1936-2017) as his replacement. Arkansas-born Campbell had started playing guitar at the age of four and in 1958 had formed his own band, the Western Wranglers. Moving to LA he joined the Champs, who had previously topped the US charts with "Tequila" in 1958. Writing songs and recording demos, he soon became a much-sought after session musician and a regular member of what was later dubbed "The Wrecking Crew," before going on to have an incredible solo career. The following year his own tour commitments would see him being replaced in the band by Bruce Johnston.

On the same day the band played the last show of the two-week tour in Chicago (without Campbell), Brian went into the studio to record the new song, as he later recalled: "I wrote that at my apartment in West Hollywood. As soon as I finished I felt I had to record it, so I called up my engineer Chuck Britz and woke him up.

'Please Let Me Wonder' was recorded at 3:30 in the morning. I drove to the studio in the middle of the night and recorded it. That song was done as a tribute to Phil Spector's music. It definitely has a good straight ahead feel to it. I knew I loved that song from the moment it was finished and I've always loved it."63

In another interview with Harvey Kubernick, Brian gave a slightly different version: "That was cut at 4:30 in the morning. I went to the studio in the middle of the night. I called my engineer…and my wife and I went to the studio. We were there 5-8am. One of my favourite recording sessions I ever had in my life."105. Although that story is oft repeated, the session logs have the instrumental track recorded between 7pm and 10.30pm with vocals by the band overdubbed two days later.

"We got the feeling we were helping create the sound…we felt like we had left some creative juice there. We weren't just playing the notes; we were writing the notes"

Mike is again credited with co-writing the lyrics, so whatever input he made must have been done around the time of the vocal session.

Now seen as another practice run for what would be *Pet Sounds,* the original title for the song was "Don't Let Me Wonder." The lyrics relate to the narrator's confessing his doubt and discomfort over whether his girl will reveal she doesn't love him, and while fearing what her answer may be, choses instead to believe that she does. Musicologist Philip Lambert had a different view: "Brian's most heartfelt statement about the circumstances of his artistic dreams…Although the lyric appears to be directed at his new wife, asking for her love and understanding while he navigates the rocky shoals of his feeling, it's easy to read a different message into it, directed at the creative partners in his band."9 The song ends with Brian softly saying, "I Love You," apparently an improvised line added during the session. The influence of drug use could well account for the dreamy air of the song, heightened by Campbell's emotive guitar line that accentuates Brian's vocal phrases just at the right moment. If this is about his wife Marilyn, it signifies that he is not the husband she wants him to be, or is incapable of being.

Brian later confessed that this was the first song he wrote while being high, admitting that by smoking marijuana it made him feel "free to explore the boundaries of my creativity…more cerebral, spiritual, increasingly analytical of how I was feeling and what I was thinking."9 But it has to be noted that Brian had already written mellow ballads before, such as "The Warmth of the Sun" and "In My Room," so that heightened creativity had always been in evidence.

Although Brian said that he produced the song as "a tribute to Phil Spector," it bore no actual similarity to his idol's 'Wall of Sound' methods.133 However, what was readily apparent with the recording was Brian's growing need for absolute perfection from his musicians, insisting on take after take to get the smallest of errors corrected. And the musicians went along with it, knowing that they were dealing with someone special. Percussionist Julius Wechter was in admiration of Brian: "He really respected musicians. There were a lot of leaders, like Spector, who just treated musicians like paid employees, like machines. The more I think of it, Brian used to come out of the booth, shake hands with everybody. It was more like a party. We got the feeling we were helping create the sound, and after the session, we felt like we had left some creative juice there. We weren't just playing the notes; we were writing the notes."72

"Please Let Me Wonder" was described by *Cash Box* as "an easy-going, slow-rocking ode about the ambiguities of a love relationship,"134 while *Billboard* saw it as an "interesting and well done change of pace ballad."135 Looking back on the song many years later, *AllMusic's* Matthew Greenwald wrote: "Through the years it has become known as one of the most treasured of Brian Wilson's more obscure album cuts. A *quantum leap* for this gifted composer."136 *Paste* magazine also reflected on the song, describing it as "pop majesty…[with] one of the lushest backing tracks in all of the Beach Boys' pre-*Pet Sounds* catalog.137

David Leaf called it "a beautiful song that is noteworthy for the lead vocals that are exceptionally tender and warm. Listen for the organ-guitar interplay in the break and for the fat bass line. The bass throughout this side was a signpost on the way to *Pet Sounds.*"116 Jim Fusilli wrote: "Brian as narrator is opening his heart to his girl for the first time and can't express himself as he wants to. Abstract but highly personal declarations are the best he can do, as if he's not precisely sure what he expects love to bring to his life. He's terrifically confused. A deep, encompassing love is foremost on his mind. Is it because of her or because it's what he most wants? Does this type of love exist or is it a product of fantasy, of will."130

Rocksucker's Jonny Abrams pointed out: "There are some things that science can't explain, and Brian Wilson's ability to reduce grown men to tears by chord progression alone is one that has perhaps been taken for granted - a tribute to the lofty standards he imposed upon himself."301

In describing the album, Leaf wrote: "At the time, it was very risky to lay your heart right on the line as Brian does in these songs. This album was a big turning point for the group, as the subject matter of their songs became more adult and ultimately less appealing to their teenage audience who still hungered for pure fun in the sun."116

With its use of dealing with each instrument individually, and deconstructing the song into tiny segments, "Please Let Me Wonder," like so many tracks on *Today!,* was another clear indication of just how far Brian had come in his music development, as well as a strong hint of what lay ahead in the near future.

41. Catch a Wave *(Surfer Girl* 1963)
(Brian Wilson, Mike Love)
Recording
12/06/63 Western Recorders, LA (tracking)
14/07/63 Western Recorders, LA (vocals and harp)
16/07/63 Western Recorders, LA (tracking)
Producer - Brian Wilson
Engineer - Chuck Britz
Band members
Brian Wilson (lead vocal, organ, piano); Mike Love (lead vocal); Carl Wilson (lead guitar, vocals); Dennis Wilson (drums, vocals); David Marks (rhythm guitar); Al Jardine (bass guitar, vocals)
Guest
Maureen Love (harp)
Album released - 16/09/63

TV/Film Performance
21/01/77 Capital Centre, Washington DC

One of the best candidates for a song that should have been a single, and another missed opportunity by the label. With perhaps one of Brian's best a capella introductions, this is *the* classic surfing song, complete with Mike's 20-year-old sister Maureen capturing the sound of rolling waves with a beautiful harp glissando. Originally titled "Sittin' On Top of the World," it invites the listener to take part in the "*greatest sport around*," while at the same time dismissing all its detractors. Despite having a cold during the vocal session, Mike shares lead vocal with Brian, with Mike's opening line on the verses being followed by Brian's falsetto on the second to great effect (Mike would also be awarded co-writing credit following his successful lawsuit in 1994).

> ***"He fantasises about the waves of the female form, also perfectly proportioned and awaiting, he thinks, physical domination"***

With Al rejoining the band in time for the *Surfer Girl* sessions, it also meant that the band would be a six-man outfit until David Marks departed later in the year. Brian recalled in 1990: "[It] was more rhythmic. The guitars were more clean and driving as if to say they didn't wanna stop. The piano was played by me and it was perfectly synchronized with the guitars. The three different sounds combined to make one unique sound. I was ecstatic about this." The instrumental track was included on the *Stack-o-Tracks* album, the band's first album that failed to chart in both the US and UK.

Phil Lambert wrote: "In a guy song like 'Catch A Wave,' the surfer brags to his friends about his success, which leaves him 'top of the world' but he also puts on a show for the waves of humanity watching from the beach. He fantasies about the waves of the female form, also perfectly proportioned and awaiting, he thinks, physical domination. He knows that there's more than one way to get to the top of the world."9

In September 1964, Brian's friends Jan Berry and Dean Torrence (Jan & Dean) released their version of the song to coincide with the current craze of skateboarding. Jan Berry approached Brian and his then-current collaborator Roger Christian to rewrite it for them, and they came up with "Sidewalk Surfin.'" It reached #25 on the Hot 100.

40. Here Today (*Pet Sounds* 1966)
(Brian Wilson, Tony Asher)
Recording
11/03/66 Sunset Sound Studio, LA (tracking for "Good, Good, Good Vibrations")
12/03/66 Western Recorders, LA (tracking for re-titled "Here Today" - 20 takes)
22/03/66 Western Recorders, LA (mixing)
23/03/66 CBS Columbia Studio, LA (vocals)
25/03/66 CBS Columbia Studio, LA (vocals - take #11 master)
Producer - Brian Wilson
Engineers - Bruce Botnick (Sunset), Chuck Britz (Western), Ralph Valentin (Columbia)

Band members
Mike Love (lead & backing vocals); Brian Wilson (backing vocals - falsetto); Carl Wilson (backing vocals); Al Jardine (backing vocals); Bruce Johnston (backing vocals)
Session musicians
Frank Capp (tambourine on snare drum); Al Casey (12-string electric guitar); Mike Deasy (12-string acoustic guitar); Larry Knechtel (Hammond B3 organ); Gail Martin (bass trombone); Nick Martinis (drums); Jay Migliori (baritone sax); Jack Nimitz (baritone sax); Ray Pohlman (electric bass guitar); Don Randi (tack piano); Lyle Ritz (upright bass); Ernie Tack (bass trombone)
Album released - 16/05/66
US single released - 18/12/67 b-side of "Darlin'" Capitol 2068#24
Film/TV performance
25/04/66 *Top of the Pops* BBC-1 London (footage of band at Lake Arrowhead, Hollywood (broadcast 04/08/66)

This was the last song recorded for *Pet Sounds* (except for mixing). Originally logged on the session sheet as "I Don't Have a Title Yet," it may have reflected the confusion in writing the lyrics, as Tony Asher later explained: "That's a song that has a number of little sections to it that are quite different, and it was not one of the easier songs to write on the album. It was, I recall, a song that I wrote quite a lot to, much of which we didn't use. It was sort of a struggle before we got the lyric that Brian was happy with, that Brian and I were both happy with. We went through quite a bit. I think I churned out quite a lot of okay-but-not-terrific lyric on that song."[72] Asher would also claim that he contributed musical ideas to this and a couple of other songs on the album, saying: "'Here Today' contains a little more of me both lyrically and melodically than Brian."[123] Brian disputed his claim.

In a 1996 interview, Brian said the song had "really good lyrics,"[72] but later revealed: "'Here Today' was probably one of the mystery songs on the album, I don't really know what it's about. I liked it, but yet I didn't. I don't really identify with that song ...It was just one of those songs in there, one little song"[72]
Whatever the different opinions of Brian and his co-writer, the song is undeniably one of the album's gems. Mike's spot-on lead vocal tells the story of a girl's ex-boyfriend warning her newfound lover that their relationship will be "here today" and gone tomorrow, leaving him heartbroken and his world a mess. Brian later claimed: "'Here Today' was a work of art in my opinion. It was an assertive track with utilization of [Ray Pohlman's] basses played up higher [thanks to engineer Bruce Botnick]. The trombones gave it that masculine touch." Interviewed about the song, Bruce was quick to point out: "Another ooh and aah thing from the band that was actually right for it. There's not a lot of room for the band to do anything other than be quickly orchestral. Brian was smart enough not to overwrite the vocals. He correctly used the vocals as another pad. If he had made the mistake of overwriting the background parts, you would never pay attention to the leads, and we would have gotten in the way."[72]

"The angriest song on the album...a masterpiece of discontent"

Like most songs on *Pet Sounds*, the band members found that when it came to the vocal sessions, Brian was a hard taskmaster demanding the very best. Mike recalled: "We worked long and hard on the vocals, and if there was a hint of a sharp or a flat [there] we would have to do it again until it was right. Every voice had to be right. The timing had to be right."

Carl also appreciated what his brother was trying to achieve: "We'd be about eight or nine bars into a song and Brian would go, 'OK' and stop us. Nobody else in the room would know what was wrong with it. But he knows that a note was wrong, or somebody hadn't played, out of all the bits that were going on. It was amazing how he heard something at the time that it occurred." Bruce Johnston, too, remembered the tension in the studio: "I was just so afraid of him yelling at me, that I thought I better sing it right. Brian was a combination of Rachmaninoff and General Patton. He was [amazingly] brutal in the studio. You can hear him yell, 'No talking' in 'Here Today.' He was the commander in chief of several countries at once."72

Using Sunset Sound Studio instead of Western was the idea of saxophonist Steve Douglas, one of Brian's session musicians and a member of Capitol's A&R department. Sunset was well known for doing the audio recordings for a number of the early Disney movies. Engineer Botnick recalled: "The Beach Boys needed to record and they couldn't get into Western, so Steve suggested they come over to Sunset Sound. The minute that I heard that I was working with Brian I was impressed, because I was really taken with their sound. The structure of the harmony and how modern it was in their approach. I immediately liked it."72

Wall Street Journal rock critic Jim Fusilli wrote: "The technical structure of 'Here Today' is intriguing because there seems to be no reason for its complexity. The choruses are seven, not eight, bars long; and the twenty-bar verses are separated into sections of various and unusual lengths: some five, some eight, some seven, etc. That kind of convolution would suggest a different lyrical theme than the one here, or lyrics that required a contrast in the music…From a fan's perspective [the song] is a valuable part of *Pet Sounds*. Because it isn't perfect, it serves to remind us that the album is the product of a human endeavour, of hard, hard work, and thus subject to highs and not-so-highs. And though it lacks the cohesion so gloriously possessed by many of the album's other tracks, it's an interesting song - and not a safe choice, particularly for someone working under the strain of high expectations and record company demands. Thus, like the instrumental title track, [it] is admirable for what it is, but more so, for what it endeavours to be: yet another extraordinary pop recording."130

According to Keith Badman, the first session had Brian recording a musical sequence for a track that had the working title of "Good, Good, Good Vibrations," maybe intending to use the opening passage for his ongoing "Good Vibrations" project. However, he completed the session by reworking it into separate piece that would later become "Here Today."11

In the original mono mix can be heard the famous studio chatter and cough, especially in the 37 second-long instrumental bridge which dramatically kicks off with a jerking thump from Larry Knechtel's Hammond organ. While recording the ooh and aah background vocals at Columbia, Bruce, or possibly Dennis (perhaps unaware that the tape was still rolling) is heard having a conversation with a photographer about cameras, and Brian shouting to them, 'No talking' and saying to Chuck Britz 'top please,' an instruction to rewind the tape and start over.74 Although some critics see this as Brian's production being a little more cavalier when it came to doing the mixing, it remains a fun part of Beach Boys lore. To satisfy the perfectionists, the studio chatter was removed for the 1997 stereo mix.

Legendary musician Al Kooper acknowledged that the use of instruments on the track influenced his later work, most notably on tracks like 1968's "I Can Love Woman," and quipped: "The verses are very Beach Boys and the choruses are very Four Seasons, so I had both coasts covered." When invited to Brian's home for a private listening to *Pet Sounds,* Kooper recalled: "I wasn't expecting *that*. It completely floored me. He was really proud of it, and if there was a part he liked, he would take the needle and put it back and play that part again. And then he played the whole album again. God bless him." On reflection, Kooper summed up his admiration for the album: "It's a religious experience. Whenever I think I'm good at what I do, I put that on and then I'm humbled again."[10]

Certainly strong enough to be considered as an A-side single, the song had to wait some 18 months before being surpringly chosen as the flip-side of the Top 30 single "Darlin" in December 1967. Critics then and now were almost unanimous in their praise, with the exception of the slightly cynical Norman Jopling for *Record Mirror,* who called it the album's "corniest song" and a "kind of condensed showcase of all the backing sounds that anyone could cram into a few minutes. Not too good at all…"[139] Mark Dillon praised it for being one of *Pet Sounds'* "most incredible instrumental arrangements,"[10] while Rick Swan described it as one of "frustration, the angriest song on the album…a masterpiece of discontent."[21]

39. (Wouldn't It Be Nice) To Live Again (*Made in California* 2013)
(Dennis Wilson, Stan Shapiro)
Recording
23/05/71 Beach Boys Studio, Bel Air
Producers - The Beach Boys
Engineer - Stephen Desper
Band members
Dennis Wilson (lead vocal), Brian Wilson, Carl Wilson, Mike Love, Al Jardine, Bruce Johnston (backing vocals)
Session musicians - unknown
Album released - 27/08/13

Jack Rieley had big ideas for the band following their fall from grace at the start of the 70's. For the making of what would become their next album, their new manager went all-out to enhance the band's credibility, even successfully pairing them up with the Grateful Dead for a well-received concert at the fashionable Fillmore West. As for their next album, he strongly recommended they resurrect the long-lost masterwork "Surf's Up" that was to have been the centrepiece of the discarded *Smile*.

But there was friction and infighting in the Beach Boys' camp, mainly over the running order of the songs for the next album. Never a big fan of pop music, Rieley had persuaded them not to include Brian, Carl and Al's charming "Loop De Loop," while it was also alleged that Dennis and Carl were unhappy (perhaps rightly so) with the inclusion of Mike's "Student Demonstration Time." Al also took issue that more of his own songs were not considered. Not only that, it was becoming apparent that Rieley was favouring the Wilsons over Mike, Bruce and Al.

But perhaps the biggest disagreement was between Carl and Dennis over the inclusion of two of Dennis's songs, "4th of July" and "(Wouldn't It Be Nice) To Live Again," resulting in a frustrated Dennis pulling both songs, saying they weren't "worthy" of them, and saving them instead for a proposed solo album, which apparently was nearing completion. Jon Stebbins later claimed that Rieley had said: "[The] others in the band voiced jealousy of the songs which Dennis sang lead, and were constantly maneuvering to exclude them."[140]

"The greatest Beach Boys song never heard"

According to co-writer Stan Shapiro, a bitterly disappointed Dennis, on the way out of the studio, told Mike to go back and write something "earth-shaking"…like a few more stupid car songs."[141] According to Shapiro, Mike replaced "(Wouldn't It Be Nice) To Live Again" with his totally-inappropriate "Student Demonstration Time." Dennis had originally visualised his song to follow Brian's desolate "Til I Die" to close the album, but Carl objected. If that had been agreed, it would surely have elevated the album and the song to legendary status.

Andrew Doe was full of praise for the song: "A classic Dennis Wilson composition featuring his best ever vocal - yes, better than 'Forever' - and stellar background vocals from his brothers. Totally majestic…"[142]. Rick Swan also saw it as a masterpiece: "Dennis tenderly croons this wistful ballad supported by a tasteful background of flutes and piano. When he leaps to a higher range, chills ripple through every sentient being within earshot. Melancholy and mournful, but ultimately triumphant, it stands not only as one of Dennis's best performances ever, but one of the Beach Boys' finest mature works…"[21]

Peter Carlin wrote: "Dennis could write and produce songs that all but rivalled Brian's for emotional power and grace."[32] Then there was the pain and weariness in his voice, sounding like sandpaper's been scraped over it, but at the same time highly emotive and totally apt for the mood of the composition. Jon Stebbins wrote for *Pop Matters*: "If the Beach Boys were all championing Dennis Wilson, the stuff would have been out a long time ago. But they don't see an upside for themselves."[143].

For whatever reasons, the surviving Beach Boys would keep Dennis's lost treasure hidden in the archives for the next 40 years.[142] After the *Surf's Up* album was completed, Dennis turned his hand to a tentative solo project in collaboration with his friend Daryl Dragon, claiming (but not too seriously) that the album might be called either *Poops* or *Hubba Bubba*. Sessions for the album continued throughout 1971 with Dennis hedging his bets on whether he was in or out of the band. Some of the tracks shortlisted for the album were "Lady," "Make It Good," "Barbara," "Cuddle Up," "(Wouldn't It Be Nice) To Live Again," "I've Got A Friend" and "Sound of Free." Eventually the project collapsed, with Dragon going on to form The Captain & Tennille with his wife Toni, and the band sequestering two of Dennis's collabs with Dragon - "Cuddle Up" and "Make It Good" - for their next album *Carl and the Passions - "So Tough."*

According to a frustrated Stan Shapiro, he claimed he had written "(Wouldn't It Be Nice) To Live Again" all by himself and dismissed it as being Dennis's tribute to his wife Barbara. In an article for *Shindig* magazine he stated:

"I wrote 100% of the words in the song…I wrote those words long before Dennis met Barbara Charren and the song had nothing to do with Barbara whatsoever…As a matter of fact I was with Dennis when we met Barbara for the very first time at the Hamburger Hamlet in the Westwood Village next door to the theater on the corner. I wrote the song as a part of a six page letter appealing to my girlfriend to come back after she moved in with an older man…I was heartbroken and pleaded with her to come back in a six page letter, in which I penned the poetic song. I sent the letter to her and a few days later it was returned unopened. I opened the envelope and left the letter on my kitchen table. Dennis then read the letter and pleaded with me to let him use it in the song. I turned him down…and, for the record, at that point Daryl Dragon had nothing to do with it…A couple of weeks later I got a call from another producer who asked me if I heard what happened to my girlfriend. I was devastated to learn that she taken her own life after falling out with the movie maker, and Dennis begged me, once again, to let him put the words to music. This time I acquiest to his persistence and let him record it…"

Record producer Al Gomes submitted the song to the Grammy Awards in 2007, making it the first time Dennis's name appeared on the Grammy ballot as a songwriter, along with Shapiro.145.

In 2013 Beach Boy archivists Mark Linett and Alan Boyd, the duo behind the Grammy-winning *Smile Sessions,* released *Made In California*, a massive collection of mainly unreleased work by Dennis and Carl. The inclusion of the song was, for all those who had petitioned for its release on Facebook, their first chance to hear the mournful, dynamic tearjerker, dubbed by some "the greatest Beach Boys song never heard." An extended mix of the song was later featured on the 2021 *Feel Flows* box set.

38. Long Promised Road (*Surf's Up* 1971)
(Carl Wilson, Jack Rieley)
Recording
03/04/71 Beach Boys Studio, Bel Air (piano track)
04/04/71 Beach Boys Studio, Bel Air (tracking)
04/05/71 Beach Boys Studio, Bel Air (vocals)
Producer - The Beach Boys
Engineer - Stephen Desper
Band members
Carl Wilson (lead & backing vocals, Wurlitzer electric pianos, grand piano, upright piano, Hammond organ, Moog synthesiser, electric & acoustic guitars, drums, tambourine, shakers, temple blocks, ride cymbal swell); Brian Wilson (backing vocals); Mike Love (backing vocals); Al Jardine (backing vocals); Bruce Johnston (backing vocals)
Guests
Marilyn Wilson (backing vocals); Diane Rovell (backing vocals)
Album released – 30/08/71
US single released - 24/05/71 b/w "Deirdre" Brother/Reprise 1015
UK single released - 06/71 b/w "Deirdre" Stateside SS 2190
US single re-released - 11/10/71 b/w "Till I Die" Brother/Reprise 1047 #89
Film/TV performance
1971 Promo

While Carl Wilson's magnificent soulful voice is best remembered for *God Only Knows*, this almost one-man show is arguably his finest achievement when it comes to writing, production and performance. At a time when the band's popularity was waning and Brian now almost in self-isolation, it was left to the other band members to step up to the mark, especially Carl.

But things were about to change. During the recording for *Sunflower,* 28-year-old local deejay John (Jack) Rieley (1942-2015) dropped in to Brian's Radiant Radish health food store in West Hollywood and invited him and the band to come down to the KPFK Pacifica radio station to do an interview for his show. "DJ John Frank," as he was called, was already a huge fan of their music, appeared to have an impressive resume, including (falsely, it turns outs) a Peabody Award recipient and Pulitzer winning journalist now working for NBC News. He could certainly talk the talk and Brian was easily taken in by it, readily agreeing to do a radio show interview, his first for many months.

In the interview on July 29th 1970 Brian. Mike and Bruce talked about subjects such as the unreleased tracks on *Smile* (especially Surf's Up"), as well as the band's current recording problems and business issues. Their co-manager Fred Vail, who had arranged the interview, recalled: "We got out to this station and Jack... is all excited and becomes very enthusiastic about the Beach Boys." Rieley later told *Rolling Stone*: "I had read some articles about Brian. They first got my interest in meeting him. I thought, 'Nobody could be that far out.' I found out they could be."11

During the interview Brian admitted to Rieley that "the clean American thing has hurt us, and we're not getting any kind of airplay today," before going on to say that the band was not "putting enough spunk in our production and I don't know who to blame...we haven't done enough to change our image...we sort of operate a democracy thing in our productions...Maybe that's the problem. I don't know." Rieley then said, "This is what you need," and then spoke about all the things he would do to make the group popular again.11

On August 8th Rieley sent Brian a six-page memo describing how he would stimulate both increased sales and popularity, and they took him at his word. After the poor showing on the charts for *Sunflower*, it looked certain that Vail's days were numbered, and, indeed, by the end of August Rieley had become the band's new manager and the Brother label's director of public relations. Almost from day one he had set out his conditions - Carl would now be the band's official leader; no more matching stage outfits. His intention was to turn them into a band of songwriters, giving each member the chance to shine, with the focus now shifted from love and romance to more socially conscious topics (although he later admitted it was not part of his master plan).

It all got off to good start when the band played to a 6,000-strong enthusiastic crowd at the Big Sur Festival in October, garnering positive reviews and re-establishing their place in rock's hierarchy as a credible live act.

Once *Sunflower* was released at the end of August, any optimism over its commercial success soon evaporated with its low chart-rating. For many critics, even those who praised the new album, the damage to the band's popularity had already been done long ago with their non-appearance at the 1976 Monterey Festival, and even now was showing little sign of being reversed. During a second meeting with Rieley, he insisted that he knew a way to make them become more relevant and thus regain their popularity. Taking his word for it, Carl sacked current manager Fred Vail and installed Rieley, reputedly at the instigation of both Mike and Bruce.

Rieley's master plan for their revival came with caveats: no more striped shirts and matching outfits; Carl was to become the official band leader; Brian was to be back for live shows, and the adoption of a new slogan - "It's now safe to listen to the Beach Boys." And it seemed to work. Subsequent shows, including the Big Sur Festival and Carnegie Hall, all had Brian in attendance, with an eclectic mix of old hits and recent album tracks. Neither were all these simple 45-minute gigs; instead the band would occasionally stretch to two-hour performances covering music from their entire career.

"I was writing personal lyrics - love songs with a sense of poetry"

It seemed Rieley was being good to his word. Carl recalled: "He was very healthy for the group. We were real sheltered. We had hit the big time in 1962 and gotten quite isolated from the real world. We had our own protective bubble. The main thing Jack did was point out to the group what its good points were and when we were a little fuzzy and didn't see things too clearly …"[98]

Rieley would co-write three songs for the next album, two with Carl and one with Brian. With the original title of *Landlocked,* it would be one of the first-ever albums with an ecological, save-the-planet theme, but it was also beset by problems within the band. Rieley was keen to have some of the *Smile* tracks resurrected, especially Brian's masterpiece "Surf's Up," but even though Brian was strongly opposed to the idea, it was not only included but also became the album's new title (although according to Bruce, it was all a sham, intended to fool the public into believing Brian was now back in charge). Carl and Dennis also locked horns over the inclusion of two of Dennis's recent songs, which subsequently had to wait more than two decades to see a release. Around this time, Dennis, apparently drunk, would accidentally put his hand through a window and sever tendons, leaving him unable to play drums for over three years.

"Long Promised Road" was the first song that Carl and Rieley wrote together. Asked about it in 2013, Rieley recalled: "Carl asked me to have a hand in it. I felt that I was on to something. Van Dyke Parks wrote ethereal lyrics. *Surf's Up* is a masterpiece but it's also ethereal. I was writing personal lyrics - love songs with a sense of poetry. I was trying to tell the tale of life and love that we go through at different times in life. I adore the English language so much [and it] gave me the opportunity to stretch out. I wanted to see Carl make something extraordinary. His vocals are so precious on it…I worked very hard with him on his performance, which was stellar."[99].

Following the near-apocalyptic images of the opening track, "Don't Go Near the Water," "Long Promised Road" looks back at a decade of ecological blunders, describing the struggle that the human spirit has in trying to come to terms with the images of pain and suffering, but also finding hope and tranquillity lying ahead on that long, promised trail. Timothy White described the song as "wistful but determined in its hopefulness, and so Brian harboured fond feelings toward it...Thus, the heroic theme and his brother's emotional investment in the saga certified the enduring worth."69.

Released as a single ahead of the album, it failed to chart (their sixth successive one to do so), and when re-released five months later, it only made #89 on the Hot 100, becoming the band's lowest-charting single of their career, a record it would sadly hold for the next 18 years.

Rieley's association with the Beach Boys would last a couple more years, and in that time would even replace Nick Grillo as their business manager. He would go on to co-write another seven songs for the band; instigate the employment of Flame members Ricky Fataar and Blondie Chaplin as bona fide Beach Boys, and then help prompt the foolhardy decision to record an album in Europe. Eventually, strong rumours of falsehoods, and even manipulating arguments among different band members, would force Carl to cut their ties with him.

But with Carl's sensitive and mellow lead vocal, striking backing vocals, stupendous synth-heavy arrangement (again, thanks to Carl), and finally, without question, Rieley's pseudo-important lyrics, "Long Promised Road" remains a perfect example of the tenor of the times, and would most certainly have become, along with Brian's "Til I Die," the album's standout tracks, had it not been, of course, for the decision to revisit and re-record "Surf's Up" in all its spectacular, sun-kissed glory.

A wonderful version of the song, recorded at the Carnegie concert, would later appear on 1998's *Endless Harmony* compilation.

37. Girl Don't Tell Me *(Summer Days (And Summer Nights!!)* (1965)
(Brian Wilson)
Recording
30/04/65 Western Recorders, LA (tracking -16 takes, inserts, Carl's lead vocal)
Producer - Brian Wilson
Engineer - Chuck Britz
Band members
Carl Wilson (lead vocals, 12-string guitar, acoustic guitar); Brian Wilson (bass guitar); Dennis Wilson (drums); Bruce Johnston (celesta)
Guest
Ron Swallow (tambourine)
Album released - 05/07/65
US single released - 20/12/65 b-side to "Barbara Ann" Capitol 5561 #2
UK single released - 02/66 b-side to "Barbara Ann" Capitol CL 15432 #3

The song often compared to the Beatles' "Ticket To Ride," which was largely the work of John Lennon. Brian had made the comment that he intended to "submit it" to his rivals, but whether they would have accepted it is doubtful to say the least. Apart from the stammered words in both songs (compare Brian's "guy-uy-uy," "write-ite-ite," and "t-i-ime" with John's "ride-i- ide,") there is not a great deal of similarity apart from slightly similar tempos and guitar breaks. Musicologists point out the lack of backing vocals on "Girl Don't Tell Me" as Brian's deliberate attempt to sound like his rivals. However, in 2002 Brian actually cited "Ticket To Ride" as the song that gave him the inspiration to write "a Beatles song."146

> *"I didn't have any way to get it down. But I just heard the whole thing up there, from start to finish"*

Whether intentional or coincidental, none of this deters from the fact that it is a great song, one that Brian wrote while on honeymoon with Marilyn. He later recalled: "I didn't have any way to get it down. But I just heard the whole thing up there, from start to finish, and I remembered it well enough to go later and write down the lyrics on a piece of paper."35

The remorseful song about a disinterested girlfriend from a previous summer and her empty promises features Carl's confident lead vocal, his first since "Pom, Pom Play Girl" and "Louie, Louie" on *Shut Down Volume 2,* and the band playing nearly all their own instruments, a practice that was becoming less frequent at this point in time.

The song was covered in October 1965 by 12-year-old singer-songwriter Keith Green. Released on the Decca label, it was produced by Gary Usher. A pioneer of the contemporary Christian music genre, Green would tragically die in a plane crash in 1982.

In its review of "Girl Don't Tell Me," *AllMusic* wrote: "The Beach Boys' recording of the song allows the song to speak for itself with a muted production, utilizing a simple guitar-bass-drums backdrop that is given a gentle bit of sonic colour by the ringing tones of a celeste. This recording is also unusual in that it forsakes the group's usual vocal harmonies for a solo lead vocal beautifully rendered by Carl Wilson...The end result is lovely and understated and communicates its strong emotions in a subtly moving fashion."147

Joseph Kyle opined: "This classic Beach Boys track captures the emotional pull of the separation caused by the end of the season. In a rare moment of masculine strength, Wilson's protagonist is strong, confident, and aware of what will happen next, and offers up a self-preserving move that exerted a unique level of maturity for a Wilson song of that era. Other than that, it's simply a lovely tune, and one of the finest in a catalog of hundreds of lovely songs."148

Long overshadowed by the album's two hits, "Help Me Rhonda" and "California Girls," and rarely discussed in the decades that followed, "Girl Don't Tell Me" is now considered to be a true masterpiece and no longer just a hidden gem.

36. Time To Get Alone (*20/20* 1969)
(Brian Wilson)
Recording (Redwood)
12/10/67 Wally Heider Studio, Hollywood (tracking for Redwood)
14/10/67 Wally Heider Studio, Hollywood (strings & horns)
15/10/67 Wally Heider Studio, Hollywood (drums & percussion)
13/11/67 Wally Heider Studio, Hollywood (vocal overdubs?)
Recording (20/20)
02/10/68 Beach Boys Studio, Bel Air (track re-recorded)
04/10/68 Beach Boys Studio, Bel Air/ I.D Sound Studio LA (vocal overdubs)
15/11/68 Capitol Studio, Hollywood (stereo mix)
21/11/68 Beach Boys Studio, Bel Air
Producer - Carl Wilson

Engineer - Jim Lockert or Bill Halverson (*Wally Heider*)
Band members
Carl Wilson (lead vocal); Brian Wilson (vocals, piano, harpsichord, organ); Mike Love (vocals); Al Jardine (vocals)
Session musicians (1967)
Dwight Carver (possibly French horn); Dick Forrest (trumpet, flugelhorn); Jay Migliori (flute, clarinet); Gene Pello (drums); 6 violins, 2 cellos, 2 violas.
Session musicians/Guests (1968)
Danny Hutton (piano); Diane Rovell (additional vocals); Marilyn Wilson (additional vocals); Ron Brown (bass); Jay Migliori (flute, clarinet); Ray Pohlman (bass); Gene Pello (drums, percussion)
Album Released - 10/02/69

Brian had originally written this song for a new trio of singers called Redwood, which consisted of his best friend, 25-year-old Danny Hutton, with Cory Wells and Chuck Negron. With the aim of signing them to the Brother label, he planned to also give them the song "Darlin," which he had written several years before, and for which Hutton had already recorded a guide vocal on October 11th 1967.

The initial recording for "Time To Get Alone" took place in the midst of the *Wild Honey* sessions. Once they realised what Brian was doing, Mike, Carl and Al all objected to the fact that he was giving away quality music that should be recorded by the Beach Boys (shades of the Murry-Brian arguments over "Surf City" being given to Jan & Dean). Mike recalled: "[Brian] had them in the studio for several days, and he was really funny. They didn't meet up to his expectations…They'd go in and they wouldn't sing well enough for him…but they went off and made billions [as Three Dog Night]"

According to Negron, the decision not to produce their songs was a result of *Smiley Smile's* lack of success and Brian seemingly becoming less committed with the band: "The other Beach Boys wanted Brian's immense songwriting and producing talents used strictly to enhance their own careers." Although claiming that the Beach Boys would have made millions in additional royalties if they had signed them to Brother, Negron went on to admit he would have done the same thing if he had been in their position.[149]

> ***To all intents and purposes, this gifted artist was being bullied out of pursuing his own artistic and personal freedom.***

It all came to a head several weeks later when Carl, Mike and Al came into the studio to hear the version of "Time To Get Alone," as Negron explained: "They manoeuvred Brian into the control booth and reduced him to tears. It was a cruel and pathetic scene…It was as if Brian had turned into a little boy. The conversation appeared quiet and calm, but we could tell it was emotional and intense. The others were doing most of the talking, like overbearing, controlling parents. Brian would move away and they would block his escape…We could actually feel Brian crumbling, and when he came out of the booth, a tear dropped down his cheek. His head was lowered and his shoulders sagged. It was the body language of a child who had just been scolded and punished."[149]

To all intents and purposes, this gifted artist was being bullied out of pursuing his own artistic and personal freedom.

Submitting to the pressure, Brian agreed to stop working with Redwood, who would indeed re-emerge later as the successful Three Dog Night. Thirteen days after their first session with Brian, the Beach Boys were back in the studio to record "Darlin" themselves. But "Time To Get Alone" would now be shelved for a year.

In October 1968, as part of the sessions for the *20/20* album, Brian re-recorded the original harpsichord-driven track at his Bel Air home, with Carl's lead, and Brian and Al's backing vocals, overdubbed two days later at both his home and at I.D Sound. The sessions were filmed and later edited as part of the promotional film for "I Can Hear Music" single in 1969, and later used for the 1985 *An American Band* documentary, with "Time To Get Alone" synched to it.

Rick Swan described the song as a "technical and creative triumph. Carl has his fingerprints all over this. He's tasteful for the most part, only occasionally lapsing into the mundane. This waltz-time song is one of the band's best songs of the late Capitol era. The vocal uniformly excellent, and the resonant "deep and wide" stuns. A hidden treasure."[21] Barry Lenser of *Pop Matters* called it "a dream, right on down the line from Carl's feathery lead vocal and the way it contrasts with the up-and-down crunch of the waltz backdrop - to the sumptuously layered arrangement of the chorus to the immaculate production job to the unadorned coda (which is from the extended version)."[150]

35. Cabinessence (*20/20* 1969)
(Brian Wilson, Van Dyke Parks)
Recording (Smile)
03/10/66 Gold Star Studio A (tracking for "Home On the Range")
11/10/66 Western Recorders Studio 3 (tracking "Child Is the Father To The Man" version 2 – logged as "Cabin Essence")
11/10/66 CBS Columbia Studio, LA ("Home On the Range" vocal overdubs for "Cabin Essence")
12/10/66 CBS Columbia Studio, LA ("Child Is Father To The Man"/"Cabin-Essence" vocals)
06/12/66 CBS Columbia Studio, LA (vocal overdubbing)
11/12/66 CSB Columbia Studio, LA ("Cabin Essence" vocals)
15/12/66 CBS Columbia Studio, LA ("Cabin Essence" vocals)
27/12/66 Western Recorders, LA (extra vocals for "Who Ran the Iron Horse" section)
Recording (20/20)
20/11/68 Capitol Studio, Hollywood ("Cabinessence" additional vocals overdubbed onto existing tapes)
22/11/68 Capitol Studio, Hollywood ("Cabinessence" chorus 2 and tag stereo mixes)
Producer - Brian Wilson
Engineers - Larry Levine (*Gold Star*), Chuck Britz (*Western*)
Band members
Brian Wilson (chorus & tag vocals); Carl Wilson (lead, chorus & tag vocals; acoustic guitar); Mike Love (lead, chorus & tag vocals); Dennis Wilson (chorus & tag vocals); Al Jardine (chorus & tag vocals); Bruce Johnston (chorus & tag vocals)
Session musicians
James Burton (guitar); Carl Fortina (accordion); Jim Gordon (drums, tambourine); Carol Kaye (bass guitar); Jay Migliori (sax & flute); Tommy Morgan (harmonica, bass harmonica), Van Dyke Parks (harmonium, upright piano); Bill Pitman (Danelectro fuzz bass); Lyle Ritz (upright bass); Tommy Tedesco (acoustic guitar, bouzouki); Oliver Mitchell (trumpet);Jimmy Bond Jr (upright bass); Jesse Ehrlich (cello); Armand Kaproff (cello)
Album released - 10/02/69
Single released - 06/11 b/w "Wonderful" Mojo MOJ 06/Capitol MOJ 06

One of the more famous relics of the unparalleled world that Brian was creating with *Smile*, and one of the most analysed by both musicologists and fans alike. Assembled from three separate *Smile* segments tentatively called "Home on the Range," "Who Ran the Iron Horse," and "Grand Coulee Dam" - which put together tell the story of the building of the great railroad that crossed America in the latter part of the 19th century. The first part describes quiet nights on the prairie, the second pictures the Chinese labourers working with their tools, and the final part describes the wonder of the finished project, with watching crows flying overhead.

The trouble is, for thousands of fans at the time, it just didn't make any sense. As one of the more divisive of the Van Dyke Parks collaborations, it was left to the writers to try and explain its meaning. In an interview with Steven Gaines, Parks said that they had been "trying to write a song that would end on a freeze-frame of the Union Pacific Railroad - the guys all coming together and have their picture taken."[123]

Parks elaborated later: "The whole thing seems to be about the taking of the territory. Folks sing a song of the grange. Granges were collectives of farms that would pool their resources so they could set their own prices, so that they weren't competing so much with each other, but so they were finding a reasonable return for their endeavours... the grange system was the backbone of the American farm. And we had to bring the Chinese into this equation, because they were working on the railroad, and the prairie was absolutely dependent on the railroads."[8]

In 1969 former band associate Michael Vosse had a different take on it, claiming the song had evolved from two pieces called "Home On the Range" and "Who Ran the Iron Horse," but that the former was about a Chinese cat working on the railroad and that a segment called "Bicycle Rider" was to become part of it. He also recalled that Brian "had a very definite visual image in mind of a train in motion, and suddenly stopped in the middle of the song with the 'Grand Coulee' refrain."[57]

"One of the very few almost-complete Smile tracks and, therefore, a solid and tangible reminder of its lost majesty"

As for Brian, he recalled: "The first movement of the teenage rock opera to God ends with 'Cabinessence,' which goes back and forth from one thing into a rock n' roll waltz, and finally ends with a creative fade tag...I'd call it contemporary American music, not rock n' roll. Rock n' roll is such a worn-out phrase. It's just contemporary American."[8] In 1990 he wrote: "All my life I've been fascinated by waltzes. By this album I rolled around to doin' what I call a rock n' roll waltz with 'Cabin Essence.'"[26]

Mike took Parks to task over his lyrics, especially the repetitive line at the end, "*over and over the crow cries uncover the cornfield*," which he felt was a drug reference, referring to it as Parks' "acid alliteration." Up to that time, the only other band member to approve the lyrics was Dennis, who felt especially "turned on" with his own line about a "truck drivin' man." To ease the growing tension, Brian called Parks to the studio where he refused to explain the lyrics to Mike, saying, "I don't know what these lyrics are about. They aren't important, throw them away."

Although Parks said later that Mike didn't appear offended by his answer, he admitted he was "physically afraid" of him after Brian had told him what Mike had done to him. Unfortunately, Parks failed to elaborate.268 In 1995 he admitted: "I have no idea what those words meant. I was perhaps thinking of Van Gogh's wheat field or an idealised agrarian environment. Maybe I meant nothing, but I was trying to follow Brian Wilson's vision at that time."269 Mike would go on to sing the line despite his reservations.

In a 2013 interview Parks summed up the whole episode by surmising: "I don't think the crows created a problem at all. I think the music created the problem for Mike, and it was perfectly understandable that he was terribly jealous of me, as it became evident that he wanted my job [as Brian's lyricist]. And I did not want a job that somebody else wanted."270

The instrumental track that appeared on the 1993 *Good Vibrations* box set is simply breathtaking. In June 2011 "Cabinessence" was chosen as an exclusive single to promote the forthcoming *The Smile Sessions*, and came free with *Mojo* magazine's "Ultimate Collector's Edition." *Mojo* also ranked it at #11 in their 50 Greatest Beach Boys tracks: "*Smile* in microcosm. Vast in scope, unprecedented in its ambition, and as much an unsolved riddle as the album it had been written for, this was the misunderstood masterpiece that caused Mike Love to crack and the project to flounder. Several curiously juxtaposed parts - springy, Disneyesque 'doiyngs,' the chain gang thud of 'Who Ran the Iron Horse' central section, a buzzy, windswept finale - create a micro-symphony to the US that's more strange than sepia-toned."25

Biographer Peter Carlin wrote: "[It] contrasted placid verses describing a frontier home with a thundering chorus giving voice to the coming railroad. The song's climatic section zoomed skyward, simultaneously evoking the Grand Coulee Dam (and the electrifying future it represents) and the eyes of a Chinese labourer as they follow the arc of a hungry crow circling a thresher working a cornfield."32 Rick Swan almost ran out of adjectives in describing the song, but summed it up perfectly: "Squabbles aside, we're left with this, a glistening pearl from *Smile*, as innovative and original as it was in 1966. That "Cabinessence' might not be an exceptional wonder from *Smile*, but just a representative track, truly boggles the mind."21

Love it or hate it, "Cabinessence" remains one of the very few almost-complete *Smile* tracks and, therefore, a solid and tangible reminder of its lost majesty. Described by Jon Stebbins as "some of the most haunting, manic, evil-sounding music the Beach Boys ever made,"140 it has polarised opinion more than any other song in the band's career, and will no doubt continue to do so for decades to come, or at least until Mr Parks has a sudden brainstorm and remembers more clearly just what those crows were all about...

34. I'm Waiting For the Day *(Pet Sounds 1966)*
(Brian Wilson, Mike Love)
Recording
01/03/66 Western Recorders, LA (tracking - take #14 master)

06/03/66 Western Recorders, LA ("Untitled Ballad" - strings & woodwind instruments, vocal overdub)
10/03/66 CBS Columbia Studio (vocal overdubs)
12/03/66 Western Recorders, LA? (alternative mix with Mike on lead)
Producer - Brian Wilson
Engineer - Chuck Britz, H Bowen David (Western), Ralph Valentin? (Columbia)
Band members
Brian Wilson (lead & bass vocals); Mike Love (bass & backing vocals)
Session musicians
Gary Coleman (timpani, bongos); Jim Gordon (drums); Billy Green (flute); Leonard Hartman (English horn); Jim Horn (sax, flute); Carol Kaye (12-string electric guitar); Larry Knechtel (Hammond B3 organ); Al De Lory (upright tack piano); Jay Migliori (flute); Ray Pohlman (electric bass guitar); Lyle Ritz (upright bass, overdubbed Arco upright bass); Sid Sharp Strings
Album released - 16/05/66

One of two tracks on *Pet Sounds* that Brian collaborated with someone other than Tony Asher, the other being the Wilson-Sachen song, "I Know There's An Answer." According to Brian, it was written around February 1964 but with no specific inspiration. It was one of the many songs that Mike was later awarded co-authorship after winning a lawsuit (apparently, for changing just eight of the original words), and also features just the two of them singing on the recording. Charles Granata would refer to the song as "a sensational reminder of the smart songs" that Mike Love co-wrote with Brian on the *Today!* album 74

Unlike many of the album's tracks, the narrator here sounds confident and optimistic, "waiting for the day" when the girl he loves is ready to begin a relationship with him after being left broken-hearted and abandoned by her former lover. He now waits patiently until her pain subsides, reminding her that he couldn't just sit back and watch what this guy was doing to her.

Musicologist James Perone gave his interpretation of the lyrics: "It is the story of friends who become lovers; however, at the point in time of the song, they seem to be in a nebulous area somewhere between the two states. Therefore, while the sentiments are more optimistic than those of some of the lyrics on *Pet Sounds*, the listener can still sense some of the unease of Wilson's character. He may be hopeful, but he is not quite where he wants to be."151

Apparently Brian felt that his vocal on the song was under par: "I thought I sounded a bit weird in my head. That's the one cut off the album I didn't really like that much. But, you know, it's okay, it's not a case of liking or not liking it; it was an appropriate song, a very, very positive song. I just didn't like my voice on that particular song."72. British singer Tony Rivers thought otherwise: "For the most part the lead is a beautifully, sweetly sung and completely convincing performance. It's a song that modulates through some haunting string parts into what almost feels like a 'false' ending, but then double tempos with Brian really rocking out the lyric."75 Carl also praised the song's dynamics: "The intro is very big, then it gets quite small with the vocal in the verse with a little instrumentation and then, in the chorus, it gets very big again, with the background harmonies against the lead. It is perhaps one of the most dynamic moments in the album."130.

The booming, attention-grabbing sound of timpanis that open and close the song is provided by Gary Coleman, and the way they rise in intensity, fall for the bridge and the interlude, and then rise again at the end, manages to evoke a "throbbing, aching heart."9 Likewise, Granata suggests Leonard Hartman's English horn urges "a sense of longing when voiced behind Brian's lead vocal."74

The song finishes with what Jim Fusilli called "a biting bit of youthful machismo" with the lines, '*You didn't think that I could sit around and let him work. You didn't think that I could sit around and let him take you... You didn't think that I could sit back and let you go*'."130 Just another glorious snippet of a song that will become a fan favourite.

What if the Beach Boys had recorded the song in 1964? Philip Lambert suggested: "Certainly the instrumental colours and vocal arrangement would have been simpler...Most strikingly, it's hard to imagine the string meditation section occurring in any form in an earlier arrangement of the song."9 Maybe the song just did not fit the band in 1964, but it certainly could (and should) have been a strong contender for inclusion on the *Today!* album the following year.

> ***"I thought I sounded a bit weird in my head. That's the one cut off the album I didn't really like that much"***

Norman Jopling, writing for *Record Mirror,* saw the song as an exhibition for "shotgun drums...string and organ, but used completely different [from "Don't Talk"]...it suddenly develops into a thumpy, heart-beating noise, which is the introduction for Brian Wilson to throw in everything including the proverbial kitchen sink, and presumably the washing up water..."139 *Mojo* described it as "one of the lavishly orchestrated gems which give *Pet Sounds* its astonishing depth. Complex both in structure and emotional meaning, it pitches Brian as the tortured suitor in an inverted 'Help Me, Rhonda' situation, as he begs his girl to give herself fully to him."25 The *Guardian* ranked it at #21 in their Top 40 Beach Boys songs.83

33. I Can Hear Music (*20/20* 1969)
(Jeff Barry, Ellie Greenwich, Phil Spector)
Recording
01/10/68 Beach Boys Studio, Bel Air (tracking, backing vocals, Carl's double-tracked lead, vocal & instrumental inserts)
11/11/68 Capitol Studio, Hollywood (mixing)
17/11/68 Capitol Studio, Hollywood (stereo mix)
Producer - Carl Wilson
Engineer - Steve Desper? (Bel Air)
Band members
Carl Wilson (lead vocal, guitar, bass, handclaps, tambourine?); Mike Love (backing vocals, handclaps); Dennis Wilson (drums, piano, handclaps); Al Jardine (backing vocals, handclaps);Bruce Johnston (backing vocals, handclaps, Fender Rhodes electric piano, handclaps)
Session musician
Mike Kowalski (snare drum, sleigh bells)
Album released - 10/02/69
US single released - 01/03/69 b/w "All I Want To Do" Capitol 2432 #24
UK single released - 14/02/69 b/w "All I Want To Do" Capitol CL 15584 #10
Film/TV performances
16/02/69 *Kraft Music Hall* NBC Burbank (broadcast 19/02/69)
01/04/69 *The Mike Douglas Show* Westinghouse, Philadelphia (broadcast 09/04/69)
03/04/69 *Top of the Pops* BBC-1 London (footage of recording sessions for "Time To Get Alone")
22/04/69 *Happening* ABC New York (footage of recording sessions for "Time To Get Alone")
16/06/69 Olympia Theater Paris TFI (filmed concert)

30/06/69 De Raiders En De Beach Boys NCRV Amsterdam (broadcast 03/07/69)

The first Beach Boys song in which Brian had no involvement, either with performing, composing or producing. After watching his older brother working in the studio for the past six years, Carl had his first chance to produce a Beach Boys' release himself, and he does it admirably with this intoxicating cover. Recording sessions for their next album *20/20* had commenced at Brian's home studio the previous May, and almost right from the start it was apparent that Brian was beginning to distance himself from the band, only participating in the recording when the mood suited him.

Produced and arranged by Carl, this was a major turning point for the band. From now on it was clear that they didn't need Brian to recreate and produce the quality sounds that he had been doing almost alone for so many years. Carl's slick and shimmering production lead Peter Carlin to write: "The song's thunderous sound revealed exactly how close Carl had observed his older brother's production techniques."32

Carl's arrangement included the familiar devices his brother had used so often. Toward the end of the song there is a glorious harmonic a capella break before the main theme returns before fading. It is simply one of those breathtaking moments, like the coda in "God Only Knows" and even the deafening silence in "The Little Girl I Once Knew," that every Beach Boy fan holds dear to their hearts.

Although the original "I Can Hear Music" was co-authored by Phil Spector and released on his label in October 1966, it was not one of his "Wall of Sound" productions. Helmed by Jeff Barry and recorded by the Ronettes, it just managed to scrape into the Hot 100, signalling the trio's last chart entry.

> **"A glorious harmonic a capella break before the main theme returns before fading. It is simply one of those breathtaking moments"**

Record World describing the Beach Boys' version as a "slow but torrid goodie,"152 while more recently *Paste* celebrated it as "one of the few post-*Pet Sounds* songs where the band actually sounds stoked to be performing together."153. In its list of the 50 greatest Beach Boys songs, *Mojo* wrote that it "perfectly captures the songs *joie de la musique*.25

32. Help Me, Rhonda *(Summer Days (And Summer Nights!! 1965)*
(Brian Wilson, Mike Love)
Recording (Today!)
08/01/65 Western Recorders, LA ("Help Me Ronda" tracking - 31 takes)
19/01/65 Western Recorders, LA ("Help Me Ronda" guitar & vocal overdubs)
Recording (Summer Days)
24/02/65 Western Recorders, LA (tracking, vocal overdubs for single version)
03/03/65 Western Recorders, LA (vocal work for single version)
21/03/65 Western Recorders, LA (live instrumental overdub, vocals for single version)
22/03/65 Western Recorders, LA (final mix, new vocals)
Producer - Brian Wilson
Engineer - Chuck Britz

Band members
Al Jardine (lead vocal); Brian Wilson (harmony & backing vocals); Carl Wilson (harmony & backing vocals, 12-string electric guitar); Mike Love (harmony & backing vocals) Dennis Wilson (harmony & backing vocals)
Session musicians/guests (Today version)
Bill Pitman (electric guitar); Glen Campbell (12-string electric guitar); Billy Strange (ukelele); Ray Pohlman (bass guitar); Leon Russell (grand piano); Hal Blaine (drums, timbales); Julius Wechter (claves); Billy Lee Riley (double-reed harmonica); Steve Douglas (tenor sax); Plas Johnson (tenor sax); Jay Migliori (baritone sax); Ron Swallow (possibly tambourine)
Session musicians (Summer Days version)
Billy Strange (12-string guitar); Glen Campbell (electric guitar); Barney Kessel (ukulele); Carol Kaye (bass guitar); Larry Knechtel (Wurlitzer electronic organ); Don Randi (grand piano); Hal Blaine (drums, timbales); Steve Douglas (tenor sax); Plas Johnson (tenor sax); Jay Migliori (baritone sax)
Summer Days album released – 05/07/65
US single released- 05/04/65 b/w "Kiss Me Baby" Capitol5395 #1
UK single released - 05/65 b/w "Kiss Me Baby" Capitol CL 15392 *#27*
Film/TV performances
21/04/65 *Shindig!* ABC New York
22/10/65 *The Andy Williams Show* NBC Burbank(broadcast 02/05/66)
21/01/77 Capital Centre, Washington DC
21/06/80 Knebworth England concert (later released on CD/DVD)
13/07/85 *Live Aid*, Philadelphia Pa.

The two versions of this classic song could not be more different. Originally written as an album track for the album *Today!* with the name spelt Ronda, it was later seen by Brian to have commercial potential as a single and so he re-recorded it with that in mind, together with slightly different lyrics and the amended name Rhonda. According to Philip Lambert, however, it was because Brian had heard that another group, the Rip Chords (Bruce Johnston and Terry Melcher) were considering releasing their own version as a single.9 The Rip Chords did record the song just two days after the Beach Boys completed the "Rhonda" version, but it was never released.

Melcher recalled that after cutting the single, "Brian came into the office; this was when we actually became friends. He came in and said, 'I have recorded this and it's going to be a Beach Boys' single. I had my version on release at Columbia. The singles were pressed, the ads shot and Brian said, 'I'm going to put this out myself, so what can you do for me?'" Melcher replied, "Well, I'll kill the release." What Melcher didn't know at the time was that his songwriting partner Bruce Johnston had just joined the Beach Boys, and according to the new recruit it was at his suggestion that Brian included the new version on their next album, *Summer Days (And Summer Nights!!)*.

Brian later claimed the song was inspired by Bobby Darin's hit "Mack the Knife," which he happened to be "fooling around" on the piano when he began to develop the music for the song. In a later memoir, he said that he had first written the music on his bass guitar and then completed it on piano.35. He also cited Buster Brown's "Fannie Mae," a Top 40 hit in 1960, for the song's inspiration. According to Brian, it wasn't based on a real person, although in the early 70's he told an Australian deejay that the "*get her out of my head*" line was about a short relationship Mike had with a blonde girl called Sandra Rice, whom he had met at a concert in Sydney back in January 1964. Falling deeply in love, he had promised her he would return after the tour and ask her parents for permission to marry her.

But Mike never did go back…65. Mike had his own version: "There are a lot of people, a lot of girls named Rhonda out there who have gotten remarks related to that song all their lives."154. Although told by Brian it was fictional, Al remembered: "I'm sure there was something down there in the psychology of it…We didn't really get into the meaning of the lyrics. They spoke for themselves."10

"Fellas…Quit screaming and sing from your hearts. You're doing fine now…So you're big stars. Let's fight for success. Let's go. OK"

Subsequently, the narrator of the song is a guy whose fiancé leaves him for another man and now begs Ronda to start a new relationship with him so he can get her out of his mind. The "Ronda" version was included on the *Today!* album and although Brian had intended to sing the lead vocal himself, he gave it to Al, only his second lead vocal following "Christmas Day" on the *Christmas Album*. According to Brian, "We did two versions of 'Help Me Rhonda.' We did one with the ukelele and we did one with guitars. We chose to use the guitar version. I heard myself singing lead on it originally and then I turned it over to Al. I produced the Beach Boys so I decided who would sing lead. I just had a sixth sense about who should sing what songs…I'd heard Al sing a lot and liked his voice and wanted to write a song for him that showed off the quality of his voice, and sure enough, I did."155.

Al recalled having a difficult time with it and considered it to be a big leap forward for him: "I was used to singing background. It was a whole different thing …quite complex…It seems quite simple now, but it's something called timber meter, and rhythm. It was a matter of getting your mind-body concentration together…Finally it came together real well."56. Al also remembered having a conflicting opinion with Brian over the line *"Ronda, you look so fine"*: "I think the part that was hard was the length of 'fine,' that was the part, to be specific with you. It could have been sung quicker or longer, and I just heard it longer and he heard it shorter. I think it kind of came out halfway in between."47. *Mojo* wrote: "With its lightweight guitar motif, girl-trouble lyrics, killer chorus and air of familiarity … 'Help Me Rhonda' resembled business as usual…Perfectionism has arrived."25

The original song ends with a succession of five rather unnecessary fake fade-outs, a headache for potential radio stations, and thankfully not repeated on the second version. Alexis Petridis of the *Guardian* described it as "undercutting the triumphant chorus with a weird sense of uncertainty."156

In an interview for *Uncut* in 2008, Mike talked about his collaboration with Brian on "Help Me Rhonda": "The song writing process itself was very spontaneous. It was either an idea that I had, or one that Brian had. On 'Help Me Rhonda' he had a great track going, and I went and wrote the lyrics, tailoring the lyrics to the melody. We'd go into the studio with a couple of musicians, and with Carl and Dennis, and we'd bang out a track…"157 Mike was awarded co-authorship of the song following his successful lawsuit in 1994.

With re-recording the song for a single now confirmed, Brian and the boys went down to Western on Wednesday February 24th for the first recording session, just a couple of weeks before the release of *Today!*. It would turn out to be the most talked-about session of their career…

Excited about the new song, Brian had invited his parents, Murry and Audree, to watch him record it that evening. Brian had fired Murry as their manager during a session for "I Get Around" the previous year. Now he was back in the control room, along with engineer Chuck Britz, as the boys rehearsed and overdubbed the complicated interlocking vocals onto the tracking tape done earlier in the day. Brian got annoyed when Murry, apparently drunk, began to continually interrupt the session over the intercom with barbs and critical comments, making everyone there feel the weight of his disapproval, especially when he came down to the studio floor to confront them. Despite Murry's attempts to stop the recording, Brian made sure Britz kept the tape rolling to preserve their exchanges. In the years that followed, they would be heard for the first time on various bootleg albums, creating both a historical document and a firm place in Beach Boys history for all eternity.

Although there are differing printed versions available, the gist of some of the exchanges are as follows. To begin with Murry tries to radiate some warmth toward the boys:

Murry: "You got a wonderful tune here. Al, loosen up a little more, say Rhonda a little more soft and sexy. Carl, "ooh" better, and we got it." ….
Murry: "Fellas, Brian, have the guys loosen up. You got a beautiful tune here! Loosen up! You're so tight, fellas, I can't believe it."
Murry (to Al): "You're too tense! Look, they have so many [hangers on] here, you shouldn't have it. But loosen up and just forget it. You're doing a great job….Look, I'm proud of you! You've got the lead, buddy, on their next single! Loosen up and sing from your heart. Right down here; that's all you need. The rest is easy."
Murry: "Fellas, I have 3,000 words to say. Quit screaming and sing from your hearts. You're doing fine now…So you're big stars. Let's fight for success. Let's go. OK. Let's go. Loosen up. Be happy. OK fellas? If you've got any guts, let's hear it. You're doing wonderful."
Brian: "Oh, shit! You're embarrassing me now! Shut up!"
Murry: "I'll leave Brian, if you're going to give me a bad time."
Brian: "Don't talk so loud. That really gets me…One ear left, and your big bad voice is killing it."
Murry: "I'm sorry I'm yelling. Let's go. Loosen up, Al. Let's roll. Loosen it up, fellas."
Brian: "I can't take it." [Murry and Audree get ready to leave]
Brian: "Go ahead, say what you want to say."
Murry: "We need Al to loosen up, Dennis is flatting, and Mike is flatting the high notes. We need help."
Brian: "Who needs help?"
Murry: "We need the honest projection we used to have. When the guys get too much money, you start thinking that you're gonna make everything a hit. I'm sorry. I'll never help you guys mix another session."
Brian: "Why?"

Murry: "Because you don't appreciate the good help that Chuck and I have given you. Listen, let me tell you something. When you guys get so big that you can't sing from your hearts, you're going downhill...downhill!"
Murry: "You think you got it made?"
Brian: "No, we don't. We would like to record in an atmosphere of calmness, and you're not presenting that."
Murry: "Look, Brian. I Love you, Your mother loves you...Son, success never comes easy. Success never comes from phony singing for money."
Murry (to Audree): "The kid got a big success and he thinks he owns the business. I'm sorry, I'm sorry dear. I'm sorry."
Murry: "Chuck and I used to make one hit after another [snapping his fingers] in thirty minutes. You guys take five hours to do it. You know why?"
Brian: "Times are changing...times are changing..."
Murry: "Because you guys think you have an image. Don't ever forget...honesty is the best policy. Right, Mike?" [Mike agrees]
Murry: "You know what I'm talking about. We've had our differences, but you know what I'm talking about...Okay, forget it."
Brian: "Times are changing...times are changing..."
Murry: "Forget your image as a producer, dear. You can live for two hundred years if you grow."
Brian: "I don't know what you're talking about."

With that, Murry and Audree departed, leaving Brian to supervise the completion of the song. When released as a single, the faster-tempo song shot up the charts and knocked the Beatles' "Ticket To Ride" off the top spot, giving them their second chart topper on the Hot 100 and leading their magazine to describe it as "an intriguing off-beat rouser."[158] *Cash Box* called it "a power-packed hard-driving romantic surfin'-rocker with an extremely infectious danceable backbeat,"[159] while more recently *AllMusic* opined: "It remains one of the best examples of Wilson's ability to turn the turmoil of life into stirring music."[160]

Bass guitarist Carol Kaye enjoyed a great relationship with Brian in the studio, but with this song he pushed her to the limit: "That's the song I got pissed off at Brian about. In those days I had my strings way high and really played hard. I worked hard. He did take after take, and then the last take he did of that, he had us doing it for about eight minutes while he held the phone up to the speakers. I guess he wanted the rest of the Beach Boys to hear the track. And there we were, my fingers were almost bleeding."[161]

Brian later said it was "one of the hits that Capitol wanted,"[35] and was therefore included on the next album. The song was also included on the band's second EP *The Beach Boys Hits* in May 1966. Johnny Rivers covered the song in 1975. With backing vocals by Brian, it scored a #22 hit in the US.

31. Feel Flows (*Surf's Up* 1971)
(Carl Wilson, Jack Rieley)
Recording
01/71-04/71 Beach Boys Studio, Bel Air

29/07/71 Beach Boys Studio, Bel Air
Producer - The Beach Boys
Engineer - Stephen Desper
Band members
Carl Wilson (lead & backing vocals, electric guitar, bass guitar, pianos, Baldwin organ, Moog synthesiser, jingle sticks); Brian Wilson (backing vocals); Bruce Johnston (backing vocals)
Session musicians/Guests
Steve Desper (Moog programming); Marilyn Wilson (backing vocals); Diane Rovell (backing vocals); Jack Rieley (vocal noises); Charles Lloyd (tenor sax, flute); Woodrow "Woody" Theus (bass drum, jingle sticks)
Album released - 30/08/71

Jack Rieley would go on to co-write a total of ten songs on the band's next three albums, the first being *Surf's Up*. The two songs "Long Promised Road" and "Feel Flows" were Rieley's two collaborations with Carl, who almost single-handedly recorded them himself. Carl had already laid down a basic instrumental track for "Feel Flows" before asking Rieley to contribute lyrics. Explaining the spiritual nature of the two songs, Carl told *NME* in November: "We believe in God as universal consciousness. God is love, God is you, God is me, God is everything right here in this room. It's a spiritual concept which inspires a great deal of our music."76

In a 2013 interview, Rieley explained: "One of the finest experiences in a studio that I had. Carl put together a raw-bones concept and gave me a tape, I took it home and listened to it over and over. The lyrics started coming out of me: a reflection of the sensitive side of life. I'm so proud of them. Carl's guitar solo might be the best he ever played. There is a point in the song where you hear a synth and then there's a "swoosh" sound. Carl and I have been told by a number of girls that that was the closest they'd heard to the sound that would go with an orgasm."99

> **"A cosmic soup spiced with manager Jack Rieley's looniest lyrics… just an accurate description of the music's pelagic fathomlessness"**

Rieley commented on his lyrics for the song: "There's an awful lot of love-song material within the texture of the lyric. But there are other elements I brought into it. I have diverse interests anyway and they're reflected in the lyrics. I was overloaded with compliments, especially from the Wilsons. Mike was sort of mystified by my lyrics and thinking, 'Where the hell is Jack Rieley taking us?' This wasn't just a comment on my lyrics but also in terms of career direction."99

Carl's incredible lead vocal was the result of using a reverse echo (an audio recording played backwards).*Aquarium Drunkard* described it as Carl "channelling his vocals through a reverse echo, like a stream merging backwards, and manning everything from lead, backing and harmony vocals to piano, organ, Moog synthesiser, guitar and percussion. The double-over saxophone and flute contributions from Charles Lloyd only elevate the song's already transcendent sonic heights, with chiming piano chords, warped production and arcane lyrics hinting at a cosmic divinity."110 Mike recalled: "It's amazing. It's unlike anything we ever did."162

Carl later explained how he achieved the keyboard sound effects: "I played piano first and then I played organ. I played piano twice, overdubbed it, and used a variable speed oscillator to make the track different speeds so that the piano would be a little bit out of tune, sort of a spread sound ... And then I put the organ on and put it through the Moog at the same time, so that one side of the stereo had the direct organ sound and the other side had the return through the Moog synthesizer."[163]

Most critics dismissed Rieley's non-sensical lyrics, one even describing them as "wandering in and out of the Twilight Zone,"[21] but the music was a sheer delight, "as modern and progressive as the majority of heavy music in the mainstream rock world of 1971."[140] *Mojo* described it as "the Beach Boys' best 100 per cent Brian-free moment ... a cosmic soup spiced with manager Jack Rieley's looniest lyrics...just an accurate description of the music's pelagic fathomlessness."[25] The song was also used in the 1972 surfing movie *Five Summer Stories*.

Carl's vision had paid off with dividends. With a little guidance from engineer wizard Steve Desper, this sonic tapestry of keyboards, synthesisers, fuzz guitar and scintillating flute solo, heralded a new stage in his career as vocalist, writer and producer, and for the next three albums he would, indeed, be the chief creative force of the Beach Boys.

The last word goes to film director Cameron Crowe, who chose the song for the soundtrack to his 2000 movie *Almost Famous,* citing it as "the happy/sad greatness that defines the group and the timelessness that allows the Beach Boys to tower over any attempt to classify them as simple poster boys for the California experience. It is the essence of the fulfilled promise of the Beach Boys and everything Brian envisioned for their creative journey." [164]

In late 1996 Carl was diagnosed with lung cancer, with secondary traces to the brain. He had been a heavy smoker since his teens, but there was no public announcement until the following year, by which time he was undertaking a course of chemotherapy. On August 31st he made his final appearance with the band on the fourth night of their residency in Atlantic City, fighting illness to take part in just two numbers, "California Girls" and "God Only Knows." Following a family gathering at Carl's house in January 1998 to watch Super Bowl, it was reported that Brian's wife Melinda had told him that they didn't think they would see Carl again. And she was right.

On February 6th 1998, at the age of just 51, Carl succumbed to the illness, just two months after the death of his mother. He was buried at Westwood Memorial Park in Los Angeles. In an interview a few months later, Brian said that he and Carl hadn't "really" spoke to one another for 25 years, and that "we couldn't deal with each other, so we didn't talk to one another...I'm the last of the Wilsons. He wasn't, of course, the last of the Beach Boys, though, and perhaps wasn't even any longer a Beach Boy at all."

Carl Wilson would forever be a Beach Boy, but now its very heart and soul had tragically been taken away.

30. She Knows Me Too Well (*The Beach Boys Today!* 1965)
(Brian Wilson, Mike Love)
Recording
05/08/64 Western Recorders, LA (tracking -16 takes; vocal overdubbing)
08/08/64 Western Recorders, LA (vocals double-tracked)
Producer - Brian Wilson
Engineer - Chuck Britz
Band members
Brian Wilson (lead vocal, harmony & backing vocals, acoustic upright piano), Mike Love (harmony & backing vocals); Carl Wilson (harmony & backing vocals, electric lead & rhythm guitars); Dennis Wilson (harmony & backing vocals, drums); Al Jardine (harmony & backing vocals, electric bass guitar)
Session musician
Carrol "Cappy" Lewis (harmonica)
Album released – 08/03/65
US single released -24/08/64 b-side to "When I Grow Up (To Be a Man)" Capitol 5245 #9
UK single released - 23/10/64 b-side to "When I Grow Up (To Be a Man)" Capitol CL 15361 #27

No other track on *Today!* (and they're nearly all great) points toward the direction Brian's music was taking him more than this haunting ballad about a man exploring his own failings in a relationship while deluding himself into thinking that everything is still okay. Like in the companion track, "Don't Hurt My Little Sister," the guy still has a lot of growing up to do. As good as it is, Capitol saw fit to relegate it to the flip-side of the equally impressive single, "When I Grow Up (To Be a Man)."

While planning and writing for *The Christmas Album*, due for release in November 1964, Brian took time out to concentrate on a song that would just ooze with sophistication and get his creative juices flowing for better things to come. It was allegedly the first song he wrote while under the influence of marijuana, which itself lead many to wonder why so many great songs are written that way. In an interview for *Record Collector*, Brian claimed the song was a tribute to songwriter Burt Bacharach,[113] although Matthew Greenwald of *AllMusic* compares it to "Don't Worry Baby," with its Spector-inspired chord changes.[114] *Cash Box* reviewed it, slightly off the mark, as a "captivating cha cha beat romancer that's…sure to please the kids."[115]

> ***"It was almost like you were hearing a cut from Pet Sounds a year before the album even existed"***

Many musicologists see this song and several others on the album as a major leap in Brian's music development and another step toward *Pet Sounds*. The eminent David Leaf spoke for many of them, claiming that by listening to the angelic harmonies and ultra-sophisticated chord changes, "it was almost like you were hearing a cut from *Pet Sounds* a year before the album even existed."[116]. Writing for *Pop Matters*, Scott Interrante described the song: "The harmonically complex song perfectly expresses the tension and confusion of the lyrics, but always manages to be accessible and tuneful in a way that only Brian Wilson can pull it off. That the track was recorded so early in the album process (before the process even began, in fact) and manages to be one of the most forward-thinking tracks the Beach Boys had put out up to that point, is quite astonishing."[117]

Jim Fusilli described the song as showing "Brian's perspective on the turmoil within his young love affair, and how jealousy and the possibility of betrayal harm a relationship. This is the rare song in which Brian gives himself a free pass...essentially forgiving himself for hurting her since she knows how he really feels: Why worry? She knows I don't mean anything by my misbehaviour."130

Michael Hann of the *Guardian* opined: "The "fat bass" throbs metronomically, a heartbeat that sounds almost human. Brian Wilson sings the lead himself, in a falsetto so pure and plaintive your heart melts. The harmonies on the chorus are like pillows on which to rest your head and dream...It's a perfectly judged piece of composition and one that highlights how undervalued Mike Love's contributions to the Beach Boys were: this is subtlety far beyond the caricature of the man reputed to have told his cousin, ' Don't f**k with the formula.'"118 Matt Mitchell, writing for *Paste* magazine, described it as "sorrowful glint of romance, jealousy and insecurity,"119 while *Rocksucker's* Jonny Abrams opined: "Right from the thrillingly unusual G# to E chord progression of the intro and killer opening verse...[the] song twists, turns and ultimately beguiles to a degree that's high even for a Brian Wilson composition."301

"She Knows Me Too Well" was another *Today!* track for which Mike was later given co-writing credit.

29. Surfer Girl (*Surfer Girl* 1963)
(Brian Wilson)
Recording
08/02/62 World Pacific Studio, LA (6 takes - take #4 master; vocal overdubs)
12/06/63 Western Recorders, LA (re-recording)
Producer - Brian Wilson
Engineer - Chuck Britz (*Western*)
Band members
Brian Wilson (lead vocal, bass guitar), Mike Love (backing vocals); Carl Wilson (backing vocals, lead guitar); Dennis Wilson (backing vocals, drums); Al Jardine (backing vocals, rhythm guitar)
Guest
Val Poliuto (piano?)
Album released - 16/09/63
US single released - 22/07/63 b/w "Little Deuce Coupe" Capitol 5009 #7
Film/TV performances
28/10/64 *The TAMI Show* (recorded at the Civic Auditorium, Santa Monica for cinema release)
16/06/69 Olympia Theater Paris TFI (filmed concert)
01/11/74 *Chicago's New Year's Rockin Eve* ABC New York (broadcast 31/12/74)
21/01/77 Capital Centre, Washington DC
21/06/80 Knebworth England concert (later released in CD/DVD)

The song that Brian often refers to as the first one he composed when he was about 19 (although some of his boyhood friends from high school dispute that, claiming he had written lots of songs prior to what was originally called "Little Surfer Girl.") The lyrics were allegedly inspired by his three-and-a-half year relationship with Judy Bowles, four years his junior, who also lived in Hawthorne. She often attended baseball games with her two brothers in the summer of 1961, and it was while at a Pirates game when Brian noticed her in the grandstand and soon after began dating. Although it's not clear that Judy was the direct inspiration for the song, Brian did write another song about her called "Judy" at the same session for "Surfer Girl," but it did not see an official release until appearing on the compilation *Lost & Found* in 1991.

The inspiration for the music came from Dion and the Belmonts' version of "When You Wish Upon a Star," the Oscar-winning song sung by Jiminy Cricket in the 1940 Walt Disney movie, *Pinocchio*. In an interview for CBS Radio in 1976, Brian revealed: "Back in 1961, I'd never written a song in my life. I was 19 years old. And I put myself to the test in my car one day. I was actually driving [along La Brea Avenue] to a hot dog stand, and I actually created a melody in my head without being able to hear it on a piano. I sang it to myself; I didn't even sing it out loud in the car. When I got home that day, I finished the song, wrote the bridge, put the harmonies together, and called it 'Surfer Girl.'168 In 1989 he gave a slightly different version: "I was in my '57 Ford, cruising around, and I started humming along to a song that was on the radio. I turned the radio off and I kept humming it, but I went into my own little composition. Then I got home, went to my piano, and doctored it up a little bit."169

In a further interview in 2022 he claimed: "The day I wrote 'Surfer Girl' I was in my car and heard a record on the radio by a guy named Dore Alpert called 'Tell it to the Birds.' [It was actually Herb Alpert]. Once that song was over, I started humming a melody to myself. Then I drove home and quickly went to the piano and finished off the melody where I wrote the bridge and the introduction and the fade. So part of it was written in my head and part of it was written on the piano. It took me a while but I got it. I knew that was a special one when it was done. It's still one of my favourites. I wasn't one of those kind of writers who'd just bang out song after song. I never wrote songs when I was not inspired.170

"The perfect soundtrack for holding hands and cuddling while the sun sets, an invitation hard to resist"

Whatever version is true, it still appears that "Surfer Girl" was written before the band's first single, "Surfin'" and his claim maybe due to his fondness for it, as it was based on the Disney classic that as a child he had sung so often to his parents. Brian later admitted: "I think 'Surfer Girl' is my best song. I believe it in my heart. It may not be the best "record" we ever made, but if you think of it as just a song, it's so simple and the bridge is so lilting. It tells a story about love. Something that will be forever."171

As for Judy Bowles being the inspiration, there is again a little controversy. Although Brian claimed in 1964 that the song was "directly inspired by a girl I was dating at the time,"172 Judy later admitted: "At the time I thought [it] was written for me, but I've read what Brian said in his book that he didn't write it within anyone in mind. I remember my girlfriend, Diana, she was real little, she begged Brian, literally begged him, if she could be the "little one" at the end of the song. And Brian kind of laughed and said okay."173

On February 8th 1962 Brian, Al and Dennis (still known as the Pendletones at the time) went down to World Pacific Studios in LA with the intention of recording potential follow-up singles to their first hit, "Surfin'" released the previous December. The songs were "Surfin' Safari," "Surfer Girl," "Judy," and the instrumental "Karate." Produced by husband and wife Hite and Dorinda Morgan and engineered by Hite, the session saw Brian allegedly bringing in Val Poliuto to play drums after Murry convinced him Dennis wasn't good enough.

Timothy White described the session for "Surfer Girl.": [It] began with nervous chatter about burping on microphone. Mike counting off into a horrible flat drone that made Brian holler, 'Stop the whole thing!' Before the second take, Brian yelled to Hite Morgan in the control room, asking, 'Can I do this without the bass this time? And dub the bass with our voices next time?' 'No!' said Morgan. 'Huh?' 'No!' 'He says no,' Mike repeated cautiously."[29] That session would not see the light of day until 1969.

A few days after the first session, Al announced he was leaving the band due to creative differences and believing the Pendletones would never be a commercial success (and not to pursue a career as a dentist as often stated). According to Stephen McParland, Brian first considered Paul Johnson of the Belairs as a suitable replacement, but Johnson opted out, citing the "differences" between the two bands' music. Within a matter of days, 13-year-old David Marks, who Johnson referred to as a "skinny kid with stars in his eyes," and who lived across the street from the Wilsons, was getting ready to go to school when the boys came over to his house and asked him, "Do you want to be in the group?" Although it would prove to be short tenure, it was one in which he would make a valuable contribution.[65]

Surprisingly "Surfer Girl," now considered one of Brian's best ballads, was not considered for either of the band's next two albums, *Surfin Safari* and *Little Deuce Coupe,* but in June 1963, days before his 21st birthday, Brian took the boys to Western, intent on proving to Capitol he was capable of being the band's producer, and re-recorded "Surfer Girl" as the title track of their next album. The result was one of the first and best examples of Brian adapting the Four Freshmen choral style, with all the voices singing the words together. Philp Lambert points out that Brian then "deviates from the choral style in the bridge as he sings the first three lines himself [but with dramatic impact] and in direct imitation of a Four Freshmen trick, the choral texture returns..."[9]

Rick Swan described its powerful lyrical attraction: "With it's memorable melody, wistful and insistent, it serves as the perfect soundtrack for holding hands and cuddling while the sun sets, an invitation hard to resist. Brian sings like's he's auditioning for heaven, the other boys do their best to match him and for the most part succeed."[21]

David Leaf: "Everything that would make Brian the preeminent arranger and produce of this time is on 'Surfer Girl.' The lush vocals, the full instrumental sound, the brilliant chord changes and the heartbreaking falsetto that came to characterize the soft side of the band's rock n roll heart."[168] *Cash Box* described it as "a lilting soft beat-ballad charmer,"[174] while *Mojo* offered: "There's a special kind of nostalgia, the most acute and piercing kind: nostalgia for something that never existed. That keen yearning is all over the first song Brian wrote, alone in his bedroom."[25]

The 1998 *Endless Harmony* compilation includes a rare split vocal version that is truly divine.

28. When I Grow Up (To Be a Man) (*The Beach Boys Today!* 1965)

(Brian Wilson, Mike Love)

Recording
05/08/64 Western Recorders, LA (tracking - 37 takes)
10/08/64 Western Recorders, LA (vocal overdubs - 14 takes)
Producer - Brian Wilson
Engineer - Chuck Britz
Band members
Mike Love (lead vocal, harmony & backing vocals); Brian Wilson (lead vocal, harmony & backing vocals, acoustic upright piano, Baldwin electric harpsichord); Carl Wilson (harmony & backing vocals, electric lead & rhythm guitars); Dennis Wilson (harmony & backing vocals, drums, hi-hat), Al Jardine (harmony & backing vocals, electric bass guitar)
Session musician
Carrol Lewis (double-reed harmonica)
Album released - 08/03/65
US single released - 24/08/64 b/w "She Knows Me Too Well" Capitol 5245 #9
UK single released - 23/10/64 b/w "She Knows Me Too Well" Capitol CL 15361 #27
Film/TV performances
04/11/64 *Discs A Go Go* TWW Bristol, England (broadcast 09/11/64)
05/11/64 *The Beat Room* BBC-2 London (broadcast 09/11/64)
06/11/64 *Ready Steady Go* ARTV London
07/11/64 *Open House* BBC-2 London
08/11/64 *Thank Your Lucky Stars* ITV Birmingham (broadcast 14/11/64)
18/11/64 *Age Tendre Et Tete De Bois* TF2 Paris

Recorded during a short break from touring in the summer of 1964, the song about impending adulthood was written by 21-year-old Brian with additional lyrics by Mike. In an interview for the *Birmingham Post*, Brian explained: "When I was younger, I used to worry about turning into an old square over the years. I don't think I will now, and that is what inspired [the song]." More recently he added that at the time of writing he looked on his future with dismay: "I was inspired about what it was gonna be like to grow up. Will I like the things then as I did now? I wrote that in my early twenties. As I look back on that I am happy with my life now and I didn't think I would be."133

Some commentators believe Brian wrote this as he had doubts about his girlfriend Marilyn Rovell, who he would marry the following December. Mike believed it was "probably influenced" by Brian's dad Murry who had a habit of challenging his son's manhood.188

The song has many attributes. It is the first in their career to employ a harpsichord arrangement as a lead keyboard instrument, which at the time was quite unusual for a pop group, and Carrol Lewis's double-reed harmonica gives the song a wonderful rhythmic texture. It was also one of the first rock songs to have impending adulthood as a theme, and possibly the first chart hit to use the phrase "turned me on," one that would become more widely associated with drug use in the years to come.

"An ode to youth's fleeting nature"

But like many tracks on the album, its Brian's sophisticated harmonic innovations that rubber stamp the song with excellence. The split lead vocal with

Brian and Mike exchanging sections - Brian taking the higher, more difficult ones, while Mike takes the lower, more simple parts - is a method used throughout the album. Then there's the 14-30 count-up in age beginning in the second verse, and the "*Won't last forever/"It's kind of sad*" vocal trade-off between Mike and Brian at the end. All these combine to make it astonishingly advanced for its time.

The tracking took an incredible 37 takes to get it to Brian's satisfaction, an example of how demanding he was becoming in the studio. Apart from harmonica-player Lewis, the band members played all the instruments, and Carl remembered how he was particularly hard on Dennis, who struggled with the complicated rhythm of the song. When it came to the vocals, Brian later expressed his disappointment with his own "whiney" vocal, and that the band were trying too hard to emulate the sound of the Four Freshmen. Reviewing the album, David Leaf wrote: "It was shocking to hear so many great ballads on one side of a record. Looking back, it's clear that these tracks were the musical and lyrical precursors to *Pet Sounds*."116

The Beach Boys gave their first live performance in the UK in November 1964, and on the top-rated *Ready Steady Go!* sang "I Get Around" and "When I Grow Up (To Be a Man)," the latter with a false start. When co-host Keith Fordyce asked Mike about surfing and Brian about his thoughts on the UK, their answers were drowned out by the screaming studio audience. Other televised appearances at the time have long since been lost.

Musicologist Charles Granata celebrated the song that "best exemplifies the [band's] musical growth."74 *Cash Box*, meanwhile, described the song as being in "jumpin' rhythmic manner that has made [the band] such big teen favourites,"138 while *Mojo* called it "an ode to youth's fleeting nature."25.

Backed with the even more sophisticated "She Knows Me Too Well," the single became the sixth by the band to reach the US Top 10. It also became the theme song to the 2009 tv comedy-drama *Men of a Certain Age,* starring Ray Romano.

27. Cuddle Up *(Carl and the Passions - "So Tough!" 1972)*
(Dennis Wilson, Daryl Dragon)
Recording
09/04/72 Beach Boys Studio, Bel Air
10/04/72 Sound City, Sepulveda CA (bass, timpani, strings)
04/72 Beach Boys Studio, Bel Air (vocals)
Producer - The Beach Boys
Engineer - Stephen Desper or Steve Moffitt
Band members
Dennis Wilson (lead & backing vocals); Carl Wilson (backing vocals, acoustic guitar); Mike Love (backing vocals - not used on original mix); Blondie Chaplin (backing vocals); Al Jardine (backing vocals - not used on original mix)
Session musicians/Guests
Frank Capp (timpani); Daryl Dragon (grand piano, co-arranger, orchestra producer); Toni Tennille (backing vocals); 12 violins, 4 viola, 4 cellos, 3 arco double basses.
Album released - 15/05/72
US single released - 15/05/72 b-side to "You Need a Mess of Help to Stand Alone" Brother/Reprise REP 1091
UK single released - 05/72 b-side to "You Need a Mess of Help to Stand Alone" Reprise K 14173

In an interview for *Uncut* Bruce was asked if he knew Dennis had it in him as a songwriter, and he replied: "None of us did, including Dennis. In January 1966 we were in Japan and had a lot of time on our hands. We played about 14 shows, so I started showing Dennis how to play the piano and how to chord. I kind of unlocked what was already in there and he started putting it all together." And put it together he certainly did, especially with this lovelorn ballad co-written with his friend Daryl Dragon.

LA-born Daryl Frank Dragon (1942-2019) came from a musical family, son of a conductor and composer, and, with brothers Doug and Dennis, a member of the 60's group The Dragons. His familiar stage name "The Captain" came from the time he was a keyboard player with the Beach Boys during the period 1967-72, and Mike referring to him as "Captain Keyboard."

On December 4th 1970 Dennis and Dragon released a stunning song called "Sound of Free" as a UK-exclusive single on the Stateside label. Written by Dennis and Mike, it was produced by Dennis, who also provided lead vocal, while Dragon's two brothers contributed backing vocals. On the flip-side was Dennis's "Lady," his loving tribute to Barbara Charren, his wife of four months, and recorded the previous December. This was one of Dennis's songs that was passed over for inclusion on both *Sunflower* and *Surf's Up*.

"The emotional dimension and the longing in Dennis's voice ... are almost too much to bear"

In his 1978 biography John Tobler made the point: "No one seems to have ever asked Dennis what the idea was behind this burst of independence, but it's possible that there's some connection with the fact that *Sunflower*, and in fact *Surf's Up*...were released in Britain on the Stateside label.[192] The single was not successful.

After the release of *Surf's Up* in August 1971 Dennis and Dragon collaborated on two songs that were intended for a possible album by the duo. One was "Make It Good" and the other was "Cuddle Up," another tribute to Barbara, that had a working title of "Old Movie." According to engineer Steve Desper, Dennis used that same working title for his Vietnam lament, "4th of July." Maybe he just liked the title.[274]

Emboldened by his wife's encouragement, Dennis now considered striking out on his own with his trusted sidekick, and sessions for a joint album with working titles of *Poops* and *Hubba Bubba* would continue throughout 1971 amid rumours that Dennis was about to quit the Beach Boys. However the project was abandoned in early 1972, and by this time the band had sequestered both "Make It Good" and "Cuddle Up" for their new album, *Carl and the Passions - So Tough!*, no doubt due to them struggling for new material.

Without knowing it, "Cuddle Up" would become the highlight of the album. In early April, the band re-recorded these and other songs at Brian's home studio and at Sound City, with Dragon there to provide his keyboard skills.

Concurrently released in two formats on May 15th 1972, one was for the album, while the other, with a slightly different mix, additional string overdubs and backing vocals, was for the flip-side to the chart-flopping single, "You Need a Mess of Help To Stand Alone."

More of a group effort than "Make It Good," "Cuddle Up" received universal retrospective praise, especially from *Mojo*: "Beneath the good looks and penchant for excess, Dennis was the Beach Boy's perennial romantic. This twilit hymn, sparsely orchestrated and led by a tender 3am vocal, remains one of the band's most unadorned songs. On the surface a simple paean to love, deeper investigation reveals a ballad that is warm and adoring *and* desperate and lonely…More than any other of his songs, 'Cuddle Up' *is* Dennis Wilson."[25]

Another reviewer opined: "The song begins in intimate fashion, with softly-played piano and Dennis's careworn vocals to the fore, before stirring strings and background vocals build to a climax steeped in equal parts anguish and ecstasy. Never one to shy away from wearing his heart on his sleeve, the sumptuously melodramatic 'Cuddle Up' might be the song that best sums up the incurable romantic inside Dennis."[271]

Matthew Greenwald for *AllMusic* saw the song as a "somewhat top-heavy, classically influenced ballad. However, the lyrics and Dennis Wilson's excellent vocals render this an emotional masterpiece, closing the album out with style.[272] In his excellent study of the band's entire catalog Rick Swan wrote: "Irrespective of all the cuddling, [the song] works as a subtle allegory for sex. Its slow build leads to a frantic climax, to a soft landing, to a gentle tingle at the coda. Heartbreaking and charming, this is the album's outstanding track."[21]

One online reviewer was more than impressed: "The emotional dimension and the longing in Dennis's voice …are almost too much to bear. Symphonic in design and prayer-like in spirit, the song mesmerises on melodic grounds: the repetition of *'The Night'* and *'has come'* in the opening verse anticipates the beautiful melodic upturn that comes at 'Cuddle Up' and the descent that follows, plus there's the transcendent middle section featuring wordless vocals and strings, and gorgeous key changes that could make Brian envious. The song also captures so powerfully the tenderness and loneliness that's at the core of Dennis's ballads. The words…may read like an invitation to another to gain comfort from his embrace, but they more likely express Dennis's desperate cry for the love and intimacy another might offer him…"[273]

26. The Little Girl I Once Knew (Single 1965)
(Brian Wilson)
Recording
13/10/65 Western Recorders, LA (tracking - 15 takes, vocal overdubs & inserts)
24/10/65 Western Recorders, LA (vocal overdubs, mono mix)
Producer - Brian Wilson
Engineer - Chuck Britz
Band members
Brian Wilson (lead & harmony vocal); Mike Love (lead & harmony vocal); Carl Wilson (lead & harmony vocal); Dennis Wilson (harmony vocal); Al Jardine (harmony vocal); Bruce Johnston (harmony vocal)
Session musicians
Frank Capp (percussion); Carol Kaye (bass guitar); Don Randi (organ); unknown (12-string guitar); Roy Canton (trumpet); Jim Horn (sax); Plas Johnson (sax), Jay Migliori (sax)
US single released - 22/11/65 b/w "There's No Other (Like My Baby)" Capitol 5540 #20

UK single released - 12/65 b/w "There's No Other (Like My Baby)"Capitol CL 15425

Perhaps one of the most underrated songs in the Beach Boys' entire career, and one hardly mentioned in a number of biographies and music studies; made even more unthinkable as it still stands as one of Brian's most daring and intricate recordings and one that at the time was never even considered good enough for an album.

It was first recorded in October 1965 following the making of the *Party!* album, and at the same session that saw the band commence work on "Don't Talk (Put Your Head On My Shoulder)," their first attempt at a future *Pet Sounds* track. "Little Girl" was also the first song recorded for their next album, which at the time had no name or release date (it turned out, of course, to be *Pet Sounds*), and on the session tape box was initially labelled "Carol K," referring to sessionist Carol Kaye, whose bass guitar features prominently on the track.

In the song the narrator meets up with a girl he hardly noticed when she was younger, but now, all grown up, has a newfound fascination for her, and despite having a boyfriend, intends to "move in" on her one day. A similar subject was covered with the band's "All Dressed Up For School," a leftover from the *Little Deuce Coupe* sessions. There is some speculation his wife Marilyn may have been Brian's inspiration for "Little Girl."

"As a composer and arranger, he was going where he wanted to, convention be damned"

Although Mike has no writing credit, biographer Mark Dillon suggests he had contributed to them, although the song was not one of the 79 listed in Mike's 1994 lawsuit.10

Brian commented on the song in 2007, especially the classic opening: "That is my very favourite introduction in a song in my whole life. It kills me every time. It might have been the first time the music stopped and started again on a record. I wrote the intro at the studio before we cut the thing, and [session musician] Larry Knechtel, it was his idea to keep the music rolling. We tried one, and then I put a second guitar overdub on top of the other guitar. And the rest of it was history. We were doing stereo but I could only hear the mono and I always put the vocals up front in the mix. Mixing in mono is good for my left ear. My right ear is broke, done and over with."175

As the years went by Brian's opinion of the song changed. In 1995 he revealed his dissatisfaction: "It was a fine song, except the intro is the only good part of it, and the rest didn't sound so good. I thought the song in itself sucked. I didn't like the harmonies, I thought they were sour and off-key." 25 years later he compared the intro as being as good as "California Girls," (and it was), that his lead vocal was "really spectacularly great," and even claimed that the band could never sound any better than they did on this song.202 The following year he repeated the comment he had made about "Let Him Run Wild" by describing his lead vocal as "too effeminate."175 With Brian there would always be conflicting reflections.

Over the years, critics have drawn comparisons with the music of Burt Bacharach, and praised the "daringly different" song as a subtly complex piece of avant-pop, with its fragmentary approach, its ambiguous arrangement, and knockout vocals by Mike and the rest of the band. Then there is the famous "dead air," dramatic pauses of several seconds that precede the chorus, leading some frustrated deejays to omit the song from their radio playlists (maybe one of the reasons for its poor sales). In 2014 Brian admitted that the song "should've gotten more attention."

Because of its poor showing on the US charts, Capitol's president Al Coury decided to rush-release "Barbara Ann" as the next single, without the band's knowledge. For that same reason, Brian decided not to place it on *Pet Sounds*. The song was eventually included on the band's second EP *The Beach Boys Hits* in May 1966, before finally appeared in album form with 1968's *The Best of the Beach Boys Vol 3*.

Comparing the song with "California Girls," Scott Interrante of *Pop Matters* wrote: "[It] feels more predatory in its excitement for a young girl who's growing up before your eyes. Still, the intricate arrangement, powerful layers of vocals, and distinctive pre-chorus pause make it a strong stand-out song."[203] *Cash Box* described it as a "rhythmic ode about a fellow who reminisces about how his gal has grown up and become a woman."[204] Rick Swan claimed: "The intro alone deserves classic status."[21]

Musicologist Jim Fusilli wrote: "Brian…demonstrates that he has refined the technique of seeming to wander far from the logic of his composition only to return triumphantly to confirm the emotional intent of the work. The technique is employed time and time again in *Pet Sounds*… As for the four seconds of dead air that occur twice in the song; though they must have driven disc jockeys crazy…somehow needs them. As the song is constructed, you simply cannot move from the verse to the chorus without them. I mean you can, but you'd destroy the flow and eliminate the tension that precedes the joyous chorus. Of course, Brian knew four-second tacets in the middle of a pop single were unacceptable. But as a composer and arranger, he was going where he wanted to, convention be damned."[130]

On its release in the UK, John Lennon sang its praises in an interview for *Melody Maker*: "This is the greatest! Turn it up, turn it right up. It's GOT to be a hit. It's the greatest record I've heard for weeks. It's fantastic. I hope it will be a hit. It's all Brian Wilson. He just uses the voices as instruments. He never tours or anything. He just sits at home thinking up fantastic arrangements out of his head. Doesn't even read music. You keep waiting for the fabulous breaks. Great arrangement. It goes on and on with all different things. I hope it's a hit so I can hear it all the time."[205]

Praise indeed! Now generally considered as a turning point in the band's sound and musical style, it was a portend of how Brian's experimentation with song structure would blossom in the years that followed.

25. Do It Again (*20/20* 1969)
(Brian Wilson, Mike Love)
Recording
26/05/68 Beach Boys Studio, Bel Air (tracking & vocals)
29/05/68 Wally Heider Studio, Hollywood (transfer)

06/06/68 Beach Boys Studio, Bel Air
12/06/68 Beach Boys Studio, Bel Air (instrument overdubs)
Producer - The Beach Boys (Brian & Carl)
Engineers - Stephen Desper (Bel Air); Bill Halverson? (Wally Heider)
Band members
Mike Love (lead & backing vocals, handclaps); Brian Wilson (backing vocals, piano, organ, possibly bass); Carl Wilson (backing vocals, electric lead & rhythm guitars, possibly bass & tambourine); Dennis Wilson (backing vocals, drums); Al Jardine (backing vocals, electric rhythm guitar, handclaps); Bruce Johnston (backing vocals, handclaps)
Session musicians
John Guerin (drums, wood block, possibly tambourine); John Lowe (bass sax); Ernie Small (baritone sax)
Album released - 10/02/69
US single released - 08/07/68 b/w "Wake the World" Capitol 2239 #20
UK single released - 19/07/68 b/w "Wake the World" Capitol CL 15554 #1
Film/TV performances
68 Promo
08/08/68 *Top of the Pops* BBC-1 London (promo film)
09/68 *Hits A Go Go* ZDF West Germany (promo film)
12/08/68 *The Dick Cavett Show* ABC, New York (broadcast 13/08/68)
12/08/68 *Happening* ABC, LA (broadcast 17/08/68)
26/08/68 *The Mike Douglas Show* Westinghouse, Philadelphia (broadcast 29/08/68)
13/10/68 *The Ed Sullivan Show* CBS New York
30/11/68 *Top of the Pops* BBC-1 London (broadcast 25/12/68)
10/12/68 *Beat Club* Radio Bremen TV West Germany (broadcast 25/01/69)
13/12/68 *Hot and Sweet* ZDF Munich (broadcast 15/02/68)
14/12/68 *Twien*, Theater De Brakke Grond, Amsterdam (broadcast 23/12/68)
16/06/69 Olympia Theater Paris TFI (filmed concert)
21/06/80 Knebworth, England concert (later released on CD/DVD)

With a working title of "Rendezvous," this classic piece of nostalgia was inspired by Mike after going surfing in May 1968 with his old friend Bill Jackson, at what at the time was an out-of-bounds "surf rat" called Trestle Beach in San Diego County. Mike wasted no time before showing Brian some of the lyrics he had in mind and together they came up with what Brian later claimed to be the best collaboration they had ever worked on.

The music was partly based on surf group The Frogmen's instrumental "Underwater," a minor hit on the Candix label in 1961, although Hank Ballard & the Midnighters' 1960 hit "Finger Poppin Time" has also been mentioned by Mike.[188]

It was a time when Brian was just starting to distance himself from recordings, just participating when the mood suited him. But if he listened to something that was interesting he would come down from his bedroom to participate. And this was one of those times, as Mike recalled: "[Brian] remembers it being at my house. I remember it as being at his house. He starts pounding at the piano, I was summoning up the words and we got a chorus together, which was basically a bunch of doo-wop inspired harmonies. We created that whole song in fifteen minutes."[190]

With one of Mike's finest lead vocals, the song is a self-conscious callback to the band's previous surf-based material which had reached a peak with *Surfer Girl* in 1963. In an interview for *Songfacts*, Mike spoke about writing lyrics before the music: "Well, with me, I might come up with a hooky lyric. With Brian it almost always starts with the music. And so me being a lyricist, in that particular song I actually went on a surfing safari, a little trip with my high school buddies, so it's really autobiographical in terms of the lyrics. Because I went to the beach with my friends and we went to the surfing spot down at a place called San Onofre, down near the Marine Corps base down south. And it was such a beautiful day and the waves were great. And then of course one of the great things about the beach is it attracts good looking girls. So I wrote the words and Brian came up with the track. I came back and we sat down at Brian's piano, and we banged that song out in maybe 15 minutes, something like that. I had the concept and the lyrics in mind, and he just got a good groove going on the piano, and our engineer at the time, his name was Steve Desper, he came up with that really interesting electronic treatment to the bass, to the beginning of the song. But yeah, I had the concept and quite a bit of the lyric thought out before I even got involved with Brian on that one."191

All they needed was the will to return to their roots and use their own past work as a starting point - to model themselves

According to musicologist Philp Lambert its infectious riff was devised by "running a series of press rolls on a snare drum through a tape-delay system, achieving a sexy metallic buzz that was sandwiched with a clap track to make the single seem to detonate," and describing it as "magnificent in every respect." Steve Desper explained the drum effect he achieved during the mixdown: "[We had] commissioned Philips in Holland to build two tape delay units to use on the road (to double live vocals). [He] moved four of the Philips PB heads very close together so that one drum strike was repeated four times about 10 milliseconds apart, and blended it with the original to give the effect you hear."

The unusual sound of hammering in the fade was apparently lifted from an unreleased *Smile* snippet titled "I Wanna Be Around" (aka "Woodshop"), recorded on November 29th 1966, and included here, as *Mojo* suggests, simply "to stoke the cult of that LP."25

In an interview for *Melody Maker*, Carl reflected on the song: "Yes, I suppose it has got the old Beach Boys surfing sound. It's back to that surfing idea with the voice harmony and the simple, direct melody and lyrics. We didn't plan the record as a return to the surf or anything. We just did it one day round a piano in the studio. Brian had the idea and played it over to us. We improved on that and recorded it very quickly, in about five minutes. It's certainly not an old track of ours; in fact it was recorded only a few weeks before it was released. We liked how it turned out and decided to release it."11

Bruce had a different opinion, explaining it to a reporter in September 1968: "I don't like it…I don't think that the group were entirely happy with it, but everything else was going back to basics, so I suppose it was inevitable that we should."192. Brian referred to it as "a primitive surf song."

In order to catch the tail end of the summer, and just two weeks after the release of *Friends*, "Do It Again" was rush-released by Capitol as the band's next single. Surprisingly it just scraped into the Hot 100 at #20, the last of their singles to do so for nearly eight years. A slightly edited version, including the *Smile* snippet, later appeared as the opening track on their 1969 album *20/20*. The song was also included on the Japanese version of *Friends*.

However, across the Atlantic it became the band's second #1 on the UK charts following "Good Vibrations" two years earlier. Mike was impressed by the British fans' continuing support, calling it "unbelievable." A rarely-seen colour promotional film was also made for the single. Directed by Peter Clifton, it was shot in LA and showed the band driving up to a surf shop to grab boards and then going to the beach to surf.

Reviewing the song for *Disc & Music Echo,* and following on from her scathing attack on the band's musical direction, Penny Valentine was more than impressed with the new single: "This is a vast improvement on The Beach Boys' last single, and thank goodness for it. It sounds like bees humming on a summer breeze and is so completely solid; there isn't room for a fly to creep in. It goes on very gently and easily and is very, very pleasant. In a way it reminds me of one of the tracks off *Pet Sounds,* which is nice to say the least, and a hit it will most certainly be. I can imagine a few people will be muttering, 'Well, she said they were finished,' but I didn't. I said they should get back to their competent, commercial sound and they have. So there."[193]

Record World opined: "The Beach Boys go back to the beach for some of that unadulterated surfing sound '68,"[194] while *Cash Box*, described it as an "ingenious production," and that "overtones of their current interest in electronic innovation are almost over-lookable in this surfin' return."[195] Philip Lambert described the song as "pure nostalgia for the old days of surfing and girls and California sunshine...The music satisfies the nostalgic urge by reaching back to the most basic three-chord progression, just like the verse of 'Surfin Safari'...It shows that the group could still make a great Beach Boys record. All they needed was the will to return to their roots and use their own past work as a starting point - to model themselves."[9]

In its review of the song *Mojo* wrote: "With innocence in short supply in 1968, the year of Tet and political assassinations, Mike Love reinvented the brand as a totem to nostalgia, youth and the beach."[25]

Apparently "Do It Again" is the only track on *20/20* recorded in mono, as engineer Desper lost the master tape while compiling the *Stack-O-Tracks* instrumental album. Fortunately, he had kept a copy. Thirty years later the tape, believed to have been stolen in 1980, was retrieved and a true stereo mix was finally made available on the excellent *Made in California* compilation.

In 1995, Brian recorded a version for his solo album, *I Just Wasn't Made For These Times,* in which he was joined by daughters Carney and Wendy. In 2011 the surviving members of the band (Brian, Mike, Al, Bruce and David) recorded a new version of the song as part of their 50th Anniversary celebration, with Brian's longtime friend Jeff Foskett handling the falsetto vocals. It was released as a bonus track on their final album, *That's Why God Made the Radio.* Mike also recorded his own version for his 2017 album *Unleash the Love*, which featured John Stamos.

The song was also featured in the movies *One Crazy Summer* (1986) and *Happy Feet* (2006).

24. In The Back of My Mind *(The Beach Boys Today!* 1965)
(Brian Wilson, Mike Love)
Recording
13/01/65 Western Recorders, LA(instrumental tracks -take #39 master)
19/01/65 Western Recorders, LA (vocal overdubs - five takes)
Producer - Brian Wilson
Engineer - Chuck Britz
Band member inc.
Dennis Wilson (double-tracked lead vocal); Brian Wilson (backing vocals); Carl Wilson (backing vocals, 12-string lead guitar)
Session musicians
Hal Blaine (temple block, timbale); Peter Christ (possibly English horn); Steve Douglas (tenor sax); Plas Johnson (tenor sax); Jay Migliori (baritone sax); Carol Kaye (bass guitar); Bill Pitman (acoustic guitar); Don Randi (Hamond B3 organ); Billy Riley (possibly double-reed harmonica); Leon Russell (Wurlitzer electric piano); Billy Strange (electric rhythm guitar); Tommy Tedesco (autoharp); Julius Wechter (vibraphone)
Album released - 08/03/65

Perhaps more than any other song on the wonderful *Today!* album, this one is a clear example of Brian testing the boundaries of his creativity and producing the kind of music that hinted at what was to come with *Pet Sounds*.

Written and recorded just after Brian married Marilyn Rovell, the rather unsettling love song had a working title of "Denny's Ballad," as Dennis, for once, was given the opportunity to sing lead vocal. And he does a sterling job, delivering "a husky, wavering vocal that fits perfectly into Brian's orchestral canvas."[5] Esteemed biographer David Leaf wrote that "Dennis's soulful lead vocal helps bring out the jazzy feel of a song that is really unique in the Brian Wilson catalogue," while musicologist Philip Lambert described the chord patterns as being "virtually unprecedented in Brian's work."[9]

> *"I told them I foresee a beautiful future for the Beach Boys group, but the only way we could achieve it was if they did their job and I did mine"*

The heartfelt lyrics have the narrator expressing the fear of losing his soulmate, speaking "from the bosom of domesticity." Feeling "blessed with everything,", he then describes a world that is safe enough for a man to "cling" to, although still having unfounded suspicions that this happy relationship will one day fall apart.[32] Biographer Peter Carlin described it as being "like an orchestra falling apart. It's about the guy's wife, and that's the most intimate relationship you can have. It radiates the complexities in Brian's inner life and how that comes through in his music and how he expresses that in music."[32]

While Dennis handles the double-tracked lead vocal almost throughout, Brian and Carl sing two lines in unison during the bridge, which is underscored with pizzicato strings. Carlin described the bridge as "a rushed, unmelodic digression that tumbles toward the climatic verse that identifies the source of the darkness in this seemingly sunny relationship as the singer doubts that it can last,."[32] while Lambert sees the arrangement as carrying "the sense of a sonic explorer, marvelling at the colouristic possibilities in various instrumental blends,"[9]

With its unprecedented chord patterns, the song is justifiably considered a masterpiece and commonly referred to as being inspired by the Tin Pan Alley style of songwriting. Brian revealed in his 2016 memoir that the melody was indeed inspired by the Skyliners' 1958 doo-wop hit, "Since I Don't Have You."

Although Brian admitted in 1995 that he felt his double-tracking of Dennis's fragile vocal was not to his liking, most commentators praised the performance. Peter Doggett said that Dennis "showed for the first time an awareness that his voice could be a blunt emotional instrument" and that his "erratic croon cut straight to the heart with an urgency that his more precise brothers could never have matched."176

The song did receive its share of criticism. Charles Granata described it as "disturbing…the antithesis of any prescribed commercial formula - a curious experiment marking an extreme deviation from the band."74 Jim Fusilli stated: "His girl knows him, loves him, but Brian isn't sure it's enough, and maybe he'd be better off elsewhere. And yet he's not sure he can survive without her or without the special feeling love brings him…no matter how much happiness Brian finds with the love of his life, he'll always wonder if the good times will last and whether he'll be the one who severs their relationship, thus destroying the wonderful thing."130

After the first session on January 13th 1965 Brian revealed to the rest of the band that he would not be going with them on the North American tour, due to commence the following month. In a 1965 interview with Earl Leaf for his Capitol-published *TeenSet* magazine, he revealed: "We were about halfway through the album when I decided to tell the guys I wasn't going to perform on stage anymore and that I can't travel. I wanted to sit at the piano and write songs while they were out touring. The night when I gave them the news of my decision they all broke down. I'd already gone through my breakdowns. Now it was their turn…I told them I foresee a beautiful future for the Beach Boys group, but the only way we could achieve it was if they did their job and I did mine…Its gonna be well worth it because I'm gonna write you some good songs"11

In 1975 Brian recorded a demo of "In the Back Of My Mind" with his own lead vocal and additional lyrics, but it remained unreleased until featured as a bonus track on the deluxe edition of his 2015 solo album *No Pier Pressure*.

23. Don't Talk (Put Your Head On My Shoulder) (*Pet Sounds* 1966)
(Brian Wilson, Tony Asher)
Recording
13/10/65 Western Recorders, LA (first vocal overdubs)
11/02/66 Western Recorders, LA (tracking, lead vocal and vocal inserts)
03/04/66 Western Recorders, LA (strings & lead vocal overdubs)
Producer - Brian Wilson
Engineers - Chuck Britz, H Bowen David (Apr 3)
Band member
Brian Wilson (vocal)
Session musicians
Hal Blaine (ride cymbal); Glen Campbell (12-string electric guitar); Frank Capp (vibraphone, timpani); Al de Lory (Hammond B3 organ); Steve Douglas (acoustic grand piano); Carol Kaye (bass guitar); Lyle

Ritz (upright bass); Billy Strange (12-string electric guitar); The Sid Sharp Strings (4 violins; 1 cello; 1 viola).
Album released - 16/05/66

Anthony D Asher was born in London in 1939 and moved with his actress mother to LA before he was six months old, while his father remained behind to serve in the US Army during World War Two. He learned to play the piano and compose music by the age of 12, and later graduated from UCLA with a degree in journalism. He found work at the Carson-Roberts advertising agency (where one of his colleagues was future Python and film director Terry Gilliam). Most sources claim that Asher met Brian Wilson in early 1963, as he later explained: "I think we were recording some music, or voice-overs for a commercial, and I had heard that the Beach Boys were in another studio [alone]...eventually we met." Another source states they met at a social gathering at the home of mutual friend Loren Schwartz, who claimed that he and Asher had been close friends at Santa Monica College.

In any case, Brian thought Asher was "a cool person" and it was he who he called in December 1965 to help him write songs for *Pet Sounds*. Asher recalled: "I got this phone call and the voice said, 'This is Brian Wilson.' And I said, 'Yeah, right. This is one of the guys in the office, right?' But it turned out it was in fact Brian Wilson. And he wanted to know if I was available to write some songs with him."[72]. Asher then took leave of absence from work and within ten days was a guest at Brian's house. Over the next two weeks or so, they put their minds together to create most of the songs for what was to become one of the greatest albums in pop history.

Seemingly underrated for so long, this wonderfully poignant song is now widely considered to be Brian at his heartbreaking best and one of the finest examples of pairing an instrumental arrangement with lyrical lines with such exquisite panache. It is also one of three solo efforts on the album (along with "Pet Sounds" and "Caroline No,") with no harmonies or instrumental contribution from fellow band members.

"The innocence of youth in my voice, of being young and childlike. I think that's what people liked"

This heartbreaking tale of unspoken love has echoes of Brian's own fragile vulnerability in its delicate description of what happens when words can fail as blissful romance turns to doubt over a lover who may no longer feel the same about you, perhaps hinted at in the line *"let's not think about tomorrow."* But we are still left with the unanswered question - is the narrator speaking to his lover or talking to himself? Brian admitted later: "I wanted to be a girl in my voice, so I did. I wanted to sing like a girl. Not consciously, but it was all figured out in my brain, waiting for me to do it. So I went in there, put some beautiful music on tape..." [73]

Asher, knowing perhaps more than anyone about Brian's inner feelings at the time, recalled: "It's an interesting notion to sit down and write a lyric about not talking. That came out of one of those conversations where we were talking about dating experiences. These conversations that we'd have would go in funny little directions, and I think at some point we were talking about how wonderful non-verbal communication can be between people. Hard subject to write a song about, but I think we pulled it off. It is a beautiful song...a really great song."72

When it came to the memorable line *"listen to my heartbeat,"* beautifully delivered with Brian's stunning falsetto along with Carol Kaye's Fender bass evoking the sound of a beating heart, it led to some musicologists musing over whether the words came even before the music was tracked. Asher recalled: "I don't remember that but I think ...that lyric line was Brian's line, and very well he may have had that in his head when he was writing it." Brian opined: "I felt very deeply about that line. One of the sweetest songs I ever sang. I have to say I'm proud of it. The innocence of youth in my voice, of being young and childlike. I think that's what people liked."72 Asher especially remembered the string arrangement: "I didn't know that [Brian] could write for a string quartet or quintet. And it sounds classical, although it has interesting passing tones. I can remember that so vividly; I just thought 'This is truly heartbreakingly beautiful stuff.' It really was. It was just wonderful. And that was really a revelation to me."72

Despite the other band members having no input, Bruce identified with the song's significance: "I think I was in awe of the string arrangement, how so few strings could do so much...He made everything sound like you could set it up in your living room and stand in the middle. And maybe add some echo later. He absolutely under-produced his sweetening."72.

Yuka Honda of the rock band Cibo Matto gave one of the best reviews: "Brian Wilson's chord progressions tell the most heartbreaking yet beautiful and silently intense story of the duality of life, all from a place of hope. The six bar intro of "Don't Talk"...is worth a thousand books. I consider it to be one of the greatest chord changes ever written."10 Legendary producer Phil Ramone recalled: "Though [Brian] might not have studied Brahms or Ravel, he heard them in his head. That is evident in these chords, and the way they were voiced. It was unusual for pop music at that time."74

With songs like this, brimming with overwhelming emotion, we find adult Brian now looking at the complexity of relationships with a deeper sense of maturity, and one plainly evident in all the other songs on side two of this great album.

Of course, it's worth pointing out that all was not happy in the Beach Boys' camp during the vocal recordings. Returning from their successful tour of Japan, the other band members were aware that Brian had already written most of the songs with a third party, but when it came to what they saw as his pre-determination of the vocal parts, it caused friction, even to the extent that Mike was reportedly unhappy about attending the vocal sessions.

Brian later recalled: "I think they thought it was for Brian Wilson only. They knew that [I] was going to be a separate entity, something that was a force of his own, and it was generally considered that the Beach Boys were the main thing. So with *Pet Sounds* there was a resistance in that I was doing most of the artistic work on it vocally, and for that reason there was a little bit of inter-group struggle. It was resolved in the fact that they figured it was a showcase for Brian Wilson, but it was still The Beach Boys. In other words, they gave in. They let me have my little stint."75 With what must have been a wry smile, Bruce, who had only been with the band for little more than a year, summed up how he felt: "*Pet Sounds* was the solo album that Brian shared with us."

Marilyn Wilson recalled: "How much more romantic can you get? Brian was very romantic when he wanted to be, and so to be able to be in your twenties and say, *'Don't talk, put your head on my shoulder.'* Other people would have thought that was sissyish, but he was very romantic, and that was just coming from two people just being close."[72]

Mojo wrote: "Only Brian could so successfully convey the reverence of lovers drinking in each other's essence among the silence…Nothing more is needed."[25]. Tony Banks of the band Genesis cites it as the song he spent the most time deconstructing: "When it came out, there had been nothing quite like it in terms of the sort of harmonies it was using. It doesn't sound as complicated as all that, but it just goes through all these key changes as it goes along. To me, it's just a wonderful construction and beautiful piece of music."[76]

But let's give Brian the final word: "[Don't Talk] was something that I think was the result of the fact that there are so many different ways to tell somebody you love them, and I think that we had a real special kind of grip on that kind of thing. No one walked in the room and said, 'Hey, you two, break it up.' There was nothing like that at all. It was like God had given us something to do together…"[72]

22. All I Wanna Do (*Sunflower* 1970)
(Brian Wilson, Mike Love)
Recording
24/02/68 (early version)
24/05/68 Valentine Studio, Studio City CA (early version)
08/06/68 Valentine Studio, Studio City CA (2nd version)
19/03/69 Gold Star Studio, LA (tracking - 39 takes)
07/69 Beach Boys Studio, Bel Air (vocals)
Producer - Carl Wilson
Engineers - Stephen Desper, Doc Siegel
Band members
Mike Love (lead vocal, harmony & backing vocals); Brian Wilson (harmony & backing vocals); Carl Wilson (harmony & backing vocals, 12-string electric guitar; Rocksichord, electric sitar); Dennis Wilson (harmony & backing vocals); Al Jardine (harmony & backing vocals); Bruce Johnston (harmony & backing vocals)
Session musicians/Guests
Hal Blaine (drums); Jimmy Bond (double bass, electric bass); Al Casey (rhythm guitar); Gene Estes (shaker); Mike Melvoin (piano); Stephen Desper (Moog synthesiser)
Album released - 31/08/70

This love song of undying devotion was bypassed by both *Friends* and *20/20* before finding a place of honour on *Sunflower*, over two years after the first recording. Now it is regarded as one of the finest of the band's songs that was a not a hit record. Carl Wilson produced the final version with a little assistance from Brian, while Mike handled the double-tracked lead vocal, surely one of his best. One of the early versions featured an electric sitar but no lyrics.

In 1995 Brian went on record to describe the song: "That was one of those songs that had a nice chord pattern, but I think it was a boring song, and I thought it wasn't done right. I thought it should have been softer, with boxed guitars," athough five years later he called it "a really nice one."[179]

In a more recent interview, Mike described the song as "totally poetic and heartfelt" and recalled rehearsing the song with his touring band for a live concert at the Royal Albert Hall: "Funnily enough, I didn't even remember the verse of 'All I Wanna Do' when we rehearsed it recently. We were in rehearsals and the lyrics were written out but they weren't right and I was struggling with it...I couldn't remember it even when listening to the song so closely as we would. Other people would say what they think was the lyrics and it wasn't completely accurate. Well, that was the case with the printout I had of the lyrics...everything else was right but not that."[180]

Noted musicologist Philip Lambert described the song: "...the lush backing chorus grows in intensity along with the love expressed in the lyric. By the time the chorus arrives, the depth and complexity of the singer's feelings are captured by an intricate layering of a main tune repeating the song title, a midrange non-texted countermelody in response, a 'doot-doot-doot' line reaffirming the mellow beat, and a foundational bass line. It's the next step beyond the elegantly transparent layered endings of 'Fun, Fun, Fun' and 'God Only Knows' and so many others."[9]

Mike Love deserves high marks for his vocal and lyric contributions, which may be his most tasteful in the scope of the entire Beach Boys canon

AllMusic's Mathew Greenwald reflected on the song: "Possibly one of the most beautiful and unusual songs and recordings on the *Sunflower* album ... is also one of the band's true lost classics. Mike Love deserves high marks for his vocal and lyric contributions, which may be his most tasteful in the scope of the entire Beach Boys canon. Brian Wilson's haunting, minor-key melody and ghostly arrangement is truly bittersweet evidence that he had certainly not lost his artistic grasp. A unique arrangement, which features a piccolo snare drum as the primary rhythm instrument, is more than effective, and this is topped off by interesting and well-executed harmonies and an almost Byrds-like guitar line."[181] *Rolling Stone's* Jim Miller described Brian's production as "mind-wrenching."[182]

In recent years, a radio station in California pranked listeners by playing "All I Wanna Do," before telling them it was new song by Australian multi-instrumentalist Kevin Parker's psychedelic music project Tame Impala. Listeners believed him and called in. Only then did he confess it was a 50-year-old Beach Boys song.

"All I Wanna Do" was another song overshadowed by greater ones at the time. The *Guardian's* Alexis Petridis wrote: "*Sunflower* is the real jewel in the Beach Boys' 70's catalogue: more of a band effort than *Pet Sounds*, packed with amazing songs, not least 'All I Wanna Do,' a blissful, reverb-drenched dream that some have claimed as a precursor to chillwave."[42]

Petridis was right. With its use of layering, reverb and delay effects, it led to the song being retrospectively cited as the earliest example of dream-pop and chill-wave, a precursor to shoegaze, and an influence for many lo-fi acts. Critic Jim Allen called the band "Godfathers" of dream pop, celebrating the song's "cinematic dream sequence" style of production.[183]

21. Let Him Run Wild (*Summer Days (And Summer Nights!!)* 1965)
(Brian Wilson, Mike Love)
Recording
16/03/65 Western Recorders, LA (tracking - take #16 master, vocal overdubs, mono mix)
30/03/65 Western Recorders, LA (alternative versions inc album version)
04/06/65 CBS Columbia Studio, LA (vocals)
Producer - Brian Wilson
Engineers - Chuck Britz (*Western*); Ralph Valentin? (*Columbia*)
Band members
Brian Wilson (lead vocal, harmony & backing vocals, handclaps); Mike Love (harmony & backing vocals, handclaps); Carl Wilson (harmony & backing vocals, handclaps, 12-string guitar); Dennis Wilson (harmony & backing vocals, tambourine); Al Jardine (harmony & backing vocals, handclaps); Bruce Johnston (harmony & backing vocals, handclaps)
Session musicians
Hal Blaine (drums, temple blocks); Jimmy Bond (acoustic bass); Frank Capp (vibraphone); Steve Douglas (tenor sax); Carol Kaye (bass guitar); Howard Roberts (archtop acoustic guitar); Leon Russell electric piano); Billy Strange (wood block hit on tambourine); Ron Swallow (handclaps); Jerry Cole (possibly electric guitar); Barney Kessel (possibly acoustic guitar); Al De Lory (possibly piano); Roy Caton (possibly trumpet); Jay Migliori (possibly baritone sax); Plas Johnson (possibly tenor sax)
Album released - 05/07/65
US single released - 12/07/65 b-side to "California Girls" Capitol 5464 #3
UK single released - 08/65 b-side to "California Girls" Capitol CL 15409 #26

If anyone buying the hit single "California Girls" in the summer of 1965 had taken the time to listen to the flip-side they would have found this incredible album track, and one that by itself should have been considered as an A-sider. According to Brian, this was one of the first songs he wrote while under the influence of marijuana.35 Allegedly inspired by his father Murry's philandry, it reminded him, as Peter Carlin points out, of a painful moment in his past "that he didn't care to relive."32

Brian described the soulful ballad as being "about a girl who was dating a guy who didn't stay close to her. The guy singing wants the girl to let her boyfriend run around and eventually leave her so he can come in and get her. He wants a bad thing to happen so that it'll turn into a good thing."35

With a working title of "I Hate Rock n' Roll," it was the first track recorded for the *Summer Days* album. Brian later admitted the song was "a sore spot," and was "real, real conscious" that his performance was "really, really lame," singling out his vocal as sounding "too shrill," "like a fairy," and "like a girl…like a chick…a sick chick."2

> ### *"You can practically smell the weed on the woozy track's languid arrangement."*

Cash Box called it an "interesting weeper which blends in generous portions of counterpoint harmony."185

Despite Brian having his regrets, the majority of critics and fans alike saw the song as another signpost pointing toward *Pet Sounds*. As far as *Mojo* was concerned, the song was "Brian's introspective ballad of jealousy and unrequited love…his deepest foray yet into the wild psychedelic country up ahead,"25 while the *Guardian* looked at it as "a wonderful song…that stirs the influence of Burt

Bacharach into a saga of heartbreak and optimism. The writing and arrangements are ever more ornate," but then adding that "the real genius of Brian might not be all the musical twists and turns but how effortlessly the finished project feels."[42] *Far Out* magazine opined: "With melancholy floating through the dreamy arrangement, Wilson conjures up a surprisingly moving lament that doubles as a look into a hazier side of Wilson's evolving musical instincts. You can practically smell the weed on the woozy track's languid arrangement."[184]

Brian had taken a simple idea, added a Bacharach-style swing chorus, and made it work as if there were no other options available that could have been as effective. Rick Swan identified the moments seen as sowing the seeds for *Pet Sounds*: "The jazz-like chords, the innovative arrangement, the bold melodic arcs, the aching voices...the plaintive guitar floating in after the first line of the verse, the entrance of the melancholy bass, the wistful marimba heard as the chorus fades... and the diminished chord heard at the end of the chorus, totally unexpected, yet utterly right.[21] Jim Fusilli saw the song as a "gorgeous track...and the sweet, pensive section after the chorus portend the sounds of a forthcoming classic. Brian's vocal is assertive, more so than anything he offers on *Pet Sounds*."[130]

Johnny Abrams of *Rocksucker* waxed lyrical in his description: "It's so beguilingly transcendent that it almost defies logical explanation. Maybe it's a well-chosen vocal harmony, or an effect on the vocals, or the feel-good factor lingering from such a monumental chorus. Whatever it is, it's proof positive of music's ability to make something so subtle sound so vast, and it's as close as any pop song has come to revealing the meaning of life."[301]

Carl and Dennis both singled out the song as the point in time where they began to see Brian's immense talent as both writer and arranger. Al was of the same opinion: "In terms of [his] musical direction, I always thought that [the song] was the turning point, the beginning of that phase when things began to get more complicated."[72]

Brian's dislike for the song led him to pull it from the 1993 *Good Vibrations* box set. However, he decided to re-record it for his 1998 solo album *Imagination*, as one of two Beach Boys songs he revisited. History repeated itself when Brian was asked about the album: "I don't like the sound. I don't like my voice on it,"[186] and in another interview admitted: "I wasn't having that much fun at the time...I just thought people were out to kill me...I just couldn't deal with it. I just sort of flipped out."[128]

The instrumental track was included on the 1966 *Stack-O-Tracks* album.

20. Kiss Me, Baby (*Beach Boys Today!* 1965)
(Brian Wilson, Mike Love)
Recording
16/12/64 Western Recorders, LA (tracking - 9 takes), two vocal overdubs)
15/01/65 Western Recorders, LA (vocal overdub, Brian's lead vocal)
Producer - Brian Wilson
Engineer - Chuck Britz
Band members
Brian Wilson (lead vocal, harmony & backing vocals); Mike Love (lead vocal, harmony & backing vocals); Carl Wilson (harmony & backing vocals, 12-string lead guitar); Dennis Wilson (harmony & backing vocals); Al Jardine (harmony & backing vocals)

Session musicians
Hal Blaine (drums, temple block); Peter Christ (English horn); Steve Douglas (tenor sax); Jay Migliori (baritone sax); David Duke (French horn); Carol Kaye (bass guitar); Barney Kessel (12-string acoustic guitar); Bill Pitman (acoustic guitar); Ray Pohlman (6-string bass guitar); Leon Russell (grand piano); Billy Strange (electric guitar); Julius Wechter (vibraphone, bell-tree)
Album released - 08/03/65
US single released - 05/04/65 b-side of "Help Me Rhonda" Capitol 5395 #1
UK single released - 05/65 b-side of "Help Me Rhonda" Capitol CL 15392 #27

The music for one of the Beach Boys' greatest ballads began life during a break in the band's 1964 European tour. While Brian and 59-year-old photographer Earl Leaf were taking a break from touring and walking around the red light district of Copenhagen, they heard someone nearby playing the piano. According to Leaf, "Brian dashed into this dancehall-opium den-chop suey joint...edged the piano player off the stool and started whomping the keys in a creative frenzy. The piano player yanked the stool away. Brian continued to bang the piano sitting on the floor...a bruiser-bouncer with Samson muscles and Frankenstein eyebrows broke his trance by slamming down the keyboard cover. Brian darted out into the roaring slum street, whistled up a Danish cab and raced back to the Royal Hotel. He spent the night composing at the piano in a shut-down hotel café." The song was "Kiss Me Baby." [187]

Despite his mindset at the time, Brian had produced one of his most complex and superbly crafted songs of his career

This most moving of songs was first recorded nine days after Brian proposed to his future wife Marilyn Rovell and inspired by their lengthy separation due to touring commitments. According to Mike, Brian's wistful bass line "led to my lyrics about a guy who [still living with his parents] has a disagreement with his girlfriend, even though they can't even remember what they fought about, leaving them both broken-hearted."[188]

Following what is another classic intro, Mike and Brian exchange their low/falsetto counterpoint vocals on the verses, each preceding a dynamite chorus that has Mike's unforgettable *"kiss a little bit/fight a little bit"* hook.

Mark Dillon described it as "a ballad that pleaded for the romantic reconciliation [Brian] anticipated with Marilyn,[10] although Scott Interrante suggests that it "doesn't seem to lyrically parallel [Brian's] personal life at the time," and that "for an album whose songs are so concerned with the future - whether worrying about it or anticipating it - 'Kiss Me Baby' is an odd man out, focusing on coming to terms with the present." He described the song as among Brian's "most interesting compositions," adding that it contained "some of the thickest and most beautiful of harmonies the group had pulled off up to that point."[189]

In his excellent study of Brian's music, Philip Lambert wrote: "One of Brian's most beautiful ballads and it's also one of his most artfully crafted. The flashback effects, for example, are enhanced by sudden reductions in the backing sound. At those points we get a keen sense of the vagaries of memory, crippled further by the pain of heartbreak. Then in the chorus, where the guy serenades his girl with romantic invitations...melodic phrases blend and overlap as a further expression of the guy's confusion and concern, with Brian's falsetto lead soaring above quickly moving group vocals in the middle and Mike's anchoring bass."9

Another study described the song's makeup: "The melody, built on a descending four-note pattern, is framed by guitars, piano and percussion, which never intrude on this intimate confessional. Brian's vocal glides effortlessly above the instrumental track, Mike delivers one of his most tasteful vocals, and the background vocals are outstanding, yet subtle. The lyrics offer wonderful turns of phrase...shattering when punctuated by Hal Blaine's end-of-phrase snare flourishes, while the chorus patter of *"kiss a little bit and fight a little bit"* is utterly magical."5

The tracking session on December 16th would prove to be Brian's last studio work before his breakdown on a flight to Houston a week later, thus making it the only *Today!* track whose recording spanned before and after the incident.

Despite his mindset at the time, Brian had produced one of his most complex and superbly crafted songs of his career, and a perfect example of teenage angst. When coupled with "Help Me Rhonda" on the chart-topping single, it became one of the best value-for-money singles of the band's entire career. *Billboard* described the song as being "good ballad material with strong arrangement and vocal performances,"276 while *Cash Box* called it "a tender, slow-moving moody ballad which effectively blends in snatches of harmony and counterpoint."277

More recently, *AllMusic's* Thomas Ward praised it as a product of Brian's "dense, multi-layered confessional songs with adult themes and exploring issues previously only developed by performers such as Bob Dylan,"275 while biographer Jon Stebbins saw it as "the pinnacle of balladry...a mammoth artistic achievement."189 A stunning a capella mix was featured on 2001's *Hawthorne Ca.*

19. Break Away (Single 1969)
(Brian Wilson, Reggie Dunbar)
Recorded
31/03/69 Gold Star Studio, LA (tracking, guide lead vocals by Carl & Al, backing vocals overdubbed)
02/04/69 I.D Sound Studio, LA (mono mix with Brian's lead vocal)
10/04/69 I.D Sound Studio, LA (horn insert, additional backing vocals)
23/04/69 Beach Boys Studio, Bel Air (horn insert and additional backing vocals)
13/05/69 I.D Studio LA (stereo mix)
Producer - Brian Wilson, Murry Wilson
Engineer - Larry Levine or Stan Ross (Gold Star);
Band members
Carl Wilson (lead vocal on verses); Al Jardine (lead vocal on chorus); Brian Wilson (backing vocals); Mike Love (backing vocals); Dennis Wilson (backing vocals); Al Jardine (backing vocals); Bruce Johnston (backing vocals)
US single released - 16/06/69 b/w "Celebrate the News" Capitol 2530 #63
UK single released - 06/69 b/w "Celebrate the News" Capitol CL 15598 #6
UK single re-released - 06/75
Film/TV performances
03/06/69 *Beat Club* Radio Bremen TV, West Germany (broadcast 07/06/69)(YT)
16/06/69 *Midi Premiere* TFI Paris
16/06/69 Olympia Theater Paris TFI (filmed concert)
18/06/69 *Bratislava Song Festival*, Czechoslovakia InterVision (syndicated from 21/06)
19/06/69 *Top of the Pops* BBC-1 London (footage of visit to Leeds Infirmary, England 08/06/69)
30/06/69 *De Raiders En De Beach Boys* NCRV Amsterdam (broadcast 03/07/69)

08/07/69 *The Mike Douglas Show* Westinghouse, Philadelphia (broadcast 22/07/69)
30/07/69 *The David Frost Show* Westinghouse, Philadelphia (broadcast 08/08/69)

Murry Wilson's relationship with his sons, particularly Brian and Dennis, is well documented, but the facts cannot be ignored that, without him, the Beach Boys would most probably never have existed. With his music background, he introduced them to all the necessary people that could help them achieve their goals. He was generous to a fault and implored on his sons that to succeed in business it took guts and hard work. But the records show he was also a strict disciplinarian and the slightest disobedience from his sons could result in physical abuse, with Dennis and Brian becoming the most convenient targets.

Once the Beach Boys had become successful, Murry continually tried to stamp his authority on what they recorded, despite being sacked as their manager by Brian, and it all came to a head during the January 1965 session for "Help Me Rhonda," which practically put an end to his interference. Al Jardine probably hit the nail on the head when later asked about Murry: "Well he had a child prodigy on his hands. He simply had a limited ability to cope with it. Murry was a salesman. Draw your own conclusions. Always selling something. Very aggressive and tough-minded. Taskmaster."47

But that didn't put an end to Murry's involvement in a Beach Boys record. On April 12th 1969 the band issued a lawsuit against Capitol for around $2 million for unpaid royalties and production fees, as well as alleged general mismanagement. It signalled the end of their seven-year relationship with the giant label and the chance to relaunch their own, Brother Records. But it also left them without a recording contract for the first time in their career.

With a little help from his dad, Brian had managed at the drop of a hat to create a bona fide Beach Boys classic

Capitol would still retain ownership of all their albums up to and including *Party!,* but as soon as it was settled Capitol deleted those albums from their roster, therefore suspending royalties. It looked like a financial disaster for the band, and they still owed the label one last original single.

Although the contract was due to end on June 30th, Capitol still appeared keen to keep them on board, despite setting the band deadlines of April 21st for the single and May 1st for the album, in order to fulfil their contractual obligations.

In order to get the cramped cashflow moving again, Murry called Brian and told him they needed his help. It had always been his ambition to write a hit for the band, and now he saw the opportunity. Although recollections differ, Brian claimed that Murry came up with the idea of a song called "Break Away" from watching the *Joey Bishop Show* and the message: "We're gonna break away for a minute and we'll be right back!"2 When father and son got together, Brian recalled that they "plunked and plunked and plunked…and finally got the song going."2 Apparently, Brian completed the song in an hour at Gold Star and recorded it without any session musicians other than a horn insert. The result was a hugely impressive production with both Carl and Al handling the lead vocals. Brian later recalled why Murry used the pseudonym Reggie Dunbar: "My dad and I wrote it. He didn't want anyone to know that he wrote it with me. Believe it or not, we wrote some of it on the doorstep outside my house and some sitting around at the piano. I was still friends with my dad after he didn't work with us anymore. He was a good buddy…"175

Asked the same question in another interview, Brian typically offered a completely different view: "I don't know. He was nutty. He was crazy, that was his fictitious name."2 Although credited as lyricist, it is uncertain as to what extent Murry's contribution was, and whether Brian also had a hand with the words. Unfortunately "Break Away" never did make it on to their next album *Sunflower*, but as a stand-alone single it once again did better in Europe, despite Capitol's reluctance to give it the promotion it deserved. It finally appeared on the 1975 *Spirit of America* compilation, along with another stand-alone single "The Little Girl I Once Knew," and again on *20 Golden Greats* the following year. A wonderful alternate take was featured on *Endless Harmony* in 1998 and on *Hawthorne Ca* three years later. Previously unheard off backing vocals were later included on the *Feel Flows* box set in 2021.

There's little doubt that this positive, life-affirming song about changing your life for the better remains a firm favourite among fans, although a number of commentators pointed out that the song's title was Brian's hidden message of relief for "breaking away" from the confines of Capitol. Others have suggested that some of the pseudonymous lyrics, such as hearing lying in bed and hearing "voices in my head," may have been referred to his tormenting father.

But with a little help from his dad, Brian had managed at the drop of a hat to create a bona fide Beach Boys classic that even today deserves a little more recognition. Brian himself went on record to say: "That's a beautiful song. I think it might be one of my most underrated songs."63 And that is simply too difficult to deny.

Two months or so after the song was released, Murry Wilson sold his *Sea of Tunes* publishing company to Irving Almo for $700,000 (equivalent to $5.59 million in 2022) on the belief that the value of the band's vast catalog had peaked. As the band's manager, he had founded the company with Brian in 1962 with the intention of publishing and promoting songs written primarily by his son. In July 1965 he had sent a letter to Brian requesting sole ownership of the company as per a verbal agreement they had reached back in 1962. According to Keith Badman: "Brian allowed Murry to take total control to stop his father's continual hassling over the matter."11 In May 1969 Brian would announce to the music press that the band's funds were so depleted that they were considering filing for bankruptcy, something that *Disc & Music Echo* described as "stunning news" and "a tremendous shock on the American pop scene."304

In his 2016 memoir, Mike revealed that the band had signed away their rights to the songs under duress.188 In the late 1980's it was discovered that the exchange had been part of an elaborate plan orchestrated over a period of two years by Beach Boy lawyer Abe Somer, who concealed the fact that he was also Irving Music's lawyer, which was a conflict of interests.188 It was estimated that over the years the Beach Boys' catalog would generate more than $100,000 in publishing royalties, none of which Murry or the band members ever received. In 2022 the catalog was valued at between $100-200 million.

Murry died of a heart attack on June 2nd 1973 at the age of 55, followed by Audree in 1997 (they had divorced in 1966). In the early 90's Brian claimed it had all been a fraud and sued for the return of his songs' copyrights. The lawsuit suggested that Brian's signature may have been forged "plus malpractice, misrepresentations, suppression of facts, breach of contract and conflicts of interest," all of which made the sale illegal. While failing to recover the copyrights in court, he was awarded $25 million in damages, that included unpaid royalties."305

In 2021 the remaining Beach Boys - Brian, Mike and Al, alongside Carl's two sons Jonah and Justyn, sold their intellectual rights to the music to Irving Azoff's Iconic Artists Group, with all those involved retaining an interest in the assets. Azoff said, "We think the Beach Boys is an unappreciated trademark. They are just not as important as they could or should be."

So how will future historians evaluate the man who many say was instrumental in the Beach Boys' ultimate success? James B Murphy wrote that "material possessions do not make a childhood happy, but Murry did his best [on a modest salary] to provide his boys with things they enjoyed. And no one fought harder for the fledgling Beach Boys than Murry."306 In his 2016 memoir, Mike recalled: [Murry] was a driving force in the Beach Boys' early success, but his greed and his vindictiveness deny him any tribute. The most forgiving thing I can say about him is that he was simply an inheritor of his own father's cruelty…What is often missed in the Wilson family history is that my aunt Audree was the true musical talent in that marriage."188

Engineer Chuck Britz, who observed first-hand the friction between father and son in the recording studio, took a more sympathetic view: "I was one of the few people who liked Murry. I always did. I admired him for the way he got the kids mad at him; that made them also conscious of what they were trying to achieve. I realise that maybe he did it the wrong way, but at the same time, he did make them work as a team which was the way it should be."6

18. I Just Wasn't Made For These Times *(Pet Sounds* 1966)
(Brian Wilson, Tony Asher)
Recording
14/02/66 Western Recorders/Gold Star Studio, LA (tracking - take #6 master, Brian's lead vocal, vocal inserts)
10/03/66 CBS Columbia Studio, LA (vocal overdubbing)
13/04/66 CBS Columbia Studio, LA (vocal overdubbing)
Producer - Brian Wilson
Engineers - Larry Levine (Gold Star); Ralph Valentin (Columbia)
Band members
Brian Wilson (lead & backing vocals); Mike Love (backing vocals); Carl Wilson (backing vocals); Dennis Wilson (backing vocals); Al Jardine (backing vocals); Bruce Johnston (backing vocals)
Session musicians
Chuck Berghofer (upright bass); Hal Blaine (drums, timpanis); Glen Campbell (rhythm guitar); Frank Capp (temple blocks, cup with sticks); Steve Douglas (clarinet); Plas Johnson (piccolo); Bobby Klein (clarinet); Mike Melvoin (harpsichord); Jay Migliori (bass clarinet); Tommy Morgan (bass harmonica); Barney Kessel (mando-guitar); Ray Pohlman (bass guitar); Don Randi (tack piano); Paul Tanner (Electro-Theremin)
Album released - 16/05/66

Brian's most introspective song since "In My Room" was one of the last tracks recorded for *Pet Sounds,* with lyrics by Tony Asher, and describing someone who doesn't fit into society, perfectly mirroring Brian's mindset at the time. Asher had once revealed that the song came about after a discussion with Brian about them both being unpopular at high school.[10] He also claimed to have contributed musical ideas to this and two other tracks on the album, going on to say that the lyrics for this song were different to their other collaborations: "In many of the other songs, when Brian would express a feeling, I would say, 'Oh, yes, I've had those feelings, maybe not in the same way or the same degree, but I understood them. But this one I didn't relate to."[85]

Asher went on to say: "I think that [the song] was Brian's way of acknowledging that he didn't conform to the norm - that he was marching to the beat of a different drummer. We were certainly aware of what we were writing about when we approached the song. It was definitely a lyric written from Brian's perspective, although during the hours we spent writing, we didn't talk about his socialisation per se. He never asked me to interpret his feelings in one of our songs, and certainly not this one…We confined our conversations to the theoretical….I remember that when we finished the song, I had the sense that it might not end up on the album. It take a lot of courage for an artist to expose himself in such a personal way…But we did it, and it took a lot of guts."[85] But what about Brian? In a 1976 interview he stated: "That song reflects my life. It's about a guy who was crying because he thought he was too advanced, and that he'd eventually have to leave people behind…Yes, it did happen to me. I did *Pet Sounds* and all my friends thought I was crazy to do it."[103]

"Ultimately, Brian's public suffering had transformed him from a musical figure into a cultural one"

Apparently the first session for the song at Western on February 14th 1966 was interrupted when it was revealed that Johnny Rivers had already booked the evening's time slot, forcing Brian and the band to move to nearby Gold Star to complete the tracking with their squad of 14 session musicians. The April 13th session would prove to be the last of 27 recordings for *Pet Sounds.*

This was also the first time the band (or maybe any rock band) employed what was known as a "Theremin," an electrical instrument that had been created in the 1920's and used to create eerie sound effects in Hollywood movies like Hitchcock's *Spellbound* and the sci-fi classic, *The Day the Earth Stood Still,* as well as the popular tv series *My Favourite Martian.* In 1996 Brian admitted that as a child he was frightened by its "witchy, bewildering sounds," but couldn't remember how he ever "arrived at a place where I'd want to get one - but we got it."[72] Biographer John Tobler stated that Brian first thought of using the instrument after watching a horror movie starring Bette Davis,[192] while engineer Chuck Britz recalled Brian walking into the studio and saying, "I have a new sound for you."[8]

For the recording a simplified "electro-theremin" was played by sessionist Paul Tanner, one that had been developed especially for him in 1958. It's quite possible that Brian believed he was employing a real Theremin for the recording, as Tanner later revealed: "Brian phoned and spoke to my wife. I was on a record date, but she knew that the person I was playing for had never heard of overtime!"85. Musicologist Mark Brend was full of praise for Tanner's performance, writing that it "demonstrates perfectly the electro-theremin's appeal. The pitching is accurate to a degree that only the very best 'real' thereminists could ever achieve, yet the tone retains the theremin's haunting ethereal quality - somehow both human-sounding and alien at the same time."196 Tanner would later be re-enlisted to play it with even greater effect on "Good Vibrations" and "Wild Honey."

In 1995 the song title would be used by producer Don Was for his documentary biography about Brian, as well as its subsequent soundtrack, which became Brian's second solo album.

On reflection Rick Swan wrote: "The singer bemoans a list of losses and disappointments, the background instruments swell and sob, the mournful melody rises, postponing the resolution until it breaks with the singer's declaration of sadness, a moment which hits the listener like a brick wall. The dazzling choir washes over you and behind the miserable singer on the bridge. Beauty and despair, rolled up into a touching, brilliant performance.21 Philip Lambert called it "one of the most extreme examples of Wilson's opera-style layering, with each part projecting its own distinct personality,"9 while *AllMusic's* Donald Gearisco, saw it as "one of the most moving and powerful tracks in the Beach Boys' catalog…[one that features] overwhelming emotion and lush musical textures [with lyrics relatable] for anyone who has ever felt 'lost in the crowd.'"197

Biographer Peter Carlin referred to the song as "the overture for a decades-long saga that would be, in its way, as influential as *Pet Sounds* has been…Ultimately, Brian's public suffering had transformed him from a musical figure into a cultural one,"32 whereas Charles Granata saw it as "perhaps the most sensitive, moving song on *Pet Sounds,* [projecting] an overwhelming sense that the lyric represents Brian's life, his view of himself and his music."28

Wall Street Journal music reviewer Jim Fusilli wrote how the song "recalls a Spector production with its flashes of harsh, almost military drumming, layers of effusive guitars, and surround-sound keyboards and saxophones. And yet it's Brian too; Brian with an expanding arsenal. The tremolo electric bass under the vocal is joined by the clip-clop temple blocks, the Theremin and instruments that can't be heard individually but contribute to the overall impression when blended with other sounds - the tack piano, for example, and a banjo. There's a harmonica in there somewhere, echoing the Theremin."130

Perhaps the final word should go to Brian, who in 2011 was asked if he still reckoned he "wasn't made for these times," and replied: "It was like saying, 'Either I'm too far ahead of my time,' or 'I'm not up to my time'…[The feeling has] stayed the same…a little bit, in some ways not…[Now] I do feel I was made for these times."198

17. Fun, Fun, Fun *(Shut Down Volume 2 1964)*
(Brian Wilson, Mike Love)
Recording
01/01/64 Western Recorders, LA (tracking - 6 takes, vocal overdubs - 19 takes, alternate version)
08/01/64 or 09/01/64 Western Recorders, LA (vocals & additional overdubs)

Producer - Brian Wilson
Engineer - Chuck Britz
Band members
Mike Love (lead & bass vocals); Brian Wilson (harmony & backing vocals, piano, Hammond B3 organ, bass guitar); Carl Wilson (harmony & backing vocals, lead & rhythm guitars); Dennis Wilson (harmony & backing vocals, drums); Al Jardine (harmony & backing vocals, bass guitar, rhythm guitar|)
Session musicians
Hal Blaine (tambourine, additional drums); Steve Douglas (tenor saxes); Jay Migliori (baritone saxes); Ray Pohlman (6-string electric bass guitars)
Album released - 02/03/64
US single released - 03/02/64 b/w "Why Do Fools Fall In Love?" Capitol 5118 #5
UK single released - 03/64 b/w "Why Do Fools Fall In Love?" Capitol CL 15339
Film/TV performances
14/03/64 NBC Television Studios, Burbank (part of concert for screening in selected US cinemas, later released in 1998 as *The Lost Concert*
21/04/65 *Shindig!* ABC New York
07/02/96 *The Des O'Connor Show* ITV London (with Status Quo)
02/96 *Talking Telephone Numbers* ITV London (with Status Quo)
02/96 *The Shane Richie Experience* ITV London (with Status Quo)
21/01/77 Capital Centre, Washington DC
21/06/80 Knebworth England concert (later released on CD/DVD)
04/07/80 Washington DC concert

A song about a rebellious teenage girl deceiving her father by taking his '63 Thunderbird to go hot-rodding instead of the library was always going to be a sure-fire success, especially as it was apparently inspired by a true story about a Salt Lake City girl called Shirley Johnson.

During their early career, the Beach Boys had developed a special bond with the Beehive State and had already performed there several times a year. College girl Johnson worked as a part-time secretary at her father's KNAK radio station, which often promoted the band and arranged interviews with them. Johnson later recalled what happened in September 1963: "I did take my dad's car, and I was going to go to the library and ended up at a place called Shore's Drive In...a hamburger shop on 33rd South and 27th East." When her father did find out, he revoked her driving privileges.

The band happened to be at the radio station the following day, September 8th, following a concert the previous evening at the Lagoon in nearby Farmington. Johnson recalled: "So I was kind of complaining to the staff at the radio station that I was in a bit of trouble, and the Beach Boys heard it." According to station manager Bill "Daddy-O" Hesterman, who drove the boys back to the airport that afternoon, Brian and Mike were amused by the incident and began jotting down the beginnings to the song.199

According to David Marks, however, the song was written in a hotel room, while biographer Steven Gaines claimed: "It was written in a car while [Brian] and Mike were discussing Dennis's obsession with young girls," and that Dennis had told Mike "about a girl [from a rich family in Palos Verdes] who borrowed her father's thunderbird, allegedly to go to the library, when in reality she was going to hang out with Dennis at his apartment."12 In yet another version, biographer Timothy White states that en route to Salt Lake City airport, Mike had told Brian about "a girl he knew who had her Thunderbird keys taken away by her father after lying about school-night trips to the library," but was actually "meeting a new boyfriend at a hamburger stand."29

"Hey, we'll make the best record ever tonight! I had that kind of spirit - and Goddamn if it didn't work, you know"

Mike revealed yet another version of the story: "As far as I knew, there was no particular person that was the inspiration for that song. It was more generic. Because, what kid, when they got their driver's license, doesn't want to borrow the family car and they go cruisin' through the hamburger stand, or they say they need to go to the library, but who knows? Sometimes other thoughts become more attractive."76

Whatever the version, the fact remains that between them Brian and Mike produced one of the most irresistible song of the band's early career. It's a song that has everything - the nostalgic theme of Californian teenage fantasy; an infectious Chuck Berry-inspired riff; a wonderful polyphonic finale with Brian's soaring falsetto, and some of Mike's finest lyrics, with end rhymes such as "stand now," "man now" and "can now," endearing in their simplicity. Altogether, we have one of the band's greatest examples of defining the California myth of having carefree, good times.

Following an earlier cancellation of a session, due to Murry's dissatisfaction, Brian rescheduled it and recording got underway at Western Recorders' Studio 3 on the first day of 1963, just a couple of weeks before the band's tour of Australia and New Zealand commenced. Prior to recording, the boys improvised a slower, blusier version of the song, followed by a quick one-take of the backing track, Mike's lead vocal, and percussion and guitar inserts added to the existing tape. To complete the recording, the whole band then took a total of 19 takes to perfect vocal overdubs. The remaining session saw tracking and vocals recorded for "The Warmth of the Sun."

In an interview for *Newsweek* in 1977 Brian recalled: "I could get a record cut and done in three f*****g hours! I was a kid and I was ready for some competition. I'd run in the studio and say, 'Hey, we'll make the best record ever tonight!' I had that kind of spirit - and goddamn if it didn't work, you know."11

Carl's glorious opening riff was based on Berry's "Johnny B Goode," while musicologist Philip Lambert identified similar chord progressions as in Spector's "Da Doo Ron Ron." Mark Dillon praised Mike's keen eye for the teenage scene: "It's all so wonderfully innocent: the narrator isn't even vindictive towards the girl whose head gets inflated by her new wheels before being busted by her old man. He still invites her to join him and his friends for less duplicitous fun, fun, fun."10

Mike later recalled: "I suggested that we write a song about a girl who borrows her dad's car and goes cruising, rather than to the library, *'like she told her old man, now.'* So I came up with the concept and the lyrics, and Brian went in and recorded the track. And I even told him, it's got to start like a Chuck Berry song with a guitar lead intro, which Carl Wilson supplied. And so that's how that came to pass."76

Sessionist Hal Blaine, who shared drums on the track with Dennis, later recalled: "It just felt so good lyrically. It was just youngsters' lyrics, but it all worked. It was perfect timing for teenagers who were thinking about the beach and having fun. It couldn't miss." Blaine was also full of praise for Brian: "Any time I worked with Brian I knew it was going to be great. It was always a thrill. I couldn't wait to get started."[10]

According to producer Russ Titelman, who visited Brian while working on the song, the original lyric was "Run, Run, Run."[200] Although Brian's wonderful falsetto ending to the song was cut short for the album version, it was corrected in an alternate mix for the single. The single was "hustled" out in the US on February 3rd 1964, just four days before the Beatles arrived in the country ahead of the so-called British Invasion, and, according to Timothy White, was because "Brian wanted Liverpool competition to hear Hawthorne's Top 40 artillery while both bands were still on American turf."[29]

Despite that, the single surprisingly peaked at #5 on the Hot 100, their highest spot since "Surfin USA." Two days before "Fun, Fun, Fun" was released the Beatles "I Want To Hold Your Hand" hit the top spot and stayed there for seven weeks until replaced by their own "She Loves You." Meanwhile, over in the UK, "Fun, Fun, Fun" failed to get a chart entry when released in March, even though it had received great reviews.

Cash Box praised it's "contagious steady rock beat" and "great teen arrangement,"[201] while, retrospectively, *Mojo* wrote: "With classic Beach Boys frissons of deceit, dangerous driving and elopement, it stays lodged in the brain with its harmonic acrobatics - an enduring vision of freedom and youth."[25]

In February 1996 the remaining Beach Boys - Brian, Carl, Mike, Al and Bruce - joined up with British band Status Quo to record a new version of the song (with an additional verse) for their album of covers, *Don't Stop*. While the Quo's Mike Rossi provided lead vocal for most of the song, Mike Love performed the new verse. It reached #24 on the UK chart and a video was made to promote it. "Fun, Fun, Fun" was another song that Mike was later awarded co-writing credit following his successful lawsuit in 1994.

16. Sloop John B *(Pet Sounds* 1966)
(Traditional, arranged by Brian Wilson)
Recording
12/07/65 Western Recorders, LA (tracking - 14 takes)
22/12/65 Western Recorders, LA (guitar & vocal overdubbing)
29/12/65 Western Recorders, LA (vocal overdubbing, lead vocals by Carl, and Carl & Dennis - *later scrapped*)
Producer - Brian Wilson
Engineer - Chuck Britz
Band members
Brian Wilson (lead & backing vocals); Mike Love (lead & backing vocals); Carl Wilson (backing vocals); Dennis Wilson (backing vocals); Al Jardine (backing vocals); Bruce Johnston (backing vocals)
Session musicians
Hal Blaine (drums); Frank Capp (glockenspiel); Al Casey (acoustic rhythm guitar); Jerry Cole (12-string lead guitar); Steve Douglas (temple blocks); Carol Kaye (electric bass); Al De Lory (tack piano); Jay Migliori (flute); Jim Horn (flute); Jack Nimitz (bass sax); Lyle Ritz (string bass); Billy Strange (12-string lead guitar); Tony Asher? (tambourine)
Album released - 16/05/66
US single released -21/03/66 b/w "You're So Good To Me" Capitol 5561 #3
UK single released - 15/04/66 b/w "You're So Good To Me" Capitol CL 15441 #2

Film/TV performances
12/05/66 *Top of the Pops* BBC-1 London (promo film shot at Brian's Laurel Way home 24/04/66)
14/12/66 *Twien* Theater De Brakke Grond, NCRV Amsterdam (broadcast 23/12/68)
16/06/69 Olympia Theater Paris TFI (filmed concert)
25/02/72 *Grand Gala Du Disque Populaire* RAI Amsterdam
23/11/76 *The Mike Douglas Show,* Westinghouse, Philadelphia (broadcast 08/12/76)
21/01/77 Capital Centre, Washington DC
21/06/80 Knebworth England (later released on CD/DVD)

The famous Bahamian folk song "The John B. Sails" was originally transcribed in an issue of *Harper's Monthly* magazine in December 1916 and based on a calamitous voyage of a dissolute, ungovernable sloop plagued with drunkenness and bad behaviour, with the narrator pleading to go home. What remains of the wreck still lie embedded in the sand at Governor's Harbour in Nassau.

The song was given a modern arrangement by music professor Alfred George Walthall, and three verses and a chorus were included in Carl Sandburg's *The American Songbag*, a collection of folk songs published in 1927. The earliest audio of the song came in 1935 with a recording of a Bahamian group singing, "Histe up the John B Sail." Fifteen years later, folk group the Weavers (including Pete Seeger) recorded their calypso-style version as "The Wreck of the John B," followed eight years later by the Kingston Trio's slightly odd version with pseudo-Caribbean vocals. Later versions included Johnny Cash's "I Want To Go Home" in 1959; Jimmie Rodgers calypso-style "The Wreck of the John B" in 1960, and British skiffle singer Lonnie Donegan, with his tango-flavoured "I Wanna Go Home (The Wreck of the John B)" that same year.

"When I brought [the song] *to Brian, I was terrified. I thought I might be wasting his time. Not so - I gave him the chords, and he soaked them up like a sponge"*

The idea for the Beach Boys to record it came from Al, a longtime fan of folk music, and one very familiar with the traditional versions. He had first suggested it to Brian as early as 1961 when a number of those versions were being played on the radio. He recalled: "I had a group in high school called the Islanders, and we sang 'Sloop John B' all the time. I'd been fooling around with the song at home, and though it might be something that would work for the Beach Boys. But, it took me quite some time to convince Brian of the song's possibilities."[85]

The summer of 1965 was a time when the fusion of folk-rock was really taking a hold in the US, thanks to artists like Dylan and the Byrds, and Al saw a golden opportunity for the band to embrace it. A year before they actually cut the record, Al took his own arrangement of the song and sat down with Brian: "Brian was at the piano. I asked him if I could sit down and show him something. I laid out the chord pattern for 'Sloop John B.' I said, 'Remember this song?' I played it. He said, 'I'm not a big fan of the Kingston Trio.' He wasn't into folk music. But I didn't give up on the idea. So what I did was to sit down and play it for him in the Beach Boys idiom. I figured if I gave it to him in the right light, he might end up believing in it. So I modified the chord changes so it would be a little more interesting. The original song is basically a three-chord song [done on guitar, banjo and keyboards], and I knew that wouldn't fly.72

The following day, July 12th 1965, the same day the band's latest single "California Girls" was released, Al got a call from Brian to come down to the Western studio and hear what he had been doing with the song. Al continued, "I was blown away. The idea stage to the completed track took less than 24 hours."85 Brian made some slight lyric changes, including swapping "*break up*" for "*broke up*," and "*the worst ship*" for "*the worst trip*," (maybe as a nod to acid culture). Without knowing it, Brian had just begun work on the first song for what would eventually become *Pet Sounds*.

After what turned out to be an intense three-hour session and a total of 14 takes, Brian, along with engineer Chuck Britz and an ensemble of top musicians, created what was a spellbinding instrumental track, casting aside any previous model for inspiration, but rubber stamping it with his own interpretation. Al recalled: "Brian had never shown the slightest interest in folk music, but he was certainly passionate about this song, and his interest manifested itself in a beautiful production."74

All of this had energised Brian, and although no further work on the song would be done for the next five months, he spent that time considering the possibility of making what would be a very special album, while the band continued with their current US tour without him.

On December 6th 1965, the same day the Beatles' *Rubber Soul* was released in the US, Brian began working with new collaborator Tony Asher and played him the track for "Sloop John B." Asher later recalled that it was the only finished tune that Brian played for him. Brian loved *Rubber Soul*, and despite the Beatles being competition, he was full of admiration for their work, which he saw as different from his own: "[They] will simplify to its skeletal form an arrangement, where I would be impelled to make it more complex."130

Vocal sessions followed, including a solo lead by Carl and a Carl/Dennis dual lead, but both were discarded in favour of what turned out to be the final Brian/Mike lead. Al recalled: "[Brian] lined us up one at a time to try out for the lead vocal. I had naturally assumed I would sing the lead, since I had brought in the arrangement. It was like interviewing for a job. Pretty funny. He didn't like any of us. My vocal had a much more mellow approach because I was bringing it from the folk idiom. For the radio, we needed a more rock approach. [Brian] and Mike ended up singing it." 72

Al felt that he never received due credit: "When I brought [the song] to Brian, I was terrified. I thought I might be wasting his time. Not so - I gave him the chords, and he soaked them up like a sponge. He made the instrumental track almost immediately, and it became a huge hit for us. But he never acknowledged my contribution to the song."74

There has been some debate as to whether Brian intended "Sloop John B" to be included on *Pet Sounds*, in light of the fact that the instrumental track had been recorded at least six months before sessions for the album officially commenced in January 1966, and that it had no mood or lyrical connection with any of the personalised songs on the album. Some commentators went so far as to claim that its inclusion actually prevented *Pet Sounds* from becoming a true concept album. Brian has always denied this, stating that it was always intended for the album, perhaps believing it was never intended to be a concept anyway. Further research unearthed a mid-February 1966 tracklist for the album, including "Sloop John B" that Brian had handed to Capitol. The truth is that Capitol wanted it on the album, a song they saw as a genuine hit single, unlike the other tracks.

Al explained Capitol's dislike for the album: "They couldn't accept it. Nobody really excepted it. Capitol hated it. I know it. They wanted some hit records. We were a hit record machine and we stopped delivering those big hits. Except for 'Sloop John B.' I think they forced [it] to be on the album because it was already a hit. They slipped it on there to increase album sales. Capitol didn't like it at all. They weren't too wrong either because after that we had the *Smiley Smile* thing and it just started to go downhill from there."47

With controversy set aside, we are left with one of Brian's greatest productions. It opens with a simple flute (Jim Horn or Jay Migliori) perhaps imitating the sound of a nautical whistle, followed by gentle guitars and ringing percussion before Carol Kaye's bass kicks in. Gradually, a whole carnival array of instruments roll in like ocean waves to create a sonic tapestry. This is one of a few songs that Brian produced where the instrumental track outshines the vocals, although that too is pretty compelling, with Brian handling lead on the first and third verses and Mike on the second. Then there's that unforgettable build up to a short but immaculate a capella break that ends the second chorus. The instrumental track was later released on their *Stack-O-Tracks* album.

When released as a single two months before the album, the song justified the label's decision by peaking at #3 on the Hot 100 and becoming a huge hit across Europe. According to pop historian Joseph Murrells, the song was the band's fastest-selling single to date, with over half a million within two weeks of its release in the US. Meanwhile the release of *Rubber Soul,* just a couple of weeks before Brian laid down the track for "Sloop John B," would have a marked effect on Brian: "It blew me f*****g out. The album blew my mind because it was a whole album with all good stuff! It flipped me out so much. It was definitely a challenge for me. I saw that every cut was very artistically interesting and stimulating."123

Spurred on by his rivals, Brian later revealed: "I suddenly realised that the recording industry was getting so free and intelligent. We could go into new things - string quartets, auto-harps, and instruments from another culture. I decided right then: I'm gonna try that, where a whole album becomes a gas…*Rubber Soul* is a complete statement, damn it, and I want to make a complete statement, too!" Legend has it he then told his wife Marilyn: "I'm gonna make the greatest rock n' roll album ever made!"29

Many would say he lived up to that claim.

15. Forever *(Sunflower* 1970)
(Dennis Wilson, Gregg Jakobson)
Recording
09/01/69 Beach Boys Studio, Bel Air
12/03/69 Gold Star Studio, LA
14/03/69 Gold Star Studio, LA
17/03/69 Gold Star Studio, LA (basic track overdubbed with strings & vocals - take #39 master)
Producer - The Beach Boys (Dennis)
Engineers - Stephen Desper (Bel Air), Larry Levine or Stan Ross (Gold Star)

Band members
Dennis Wilson (lead vocals, harmony & backing vocals, piano, tambourine); Brian Wilson (harmony & backing vocals); Carl Wilson (harmony & backing vocals, Rocksichord); Mike Love (harmony & backing vocals); Bruce Johnston (piano)
Session musicians
Mike Anthony (electric guitar); Jimmy Bond (arco double bass); Lyle Ritz (bass); Daryl Dragon (vibraphone); Gene Estes (drums); Frank Capp (timpani); Orville "Red" Rhodes (pedal steel guitar); Paul Beaver (Moog synthesiser); 4 violins
Album released - 31/08/70
US single released - 03/71 b-side to "Cool, Cool, Water" Brother/Reprise 0998
Film/TV performances
25/01/71 *The David Frost Show* Westinghouse, Philadelphia (broadcast 24/03/71)
02/07/71 *Good Vibrations From Central Park* NBC (broadcast 19/08/71)

Brian once described this yearning ballad by his brother as "the most harmonically beautiful thing I've ever heard. It's a rock and roll prayer,"69 while cousin Mike wrote that it "captured the raw emotion and bluesy sensibility that he brought to his vocals."

Dennis would write some wonderful songs during his burst of creativity during the period 1968-1969, but this ode to everlasting love and faithfulness is arguably his finest work. He first met his Minnesota-born friend Gregg Jakobson in Hawaii through Bruce Johnston and Terry Melcher, who were still performing together as the Rip Chords. Jakobson lived in Benedict Canyon, not far from Dennis's home, and the two became close friends. Jakobson was a burgeoning songwriter and witnessed how Dennis's artistic birth happened almost overnight: "It was like, one day he couldn't play the piano - you know, he could plonk on it like I do - and the next day he could sit down and play you a whole complicated melody line of blues or a jazz or a rock & roll influenced melody line."206

In August 1968 Dennis moved out of his Sunset Boulevard home to get away from Charles Manson, whose "family" had been using his house for the last six months, and went to live with Jakobson in the Palisades near Santa Monica. Dennis had introduced Manson to Jakobson, who later paid the expenses for him to record some of his own compositions. Following the Tate/La Bianca murders on August 9th 1969, Jakobson was a key witness at Manson's trial, bravely coming forward to testify what he know about his behaviour. Dennis never testified or discussed his relationship with anyone, allegedly receiving death threats from some members of Manson's followers. As a result, he would live in fear for his life for years to come.

> *This was his masterpiece, simple, yet adoringly sensitive, and he would never write a better one.*

Five months later, sessions began for the band's next album, their first for new label Warner, and one that eventually would be called *Sunflower* (the band would fulfil their contract with Capitol with the release of *Live In London* in May 1970). From a pool of forty or so songs that had been written, the final selection for *Sunflower* included three of Dennis's collaboration with Jakobson, "Slip on Through," "Got To Know the Woman," and "Forever." The first two were originally credited to Dennis alone, but Jakobson had his name added in 2021 following consultation with the Wilson estate.

With help from Brian on the arrangement for "Forever" Dennis delivered a song that would rival his brother's most emotionally complex ballads. Gary Gidman described it as "widely regarded as one of Dennis's best songs. It's haunting melody, delivered with soulful restraint…unfolds over acoustic guitars, lap steel guitar, and the tick-tocking tambourine and snare idea used in [Dennis's] 'Celebrate the News.' Subdued group vocals give way first to crescendos bolstered by timpani, and finally to a powerful chorale during which Brian (who can be heard throughout the song echoing the melody with a sympathetic descant of nonsense syllables) improvises brilliant vocal counterpoint."207

Matthew Greenwald, writing for *AllMusic*, wrote: "Easily one of the standouts on the *Sunflower* album…There is a timeless quality to the whole piece, which is not unlike some of the more refined Elton John/Bernie Taupin ballads that would dominate the pop charts in the 1970's."208. In its review, *Mojo* wrote: "The lyrics read like a clumsy teenage love poem - but then he sings, his voice cracking as though red-raw from sobbing, locked out from the production's warm, dreamy reverb. By the last verse those simple words feel strangely profound: a final, weary plea from a broken man who is simply trying his best."25

Jonny Abrams wrote for *Rocksucker*: "Guiding the song from such fragility to such grand elegance, it is abundantly clear that Dennis had by now well and truly arrived as both songwriter and a singer."302

Although the production qualities are top notch, and the backing vocals sublime, its Dennis's heartfelt lead vocal that steals the show, a voice that would later be ruined by his excessive lifestyle. Despite his restless and sometimes maverick lifestyle, and apparent disregard for authority, Dennis had a big heart that always reflected in his songs.

Looking back on the song in 2008, Jakobson pondered: "God, what would it be like if Dennis had lived these last thirty years? because he was just starting to scratch the surface, musically... I'm convinced he would have gone well past his teachers, his brothers and so on. You couldn't ask for a greater teacher than Brian Wilson, of course, but I'm sure he would have gone past Brian."206

Eminent biographer David Leaf once remarked to Brian about seeing Dennis perform the song live: "I don't know why, but it was on that song that I missed Dennis the most. You know, the way he stands at the microphone, with his hand in his ear, his eyes closed, singing and swaying with the music. It's just not the same when he's not there."209

Peter Carlin surmised that Dennis could have been singing about the complicated relationship he had with his father: "All he wanted to achieve with his own music was a glimmer of respect from his father. The mutual disdain that divided Murry from his middle son during his adolescence and beyond had given way at first to tentative acceptance and then real affection."32 Jakobson would go on to write with Dennis on his celebrated solo album *Pacific Ocean Blue* in 1977.

The song was also re-re-recorded by Brian in 1972 for American Spring, (sisters Marilyn Wilson and Diane Rovell), while a stunning a capella version can be found on 2003's compilation *Hawthorne Ca,* and later on the 2021 *Feel Flows* box set.

There has been universal praise for Dennis, both as a Beach Boy and as a solo singer: "Lyrically Dennis was the diametric opposite to Van Dyke Parks,

Brian's *Smile* wordsmith. Masterfully evocative and baroque couplets like Parks' *"Columnated ruins domino"* ("Surf's Up") have no place in Dennis's universe. Instead, his lyrics are as direct and nakedly expressive as words can be, and probably no one got as much mileage out of the word 'love' as he did.210

By 1983, Dennis had become both unpredictable and unreliable, more so than his older brother, and as a result began to miss concerts. On September 26th, he made what would be his last appearance on stage with the band at the Pomona County Fairground. For the second show the following night, he turned up too drunk to play and was banned from the stage by the other band members. For the next three months, he hit a downward spiral, fuelled by drug and alcohol abuse. At Marina del Rey on December 28th, he went on another drinking binge and dived into the water from a yacht called *Emerald*, allegedly searching for objects he had previously thrown into the sea from a yacht he once owned called *Harmony*, which had since been repossessed for lack of regular payments. Now he desperately wanted them back. Although his girlfriend Colleen McGovern and his friend and yacht owner Bill Oster warned him not to keep diving, he ignored them.

At around 4.15pm he dived in one last time and never surfaced. His body was pulled from the water at 5.30pm, with tv news cameras there to report it, even before his fellow band members had heard about the tragedy. On January 4th 1984 a Federal law was waived to allow Dennis to be laid to rest at sea, as per the wishes of his wife Shawn, their divorce still having not been finalised. He was 39 years old.

Dennis once said: "Everything that I am or will ever be is in the music. If you want to know me, just listen." In listening to this song we may have a better understanding of this gentle soul who craved love, peace and harmony. He lived a life without compromise and loved music as much as he loved life itself, and in this wonderful song his voice conveys both a melancholic intimacy and a fragile vulnerability. He was every inch a victim of the California myth and the dream that died amid the reality of the changing times. He held a conviction that he could make it a better world with the sheer beauty of his songs, and there's nothing more compelling than "Forever."

This was his masterpiece, simple, yet adoringly sensitive, and he would never write a better one.

14. This Whole World (*Sunflower* 1970)
(Brian Wilson)
Recording
13/11/69 Beach Boys Studio, Bel Air (basic track, vocals)
18/02/70 (initial mastering)
Producers - The Beach Boys (Brian Wilson)
Engineer - Stephen Desper
Band members
Brian Wilson (intro lead vocal, backing vocals, piano); Mike Love (intro lead vocal, backing vocals); Carl Wilson (lead vocals, acoustic guitar); Dennis Wilson (backing vocals); Al Jardine(backing vocals); Bruce Johnston (backing vocals)
Session musicians/Guests
Jerry Cole (rhythm & lead guitar); David Cohen (lead guitar); Jack Conrad (bass); Ray Pohlman (6-string bass); Daryl Dragon (electric harpsichord, chimes, tubular bells); Dennis Dragon (drums); Gene Estes (chimes, glockenspiel); Marilyn Wilson (backing vocals); Diane Rovell (backing vocals).

Album released - 31/08/70
US single released - 29/06/70 b-side of "Slip on Through" Brother/Reprise 0929

The release of the album *Sunflower* in the summer of 1970 found the band gaining mastery of the studio, and, above all, enjoying what they were accomplishing. With much of the credit going to Carl, Dennis, engineer Steve Desper, and a temporary revived Brian, they managed to pull together long enough to produce what is arguably their most technically accomplished album.

With their new label Warner, the band could now take control of their own affairs, something that had been sadly lacking during their seven-year contract with Capitol. Whatsmore, in a short space of time they amassed over 40 new tracks of varying quality. Three potential playlists for the new album were submitted and rejected by sceptical label boss Mo Ostin, who felt they just weren't commercial enough. As a result songs like "Soulful Old Man Sunshine," "H.E.L.P Is On the Way," "When Girls Get Together," "Games Two Can Play," "Susie Cincinnati" and "Good Time," were shelved for one reason or another, although resurrected for later studio albums or compilations. In the meantime, Warner saw potential in at least one of the tracks and released "Add Some Music To Your Day" as a single in February 1970, although only peaking at #64 on the Hot 100.

"No one could consistently match the elegance of Brian Wilson. Here's proof"

Ostin, despite being a longtime fan of the band, showed little interest in some of the wonderful songs submitted by Carl and Dennis, and wanted Brian to reproduce some of the magic he had created during the *Smile* period. Warner's A&R executive Lenny Waronker even asked him to revisit "Cool, Cool Water," although it was Carl who expanded and completed the song as the album's finale. With the inclusion of the revised *Smile* track, Warner finally accepted the album.

All six band members contributed songs on the album, half of which are now considered masterpieces, but it was Brian's solo effort "This Whole World" that took fans and critics by surprise. In a 2011 interview, Brian explained that the song "was written in about an hour and a half [at his Bellagio mansion]. One night about two in the morning I got up and went to my white Baldwin organ and I was playing around and thinking about the love of this whole world and that's what inspired me to write the song."[63] In his since-discredited 1991 memoir he related that he was "stoned and confused" at the time.[28]

According to Brian the song is "about love in general…That song came from deep down in me, from the feeling I had that the whole world should be about love. When I wrote that song I wanted to capture that idea."[35] He would return to that message in 1988 with his signature solo song, "Love and Mercy."

"This Whole World" was produced and recorded in just one session at Brian's home studio, although he later claimed it took a "lot of hard work" over "a couple of days," and that "the guys in the band loved it too."[170] According to him, he taught Carl to sing lead and the others to do the background vocals, "especially the meditation part at the end: 'Om dot dit it.'"[35]

According to Keith Badman, the original track was longer but was then trimmed down. An insight into what it may have contained would emerge two years later when Brian, with co-producers Steve Desper and David Sandler, re-recorded it for the *Spring* album by Marilyn Wilson and Diane Rovell. Brian would also go on to re-record the song for his 1995 soundtrack album, *I Just Wasn't Made For These Times*.11

Before the release of *Sunflower*, Warner included the song on their first $2 mail-order *Big Ball* album, the first in a series of Lost Leader samplers that featured tracks from a selection of their signings. They also released "This Whole World" as the flip-side to the single of Dennis's "Slip On Through," but it failed to get into the charts.

This utterly magnificent song of a little under two minutes has been widely celebrated over the years for its astounding arrangement. Musician Scott McCaughey noted that although it followed an A/B/C/A/B/C pattern, "it seems to never repeat itself once." As for the background vocals building to what Mark Dillon calls "a spine-chilling intersection of four vocal parts," McCaughey wrote: "That's one of the most brilliant things about it - it builds to that majestic a capella ending and then fades so quickly. You want it to go on forever."10 Philp Lambert described it as "tonal transience,"211 and *AllMusic's* Matthrew Greenwald confirmed: "Brian reestablished his reputation as one of the most brilliant melody writers and arrangers. With a buoyant melody and an effervescent, classy vocal arrangement, Brian wipes away three years of artistic cobwebs."212 In 1978 Daryl Dragon commented on the various key changes: "From a harmony standpoint, I've never heard a song like that since I've been in pop music. I've never heard a song go through that many changes and come back."122

Perhaps the best praise came from Rick Swan: "Following a rocker from Dennis Wilson ["Slip on Through"], the song blasts off into the Milky Way, changing keys and direction seemingly at random, accompanied by a heart-wrenching melody and an irresistible backing chorus of doo-wop syllables... A silky smooth verse eases into an elegant bridge of breathtaking harmonies, climaxing with a thrilling a capella section that in turn serves up a final, gorgeous multi-part rendering of the title, pure Beach Boy heaven. Of all the first-class rock composers - the Beatles, Jimi Hendrix, the Stones, anybody - no one could consistently match the elegance of Brian Wilson. Here's proof."21

13. 'Til I Die (*Surf's Up* 1971)
(Brian Wilson)
Recording
04/11/69 Beach Boys Studio, Bel Air (piano demo)
15/08/70 Beach Boys Studio, Bel Air (*Surf's Up* version - 5 takes)
01/09/70 Beach Boys Studio, Bel Air (mastering for *Landlocked* album - minus Brian's lead)
30/07/71 Beach Boys Studio, Bel Air
Producer - The Beach Boys
Engineer - Stephen Desper
Band members
Brian Wilson (lead & backing vocals, Hammond organ; Rocksichord, snare drum, Maestro Rhythm King MRK 2 drum machine); Mike Love (lead & backing vocals); Carl Wilson (lead & backing vocals, acoustic guitar); Al Jardine (backing vocals); Bruce Johnston (backing vocals, Hammond organ)
Guests

Daryl Dragon (bass guitar, vibraphone); Steve Desper (Moog synthesiser).
Album released - 30/08/71
US single released - 11/10/71 b-side to "Long Promised Road" Brother/Reprise 1047 #89

One of the few songs in which Brian wrote both the music and the lyrics, and, according to *Mojo*, "one of his most beautiful, sophisticated, moving songs."25 On the surface, the lyrics seem almost suicidal with his dark descriptions of death and hopelessness. According to Brian it was written while suffering from an existential crisis over personal identity and strong belief that life lacked meaning, symptoms that apparently were not taken seriously by family and friends. In an earlier interview in November 1970, he admitted: "I'm not unhappy with life; in fact I'm quite happy living at home."11

Brian, perhaps through a ghost writer, described where the inspiration for the song came from: "One night, I drove to the beach, parked the car, and walked out into the deserted sand...Lately, I'd been depressed and preoccupied with death. I'd ordered the gardener to dig a grave in the backyard and threatened to drive my Rolls off the Santa Monica pier...Looking out toward the ocean, my mind, as it did almost every hour of every day, worked to explain the inconsistencies that dominated my life; the pain, torment, and confusion and the beautiful music I was able to make. Was there an answer? Did I have no control? Had I ever? Feeling shipwrecked on an existential island, I lost myself in the balance of darkness that stretched beyond the breaking waves to the other side of the earth. The ocean was so incredibly vast, the universe was so large, and suddenly I saw myself in proportion to that, a little pebble of sand, a jellyfish floating on top of the water; traveling with the current I felt dwarfed, temporary. The next day I began writing 'Til I Die,' perhaps the most personal song I ever wrote for The Beach Boys...In doing so, I wanted to re- create the swell of emotions that I'd felt at the beach the previous night. For several weeks I struggled at the piano, experimenting with rhythms and chord changes, trying to emulate in sound the ocean's shifting tides and moods as well as its sheer enormity. I wanted the music to reflect the loneliness of floating a raft in the middle of the Pacific. I wanted each note to sound as if I was disappearing into the hugeness of the universe."11

"The most beautiful suicide note you'll ever hear ... the last song of this stature he'll ever write"

The first thing that came to him when writing was being like a cork in the ocean, a rock in a landslide and a leaf on windy day - all small, helpless, inanimate objects being moved inconceivable distances by forces beyond his comprehension: "I struggled at the piano, experimenting with rhythms and chord changes, trying to emulate in sound the ocean's shifting tides and moods as well as its sheer enormity. I wanted the music to reflect the loneliness of floating a raft in the middle of the Pacific. I wanted each note to sound as if it was disappearing into the hugeness of the universe"11

Brian recorded a solo piano demo of the song in November 1969 and presented it the band members. With one member voiced his concerns, according to Bruce, Brian "decided not to show it to us for a few months. He just put it away. I mean, he was absolutely crushed."122 Various sources pointed at Mike calling the song a "downer" and that the song's lyrics were drug-derived.213 In response, Brian changed some of the lyrics (which can be found on the 2021 *Feel Flows* box set), but was urged by the other members to keep the original ones. Dennis was absent at the first session due to filming for the movie *Two Lane Blacktop,* and a Maestro Rhythm drum machine was brought in for the basic track.

Record producer Don Was described meeting Brian at the presentation for his Les Paul Award in November 1996: "I wanted to know what was going through his mind when he wrote 'Til I Die'…specifically, what prompts a person to write a song so chordally complex that it is impossible for me to tell you what key it's in. He told me that he was sitting at a piano, creating geometric patterns with his fingers, trying not to move the fingers on the outside of the patterns, but limiting changes to internal movements. When he landed on a shape that both looked cool and sounded good, he wrote it down. So, essentially he created this masterpiece by contorting his fingers into really groovy shapes. Well, I thought that this was one of the most brilliant things I'd ever heard. If I were to sit at a piano for 200 years, I don't believe such a method of songwriting would ever occur to me. But I must tell you that I've absolutely no idea whether he was just making it up on the spot to entertain me."94

Brian's bandmates were equally impressed. Al described it as "really a good vocal sound. I think Desper deserves all the credit on that one. I mean we just had the best microphones, the best microphone technique and engineering on that particular piece and that particular time." Bruce described it as the last great Brian Wilson song, and went on to say: "The track is very simple…and the great, great vocal arrangement that he wrote. Really, a great piece of work…the words absolutely fit his mindset." Even Mike admitted in a 2015 interview that the song was his favourite of any written solely by Brian, and although saying he didn't like the line "*it kills me soul,*" understood what he was saying.214. Even Brian went on to say that the song "summed up everything I had to say at the time."11

In 1995 Brian re-recorded a sparser version of the song for his solo album and documentary, *I Just Wasn't Made For These Times.*

The critics were unanimous in their praise. *Rolling Stone* opined: "There are many myths surrounding the Beach Boys, but the most persistent one is that Brian Wilson never contributed anything of value to the band after *Smile* collapsed in 1967. There are mountains of evidence to contradict that, but none are quite as persuasive as 1971's achingly-gorgeous 'Til I Die.'"216. Jon Stebbins was in agreement, writing that the song "proves that Brian could not only write beautiful music, but that he had the ability to communicate honestly and artfully with his lyrics as well. The track is decorated with a haunting vibraphone and organ bed, which frames the strong harmony vocal arrangement perfectly."140

Rick Swan described it as "the most beautiful suicide note you'll ever hear…It is an achingly poignant song of desperation and longing, a song that ranks with Brian's peak accomplishments and, sadly, the last song of this stature he'll ever write…It's a depressing song, but also opulent, sensuous and stunning."21

Christian Matijas-Mecca called it an "excellent and all-embracing song that taps into the era of peace and harmony. The melody and accompaniment seemingly comes from two distant points in Brian's colour scheme, as the melody gently floats from one cadence to the next in an irresistible groove. This glorious work is under two minutes in length and ends all too quickly."5 The *Guardian* described it simply "as spine-tingling as anything in the Beach Boys Catalogue."42

12. In My Room (*Surfer Girl* 1963)
(Brian Wilson, Gary Usher)
Recording
16/07/63 Western Recorders, LA (basic vocal track - take #13 master)
26/08/63 Capitol Studio, Hollywood (mastering)
03/03/64 Western Recorders, LA (German language version - "Ganz Allein")
Producer - Brian Wilson
Engineer - Chuck Britz (*Western*)
Band members
Brian Wilson (lead vocal, organ, bass); Mike Love (backing vocals); Carl Wilson (backing vocals, guitar); Dennis Wilson (backing vocals, drums); Al Jardine (backing vocals); David Marks (guitar)
Session musicians/Guests
Hal Blaine (triangle, wood block or temple block), Maureen Love (harp)
Album released - 16/09/63
US single released - 28/10/63 b-side to "Be True To Your School" Capitol 5069 #23
Film/TV performances
14/03/64 NBC Television Studios, Burbank (part of concert for screening in selected US cinemas; later released in 1998 as *The Lost Concert*
12/05/64 *The Red Skelton Show* CBS Hollywood
16/06/69 Olympia Theater Paris TFI (filmed concert)
21/01/77 Capital Theatre, Washington DC
21/06/80 Knebworth England concert (later released on CD/DVD)

With the Beach Boys' focus firmly on sun, surfing, cars, and other teenage fantasies during the period 1962-63, it was quite unexpected that two of Brian's greatest introspective and prophetic songs of the period, "Lonely Sea" and "In My Room," were co-written by Gary Usher, a 23-year-old bank teller from Beverly Hills, who, after visiting his uncle's house across the street from the Wilsons one Sunday in January 1962, strolled across and introduced himself to the boys while they were rehearsing in their converted garage. After contributing five songs for the band's debut album *Surfin' Safari* and the wonderful "Lonely Sea" for *Surfin' USA* just six months later, Usher once again joined Brian to write perhaps their finest song.

Usher recalled: "Brian was always saying that his room was his whole world," and Brian agreed: "I had a room, and I thought of it as my kingdom. And I wrote that song, very definitely, that you're not afraid when your'e in your room, Its absolutely true." He went on to say: "Gary recognised that the music room [in the Wilson house] served as a sanctuary to me. He never got over the fact that I slept there, right beside the piano."

Musicologist Philp Lambert described its significance: "So different from everything else on the album - no surfing, no cars, no celebration of teenage fun and games, just a guy alone in his room, contemplating the meaning of life…it's an idealised sanctuary, an escape from the sensory stimulation just outside the walls…For a twenty-one-year-old prodigy feeling the pressures of art, business and family, and for the kids buying his records, it's a very important place indeed."9

In the 1998 *Endless Harmony* documentary, Brian described the song as being about "somewhere where you could lock out the world, go to a secret little place, think, be, do whatever you have to do…I wrote it with a friend of mine, Gary Usher. We wrote it and then later on I said, 'Hey, these lyrics. I could use these lyrics.' After I had done the whole song, I looked back and said , "Oh, I know what I did. I was writing about myself."11

> ### *"For a twenty-one-year-old prodigy feeling the pressures of art, business and family, and for the kids buying his records, it's a very important place indeed"*

Usher described the time they worked together on the song: "'In My Room' found us taking our craft a little more seriously. Brian and I came back to the house one night after playing "over-the-line" (a baseball game). I played bass and Brian was on organ. The song was written in an hour…Brian's melody all the way. The sensitivity…the concept meant a lot to him. When we finished, it was late, after our midnight curfew. In fact, Murry came in a couple of times and wanted me to leave. Anyway, we got Audree, who was putting her hair up before bed, and we played for her. She said, 'That's the most beautiful song you've ever written.' Murry said, 'Not bad, Usher, not bad' which was the nicest thing he ever said to me."168

In 1990 Brian recalled another story behind the song: "When Dennis, Carl and I lived in Hawthorne as kids, we all slept in the same room. One night I sang the song 'Ivory Tower' to them and they liked it. Then a couple of weeks later, I proceeded to teach them both how to sing the harmony parts to it. It took them a little while, but they finally learned it. We then sang this song night after night. It brought peace to us. When we recorded 'In My Room', there was just Dennis, Carl and me on the first verse…and we sounded just like we did in our bedroom all those nights. This story has more meaning than ever since Dennis' death."168

During the recording session, much to the frustration of the boys, Murry Wilson was in the control room giving his usual orders over the studio intercom.

The wonderful guitar/harp introduction to the song was partly inspired by the doo-wop group The Jive Five and their "What Time Is It?" a #67 Hot 100 hit in 1962. The demo version of the song starts with an intro that was later discarded before launching into full group vocals on the first verse, unlike the finished recording which has Brian's voice first, then Carl's, and finally Dennis's. For the title/hook in the final verse, Al and Mike's bass voices join the others to complete the vocal mix. Christian Matijas-Mecca described Brian's impressive arrangement: "The finger cymbals and harp glissando in the introduction lift this song from the predictable into the very personal and private realm of Brian's inner world. His arrangement of the triplet accompaniment figure that runs through the song never becomes boring as he foregrounds and accumulates more colours that allow the richness of the song to climax in the final verse."5

It is still unclear whether the fully developed demo which is featured on the 1993 *Good Vibrations* box set was recorded the same day as the final version. With all six members present, it signalled the last of eight charting songs that included David Marks, and would remain so for nearly 50 years when he performed on "That's Why God Made the Radio" in 2012.

Beach Boy historian James B Murphy identified with the song's impact on teenagers: "[It] helped teens better understand their world, exploring their feelings without condescension, trivialisation, or melodrama. It gave voice to emotions most kids could not verbalise. Brian and Usher made it okay, daresay normal, to reveal that you felt safe and comforted in your room, even in the dark...They knew, however subconsciously, that your room was your sanctuary, an impenetrable refuge where you left the world's troubles outside. It was your friend, confidante, and confessor. Great art is personal, resonating within us some mysterious and permanent way."[3]

Other artists later reflected on the impact of the song. Journey's Steve Perry told *Rolling Stone*: "This was an anthem to my teenage isolation. I just wanted to be left alone in my room, where I could find peace of mind and lay music." David Crosby, a huge fan of Brian's, admitted: "He was the most highly regarded pop musician in America. Hands down. Everybody by that time had figured out who was writing it all and who was arranging it all. 'In My Room' was a defining point for me. When I heard it, I thought, "Okay, I give up. I can't do that. I'll never be able to do that.'" Many years later he would get the chance to sing it, along with Carly Simon and Jimmy Webb, at *An All-Star Tribute to Brian Wilson* concert in 2001. Linda Ronstadt recalled: "What a heartrending song. When you think about it, I won't be afraid. A place where I'll be safe. They were really deep, profound emotions that came out of a lot of pain. There was nothing shallow about it."[3]

Cash Box described the song as "a tearful, oh-so-smooth ballad,"[259] while in its retrospective review, *Mojo* opined: "This idea of the teenage bedroom as a cloistered shrine is underlined by the song's sparse arrangement, the group's sweet-sad harmony vocals, and faint hint of organ bringing a churchly calm to Brian's confessional."[25] Rick Swan stated: "Maybe Brian - the Reflective Introvert - is trying to tell us that alone in his room, he's in his own universe, a perfect place. Sad and true, but also powerful, revealing Brian as an insightful young man who was quickly outgrowing the fluff of '409' and 'Shut Down.'"[21]

In March 1964 the band recorded a German-language version of the song called "Ganz allein," with lyrics apparently written by a German ex-girlfriend of Mike's. Unlike the Beatles' similar versions of two of their early songs, the Beach Boys' version was never released, remaining shelved until appearing on 1983's *Rarities* album. As an indication of its impact, "In My Room" went on to be inducted into the Grammy Hall of Fame in 1999.

Usher's success with Brian would turn out to be short-lived. Despite their incredible work together, he made no secret of his dislike for Murry Wilson and showed nothing but contempt for his musical ideas. Murry knew it very well and went out of his way to get him out of the picture by nit-picking over song credits and criticising the quality of his work. According to Brian, he believed Murry's suspected that Usher was trying to drive a wedge between him and his brothers, and that he was thinking of his own concerns and not what was best for the band. While looking for another collaborator to replace him, Murry formed his own publishing company, Sea of Tunes, to personally handle all of Brian's songs. That meant if Usher was going to write songs with Brian, he would split the publishing three ways between Brian, Usher and himself. Usher wrote: "When the deal was made, if I wanted my money, I had to sign a contract," meaning as a writer his royalties were limited.

At one time it was alleged that Usher had stolen a microphone at one of the Western sessions, and when Murry heard about it he threw him out of the fold, only for Capitol's promotion man Mike Borchetta to persuade him to let him back in. But it caused hard feelings about Usher for both Murry and his wife Audree, and his work with Brian soon began to diminish. Once Brian followed Murry's advice and started collaborating with Roger Christian, Usher felt crushed by their new friendship: "I no longer enjoyed Brian's company. It was a great relationship and it slowly drifted apart for no reason..."123

It all came to a head when Murry found out that Dennis, after a heated argument with him, had moved out and become Usher's roommate. Usher recalled: "When Murry found out I might as well have been dead." It sealed his fate, and Murry ordered him out of the band's professional circle forever. To rub salt into the wound, Capitol then released two of Usher's collaborations, "Ten Little Indians" and "County Fair" as the next single.

Usher was not the only one to leave the Beach Boys circle. Around the same time, 15-year-old David Marks got into an argument with Murry, leading him to quit the band on July 30th 1963: "We were in a car on the way to Chicago when I announced I was quitting the group. Murry went, "Well, all right man. Does everybody hear that? And all the guys went, 'Ah, that's bullshit!' It turned out I still had seven months' worth of contracts, so could've stayed after that if I hadn't started pushing it..."11

Murry's dominating influence on the band in these early days was a two-edged sword. Without him, they would never have become a successful band; but with him, his unwelcomed and unnecessary interference in their career would prove both damaging and detrimental to Brian's development as both writer and producer. It was only a matter of time, but something had to give...

11. You Still Believe In Me *(Pet Sounds* 1966*)*
(Brian Wilson, Tony Asher)
Recording
14/10/65 Western Recorders, LA (tracking for "Untitled")
01/11/65 Western Recorders, LA (tracking for "In My Childhood")
24/01/66 Western Recorders, LA (tracking for "You Still Believe In Me" inc intro - 23 takes, vocal overdubs)
16/02/66 Western Recorders, LA (vocals)
Producer - Brian Wilson
Engineer - Chuck Britz
Band members
Brian Wilson (lead vocal, plucked piano strings); Mike Love (bass vocals & backing vocals); Carl Wilson (backing vocals); Dennis Wilson (backing vocals); Al Jardine (backing vocals); Bruce Johnston (backing vocals)
Session musicians/Guests
Hal Blaine (bicycle horn, finger cymbals); Glen Campbell (double-tracked 12-string electric lead guitars); Al De Lory (harpsichord); Steve Douglas (acoustic grand piano); Bill Green (contra-clarinet); John Horn (clarinet); Plas Johnson (clarinet); Carol Kaye (electric bass); Barney Kessel (double-tracked 12-string electro mando-guitars); Jay Migliori (bass clarinet); Lyle Ritz (upright bass); Julius Wechter (bicycle bell, timpani); Tony Asher (plucked piano strings); Marilyn Wilson (possibly additional vocals on intro)

Album released -16/05/66

On January 24th 1966 Brian sat down at the piano with new lyricist Tony Asher to develop a song that Brian had written during the latter part of the previous year with the title "In My Childhood." The instrumental track had been recorded on November 1st, along with another called "Trombone Dixie, and tentative lyrics had also been written, ones that Brian was not too happy with. Nothing more would be done until sessions got underway for *Pet Sounds* at the start of the new year.

Asher recalled: "On the first day of our collaboration, Brian played me the melody for a song he'd written called 'In My Childhood.' If I remember correctly, the original melody sounded exactly the way it does on the album, and someone had already written lyrics. Brian never played me the existing lyric - he played the instrumental track and said, 'I don't even want you to hear the lyric that's been written.' He gave me a tape of the track - a cassette - and then went to the piano and made a second tape, with him playing the melody and singing dummy lyrics. I took the two cassettes from that first day home and wrote the lyric…apart from Brian. He liked the lyric I came up with, and though we may have tinkered with few lines here or there, it's the song you hear on the album."85

"…[the] *moment that you realise that something in pop music has irrevocably crossed the line and merged with a classical sensibility"*

In an earlier interview, Asher commented on Brian's original song: "We wiped off those vocals and that melody and rewrote it…The [chord] changes were the only thing that stayed the same."122

In their first collaboration since Brian first contacted Asher in December 1965, the song was given a new title, "You Still Believe In Me," with revised lyrics (apparently including some input from Mike) that have the narrator confessing his inadequacies before the girl he loves, while at the same time acknowledging her undying loyalty to him. Mark Dillon described it simply as "a musing about the ups and downs of adult romance."10

Marilyn Wilson later surmised how the song could reflect on their ongoing marital struggles at the time. When asked about the song, she responded: "He knew that he was not a good husband and that I was lonely, and really didn't get much back from him, and he made me cry all the time. It was like there wasn't much of a relationship. The only way we related was musically. I could always sing the part he needed me to…I understood, and I could hear, and I could sing."130

This was something that biographer Timothy White also noticed: "[The song] was an interior monologue of self-doubt, exploring and debating Marilyn's patient capacity to forgive Brian's selfishness and creative absorption. Contrasting the rude force of their frequent breakups with the softer tone of their reconciliations, Brian admits the only time he feels in control of the relationship is when she's providing the stability, although he's unable to be what she wants him to be. There is no resolution of the problem, Brian concluding that he wants to 'cry.'"32

After just a single day in his company, Asher had seemingly learned a lot more about Brian's inner feelings than many others, with the possible exception of his wife. Brian explained his thoughts on the song: "[Its] more of what I would call a man who would be afraid to take all of his clothes off and sing like a girl because he had feelings for people from that perspective. I was able to close my eyes and go into a world and sing a little more effeminately and more sweet - which allows a lot more love to come down through me...."72

With just this one song under their belt, Brian was now convinced he had found the perfect lyricist for the album, summing it up as a 'little "Boys Choir" - type song, and one that was "very, very spiritual."72. Asher also found comfort and confidence in their new relationship: "I wasn't petrified when I handed that lyric to him. I was hopeful he would like it, but I wasn't shaking in my boots. Usually when you create something like that, it's pretty fragile."10

The song's placement on the album, immediately following "Wouldn't It Be Nice," was an intended inspiration, and one that *AllMusic's* Jim Esch identified with: "'You Still Believe in Me' develops a theme inaugurated and suggested by 'Wouldn't It Be Nice': fragile lovers buckling under the pressure of external forces they can't control, self-imposed romantic expectations and personal limitations, while simultaneously trying to maintain faith in one other. It is a theme that keeps reverberating sweetly, and hauntingly, throughout *Pet Sounds*."221

Bruce wrote of his pleasure to be a part of the recording: "[Brian] accommodated six voices...and he didn't really have to. He found a part for each of us in the room, which was really great, because if you think of it, he really only needed four parts. He didn't have to be that kind to me, but while he was training me, he allowed the spotlight to shine on me at the same time."72

With a mature lyric and a graceful and spiritual melody, Brian tops it off with one of the most remarkable vocals of his career, something that didn't escape the many reviewers. Kingsley Abbott wrote: "The delicacy of relationships is echoed in the arrangement that interweaves the instruments in a gossamer mix highlighted by finger cymbals. Everything is gently restrained, and the incongruity of a bicycle bell and a bull horn serve to catch the listener's closer attention. Brian's tender lead is boosted by the group unison vocals on the title, and the *'I wanna cry'* end tag introduces another musical motif, with the vocals following gradually descending notes. These descents can be found in more obvious patterns on the bass guitar elsewhere on the album, most notably on 'Here Today.'"75

Jim Fusilli opined: "The vocals...are nothing short of remarkable. After opening with a unison statement in which the group issues a gloomy hum, Brian enters with a subdued lead that builds steadily to the top of his falsetto. The group re-enters to sing the title and Brian repeats the melody of the first verse. Brian sings *'I wanna cry'* by himself, his voice soaring then coming down, note by extended note. Mike and Al restate in the baritone range what Brian sang, and then all the voices, with Brian on top, join in to dart around and under Brian's original line, repeatedly referring to the B note that begins the phrase. Yet another temp change and the kettledrums reinforce the majesty of the moment. The finger cymbals tap on the two. And to confuse us even further, the bicycle horn bleats on every other four into the fade."130

Musicologist Philip Lambert noted how "the chordal underpinning of the main verse and chorus contributes to the theme...as it repeats simple chord progression over and over, almost as if 'motorised' by a few turns of a crank at the back of the box...The repetitive predictability of the track thus comes to represent the constancy of the girl's faith and spirit, while the overall 'juvenile' sound captures the guy's immaturity."9

And then there's what's Rick Swan calls that gorgeous "tinkling jack-in-the-box" opening that has been a subject discussed by musicologists for decades.21 Asher wrote in 1996: "We were trying to do something that would sound sort of, I guess, like a harpsichord but a little more ethereal than that, and I think it was successful, an interesting little part of the song. He was doing the hard part; he was holding down the right notes. On a piano, if you pluck that has the hammers down on it, nobody can really tell, but if you hit the open strings, it sounds good if they're the right open strings. And he made sure they were the right open strings."72 In another interview, he described plucking "the strings with paper clips, hairpins, bobby pins and several other things until Brian got the sound he wanted."72

As for the sound of the bicycle bell and horn, a remnant of Brian's original recording, Asher admitted: "That was kept ... not because anybody thought it was a good idea to keep it [but] because it was mixed down into a track. You didn't have twenty-four tracks in those days, and you mixed some tracks that would lock in." According to Charles Granata, their imaginative use "evoke a juvenile air that [would mirror] the immature attitude projected by [Asher's] lyric."85

Record Mirror's Norman Jopling, who may have been having ear trouble at the time, called the song "slightly off-tune...[it has] a delicate backing which thank heavens doesn't interfere with the complicated but smooth-flowing harmonies,222 while, on reflection, *Mojo* offered: "Amid the music-box melancholia, the bicycle bell and antique car horn betray an infant playfulness, along with the head-in-the-piano string plucks that opens its utterly gorgeous two-and-a-half minutes."25 *AllMusic* also looked back on the song, describing it as signalling to listeners "that something new and wonderful was happening to pop music" with its end coda being the "moment that you realise that something in pop music has irrevocably crossed the line and merged with a classical sensibility."221

Perhaps the greatest compliment came from longtime Beach Boy fan Sir Paul McCartney, who revealed in a 1990 interview his admiration for Brian's falsetto on the *'I Wanna cry'* part: "I love that melody. That kills me, that melody...That's my favourite, I think. The way that's arranged, where it goes away very quietly. I was in the car the other night, and I was telling the kids, saying, 'wait, wait, here it comes.' And then it comes back, and it's so beautiful right at the end, comes surging back in these multi-coloured harmonies. Sends shivers up my spine. That's one of my favourite tracks."72

10. The Warmth of the Sun *(Shut Down Volume 2 1964)*
(Brian Wilson, Mike Love)
Recording
01/01/64 Western Recorders, LA (tracking & vocal overdubs)
08/01/64 Gold Star Studio, LA (vocals)
Producer - Brian Wilson

Engineer - Chuck Britz
Band members
Brian Wilson (lead vocal, backing vocals, piano); Mike Love (backing vocals); Carl Wilson (backing vocals, lead guitar); Dennis Wilson (backing vocals, drums);Al Jardine (backing vocals, rhythm guitar)
Session musicians
Ray Pohlman (bass guitar); Hal Blaine (bell tree, clinking percussion); Steve Douglas (tenor sax); Jay Migliori (baritone sax)
Album released - 02/03/64
US single released - 26/10/64 b-side to "Dance, Dance, Dance" Capitol 5306 #8
UK single released - 01/65 b-side to "Dance, Dance, Dance" Capitol CL 15370 #24
Film/TV performance
16/06/69 Olympia Theater Paris TFI (filmed concert)

One of Brian and Mike's most poignant ballads, mainly as being partly inspired by the tragic assassination of President John F Kennedy on November 22nd 1963. Together as a tribute the two of them composed an extraordinarily beautiful song about the pain and heartbreak of a failed romance and the consolation given by the warmth and light shining down from above. Accounts vary as to where and when the song was written.

According to Peter Carlin, Brian and Mike had started writing the song a day or two before the assassination and were still working on it on the day.32 Mike recalled in 2008: "The melody that Brian came up with was very melancholy. I'd had an experience where this girl I liked decided she didn't want to reciprocate, so I wrote the lyrics from the perspective of, 'Yes, things have changed and love is no longer there, but the memory of it is like the warmth of the sun.' I think it's really impactful and memorable…I was looking for a silver lining in that cumulus nimbus, accentuating the positive. I wanted our music to provide a sonic oasis, a place where literally you could go, like in 'In My Room,' and tell your troubles to - or at least lose yourself in the music."157

> **"The best Brian-and-Mike song ever written…When you listen to the intro there are no words, and you think, What's coming next?"**

19-year-old concert promoter Fred Vail takes up his version of the story: "[November 22nd 1963] was just another work day for me: putting the finishing touches on my Beach Boys' *Dance and Show* that night, fifty miles north of Sacramento, in Marysville, California. Before the band took to the stage at around 9.30pm, Vail asked the audience for a moment of silence for the late President, and, following the performance, he recalled: "We headed back to the El Dorado Hotel [in Sacramento], excited about the success of the evening's performance, but still very mindful of the tragic events that had happened just twelve of fourteen hours before…It was probably about 1am when we got back to the rooms... the boys were amazed, perhaps shocked, to see three of four thousand dollars in cash sitting on the bed and it was all theirs… As we all began to wind down from the events of the day, I looked over at Brian and Mike as they began working on a song that they'd already started earlier that morning. They were in the corner of the small room, still tightening up lyrics, working on the melody, and humming and singing a few lines there. By about 2am or so, the song was nearly complete. It would be a special tribute to our nation's 35th President…"217

Mike later recalled writing the song: "We woke up in the morning to the news that President Kennedy had been shot and was on his way to Parkland Memorial Hospital. We all know the result of that incident. But it was such a haunting, melancholy, sad musical composition…And the only thing I could relate to in terms of lyrics was the loss of someone you love. In that lyrical treatment, it was about somebody who you were in love with, but they don't feel the same way anymore. So they fell out of love with you. And that's a loss of love, but not quite as dramatic as being shot and killed. We didn't change the lyrics to conform to the event, but because of that event, when we recorded the song just a day or two later, it was charged with emotion. There's no doubt about that. And I think you can feel it in the lyric and the music combined…"217

In his 2016 memoir, Brian described a completely different version: "When the shooting happened, everyone knew instantly. It was all over the tv and on every kind of news. I called Mike and he asked me if I wanted to write a song about it. I said sure. It seemed like something we had to think about, and songs were the way I thought about things. We drove over to my office and in a half hour we had 'The Warmth of the Sun.' We didn't think of it as a big song. It was a personal response but it got bigger over time because of the history linked to it."35

When asked whether the song had been written prior to the assassination, or had been written in Brian's office in Hollywood, Veil replied: "They had already been working on the melody and a few of the lyrics written before we got back to the hotel. I've heard stories over the years about problems with Brian's girlfriend or Mike's girlfriend being part of the inspiration for the lyrics and this very well may have been true at the beginning of the writing process. But by the time they finished the song up that night, there was no question that the lyrics took on a more sombre meaning as they related to the events in Dallas earlier that day."217

In the 1995 documentary *I Just Wasn't Made For These Times* Brian recalled the natural despondency when they heard about the shooting: "It was a spiritual night. We got going and a mood took over us. Something took over. I can't explain it…Mike flipped out. He said, 'That's one of the most spiritual songs I've ever heard.' I said, 'Those lyrics are beautiful' He wrote those lyrics. You know, stuff like that happens every 20 years. It doesn't happen every day. JFK gets shot to death and the Beach Boys go write 'The Warmth of the Sun.'"11

Speaking to BBC Radio 1, Mike revealed: "We wrote [that song] about losing someone close. I had someone in mind. 'It didn't work out but I still had the warmth of the sun,' meaning the warmth of the memory within…"11

Despite the controversy and the conflicting anecdotes, the song remains one of the three bona fide classics that grace the *Shut Down Volume 2* album (along with "Fun, Fun, Fun" and "Don't Worry Baby.") The song has even been cited as Brian pioneering the use of adventurous chord changes in pop music, with its amazing transition from C to A-Minor to E-Flat apparently unheard of in 1964.218

Cash Box described the song as "an ultra-lovely, lazy paced ballad that the boys deliver in oh-so smooth, ear-arresting fashion,"219 while *Mojo* praised Brian's lead: "In his purest, most aching falsetto, Brian, assuaged by others, transcends the pain to deliver words of hope and comfort"25 Donald Guarisco of *AllMusic* wrote: "The sublime balance of lush vocals and sensitive songwriting made [the song] one of the Beach Boys' finest and most moving ballads."220. Even Murry Wilson liked it enough to record it himself for his 1967 solo album, *The Many Moods of Murry Wilson*, and in 2002 Brian had the honour to perform it at Queen Elizabeth's Jubilee Concert in London, with a little help from Eric Clapton on vocals.

Bruce described it as "the best Brian-and-Mike song ever written. I flipped out with the harmony and the chord changes. When you listen to the intro there are no words, and you think, What's coming next?"25

Seven days after the assassination, Capitol released the Beatles' "I Want to Hold Your Hand." marking the start of the British Invasion and ushering in what would be one of the most exciting periods in the history of popular music.

9. I Get Around (*All Summer Long* 1964)
(Brian Wilson, Mike Love)

Recording
02/04/64 Western Recorders, LA (tracking - take #15 master, vocal overdubbing, guitar & keyboard inserts)
10/04/64 Western Recorders, LA (vocals)
Producer - Brian Wilson
Engineer - Chuck Britz
Band members
Brian Wilson (chorus falsetto lead vocal, harmony & backing vocals, piano, harpsichord, Hammond B3 organ); Mike Love (lead vocal, harmony & backing vocals); Carl Wilson (harmony & backing vocals, electric lead & rhythm guitars); Dennis Wilson (harmony & backing vocals, drums); Al Jardine (harmony & backing vocals)
Session musicians
Hal Blaine (timbales with brush, rim with thin stick); Glen Campbell (6-string electric bass guitar); Ray Pohlman (6-string electric bass guitar); Steve Douglas (possibly tenor sax); Jay Migliori (possibly baritone sax)
Album released - 13/07/64
US single released - 11/05/64 b/w "Don't Worry Baby" Capitol5174 #1
UK single released - 06/64 b/w "Don't Worry Baby" Capitol CL 15350 #7
Film/TV performances
12/05/64 *The Red Skelton Show* CBS Hollywood
27/09/64 *The Ed Sullivan Show* CBS New York
28/20/64 *The TAMI Show* (recorded at the Civic Auditorium, Santa Monica for cinema release)
05/11/64 *The Beat Room* BBC-2 London (broadcast 09/11/64)
06/11/64 *Ready Steady Go!* ARTV London
18/11/64 *Age Tendre Et Tete De Bois* TF2 Paris
16/06/69 Olympia Theater Paris TFI (filmed concert)
21/01/77 Capital Centre, Washington DC
21/06/80 Knebworth England concert (later released on CD/DVD)

On February 7th 1964, the Beatles landed at JFK International Airport. From that day, the country's teenage girls would never be the same again. Signed to Capitol, the Fab Four shared the same label as the Beach Boys, and their arrival was followed by a series of raucous concerts and legendary appearances on the Ed Sullivan Show (the first attracting a tv audience of some 74 million). Almost five days before they landed, the Beach Boys had returned from their successful tour of Australia and New Zealand and on February 3rd their electrifying single "Fun, Fun, Fun" was released in the US. Although widely believed to be heading for the top of the charts, it stalled at #5 on the Hot 100, behind the Four Seasons' "Dawn (Go Away)" and the trio of recently released singles by the Liverpool Four.

The mass hysteria created by the Beatles' arrival was seen as a big test for Brian and the band. 17-year-old Carl was already a fan, having their pictures adorning his bedroom walls, and even Brian would soon go on to say that "I Want To Hold Your Hand" had blown his mind, admitting that: "I knew we were good, but it wasn't until the Beatles arrived that I knew we had to get going. The Beatles invasion shook me up a lot. They eclipsed a lot of what we'd worked for. We were naturally jealous. I just couldn't handle the fact that there were these four guys from England coming over here to America to invade our territory. When we saw how everybody was screaming for the Beatles, it was like, Whooa! We couldn't believe it. I was shook up as hell."11

Brian recalled going out to dinner with Mike a week after "I Want To Hold Your Hand" was released, and a discouraged Mike "scratching his head, saying, 'What the f**k is going on here?' Brian told him that they shouldn't quit, and went on to say: "We were very threatened by the whole thing. The Beach Boys' supremacy as the number one vocal group in America was being challenged. So we stepped on the gas a little bit… I think that as a songwriting idea, the Beatles beat us. But as an overall, versatile group sound, I think we tied 'em. I think we tied."11

With their own label now putting all their efforts into promoting their newly arrived cash cows at the Beach Boys' expense (something that Murry Wilson would vent his spleen over with Capitol's Nick Venet), it was left to Brian to hit back. But it would take time.

By April the Beatles held all top five spots on the Hot 100, eventually returning home to film the iconic movie *A Hard Day's Night*. Brian's only response was to cut three new songs and make appearances in what would soon become a long-forgotten movie called *Girls On the Beach*. Capitol executives were becoming convinced that the Beach Boys could no longer compete with the Beatles as album artists, and now predicted their future as being a band that just made singles.

> **"I knew we were good, but it wasn't until the Beatles arrived that I knew we had to get going"**

The lacklustre response to their last album *Shut Down Volume2* was considered by critics to be Capitol's fault for promoting it as another "hot-rod" album, following on from their *Shut Down,* a compilation album of car songs by various artists, including the Beach Boys' tracks "Shut Down" and "409," which became a Top Ten hit on the Hot 200 in June 1963. *Volume 2,* despite its three classics tracks, only contained four actual car songs, and the rest were considered 'fillers.' Brian, dissatisfied with his own production, saw it as being both rushed and uncomplicated, and as a result felt his musical ambitions were being stymied. He was determined not to make the same mistake on their next album. But, to appease Capitol, what was needed the most was a chart-topping single, and the result would be a major milestone in Brian's evolution as both songwriter and producer, unlike anything the band had done before.

Their new album, *All Summer Long,* would see a marked improvement with the production and no longer hampered by unnecessary fillers (although, unfortunately, there would still be one). Although a couple of tracks would be car-inspired, the rest were considered a collection of artistically unified songs with complex arrangements and mainly semi-autobiographical themes.

The first track recorded for the album was "I Get Around," another song that Mike would later win co-authorship. During the court proceedings, Brian admitted: "[I wrote it], with the exception of a possible - possibility that Mike wrote the intro, the 'round, round,'"[188] He later cited the Chiffons' 1963 hit, "One Fine Day," as one of the songs inspirations.

According to Jon Stebbins, the song was another that Brian had based on brother Dennis's life experiences,[43] as indicated in the original lyrics for the first verse: "*Well there's a million little girls just waitin' around/But there's only so much to do in a little town/I get around from town to town.*" Apparently, Mike described these as "pussy lyrics" and subsequently revised them: "I tinkered with Brian's first verse, which was about this bored kid driving around but was really about our own experiences: how we had this instant fame, some fortune, had travelled all over the country, but did any of that bring us happiness? Maybe we needed to find a different kind of place."[188]

Describing it as a "snapshot song, Canadian producer Daniel Lanois wrote: "It's like a Polaroid of a moment or a feeling. I like the way Brian wrote about specifics of a rising culture. He brings the listener in through one philosophical moment - one thought, one emotion - and that is often the most powerful way. You could write a much bigger song, but by writing a small one, you address a big subject. Funnily enough, Brian may not have been personally experiencing all those moments, but he was watching them happen."[10]

Perhaps unnoticed by the casual listener, the compositional sophistication of "I Get Around" was something that, at that moment in time, the Beatles could only aspire to, and it would serve to kick off one of the great rivalries in pop music. With its now much-imitated cover showing snapshots of SoCal teenage life, the *All Summer Long* album was a seasonal document to all the good times to be had by sun-loving guys and girls. But it was "I Get Around," that perfectly captured Brian's state of mind at the time.

With it's unexpected a capella intro, the song then bursts into life, as wonderfully described by Rick Swan: "{It} then launches into Mike's bold declaration of the theme, followed by an avalanche of harmonies, a thrilling vocal drive, then Brian's heart-stopping falsetto swoop. Unbelievably all this sonic image happens in the first four bars, proof that the Beach Boys were capable of more in the first few seconds of a song than rival groups could manage in entire albums, or even careers. The pounding rhythm track enters next, with Brian's lead whizzing overhead, navigating a clever chord change which sets up two delicious verses. Then handclaps, delirious backing vocals, and gorgeous melody lines swirling and diving in and out of each other. Beautiful stacked harmonies, a solid instrumental section, and out of nowhere, a modulation that elevates the song into the stratosphere."[21]

If 23-year-old Mike did re-write most of the words, and who are we to disprove it, then he came up with some of the finest lyrics and percussive vocals of his career.

When released as a double A-side single in May 1964, and coupled with "Don't Worry Baby," it made a strong contender for one of the greatest double-A's of all time. Debuting on the Hot 100 on May 23rd it overtook Peter and Gordon's "A World Without Love" to reach the top spot on Independence Day, remaining there for two weeks. It was America's first chart-topper by a homeland group since November 1963, and rated the fifth biggest-selling single of 1964 by both *Billboard* and *Cash Box*. The single also topped the Canadian charts and peaked at #7 in the UK, where it became their breakthrough single, thanks in no small way to the Stones' Mick Jagger, who, after hearing the song been played whilst on their first US tour that spring, effusively pushed the single on the popular tv show *Juke Box Jury*, endorsed it on *Ready Steady Go*, and personally circulated copies to the country's offshore pirate radio stations.

Despite shifting close to two million units in the US, it would be another 18 years before Capitol submitted the song to the RIAA (Recording Industry Association of America) for auditing, and only then was it awarded a gold disc. However in 2017 the song was rewarded at last by being inducted into the Grammy Hall of Fame.

The recording of "I Get Around" proved to be another milestone in Brian's career, but not for his music. At the first session on April 2nd, Murry Wilson was again in attendance and causing disruptions from the control room. Having already been fired as manager by Brian in February, he had continued to turn up for some of the sessions.

This time the friction over his interference got the better of Brian, as biographer Steven Gaines recalled: "Murry would not stop criticizing the song and Brian's production techniques...rambl[ing] on about what a loser Brian was, how poor the music was, and how only Murry had the real talent in the family. At one point he insisted that Brian end the session because something was wrong with the bassline."[123] Although Gaines went on to say that Brian threw his dad against the wall, shouting, "Get out of here! You're fired! Do you understand? You're fired!"[123], the general consensus is that he had already been fired two months before. According to biographer Timothy White, Murry also scolded Dennis, who then punched the wall in anger and left the studio.[32] Mike recalled: "Brian had a hard time standing up to his father, but this time...he shoved his dad, who went sprawling backward. That was the only time I ever saw Brian defy him personally, and Murry, defeated, left the studio."[188]

In one foul swoop, Brian had shook up both the record-buying public and the music industry as a whole. From that day on, the Beatles recognised they now had a formidable opponent and a rivalry that would continue for the next two years or so. *Cash Box* described the song as "an exciting, tailored-for-teen-tastes hot rod stomper...that should be getting around at a quick clip,"[223] while *Rolling Stone* later praised Brian's ability to be "very complex and have every single thing you do have an emotional impact, and have the listener not even aware of it - just hear it the first time and get it. That's hard."[224]

Rocksucker described it as "their most sophisticated single to date, the effortless weaving in and out of hithero rarely juxtaposed keys...truly became a trademark of Brian Wilson's songwriting on this album. [It] sets the stage for a melody so exhilaratingly sunny and mischievous that the contemporaneous dismissal of Murry Wilson...feels intrinsic to the song's air of gleeful and uninhibited rebelliousness."112

Jon Stebbins summed the song up perfectly: "'I Get Around' is clearly ahead of its time, and it signals the speed at which Brian had developed. With its edgy guitar/sax bursts doubled with trebly reverbed Fender flicks, electric-organ fills, and an arrangement that stops, goes, accelerates, and then stops and goes a few more times, the song is nearly otherworldly in its inventiveness. Each band member's voice is showcased, and this helps to make this single as good as any pop record ever made."43

As for the recording, a true stereo version of the song to yet to surface. The instrumental track was featured on 1993's *Good Vibrations* box set, although it was actually the track that the band recut for their following *Concert* album and not the original.

If Brian had filled the album with songs as good as this one, it would surely have rivalled *Pet Sounds*.

8. Caroline No (*Pet Sounds* 1966)
(Brian Wilson, Tony Asher)
Recording
31/01/66 Western Recorders, LA (tracking - 17 takes), lead vocal, instrumental insert)
02/02/66 Western Recorders, LA (further tracking inc keyboards, second bass, drums and sax)
03/02/66 Western Recorders, LA (tracking completed)
09/02/66 Western Recorders, LA (vocal double overdubs)
22/03/66 Western Recorders, LA (dogs/train tag)
Producer - Brian Wilson
Engineer - Chuck Britz
Band members
Brian Wilson (lead vocal); Banana and Louie (barking dogs)
Session musicians
Hal Blaine (Sparklet's water jug, overdubbed drums); Frank Capp (vibraphone); Carol Kaye (12-string electric guitar, overdubbed Danelectro 6-string bass); Glen Campbell (12-string electric guitar); Steve Douglas (woodblock or tambourine, overdubbed alto or tenor sax); Barney Kessel (acoustic guitar); Lyle Ritz (double bass); Al De Lory (harpsichord); Billy Green (flute & bass flute); Plas Johnson (alto flute); Jay Migliori (bass flute)
Album released - 16/05/66
US single released (solo) - 07/03/66 b/w "Summer Means New Love" Capitol 5610 #32
UK single released (solo) - 04/66 b/w "Summer Means New Love" Capitol CL 15438

There's a wistful innocence in *Pet Sounds* closing track that outshines anything else on the album. Possibly written by Brian and Tony Asher within a few days of "Wouldn't It Be Nice," both songs - polar opposites to one another in style - were destined to become the perfect bookends to the incredible album. Although Brian credited Asher with writing the beautiful lyrics, his collaborator also claims he contributed musical ideas to this and two other *Pet Sounds* tracks - "That's Not Me" and "I Just Wasn't Made For These Times."123

As for the subject matter, Asher gave all the credit to Brian, as "he'd always wanted to write a song about lost innocence, a young girl who changes as she matures and somehow, something's lost.72. In his since-discredited 1991 memoir, Brian recalled that after discussions over the proposed theme, Asher "took a tape home, embellished on my concept, and completed the words."28. In the same memoir, Brian had referred to the song as being "about how, once you've f****d up or more you've run your gamut with a chick, there's no way to get it back. It takes a lot of courage to do that sometimes in your life...I just felt sad, so I wrote a sad song."28

But who was Carol? According to Jim Fusilli, there was a conversation between Brian and Asher in which one of them (Asher can't recall who) "brought up the memory of a sweet girl who had been a high school crush. After graduation they had gone their separate ways, and when they ran into each other years later, she had changed. Her once-long hair was cut short and the qualities he had loved about her seemed to have similarly disappeared. She had hardened."10

This, of course, led to much speculation among fans over her identity. While some suggested it was Brian's former schoolmate Carol Mountain, for whom he had unrequited feelings and never forgot her, some others pointed to his wife Marlyn. Both ideas were summarily dismissed by Brian. According to biographer Peter Carlin, he had tracked down Mountain, who recounted how years after seeing each other, Brian would call her in the middle of the night just to have a conversation, waking up both her and her husband.32

"Brian wants teenage-style romance, not the intricacies of dealing with a woman out in the world, learning every day, growing"

In the 1991 memoir, heavily criticised for the implausibility of Brian being its actual author, he commented on his past infatuation with Carol (if it is to be believed): "I'd reminisce to Tony about my high school crush on Carol Mountain and sighed, 'If I saw her today, I'd probably think, God, she's lost something, because growing up does that to people.' But the song was most influenced by the changes Marilyn and I had gone through. We were young, Marilyn nearing twenty (*sic*) and me closing in on twenty-four, yet I thought we'd lost the innocence of our youth in the heavy seriousness of our lives."28

Asher went on record to confirm that Brian never mentioned Mountain to him, but their discussions did revolve around "how wonderful it is when you first meet a girl and she looks great, and how terrible it is when you know you'll be breaking up at any moment."85 He also recalled that "Caroline No" was originally written as a happier song until Brian took it a different direction when he "was saddened to see how sweet little girls turned out to be kind of bitchy hardened adults," 122) and later attributed some of the inspiration to "Brian's wish that he [and the band] could go back to simpler days...when the whole thing was a lot of fun and very little pressure"61

This left a girl called Carol Amen, who Asher had dated at high school and for a couple of years after they graduated before moving to New York to become a Broadway dancer: "When I went east to visit her a scant year after the move, she had changed radically. Yes, she had cut her hair. But she was a far more worldly person, not all for the worse."61

When Marilyn first heard the lyrics, she recalled: "I wasn't ready for how intense it was...from a romantic standpoint, which is the way I was thinking in those days. And then, I thought it was about me, because I had cut my hair...He always used to talk about how long hair keeps a girl feminine."72. Brian would revisit the subject in his "Baby Let Your Hair Grow Long" on his 1998 solo album *I Just Wasn't Made For These Times.*

In response, Marilyn revealed that Brian "constantly remembers his past and still relates to it and everybody in it. And that's another thing at seventeen years old that was hard for me to understand. You want this man to talk about you, and he was talking about all his old girlfriends."72. But in his 2016 memoir, Brian confessed that the song was "sort of about Marilyn, but, as time went on, sort of also about me...I know Tony didn't write it that way."35

The controversy continued. Bruce made a comment in 1975 about the song being "directly about Brian himself and the death of a quality within him that was so vital. His innocence. He knows it too."73. The following year Dennis claimed that the song was "about a girl that Brian was really in love with in high school. He saw her again years later, and it all came back to him, and he wrote the song."225 In 2006 Brian stated that the song "wasn't written about anyone. I just used the name Caroline."2 According to David Leaf, Asher told him that Brian had in mind "sweet little girls...and his wife's sister."122. Maybe, after all, Brian just wanted "the little girl he once knew."

When it came to the much-discussed song's title, it has become part of Beach Boys lore how Brian conceived it to be "Carol, I Know," but on hearing it played back, sounded more like "Caroline, No." After a short discussion it was decided to keep the new title, especially as it brought added poignancy to the song.

Wall Street Journal rock critic Jim Fusilli offered a more sympathetic reasoning: "*Pet Sounds* is about a man who looks into the future, doesn't like what he sees and prefers to remain a teenager. This song really expresses that. It's about the innocence and optimism of youth and the loss of youth. It's not so much about a person. It's about an emotion dying, a perspective dying. It's irrelevant who the 'Carol' is. Its more to the point that Brian's facing what we now know would be his abyss."10

In his own study of *Pet Sounds,* Fusilli wrote: "Brian wants teenage-style romance, not the intricacies of dealing with a woman out in the world, learning every day, growing. It's as if he doesn't realise she's already gone, that she doesn't want to have what they once shared - at least not with him. Or perhaps he does realise it, for the song concludes with him unleashing his falsetto, repeating the song title in a painful cry that disappears into the ether."130

This is just one of two songs on the album in which Brian is the only vocalist (the other being "Don't Talk").

There has been discussions that during the recording the band were still on the road, leaving an impatient Brian to do the vocals alone. However, after closer investigation, the band were indeed available and could have been used. Fusilli suggests that he could have used them on the bridge, but in the end he wanted this to simply be a Brian Wilson song.10

Asher commented on the final recording: "I had always heard it as only Brian singing it. With the other songs, he often played them at the piano with counter melodies and parts that others could sing, but that was never the case with 'Caroline, No.' In some ways, it was the least 'Beach Boys' of all the songs we worked on. I don't think it was inferior, but at the same time, I did think it was not at the same level of musical integrity as the other songs we were doing. I did like it. It just didn't seem to me to be as sophisticated a song as our other work."72

During the recording session bass player Carol Kaye noticed a change in Brian: "Something must have happened to Brian. I can remember he looked so sad. When he'd catch me checking out his face, he'd look back at me with a kind of deep, unexplainable sad look. I had never seen him like that before. He was happy with the music, though. It seemed to be his expression of some feeling he couldn't put into words. Not much of a tune, just a mood."72

Jim Fusilli described the intricate parts to the mournful track: "[It] begins with what sounds like a shaker, followed by a hollow, echoed percussion effect revealed by journalist Jules Siegel to be Hal Blaine hitting the bottom of an empty plastic Sparkletts water bottle [with a hard percussion mallet]. It is joined by the bittersweet harpsichord of Al de Lory and guitar of Glen Campbell and Barney Kessel, Frank Capp's 50's style vibraphone and Carol Kaye's very modern bass. Asher says the bass flutes were his idea, as was the hiring of Bill Green to play flute on the track along with Bill Horn, Plas Johnson and Jay Migliori. In many ways it's a jazz tune. Some of those chords are jazz chords."10

According to Dennis, when Murry first heard the song, "he went to pieces."122. Although loving the song, he suggested speeding up the tape and therefore raising Brian's pitch to make him sound younger. For once, Brian took his father's advice, and, during the mono mastering process, engineer Chuck Britz sped up the track a semi-tone, increasing the song's tempo by 6% while the key was raised from C to C♯.85 Not only that, Britz double-tracked Brian's vocal "live-to-tape" the same way he had done with "You Still Believe In Me." According to Fusilli, the change lost some of the nuances of the instrumentation: "I like the un-sped version, because to have a boy sing these lyrics makes no sense. But to have a man on the edge of psychological collapse sing them is a whole different story."10 The version of the song that Brian intended was later included on the *Pet Sounds Sessions* box set in 1997.

The album version of the song was edited to include the now-famous non-musical tag, recorded before Asher had re-written the lyrics. Brian returned to the studio to capture the barking of his two dogs, Banana (a beagle) and Louie (a Weimaraner), thus inspiring the album's title. Brian also recorded the sound of a locomotive train, sampled from the 1963 sound effects album *Mister D's Machine,* featuring the Owl, a Southern Pacific Railroad train that ran between San Francisco and Los Angeles from 1898 to 1965.

Reportedly at Brian's insistence, Capitol released "Caroline, No" as a single under his name, backed with the instrumental "Summer Means New Love," lifted from the *Summer Days* album. Peaking at a disappointing #32 on the Hot 100, it failed to chart in the UK. To mitigate its "unimpressive" sales, Capitol released "Sloop John B" as the next single just two weeks later. But had it really been Brian's decision?

According to Keith Badman, "everyone close to [Brian was] certain the disc (would) be a monster hit,11 with Marilyn going on to say that she felt Capitol released it as a single because they believed "it was so good," and, with it having no customary backing vocals from other band members, looked on it as a Brian

Wilson solo effort.72 Steven Gaines went so far as to say that Capitol "knew it was not a hit" but went ahead and released it anyway so as to "encourage Brian to complete the forthcoming album,"123 while Asher claimed that it was the band's criticism over the song being referred to as not being "Beach Boy enough," that led to it being released as a solo single. Even sessionist Steve Douglas claimed that he had instigated Brian with the decision.72

When asked in a 2002 interview whether he would have issued *Pet Sounds* as a solo album if the single had fared better, Brian replied that he "probably" wouldn't have done so, later admitting, "No, I just wanted to do that one. "Caroline No" fit my voice more than the other guys…"63

Cash Box referred to the song as a "tender, slow-moving gentle ode about an unhappy fella who desperately wants to get back with his ex-gal,"226 while journalist Nick Kent described it as "arguably the most beautiful song [Brian] has ever written."73 The wonderfully descriptive Rick Swan wrote: "Following the unusual percussive opening - a tambourine with an empty water bottle – the simple melody drifts over two chords, one major and one with an offbeat root, signifying the uncertainty of the lyric. The water bottle becomes, strangely enough, a gunshot through the heart, preceding a plaintive sax that emerges in the bridge to finish you off. An instrumental break arrives near the end, a pause for the singer to ponder whether there's any way back to love that's fading like the sunset, only to receive the blunt terrible answer - No. Then there's the train, a poignant sound symbolising the singer's solitude, maybe forever, maybe not. And the barking dog, putting the final period on the final sentence."21

Apparently, Brian tried to reconnect with the now-married Carol Mountain a few months after the album's release, but after visiting her once with his friend Stan Shapiro, and then making nuisance calls to her in the middle of the night, all efforts came to nothing.123

7. Heroes and Villains (*Smiley Smile* 1967)
(Brian Wilson, Van Dyke Parks)
Recording (Smile)
11/05/66 Gold Star Studio, LA (experimental session - later scrapped)
17/10/66 CBS Columbia Studio, LA ("I'm In Great Shape" rough vocals)
20/10 66 Western Recorders, LA (tracking - Verse & "Barnyard")
27/10/66 Western Recorders, LA (tracking - "I'm in Great Shape")
04/11/66 Western Recorders, LA (piano demos)
14/11/66 Gold Star Studio, LA (tracking - "My Only Sunshine")
13/12/66 CBS Columbia Studio, LA (vocals)
19/12/66 Western Recorders (new tracking)
22/12/66 CBS Columbia Studio, LA (vocals)
27/12/66 CBS Columbia Studio, LA (vocals - "Children Were Raised," "Part 2" "Whistling Bridge" etc)
28/12/66 CBS Columbia Studio, LA (vocals)
03/01/67 CBS Columbia Studio, LA (additional music, inserts & vocal overdubs)
05/01/67 Western Recorders, LA (tracking for "Part 2"; vocal chorus for "Bicycle rider")
20/01/67 CBS Columbia Studio, LA (new vocals)
27/01/67 CBS Columbia Studio, LA (vocals - "In the Cantina" section)
31/01/67 CBS Columbia Studio, LA (vocals)
02/02/67 Western Recorders, LA
03//2/67 CBS Columbia Studio, LA (vocals)
07/02/67 CBS Columbia Studio, LA (guitar overdubs, additional vocals)

10/02/67 Western Recorders, LA (solo vocal by Brian; "In the Cantina" mix-down tape)
15/02/67 Western Recorders, LA (revised instrumental track -"Prelude to fade")
18/02/67 Western Recorders, LA ("sweetening" session for Part 1 - song "completed")
20/02/67 CBS Columbia Studio, LA ("Part 2 (Gee)")
21/02/67 CBS Columbia Studio, LA (further vocals for "Part 1")
24/02/67 CBS Columbia Studio, LA (further vocals for "Part 1")
26/02/67 CBS Columbia Studio, LA (final vocals for "Part 1")
27/02/67 Western Recorders, LA (new instrumental backing for "Part 2")
28/02/67 Western Recorders, LA ("Fade to H&V" segment – 25 takes)
01/03/67 Western Recorders, LA (tracking session, verse remake & organ waltz/intro)
02/03/67 Western Recorders, LA (tracking insert for "Part 2")
Recording (Smiley Smile)
12/06/67 Beach Boys Studio, Bel Air (chorus, barbershop, children were raised vocal remakes)
13/06/67 Beach Boys Studio, Bel Air (vocal sessions)
14/06/67 Beach Boys Studio, Bel Air (tracking & vocals completed)
Late June 67 - Wally Heider Studio, Hollywood (vocals)
Producers - The Beach Boys
Engineers - Chuck Britz *(Western),* Larry Levine (*Gold Star*), Ralph Valentin? (*Columbia*), Jim Lockert (*Bel Air*)
Band members
Brian Wilson (lead vocals on "Barbershop", harmony & backing vocals; tack piano on chorus, overdubbed harpsichord, possibly sandpaper percussion, Baldwin organ, overdubbed electric harpsichord); Mike Love (co-lead vocals on "Barbershop," harmony & backing vocals); Carl Wilson (harmony & backing vocals); Dennis Wilson (harmony & backing vocals); Al Jardine (lead vocals on "chorus," harmony & backing vocals); Bruce Johnston (harmony & backing vocals)
Session musicians/Guests
Van Dyke Parks (tack piano on verse); Gene Estes (slide whistle, possibly shaker & "clank"); George Hyde (French horn); Jim Gordon (drums); Bill Pitman (Danelectro bass); Lyle Ritz (upright bass); Carol Kaye (possibly acoustic rhythm guitar); Al Casey (electric guitar); Jerry Cole (electric guitar); Steve Douglas (tenor sax); Dorothy Victor (harp); Billy Hinsche (backing & harmony vocals)
Smiley Smile album released - 18/09/67
US single released - 31/07/67 b/w "You're Welcome" Brother 1001 #12
UK single released - 18/08/67 b/w "You're Welcome" Capitol CL 15510 #8
Film/TV performances
31/08/67 *Top of the Pops* BBC-1 (16mm film of surfers directed by Peter Clifton)
25/02/72 *Grand Gala Du Disque Populaire* RAI Amsterdam
21/01/77 Capital Centre, Washington CD
21/06/80 Knebworth England concert (later released on CD/DVD)

Without any doubt, "Heroes and Villains" is the most complex recording of the Beach Boys' entire career, the result of months of experimentation, changing themes, and variation of themes, many of which were recorded and then discarded, resulting in studio expenses running up to around $40,000. During a period of nearly ten months, Brian and new collaborator Van Dyke Parks assembled and recorded a myriad of musical segments for what were four almost entire different versions of the song, with some of those segments even initially chosen to be dedicated songs of their own. In hindsight, it became the only *Smile* track in which Brian recorded vocal parts before the different sections were arranged. Ironically, the final and totally different album version for *Smiley Smile* was assembled in just three days at Brian's makeshift home studio. Its failure to get the recognition it deserved at the time would serve as a pivotal moment in Brian's psychological decline.

In an interview for KHJ radio in 1977, Brian recalled: "I said to my dad, 'I'm going to make a record that's better than "Good Vibrations," something that *you* could never do'. I don't know why in hell I said that. He goes, 'What are you talking about? What the hell do you mean I couldn't do it? Shut up!' And he started whacking me and we got into a fight. And then he started crying and goes, 'Oh, I'm sorry son. I'm sorry. I didn't understand.' I was just in a playful mood. I get that way. Just before I go in and do something great, I get a little egotistical. I pump it up."[11]

With recordings spanning almost the entire *Smile* sessions, Brian and Parks made an initial attempt at recording the song in May 1966, and then set it aside until October, when, with the success of "Good Vibrations," returned to it with renewed enthusiasm. At one time, the song's length was rumoured to be getting close to seven to ten minutes, but Brian would finally settle on a mix of a little over three and a half minutes for the final single release in July 1967.

Like *Smile* itself, sifting through the vast collection of "Heroes and Villains" segments that appeared on bootlegs over the years was like taking a glimpse inside a watery cave and discovering golden nuggets amid a mountain of somewhat confusing and down-right weird musical flotsam. Taking these to be pieces of a larger puzzle, it had musicologists and fans around the world assuming the mantle of detective and psychologist by taking a closer look at how this unfinished *Smile* centrepiece would have looked like in Brian's head.

"In truth, every beautifully designed , finely wrought, inspirationally-welded piece of music, made these last few months…have been SCRAPPED"

Following the critical success of *Pet Sounds*, Brian set his mind on exploring new directions for the next album. For that, he needed a lyricist who not only possessed a similar unbridled imagination as his own, but one who could translate his wild concepts into meaningful words. With Van Dyke Parks he found the one who could achieve his ambition. They had first met in December 1965 through mutual friend David Crosby of the Byrds, who, while at the Troubadour Café in Santa Monica, had invited Parks up to Brian's house, where they listened in the makeshift studio to a dub of the new single, "Sloop John B." Right from the start, Parks was impressed with Brian's deep understanding of the recording process.

Parks had already gained a foothold in the music business, having had two folk albums with his brother Carson, who would go on to write "Something Stupid" for Frank and Nancy Sinatra. After meeting him for the first time Brian was immediately impressed with his intelligent and articulate manner, and later recalled: "I said, 'I'll bet he'll be a good lyric writer. Sure enough, he turns out to be great, and I had to get used to the idea of kicking ideas around.'"[8]

Parks remembered the first conversation: "We spoke about what Brian was doing, because I had been with him in the studio, and he was working on this *Pet Sounds* thing but hadn't had much talk…and that was the first time we had a conversation together - a real, direct conversation with no bullshit, nobody hustling any business or anything and he said he was looking for a lyricist, which surprised me. He asked me if I did that, and I lied and said, 'Yes, I can be a lyricist.'"[8] In reality, Parks was more into poetry, one of the reasons he was attracted to LA, and whether he came clean about the truth or not, he was now on board with one of the most celebrated musicians on the planet. After that, Brian embarked on what Parks referred to as "an American Gothic trip," with his new collaborator steering him away from familiar romantic to a new kind of writing: "I tried to contribute to the idea that perhaps all music did not have to be for dancing."19

After sitting down at the piano at Gold Star for the first time, it wasn't long before Brian played Parks a few chords of a work-in-progress song that biographer Peter Carlin described as a "hurtling countryside tub-thumper," and one that reminded Parks of Marty Robbins' genre-classic single, "El Paso," which had itself become the first US chart-topper of the 1960's. Brian saw the connection straight away, and admitted that he had the Old West on his mind when writing the song, with the title of "Heroes and Villains."

For the next four hours or so, Parks took a pencil and pad and scratched down lyrics as Brian played, using syllables that matched the rhythm of the music. As Brian played him the long descending melody line, Parks immediately came up with the line, "*I've been in this town so long ...*" In a later interview for BBC Radio-1 he recalled: "Brian always made a melody and the words were slapped on that melody. I had no input whatsoever in the music. I was a total lyricist and sometimes an instrumentalist,"11 going on to say: "I had no ideas if it was day or night. Probably both. But we had the whole thing, apart from one section, in one sitting. That was the enthusiasm."32

According to *Smile*-aficionado Domenic Priore, the melodic idea for "Heroes and Villains" was inspired by the base line of the old 1917 standard, "The Bells of St Mary," made famous in the 1945 movie of the same name featuring Bing Crosby. Phil Spector put his rock and roll spin on it with Bob B. Soxx and the Blue Jeans' version on his celebrated Christmas album, and there are also traces of it in his "River Deep, Mountain High" classic. Some other accounts suggest that Brian may even have developed the melody by reworking the 1939 standard, "You Are My Sunshine."

Inspired by the Western storytelling of "El Paso" and the Spector-inspired melody of an old standard, Brian and Parks conjured up a "visual effort" based on the early history of the US Southwest, with references to the Spanish and Native American Indians.8 The original idea was that it would be a stand-alone single, but the broad cinematic landscape it created led to other *Smile* tracks being given Western-themed music and lyrics referring to barns, cabins, grits and eggs, and railroads, and the recolonisation of the American West. Beginning with the *Mayflower* and Plymouth Rock, the album would resemble a 5,000-mile journey across America from New England to Hawaii as seen as a recurring dream through the eyes of a bicycle rider. Parks went on to say. "It had to do with gambling and so forth. And the church of the American Indian, of course, is the very property which we claim now. They would never have thought of ownership of the land as anything other than an obscene presumption. It's just a different attitude, but an important one."8

Parks later recalled: "I'd just come off this personal Everest and was trying to make reason of my own life. We were panning for good information, and it all felt very California and very frontier. The whole state of California felt like a frontier to us. And the whole record seemed like a real effort toward figuring out what

Manifest Destiny was all about. We'd come as far as we could, as far as Horace Greeley ["Go West, young man"] told us to go. And so we looked back and tried to make sense of that great odyssey."8

Biographer Peter Carlin interpreted the song as "a lawless boomtown somewhere out on the fringes of the Old West...a world lit up by ambition and riddled with gunfire. The narrator speaks as a man who has become a part of the scene, but not of it, exactly, because he's still so thrilled and terrified by everything he sees...The indictment, if that's what it is, later expands to take in the sweep of the nation around them...By the time it ends, the narrator has aged and seen his own children grow to adulthood. But if he has been transformed by the decades spent in the boomtown, has he become a hero or villain? That's one question he won't, or can't, answer."32

Controversy remains on which author came up with the title, although Parks recalled: "I think it was a great title, and [Brian] suggested it...This Spanish and Indian fascination is a big chapter in Californian history, and that's what it's supposed to be - historically reflective, to reflect this place. I think he did it."8

Apparently before sessions got under way Brian bought several thousand dollars' worth of marijuana and hashish for himself and his newfound friends, which included Parks, David Anderle (the "hip" associate who helped him set up Brother Records) and Michael Vosse (the young fan-mag reporter introduced to him by publicist Derek Taylor). By the end of their first session, Brian had recorded the track for the new song, even before he had completed work on his next single, "Good Vibrations," which was eventually completed over the next two months. Brian then returned to the studio in August to work on other tracks for an album that was originally called *Dumb Angel*.

Toward the end of October, with the band on their second official tour of Europe, Brian undertook further work on "Heroes and Villains" with snippets called "I'm in Great Shape" and "Barnyard," described by Mark Dillon as turning "a day at the farm into slapstick ballet."10 This humorous thread probably convinced them to change the album's original title *Dumb Angel* to *Smile*. Switching to recording at Western, engineer Chuck Britz remembered the song being "as big if not bigger than "Good Vibrations" in its original form. I thought it was a fantastic song, a great, rich full sound."56

Over in the UK, *NME* announced: "While the Beach Boys are rocking Europe, BB-mastermind Brian Wilson has not been resting on his laurels. This week Brian's working on the next Beach Boys single, another adventure in pop music, called "Heroes and Villains," which will be, as the BB boss describes it, "a three-minute musical comedy."8

Despite all this activity, Capitol could not get Brian to deliver the long-awaited new album before Christmas. On December 15th, Brian notified Capitol that the album and its lead single "Heroes and Villains" would probably be delivered to them in a month's time. To ease the labels concerns, Brian sent them a preliminary, unordered track list with "I'm in Great Shape" listed as a separate track from "Heroes and Villains." In anticipation, the label had hired Frank Holmes to design the now-iconic "smile shop" cartoon for the album's cover and ordered some 466,000 copies, together with an elaborate booklet and the track list sent by Brian.

Returning from their successful tour of Europe, the band were on top of the world, with a chart-topping single in "Good Vibrations," and having been voted by the UK music press as surpassing the Beatles as the world's top vocal group. But back in LA, they were surprised to find, not just some unfamiliar faces in the company of Brian, but also his creativity at an all-time peak, attempting something both new and radically different in pop music. Intrigued by the music they heard, it would be a completely different story when it came to the lyrics.

With increasing pressure from Capitol, Brian now halted work on other *Smile* tracks until April to focus on "Heroes and Villains." Meanwhile, Parks was receiving continued criticism for his lyrics from band members at vocal sessions. Much of it came from Mike, who repeatedly asked him to explain the meaning of his lyrics, only to be told that they had no specific meaning. With this and all the musical modules surrounding "Heroes and Villains," and the possible direction each one might take, Brian began to lose control of the process.

After the final session for "Heroes and Villains" on March 2nd 1967, Parks temporarily dissolved their partnership after disagreements with Brian (possibly over lyrics). His final *Smile* collaboration with Brian came at Western on April 14th and a session for "Vegetables." Tired of constantly defending his lyrics and being dominated in the studio by Brian, he took up the offer of a recording deal with Warner. In a radio interview in 1974, he claimed: "I was fired, that is I resigned, that is I dissolved my relationship with the Beach Boys. I was fired because it was already decided by Mike Love, as well as by the least known members, that I had written some words that were indecipherable and unnecessary. In short, they had a better lyricist on *Pet Sounds* than the one they had on *Smile*."[11]

In February the *Village Voice* reported that the forthcoming "Heroes and Villains" single would comprise "five movements, each with a distinct melodic and rhythm line,"[227] while four days later *NME* stated it would be released once that Brian had decided on the b-side, quoting him as saying that he wanted to "keep as much of *Smile* a surprise as possible…"[11]

Beach Boy publicist Derek Taylor (1932-1997) announced on March 21st that "only a scoundrel would dispute the claim that "Heroes and Villains" is the most famous single not yet recorded…It is a fact that the single, at the time of writing, is not completed and many people here are troubled. But Brian Wilson is not one of them."[228] That very same day, Taylor, in a press release published in both *NME* and *Record Mirror*, said that the single was delayed due to "technical difficulties."[229]

Finally on May 6th Taylor made his famous announcement in *Disc & Music Echo:* "In truth, every beautifully designed, finely wrought, inspirationally-welded piece of music, made these last few months by Brian and the Beach Boys craftsmen have been SCRAPPED. Not destroyed, but scrapped. For what Wilson seals in a can and destroys is scrapped. As an average fan of the Beach Boys, I think its utterly disappointing."[11]

When Parks quit the project citing a number of reasons, Brian's creativity suffered. Any momentum had been lost as paranoia set in, even with him becoming unsure of the album's concept or even its structure. With this and the band's on-going litigation with the label over royalty issues, Brian decided to abandon the

Smile project altogether, fearing that to carry on it would kill him and put an end to the Beach Boys' career.

But "Heroes and Villains" was not dead. A week after the Beatles' ground breaking album *Sgt Pepper* was released in the US on June 2nd, and over a year since the release of *Pet Sounds*, the Beach Boys were still looking for material for their next album. Over the next six weeks, as part of the process, Brian and the band revisited *Smile* to re-re-record a number of tracks in what would turn out to be in distinctly simplified and accessible form, and nearly all done from their makeshift studio at Brian's home. Engineer Jim Lockert recalled: "We found a room adjacent to the large music room and built a control room in there, [installing] a remote console and speakers…We physically changed the music room into a recording studio with isolation and baffles and sound treatment so we could do some recording in there without problems."[11] According to Carl, "we did part of [the album] in his gym, part in his backyard, and even in his swimming pool…All over the place."[11]

The centrepiece for the new album, *Smiley Smile,* would, of course, be "Good Vibrations," but a re-recording of "Heroes and Villains," was, according to Steven Gaines, the only track that Brian "really cared about."[123] Lockert recalled: "We had the complete song, but they just wanted to use part of it. Brian wanted to change what had been done on the rest of it. I think he wanted instrumentally and vocally to make it more complex. I think he wanted to finish the song, it was a challenge to him."[56] On June 12th they recorded an entirely new vocal track and re-recorded parts of the instrumental track.

The completed song ran for 3:36 minutes, and the only remnant of the earlier *Smile* recordings that were used were snippets of the backing track recorded in October 1966, even creating an echo-chamber effect by recording some instrument parts in Brian's drained swimming pool, with a microphone fed out from the house.

Meanwhile the band were scheduled to headline the Monterey Pop Music Festival on June 17th, and, despite being one of the festival's board members, dropped out at the last minute. In a press release by the band, the reason given was their commitment to deliver the "Heroes and Villains" single to a frustrated Capitol. Without realising it, this single act would cause repercussions for the band for the next few years.

On its release (the first on the Brother label), the song made a respectable showing at #12 on the US chart, as well as peaking at #8 in the UK. It would also be the band's last US top 20 entry until "Rock and Roll Music" in 1976. The album, with "Heroes and Villains" as the opening track, was released some three months later. Reviewing the single, *Billboard* saw it as "clever off-beat rock material with an arrangement that encompassed barbershop harmony and jazz!"[231] while *Cash Box* called it a "creatively delivered conglomeration of sounds that run the gamut from amusement park hoopla to barbershop harmony," with lyrics that "pose some interesting questions."[232] *Melody Maker's* Nick Jones celebrated it as "another masterpiece of production from Wilson and another move in his flowery progression."[11] *Mojo* retrospectively called it "a gorgeous light opera of razzle-dazzle wonkiness, and more brilliant notions than occur to most musicians in a lifetime."[25]

Not all reviews were positive. Penny Valentine, writing for *Disc & Music Echo*, was impressed by some of the song's finer points, but "the record as a whole...is disappointing...One has, perhaps, just come to expect too much from the Beach Boys. And that isn't it!"233 *Rolling Stone's* Jann Wenner was even more scathing, calling it "pointless" and "weak" when compared to "Good Vibrations."11

Many critics saw the song's apparent "failure" as signalling Brian's professional and psychological decline. Future manager and lyricist Jack Rieley wrote that it "shook [Brian] to the foundations of his being and self-respect...This is when he started disappearing into his bedroom for a long time..."99 More recently, Rick Swan summed up the song's appeal: "Nonetheless, what remains is a dazzling vocal display, and an excellent example of how Brian constructed the *Smile* songs out of diverse melodic fragments. That such an experimental work could be released as a single and still go top 20 hints at the possibilities lost. Wilson's handling of Parks' elliptical lyric - which purportedly concerns Brian's battle with Capitol as much as it addresses the Old West - is surefooted, and the band deliver the incredibly complex vocals with a confidence born in familiarity."21

In the years that followed, the public had the chance to hear the song as Brian originally intended it. Beginning in 1990 the long-lost "cantina" section was released of the *Smiley Smile/Wild Honey* cd, and three years later the *Good Vibrations* box set included some ten minutes of H&V discarded segments. All these were eclipsed with the later releases of *The Smile Sessions* and then *Brian Wilson Presents Smile*, which finally gave the fans all that was needed to whet their appetite for a lifetime.

But let Mike Love have the last word. Although having little involvement in the song's development, he referred to it as the "last dynamic moment in Brian's music,"11 and it's hard not to believe he was right. His cousin would never again produce a song so dynamic, or so breathtakingly thrilling, as this one.

6. Wouldn't It Be Nice (*Pet Sounds* 1966)
(Brian Wilson, Tony Asher, Mike Love)
Recording
22/01/66 Gold Star Studio, LA(tracking - 21 takes, vocal overdub)
16/02/66 Western Recorders, LA (mono mix, vocal rehearsals)
03/03/66 CBS Columbia Studio, LA (alternate mono mix)
03/03/66 Western Recorders, LA (mono mix with incomplete vocals)
10/03/66 CBS Columbia Studio, LA (vocal overdubs & inserts)
11/04/66 CBS Columbia Studio, LA (lead vocals by Brian & Carl, harmony vocals and inserts)
Producer - Brian Wilson
Engineers - Larry Levine (*Gold Star*), Chuck Britz (*Western*), Ralph Valentin? (*Columbia*)
Band members
Brian Wilson (lead vocal, backing vocals); Mike Love (bridge & outro lead vocals, backing vocals); Carl Wilson (backing vocals); Dennis Wilson (backing vocals); Al Jardine (backing vocals), Bruce Johnston (backing vocals)
Session musicians
Hal Blaine (drums); Frank Capp (timpani, jingle stick, glockenspiel); Roy Caton (trumpet); Jerry Cole (12-string lead guitar); Steve Douglas (tenor sax); Carl Fortina (accordion); Plas Johnson (tenor sax); Carol Kaye (bass guitar); Barney Kessel (12-string mando-guitar); Larry Knechtel (tack piano); Al De Lory (grand piano); Frank Marocco (accordion); Jay Migliori (baritone sax); Bill Pitman (acoustic rhythm guitar); Ray Pohlman (Danelectro 6-string bass); Lyle Ritz (string bass)

Album released - 16/05/66
US single released - 18/07/66 b/w "God Only Knows" Capitol 5706 #8
UK single released - 22/07/66 b-side of "God Only Knows" Capitol CL 15459 #2
Film/TV performances
14/12/66 *Twien* Theater De Brakke Grond, NCRV Amsterdam (broadcast 23/12/68)
16/06/69 Olympia Theater Paris TF1 (filmed concert)
07/05/71 *The David Frost Show* Westinghouse, Philadelphia (broadcast 28/05/71)
21/01/77 Capital Centre, Washington DC
13/07/85 *Live Aid*, Philadelphia Pa.

The perfect opener for a perfect album, and one of the best examples of describing the anticipation of the romantic freedom that all young couples crave for. According to lyricist Tony Asher: "It's a song that people who are young and in love can appreciate and respond to, because it revolves around the things they've always wanted to do; live together, sleep together, wake up together - do everything together."[85]

Unusually suggestive for a Beach Boy song, Asher went on to recall how it developed: "Over a period of days, Brian kept saying he was working on a melody, but he didn't want to play it for me until he had the structure finished. One day, he said, 'It's done.' He sat at the piano and played what turned out to be 'Wouldn't It Be Nice' ... He immediately said, 'Let's start writing the lyric.' I got a legal pad and a pencil and sat next to him. Writing [it] was different from the way we wrote the other songs for *Pet Sounds*, because once he had perfected the melody, Brian's job was finished and the focus was on me writing the lyrics. When we first attacked this song, Brian kept looking at the page to see what I had written. He'd say 'No, no, no - I don't like that. Let's do something else.' I would write three words, and he's make some comment about those three words. After a short time, I realised that he was micro-analysing the individual words because he had nothing else to do! I said, 'Brian, let me take a tape of this home. I'll write the lyrics then come back.' Thank God he agreed, because it would have been tortuous writing the whole album under so fine a microscope."[85]

In a 1996 interview Asher revealed that he and Brian "both had the experience of being too young to have what the rest of the world would call a serious relationship with a girl and yet wanting to be able to have it taken seriously...It was autobiographical from the point of view of both of us. We were writing about what we both knew and had experienced."[72]

Brian revealed in a 1976 radio interview that he wrote the song to express "the need to have freedom to live with somebody...The idea is, the more we talk about it, the more we want it, but let's talk about it anyway. Let's talk it over, let's talk about what we might have if we really got down to it."[234] Singer-songwriter Zooey Deschanel wrote: "The whole song is a big question. It's a rhetorical question, which lyrically is very interesting and makes you want to listen to it more. You can see the naïveté in the narrator, but that makes it even better. That song is all hope."[10]

Although there has been suggestions that Brian was inspired to write the song by his infatuation for his sister-in-law Diane Rovell, especially in his since-discredited 1991 memoir, Asher did recall that while writing the song, Brian was "definitely infatuated by her and this innocent aurora that she seemed to possess," repeatedly mentioning how "sweet and beautiful she was."[32]

During the recording, the band struggled to perform the complex vocal parts to Brian's satisfaction, making the song the longest track on the album to record. With Brian singing the verses and Mike the bridge, Mike recalled that he was made to do 30 takes singing one background section, and, around the 20th take, he affectionately referred to Brian as "dog ears," as he could hear things that humans couldn't: "Brian must have been part canine because he was reaching for something intangible, imperceptible to most, and all but impossible to execute."76

"Brian must have been part canine because he was reaching for something intangible, imperceptible to most, and all but impossible to execute"

According to Mike, who affectionately dubbed his cousin the "Stalin of the studio," Brian "was looking for something more than the actual notes or the blend: he was reaching for something mystical - out of the range of hearing."85

Al also recalled the difficulties of meeting Brian's standards, calling it "painful beyond belief,"188 while Carl wrote: "We did at least ten sessions on that one, and it still wasn't right. I still think we sang it a little rushed."11 In a 1996 interview, he wrote: "Brilliant parts. It was hard to sing without getting tears in your eyes. We all seem to remember singing it a lot. Many times. Many days."72

Bruce revealed: "I now know why Brian made us re-record this vocally. As big as 'California Girls' was, he was unhappy with our rhythm of singing. And with that high of a standard to get it right [the song] required a lot of perfect vocal rhythm…One time, he had a 4-track Scully [tape recorder] sent to his home, but that didn't really work out."72 Bruce also remembered the tension in the studio: "We re-recorded our vocals for 'Wouldn't It Be Nice' so many times that the rhythm was never right. We'd slave [away] singing this thing and then Brian would say, 'No, it's not right! It's just not right!'"11

While studio technology was quickly developing and becoming more sophisticated, Brian's preferred recording studios Western and Gold Star, which still had four-track recording machines which limited Brian's recording ability. While he would take advantage of Columbia's new eight-track technology (as he had done with "California Girls,") he recorded all the instrumentals onto one of the four tracks, and used the remaining three for vocals. Meanwhile, engineers Chuck Britz at Western, and Larry Levine at Gold Star, would often use two four-track machines and then transfer the recording onto an eight-track, thus allowing Brian seven tracks for vocal overdubs.75 Brian would only use Gold Star once more on *Pet Sounds*, and that was for "I Just Wasn't Made For These Times."

Beach Boy publicist Derek Taylor described the energy and intensity of one of the vocal sessions at Columbia: "Brian races from studio to control booth, in his efforts to be both singer and producer…not only must he manipulate the sounds which go down on tape, but the separate and unequal egos of the Beach Boys. They listen to the tracks that Brian has spent hours recording. They listen in wonderment and awe. After swallowing the lumps in their throats and exchanging uneasy glances, work begins. First Bruce and Al step up to the mike to do that *dumdedums*, then Carl, Al and Dennis for the *runrunweeoos*. And Carl and Bruce for hums with

Brian on falsetto. And on and on into the night, overdubbing, rearranging, softening, strengthening, shifting voices, moving Al farther away, Dennis back a step, Carl closer, Mike lower. Patiences wear out. Brian will accept nothing less than perfection."75

The final round of vocal overdubs were done at Columbia. Brian recalled that one of the features of the song was Dennis singing his harmony parts by cupping his ears: "I had thought for hours of the best way to achieve the sound and Dennis dug the idea because he knew it would work."85

Mark Dillon described one of the song's most daring aspects - the ritardando (decrease in speed) before the bridge - like "a music box winding down," and went on to say: "If you were dancing to the song, what were you supposed to do during this section? And not every musician can master such a temp change." Apparently, when it was later sung live, with Al taking over Brian's lead vocal, they often skipped the part and jumped to the closing tag.10

While many listeners believed the song's lifting eight-beat intro was played on a harp, it was actually Jerry Cole's detuned 12-string guitar run directly into the console with live reverb added. This is brought to an abrupt end with Hal Blaine's single hit on a snare drum. The driving force behind the verses that follow is provided by two accordions, which in the bridge sound more like mandolins. Mike's amazing middle eight vocal is enhanced by both trumpet and a trio of saxophones, while Frank Capp's percussion hits the bells just as Brian sings about getting married. The verse base line was inspired by Brian's favourite song, "Be My Baby," as he later described: "It's just a feel you get. I sort of feel my way through the line. I can't explain how it's done, in terms of words. [The verses are] similar to the Phil Spector-type bass. It's a one-note walking bass that goes "bom-buh-bum-bah, bom-buh-bum-bah..." It keeps going one scale tone up ["bah"], then down like a walking bass."235

Due to the restrictions at Gold Star the player had to perform his instrument in the control room, away from the other musicians, who could not hear his playing in the regular recording space. The only exception was drummer Hal Blaine, who wore headphones and signalled the other musicians to play on cue. As a result, all the instruments were played live in a continuous take, without overdubbing.72

Jim Fusillo describes the opening notes to the song: "Jerry Cole's twelve-string guitar kicks off the song, playing a pattern that sounds like nothing so much as a child's toy, making a statement of innocence, of unbridled happiness. And then, at the end of the fourth bar, Hal Blaine, per Brian's instructions, smacks the drum hard, delivering a harsh, ominous sound that echoes like a shut door, a slamming gate. So much for innocence. So much for happiness. Here, gone in six seconds."130

Asher commented on the finished song: "I love the fact that the song has such a nice, bouncy feel to it. When we were writing, I was aware of the intricate rhythms that Brian had accomplished musically. There are changes in temp and legato parts that make it very interesting."85 This was one of 35 songs for which Mike Love was awarded co-writing credit following his successful lawsuit in 1994. Asher later (under oath) stated Mike's contribution was the closing line, "*goodnight my baby/sleep tight, my baby*" (actually developed during the recording), as well as some possible minor vocal arrangements.

"Wouldn't It Be Nice" was one of two songs on the album that was conceived by Brian alone and then presented to Asher, requiring only a lyric (the other being "You Still Believe In Me"). It could also be seen as the pinnacle in a trio of similarly-themed songs that had begun with "We'll Run Away" on *All Summer Long* and "I'm So Young" on *Today!* Nick Kent identified with their "teenage angst dialogue," and wrote: "This time [Brian] was out to eclipse these previous sonic soap operas, to transform the subject's sappy sentiments with a God-like grace so that the song would become a veritable pocket symphony."73 Meanwhile, the incisive Philp Lambert took the themes to be "a significant twist" on Brian's past songs: "Now the young lovers just want to be monogamous and draw strength and happiness from each other, *"in the kind of world where we belong."*9

Like some other tracks on the album, the song had a technical flaw in the final mix, with an audible tape splice in evidence between the chorus and Mike's vocal entrance in the bridge. On the 1996 *Pet Sounds Sessions* stereo mix, Mark Linett corrected the mistake: "The abrupt edit...was an edit that took an older mix with Mike Love singing and out it in the bridge. I didn't figure that out for years!" In the stereo mix, Brian sings the bridge, as the tape with Mike singing was not available at the time.85

First released as the opening track to the album, "Wouldn't It Be Nice" was released as a single two months later, backed with "God Only Knows," while in the US and other countries the sides were reversed. Either way, with two such iconic songs, it remains one of the greatest 45s of all time. While the song peaked at a respectable #8 on the Hot 100, it's UK release, with both sides receiving equal airplay, shot to #2, only being pipped to the top by (who else?) the Beatles "Yellow Submarine/Eleanor Rigby."

In his review for *Record Mirror*, the hard-to-please Norman Jopling wrote that the song "starts off prettily, and develops into a complicated ponderous beat number taken at a reasonably fast temp. It slows down half-way through but brightens up again, and the lyric is pleasant. But not exceptional Beach Boys."236 *Cash Box* described it as a "rhythmic, medium-paced, danceable sincere pledge of devotion."237 In its retrospective review, *Pitchfork* wrote: [It] has everything you love about the Beach Boys in spades...It's the ultimate starry-eyed teenage symphony to God, and it perfectly captures the earnest devotion we only seem capable of in a small window of years."238 *Mojo* called it "the perfect overture to the album's tussle between Brian Wilson's new avant-garde pop and the Boys' fidelity to he-man Americana."25

Rick Swan, as always, hit the nail on the head: "If Brian surpassed this performance, its yet to be heard. If he created a superior rock song - well, he didn't."21

5. California Girls *(Summer Days (And Summer Nights!)* 1965)

(Brian Wilson, Mike Love)
Recording
06/04/65 Western Recorders, LA (tracking - 44 takes)
04/06/65 CBS Columbia Studio, LA (lead vocal, backing vocals)
Producer - Brian Wilson
Engineer - Chuck Britz (*Western*); Ralph Valentin? (*Columbia*)
Band members

Mike Love (lead & bass vocals); Brian Wilson (harmony & backing vocals); Carl Wilson (harmony & backing vocals, 12-string guitar); Dennis Wilson (harmony & backing vocals); Al Jardine ((harmony & backing vocals); Bruce Johnston ((harmony & backing vocals)
Session musicians
Hal Blaine (drums); Frank Capp (vibraphone); Roy Caton (trumpet); Jerry Cole (12-string guitar); Al De Lory (Hammond B3 organ); Steve Douglas (tenor sax); Jay Migliori (baritone sax); Jack Nimitz (bass sax); Carol Kaye (bass guitar); Lyle Ritz (upright bass); Howard Roberts (electric guitar); Leon Russell (piano); Billy Strange (tambourine)
Album released - 05/07/65
US single released - 12/07/65 b/w "Let Him Run Wild" Capitol 5464 #3
UK single released - 08/65 b/w "Let Him Run Wild" Capitol CL 15409 #26
Film/TV performances
23/10/65 *The Jack Benny Hour* NBC Burbank (broadcast 03/11/65)
12/12/68 *Beat Club* Radio Bremen TV, Bremen West Germany (broadcast 25/01/69)
14/12/68 *Twien* NCRV Theater De Brakke Grond, Amsterdam (broadcast 23/12/68)
16/02/69 *Kraft Music Hall* NBC Burbank (broadcast 19/2/69)
16/06/69 Olympia Theater Paris TFI (filmed concert)
21/06/80 Knebworth England concert (later released on CD/DVD)
13/07/85 *Live Aid* Philadelphia Pa

    This most perfect of all the Beach Boys' fun-time songs was written, according to some accounts, while Brian was taking his first LSD trip. He had been introduced to the drug by Loren Schwartz in late 1964. Schwartz had gone to the same high school as Tony Asher, although Brian first met him at a Hollywood studio and soon became the closest of friends. Through him, Brian became not only exposed to drugs, but also a wealth of literature, philosophy, world religion, and other mystical topics, all of which he developed a deep fascination for.
    Their relationship caused friction between Brian and Marilyn. According to her, Brian only took LSD one more time, once again under Schwartz's supervision,[123] but he hit back at her by saying he never did and called her a "moronic, bovine wife."[127] In 2012 Schwartz stated: "I became the villain in this drama. I was the 'Hollywood hipster' who had ruined Brian's life…All I can say in my defense is that it is universally understood that Brian's best work followed in the next two years…"[123]
    In his 2016 memoir, Brian recalled: "The idea for 'California Girls' is that there's this guy who thinks about girls all the time, so much that he starts to imagine all kinds. But there's only one kind he really wants, and that's right there at home. The music started off like those old cowboy movies, when the hero's riding slowly into town, *bum-ba-dee-dah*. I was playing that at the piano after an acid trip. I played it until I almost couldn't hear what I was playing, and then I saw the melody hovering over the piano part."[35] In the 2021 documentary *Long Promised Road*, however, Brian stated that he actually wrote the song during the week following the trip when he was sober.

"The song was a big record for us but I never really liked anything other than the intro"

    In a 2007 interview for the *Los Angeles Times*, Brian revealed he had intended to encapsulate the sonic feel of the Drifters' hit, "On Broadway,"[245] while in other interviews he said that the shuffle beat of the song had been influenced by Bach's "Jesu, Joy of Man's Desiring."10

Brian discussed the writing process in a 1966 interview: "It all starts with religion. I believe in God - in one God, some higher being who is better than we are. But I'm not formally religious. I simply believe in the power of the spirit and in the manifestation of this in the goodness of people. I seek out the best elements in people. People are part of my music. A lot of the songs are the results of emotional experiences, sadness and pain. Or joy, exultation, and so on. Like 'California Girls' - a hymn to youth. I find it impossible to spill melodies, beautiful melodies, in moments of great despair. This is one of the wonderful things about this art form - it can draw out so much emotion, and it can channel it into notes of music in cadence. Good emotional music is never embarrassing. Music is genuine and healthy, and the stimulation I get from moulding it and from adding dynamics is like nothing on earth.85

According to Brian, he completed the song with Mike the following day, although they later disagreed over the extent of their lyrical contributions. Mike later claimed in *Rolling Stone* that he wrote "every syllable" of the song except the line, "*I wish they all could be California girls*,"246 and that it was all done in less than an hour while in the hallway of the recording studio during the tracking.188 Brian disputed this in an article for the *Los Angeles Times*: "I wrote a lot of those lyrics too; it was line for line, back and forth between us. That's what happened." As well as coming up with the subject matter and writing the opening lines, Brian went on to claim: "Every other line was his or mine…Everybody loves girls, right? Everybody loves California and the sun. That's what I wanted from the song…"245

When Mike found out he was not listed as the song's co-writer on its release, he was told by Brian that Murry Wilson, the band's publisher, was at fault.188 Brian later took the responsibility: "I knew that my Dad made a mistake by putting only my name on there."19 Mike would eventually be awarded co-writing credit after his 1994 lawsuit.

According to Mike, he found inspiration for the lyrics from the band's first tour of Europe and the UK the previous November, but felt he had failed to convey the message originally intended: "I wanted the song to be a tribute to girls everywhere - not just in the United States, let alone California, but everywhere in the world."188 In 2018 he admitted: "Some people misunderstood and thought we were saying that California girls were best, but California is a microcosm of the US, which is the microcosm of the world, and we were trying to be inclusive.247 Mark Dillon saw it as Mike's way of keeping concert-goers in mind. By celebrating the attributes of girls coast to coast, North and South, and inbetween, it allowed the band to sing it live and pay homage to every American girl in each relevant audience. Apparently, the line, "*The Midwest farmer's daughters really make you feel alright*," always got the most raucous applause.10

In a 2011 interview for *Goldmine*, Brian recalled: "I came up with the introduction first. I'm still really proud of that introduction. It has a classical feel. I wrote the song in the same key as the introduction. It took me some time. I wanted to write a song that had the traditional country and western left hand piano riff, like an old country song from the early 50's. I wanted to get something that had a kind of jumpy feeling to it in the verses."

For the first session in April, the song had a working title of "We Don't Know," and even in June it was referred to by Brian as "Yeah, I dig the girls." He spoke about the long tracking session in a Capitol interview: "Everybody was up. The whole gang was there. It became my favourite session. The intro to this song is the greatest piece of music that I've ever written. I was looking for an introduction which would be totally different to the rest of the song, but would lead into it. The song was a big record for us but I never really liked anything other than the intro."[11]

In his description of the music, Mark Dillon wrote: "The song boasts one of pop music's great intros. The sublime opening bars - which constitute Brian's favourite self-penned piece - stand apart from the rest of the song while leading into it beautifully. Carl and session player Jerry Cole open with magnificent electric 12-string guitar chords played in chamber echo. Kaye does her tumbling bass part, Hal Blaine lightly taps the cymbals, and the subtle, majestic horn of Roy Caton and saxophones of Steve Douglas, Jay Migliori and Jack Nimitz put it over the top."[10]

Carol Kaye recalled: "I love what Brian wrote there. He got a very deep feeling and we all felt it when we first played it."[10] Dillon continues: "The 22-second passage was Brian's proclamation to the rest of the music biz that he was a composer to take seriously. Unfortunately the message was often buried by DJ's who talked over the intro until Al de Lory's sexy roller-rink organ comes in ahead of the vocal."[10] Kaye also remembered the time when the other band members would turn up at a tracking session: "They were nice, cute young guys. They would exchange a joke with Hal. They seemed thrilled that we were playing it for them. My respect really grew for them when I heard takes of the vocal overdubs, because Brian really had to help them shape up to get the best vocal performances. They did a good job."[10]

Even though Brian called it his favourite session, the same could not be said for the dozen-plus musicians. Due to problems with the tempo and guitar parts for the intro, it required a mammoth 44 takes until Brian was satisfied, and by then it was past midnight. Kaye remembered it only too well: "[Brian would] spend three or four hours on one song, whereas usually in a three-hour record date we'd cut four or five tunes. We played every tune and every take like a hit record. It got a little boring because Brian would change things back and forth all the time. But we stuck it out because we knew what he was doing and we admired him. And that admiration and respect got across to him and helped him to grow and feel safe with us."[10]

In his 2016 memoir, Brian recalled: "When we got into the studio with Chuck, he said that he wanted Carl's twelve-string guitar in the intro to sound more direct. I didn't know what that meant. 'Can he play it in the booth?' Chuck said. I had never thought about that before, but it seemed like a good idea. Carl was standing next to me in the booth and all the other musicians were out in the studio. I conducted it like an orchestra."[35] Apparently, Murry had urged Brian to "simplify" the grand orchestral into and make the song less complex, but Brian would have none of it.

For the vocals, Brian welcomed the arrival of 20-year-old Bruce Johnston for his very first recording session with the band. Midway through their US tour in April, Glen Campbell, the band's regular stand-in for Brian, was unable to continue due to his own solo tour commitments. Brian told *Melody Maker*: "The Beach Boys were really in trouble now because they couldn't cancel out of the tour. So Mike, in the last minute, phones up Bruce Johnston back in Los Angeles to see if he can find a fill-in."11

At the time, Bruce was a record producer at Columbia and had been known to the band for a couple of years. At first he suggested Ed Carter, who declined the offer. In a 1974 interview, Bruce recalled: "Mike called me and said he'd like me to stand in for two weekend concerts because Brian was sick...They wanted someone yesterday - it was a real rush thing. I said, Look, Mike, I can't find anyone, so I'll come. I don't play bass, I play piano, but I suppose I could sing all the high parts if you show me what to do."11 Bruce joined the band in New Orleans the next day in time for Carl to teach him the band's repertoire. Bruce ended up staying with them for the rest of the tour, even learning to play bass along the way.

Bruce continued: "I came home from the [tour] and they said, 'Why don't you come and sing on our next album?' The first song I sang on was 'California Girls.' At that point I still wasn't a proper member of the group. I was still working at Columbia Records...and was reluctant to leave because I felt that Brian would come back to the [stage] group at any time."11

Brian told *Teen Beat*: "Bruce sounds somewhat like me when he sings falsetto. He sings and plays well. Bruce ended up making the Beach Boys his living. We love Bruce. He came just at the right time when we were against the wall.."11 Bruce also remembers Mike writing the lyrics: "Mike Love was brilliant. I was in the hallway of Western and Brian kind of popped his head out of the door and said, 'Hey Mike, I've just recorded this track. I want to call it 'California Girls' Write some lyrics.' So I just hung out with Mike in the hallway and watched him write, like a runaway fax machine. Two hours later, he had the words for 'California Girls.'"253

The single was released on July 12th and peaked at #3 on the Hot 100, just behind the Beatles' "Help!" and Dylan's "Like A Rolling Stone," but a month later only managed to reach a rather disappointing #26 in the UK charts. *Record World* described it as "a ballad with a beat extolling the Coast female...[an] extremely strong item,"248 while *Cash Box* called the song an "easy-going shuffle which touts the many positives of the Golden Gate state distaffers."249 Geoff Boucher of the *Los Angeles Times* praised the opening lyrics as "one of the most famous...in pop music," with the music being "equal parts symphony hall and amusement park, 2 ½ minutes of nuanced musical complexity and beach-blanket simplicity."250

According to biographer Peter Carlin, Paul McCartney met up with Mike while in India and played him the first two verses of "Back in the U.S.S.R." As Mike loves to point out, at that very moment he "told Paul exactly how he should write the bridge of the song, talking about how the girls in this place were so hot and the girls in that place so cool...like 'California Girls.'32 Talking to *Songfacts,* Mike gave another version: "Paul came down to the breakfast table one morning saying, 'Hey, Mike, listen to this,' and he starts strumming and singing, "Back in the U.S.S.R" the verses. And I said, 'Well, Paul, what you ought to do is talk about the girls around Russia, Ukraine girls and then Georgia on my mind, and that kind of thing.' Which he did."254 Paul later said that he wrote it as "a kind of Beach Boys parody."251 Mike added: "Of course, [Paul] needed no help writing a song, but he later acknowledged that I helped him out on the bridge. A tape still exists of he and I playing around with the song."260

In 2010 "California Girls" was inducted into the Grammy Hall of Fame, which honours records for their "lasting qualitative or historical significance."

4. Don't Worry Baby (*Shut Down Volume 2* 1964)
(Brian Wilson, Roger Christian)
Recording
07/01/64 Western Recorders, LA (tracking)
08/01/64 or 09/02/64 Western Recorders, LA (vocals & guitars overdubbed - take #12 master)
Producer - Brian Wilson
Engineer - Chuck Britz
Band members
Brian Wilson (lead vocal, backing vocals, piano); Mike Love (backing vocals); Carl Wilson (backing vocals, electric rhythm guitar); Dennis Wilson (backing vocals, drums); David Marks (possibly overdubbed lead guitar solo)
Album released - 02/03/64
US single released - 11/05/64 b-side of "I Get Around" Capitol 5174 #1
UK single released - 06/64 b-side of "I Get Around" Capitol CL 15350 #7
Film/TV performances
14/03/64 *American Bandstand* ABC Hollywood (broadcast 18/04/64)
16/06/69 Olympia Theater Paris TFI (filmed concert)

"I really did flip-out. Balls-out totally freaked out when I heard [it]...In a way it wasn't like having your mind blown, it was like having your mind revamped. It's like, once you've heard that record, you're a fan forever."[239]

This was Brian talking in 1995 about a song that, in no small way, would have a profound lifelong impact on him, and one that biographer Peter Carlin described as becoming his "spiritual touchstone."[32] The song, which has become part of Beach Boys lore, was "Be My Baby," a #2 Hot 100 smash hit for the Ronettes in August 1963. Produced and co-written by 24-year-old Phil Spector, it has since been regarding as one of the greatest pop songs of all time. Brian, of course, was already a disciple of Spector's music, but this, his masterpiece, was for Brian a never-ending object of desire and an enduring part of his mythology.

Musicologist Luis Sanchez described how the song "etched itself into Brian's mind," and with its mention in countless interviews, displayed varying themes of deep admiration, consolation, and a "baleful haunting of the spirit...an image of wretchedness." He visualised Brian in the early 70's, alone in his bedroom with curtains drawn shut, catatonic, listening to the song "over and over at aggressive volumes, for hours," as the rest of the band record something in the studio below."[240]

Brian would go on to cite other songs that "hit almost as hard," including Bill Haley's "Rock Around the Clock," Freddie Scott's "Hey Girl," and the Spector-produced "You've Lost That Loving Feeling" by the Righteous Brothers, but none had the lasting effect that "Be My Baby" had on him. Just to hear Hal Blaine's "bom bom bom -pah" drumbeat was enough to send him into raptures.

Brian often stated that he first heard the song on the radio while driving around with Marilyn, and was so excited he pulled to the side of the road to analyse the chorus. In those few seconds, he concluded that it was the greatest record he had ever heard. Once he bought the single, copies would be found around the house, in his car, and in the studio. In his 2016 memoir he conceded that "it's hard to recreate the feeling of first hearing [the song]."[35] Engineer Steve Desper recalled Brian asking him in the early 70's to create a tape loop consisting of just the song's final chorus, and he would then sit and listen to it for several hours as if in "some kind of a trance."32 Brian's belief that he would never be able to do anything as good was short-lived, and anxiety quickly turned to a feeling of burning competitiveness.

According to Brian: "I called lyricist Roger Christian and told him I had an idea. He met me one afternoon at my parents' house where in one of our last collaborations, we wrote a lush ballad whose title and chorus came directly from Marilyn's comforting words, 'Don't Worry, Baby.' I knew the song was a smash before we finished writing it."28 Mark Dillon recalls that the title did indeed come from a phrase that his then-girlfriend Marilyn used to comfort Brian after difficult days in the studio and comments made like, "I don't think I can do it, it's not good enough," to which she would unburden his soul and respond, "Don't worry baby, it's going to be great."10

Whether he believed it or not, he had created something that matched and perhaps even surpassed - his idol

In another statement Brian recalled: "I met [Roger] in the parking lot at KFWB and he presented the lyrics for me. I went home and wrote the song in about an hour-and-a-half."241 In a 2009 interview he said that the song was composed over two days: "I started out with the verse idea and then wrote the chorus. It was very simple and beautiful song. It's a really heart and soul song, I really did feel that in my heart. Some say it's about a car and others say it's about a girl, who's right? It's both. It's about a car and a woman."63

Brian actually contemplated offering the song to Spector, but decided not to after discussing it with Christian. Biographer Philp Lambert wrote that Brian "passed the word through the LA studio pipeline that [the song] was Phil's for the asking," but that "Spector declined, having no yen for material he couldn't own."9 Ronnie Spector, who sang lead vocal on "Be My Baby," recalled meeting Brian in 1963 and talking about "Don't Worry Baby": "Brian] came running into Gold Star Studios and said, 'I wrote a great song for you,' But of course [Phil] didn't do the writing on it, so [we didn't record it]."29

Although Brian may not have intended it to be a fully-fledged car song, Christian's lyrics indirectly relate to car themes, specifically a drag race in which the narrator has regrets over instigating it, fears losing his masculine image by backing out, only to be reassured by his girlfriend that she loves him and nothing will go wrong. In that respect, it's not just a love song, but one of the greatest romantic ballads of Brian's career, made even more astonishing, as Rick Swan points out, to think it "was produced and performed by a kid barely in his twenties."21

When compared with "Be My Baby," the music for which was provided by a host of seasoned session musicians later to be dubbed "The Wrecking Crew," it is even more remarkable that Brian manages to imitate that sound in the studio with just the five band members and their instruments.

In his wonderful description of the narrative, Timothy White writes: "Don't Worry Baby" is a rock rosary of a young braggart so enamoured of his street rod that he pushes the other guys in his clique into a potentially lethal shut down. Gripped on the eve of the race by a premonition of his own demise, he peers through the panicky spell of his self-pity to see that the only worldly possession not worth losing is the unconditional love of his girl. He confesses his shame, and she restores his courage with the loving counsel that comes as second nature..."29

Mark Dillon described the song as Brian elevating "suburban teenage melodrama into the realm of art - a musical equivalent to *Rebel Without a Cause*," and goes on to describe it: "Coming in after a Dennis drum intro that recalls Blaine's work...the group's cascading harmonies buttress Brian's soaring falsetto in a vocal arrangement so lush and complex the lyrics are easily lost. But it doesn't matter, because the singing is pure aural beauty. Brian's lead is one of his defining performances on one of his greatest records. Whether he believed it or not, he had created something that matched - and perhaps even surpassed - his idol."10

Timothy White saw it as avoiding "the darker chills" of the Ronettes' song: "[Brian] composed a hapless love token that showed its strength in it's sudden, surpassing humility,"29 while Peter Carlin suggests that Christian's lyrics were partly inspired by Brian's "stage fright and romantic insecurities," adding that: "The earlier verses contrasted the narrator's lust for his girl - with his fears regarding the power of his car...But when his lover keeps telling him not to worry, her reassurances lead to the sexual encounter in the final verse, and the intriguing reversal in the transitive verb that describes it. She's making love to him, which implies a sexual assertiveness (if not aggressiveness that the narrator won't, or can't claim for himself."32

In its retrospective review, *Pitchfork's* Mark Richardson wrote: "Maybe the appeal of this one has nothing to do with then specifics of the story, but surely we can all relate to the idea of support, how knowing that someone cares for you regardless of what happens gives you strength to do great things. And the music is such a perfect accompaniment to this theme, so damn cozy and warm, a tender respite from the stressful reality of the main narrative."242 *Mojo* opined: "It's beauty masks concern and doubt. Brian's confession... *'something's bound to go wrong'* pointed towards the rest of the decade with ominous accuracy."25 Speaking to *Mojo*, Al cited the song as his favourite record: "Chuck Britz got such a great sound on that song; the drums, the singing, the clicky sound on the Fender Precision bass. There's something about the way the track sat. Just about everything about it was an era-change for us."25

"Don't Worry Baby" was released in May 1964 as the flip-side to the chart-topping "I Get Around" and charted separately from the A-side as a result of differences in radio plays, finally peaking at #24. *Cash Box* referred to it as an "attention-getting shuffle beat cha cha ...[that] has the big hit goods."243

Referring to the song in a 1970 interview, Brian called the song "probably the best record we've ever done...It has about the best proportion of our voices and ranges,"11 and, in another comment, admitted: "I think I sang it sweetly enough that you could feel the love in my voice."244

Rick Swan summed the song up in his usual straightforward manner: "This is a song that perfectly expresses the longing that your lover will somehow make it better, but secretly doubting she might not."21

3. Good Vibrations (*Smiley Smile* 1967)
(Brian Wilson, Mike Love)
Recording
17/02/66 Western Recorders/Gold Star Studio, LA ("Untitled" rehearsals, tracking session - 26 takes)
18/02/66 Gold Star Studio, LA (new tracking session - take #28 master)
23/02/66 Western Recorders, LA (instrumental inserts - 27 takes)
24/03/66 Western Recorders, LA (new arrangements, decision not to put it on *Pet Sounds*)
09/04/66 Gold Star Studio, LA (new tracking session)
04/05/66 Western Recorders, LA (sixth tracking session)
24/05/66 Sunset Sound Studio, LA (music recorded in four separate sections)
25/05/66 Sunset Sound Studio, LA (two new tracking sessions)
27/05/66 Western Recorders, LA (tracking session)
02/06/66 Western Recorders, LA (work on a tracking section called "Inspiration")
12/06/66 Western Recorders, LA (work continues on "Inspiration")
13/06/66 Western Recorders, LA (further work on tracking - 21 takes)
16/06/66 Western Recorders, LA (tracking & overdub sessions)
18/06/66 Western Recorders, LA (further tracking with instrumental inserts)
24/08/66 Sunset Sound Studio, LA (tracking, guide vocal)
25/08/66 Western Recorders, LA (tracking session)
01/09/66 Western Recorders, LA (tracking, backing vocals by Carl & Dennis)
03/09/66 Western Recorders, LA (mixing)
05/09/66 Western Recorders, LA (final mixing)
12/09/66 Western Recorders, LA (final tracking session)
21/09/66 CBS Columbia Studio, LA (final lead vocal overdub; electro-theremin overdub)
Producer - Brian Wilson
Engineers - Chuck Britz (*Western*); Cal Harris, Larry Levine (*Gold Star*), Jim Lockert (*Bel Air*); Ralph Valentin? (*Columbia*), Bruce Botnick (*Sunset*)
Band members
Carl Wilson (lead & backing vocals, electric rhythm guitar on choruses and chorus fade, shaker); Brian Wilson (lead & backing vocals, tack piano on choruses, overdubbed tambourine on choruses); Mike Love (lead & backing vocals); Dennis Wilson (backing vocals, Hammond organ); Al Jardine (backing vocals); Bruce Johnston (backing vocals)
Session musicians/Guests
Hal Blaine (drums, timpani on choruses, shaker, possibly tambourine); Jimmy Bond (upright bass); Frank Capp (bongos with sticks); Gary Coleman (sleigh bells); Steve Douglas (tenor flute); Jesse Ehrlich (cello); Jim Gordon (drums on third bridge & chorus fade); Bill Green (contra-clarinet, bass sax); Jim Horn (piccolo); Larry Knechtel (Hammond organ on verses); Plas Johnson (piccolo); Al De Lory (tack piano); Mike Melvoin (upright piano on chorus fade); Jay Migliori (flutes); Tommy Morgan (bass harmonica, jaw harp); Bill Pitman (Danelectro bass); Ray Pohlman (Fender bass); Don Randi (electric harpsichord); Lyle Ritz (upright bass); Paul Tanner (electro-theremin); Terry Melcher (tambourine on verses)
Album released - 18/09/67
US single released - 10/10/66 b/w "Let's Go Away For a While" Capitol 5676 #1
UK single released - 28/10/66 b/w "Let's Go Away For a While" Capitol CL 15475 #1
Film/TV performances
26/10/66 *Tilt Magazine* TFI Paris (broadcast 25/01/67)
10/11/66 *Top of the Pops* BBC-1 London (promo #3)
17/11/66 *Top of the Pops* BBC-1 London(edited promo #3)
24/11/66 *Top of the Pops* BBC-1 London (promo #1 shot in LA 23/10/66)
31/12/66 *Beat Club* Radio Bremen, Germany (promo #3)
02/67 *Cinq Colonnes a La Une* France (promo #2)
15/12/67 *UNICEF Christmas For the Children of the World* TFI Paris (broadcast on BBC-1 London 27/12/67)
13/10/68 *The Ed Sullivan Show* CBS New York
14/12/68 *Twien*, Theater De Brakke Grond, Amsterdam (broadcast 23/12/68)
16/06/69 Olympia Theater Paris TFI (filmed concert)
30/06/69 *De Raiders En De Beach Boys* NCRV Amsterdam (broadcast 03/07/69)
28/05/70 *Something Else* New Orleans (syndicated 04/04/70)

26/11/76 *Saturday Night Live* NBC New York (Brian solo, broadcast 27/11/76)
27/04/79 *The Midnight Special* NBC Burbank
21/06/80 Knebworth Concert, England (DVD *Good Timin' - Live at Knebworth*)
13/07/85 *Live Aid* Philadelphia Pa.

"[My mother] used to tell me about vibrations. I didn't really understand too much of what it meant when I was just a boy. It scared me, the word 'vibrations.' She told me about dogs that would bark at people and then not bark at others, that a dog would pick up vibrations from these people that you can't see, but you can feel."11

So Brian recalled in 1966. Ten years later, he would declare in *Rolling Stone*: "It scared me, the word *vibrations*. To think that invisible feelings, invisible vibrations, existed scared me to death," but, as the years went by, anxiety turned to fascination for "cosmic" vibrations, and in his substance-broadened mind of the mid-60's, Brian would be comparing those feelings to lovers "communicating on that same non-verbal plane."32 By doing so the seeds for what many still consider to be his greatest achievement and certainly the song that has received the greatest kudos of the Beach Boys' entire career.

Mojo ranked it second in the list of the band's greatest songs: "Even now, writers and producers take its blueprint for unfathomable spirituality as their goal, trying to make sounds we don't think we've heard. You can still hear 'Good Vibrations' today, moving through words and melodies, endlessly nourishing future visions of inner-space: a song that everyone recognises, but only one man knows for sure what it really means"25

It all began during the sessions for *Pet Sounds* when Brian started putting together a kind of R&B-flavoured song called "Good, Good, Good Vibrations." He played the melody to his *Pet Sounds'* co-writer Tony Asher, who, despite what he described as Brian's "primitive" piano playing, manged to jot down some preliminary lyrics: *"It's weird how she comes in so strong/ And I wonder what she's pickin' up from me/ I hope it's good, good, good vibrations…"* Asher recalled: "Brian was playing what amounts to the hook of the song: *"Good, Good, Good Vibrations."* He started telling me the story about his mother…He said he'd always thought it would be fun to write a song about vibes and picking them up from other people…So as we started to work, he played this little rhythmic pattern - a riff on the piano, the thing that goes under the chorus."8

In his mind, he had just made the ultimate album; now he was going to make the ultimate single

The lyrics they wrote between them would later be discarded. Sometime later, Brian would ask his new friend Van Dyke Parks to finish off the still-incomplete lyrics, but fortunately for us all, he declined, preferring to collaborate on something they both created. Brian remembered: "I had a lot of unfinished ideas, fragments of music I called 'feels.' Each feel represented a mood or an emotion I'd felt, and I planned to fit them together like a mosaic."52 Describing the song as "his whole life performance in one track," Brian would claim at the time: "This is going to be better than 'You've Lost That Lovin' Feelin.'"11 Although Brian initially wanted to call the song "Good Vibes," he was advised by Asher that it was a "lightweight use of the language" and, instead, suggested changing it the more trendy "Good Vibrations."

With the original intention of recording it for the new album, Brian assembled some of his regular sessionists at Western Recorders on February 17th 1966 to lay down a backing track for the song that was logged "#1 Untitled." Further recording were carried out the same night at nearby Gold Star. Among the instruments on hand was Paul Tanner's electro-theremin which had been used on the recording for "I Just Wasn't Made For These Times' just three days before. Tanner recalled: "Brian came over to me and sang such and such a thing, and I said, 'Well write it down and I'll play it,' and he said ,'Write it down? We don't write anything down.'"

Brian, still a little unsure of its workings, recalled: "When 'Good Vibrations' was forming itself in my mind, I could hear the theremin on the track. It sounds like a woman's voice or like a violin bow on a carpenter's saw. You make it waver, just like a human voice. It's groovy!"11

After the first session, Brian returned to Gold Star the following day to tape a new instrumental base and tape a first guide vocal. Only then was he beginning to question Asher's lyrics. Over the next few days further sessions saw Brian building the song with insert recordings and re-working arrangements to complete the tracking for the verses. On February 24th, realising just how much time and effort will be required to complete the song to his satisfaction, Brian made the decision to leave it off *Pet Sounds,* despite Capitol having a memo the previous day with a preliminary track list for the album which included "Good, Good, Good Vibrations." The reason was that Brian felt the song wouldn't fit in with the introspective tracks that formed the core of the album. At one stage, according to his friend David Anderle, he pondered over scrapping it altogether or handing over to an R&B group or a soul singer such as Wilson Pickett at Warner; even, as Anderle suggested, giving it to Brian's young musician friend, Danny Hutton, who Anderle apparently managed at the time. But Brian held on to it.

For the next two weeks, work was completed on the album, and on March 11th Brian used Sunset Sound to record a new tracking session. Still without a definite title or even a solid idea where the song was going, he made the decision to rework it into a separate piece that would ultimately become *Pet Sounds'* "Here Today."

The session at Gold Star on April 9th was considered to be the finished version for the instrumental tracking and ready for mixing. But Brian was still not satisfied, and almost a month later, to the exasperation of musicians and band members, completed a sixth tracking session at Western. Under increasing pressure from both the label and his band Brian had reached a point where he was losing his cool. As he saw it he was "creating art" and time was of no concern to him. In his mind, he had just made the ultimate album; now he was going to make the ultimate single.

Biographer Peter Carlin wrote: "Brian began to think of 'Good Vibrations' as a smaller, psychedelic version of 'Rhapsody in Blue.' A little 'pocket symphony,' as publicist Derek Taylor dubbed it, built from parts whose distinct rhythms, moods and sounds would flow together to form a larger, cohesive piece."32 In an interview for BBC Radio, Brian revealed: "We ran wild with [marijuana]. We were being very creative on drugs. To satisfy our fantasy, we would try different studios with different parts of the song."11

In fact, Brian was so perplexed with the arranging of the song that he would, according to engineer Chuck Britz, sometimes arrive at a session, contemplate the possibilities, and then leave without recording anything. It was estimated that while Brian was on his journey of discovery from February to September, sessions for the "pocket symphony" would consume some 90 hours of tape, with an eventual overall cost of between $50,000 and $70,000 dollars in studio time, although this was disputed by Brian, who gave a figure closer to $25,000.

Always in the back of Brian's mind, of course, were the Beatles. He envisioned the Beach Boys replicating their rivals' huge fanbase that faithfully followed every move they made, expecting each successive album to be a marked leap forward in creativity. In an interview for *Go!* magazine, Brian remarked: "While Lennon and McCartney were exciting everyone with their new sounds, we were static. That's why I concentrated on giving the group a sound that would have lasting appeal."8

Following the release of *Pet Sounds* in May, work resumed on "Good Vibrations" at both Western and Sunset Sound, with Brian now abandoning the idea of taping the instrumental base in one take and, instead, recording the song in four separate sections. He also now had the lyric "*Gotta keep those lovin good…*" in his mind. Further sessions saw recording of a piece called "Inspiration," another part of the jigsaw.

According to Brian, it was Carl who suggested he employed the cello on the track, as well as using a triplet beat for the chorus, based on the Crystals' "Da Do Ron Ron." This was disputed by Parks, who claimed the credit and said it encouraged their collaborative work on *Smile*.

By June work continued on the song with Asher's lyrics, and following a "sweetening" session on the 18th, it was considered good enough to become the next single. But Brian soon thought otherwise. Frustrated and dejected with it all, work ceased on the song for the next nine weeks. Following the band's tour of the US and Canada in August, Brian was back in the studio, feeling invigorated with less pressure put on him from Capitol. On August 24th he overlaid a guide vocal with different lyrics, with the first verse including the lines: *"She's already working on my brain/I went and looked in her eyes/But I picked up something I just can't explain."*11

Meanwhile in July an ad appeared in *Billboard* with the band thanking the music industry for the sales of their album: "We're moved over the fact that our *Pet Sounds* brought on nothing but Good Vibrations." Without hardly any reader realising it, this was a subtle hint about the new single.

The final lyrics for the song were instigated by Mike, who recalled coming up with the iconic lines while on the Hollywood freeway just ten minutes before arriving at the August 24th session: "I was dictating the words *'I'm picking up Good Vibrations*' as we drove down the road. It was a kind of cliffhanger. Brian said, 'We need some words,' " and I said, 'Well, OK, Let's see.'"32 He continued: "On one passage …we did it over and over, not only to get the note right, but he wanted the timbre and quality of each note and how the four parts would resonate together. Then, Brian would be hearing something that nobody else could hear, including a dog, y'know? He would say, 'Do it again' and we'd say 'Do it again? Are you crazy?' It was so exhausting, I can remember doing 25 to 30 vocal overdubs of the same part…"11

On hearing the finished track for the first time, Mike recalled: "[It] was already so avant-garde, especially with the theremin, I wondered how our fans were going to relate to it. How's this going to go over in the Midwest or Birmingham? It was such a departure from 'Surfin' USA' or 'Help Me Rhonda.'"288 He felt that the song could be the band's "psychedelic anthem" or "flower-power offering," and based lyrics that reflected the burgeoning Flower Power movement in southern California: "[They] were just a flowery poem. Kind of almost like 'if you're going to San Francisco, be sure to wear some flowers in your hair,' and there were love-ins and all that kind of thing starting to go on. So the track…was so unique and so psychedelic in itself…I wanted to do something that captured this feeling of the track and the times, but also could relate to people."287

Mike continued: "Because I thought that the music was such a departure that who knows how well it would relate to Beach Boys fans at that time. The one thing that I figured is an absolute perennial is the boy/girl relationship, the attraction between a guy and a girl. So I came up with that hook part of the chorus. It didn't exist until I came up with that thought…It was kind of a flower poem to suit the times and complement the really amazing unique track that Cousin Brian came up with."287.

A second unsatisfactory attempt at the vocals had Brian and Carl singing on one track, Bruce, Carl and Al on the second, and Mike and Bruce on the third. Finally, after a mixing session at Western on September 5th, Brian informed Derek Taylor that the track was "ready to go." However, just a week later, he arranged another tracking session with unsatisfactory results, and out of frustration, told the session players, "I'm gonna play all the instruments myself." Once he calmed down, he realised the session held on the 5th could not be improved upon.

In one seven-hour session at Columbia on September 21st, Brian worked on a final theremin and lead vocal overdub, followed by final mixing. Although Dennis had been earmarked to sing lead, he was suffering from laryngitis and was replaced by Carl at the last minute. Brian recalled his excitement: "It was at Columbia. I remember I had it right in the sack. I could just feel it when I dubbed it down, made the final mix from the 16-track down to mono. It was a feeling of power, it was a rush. A feeling of exaltation. Artistic beauty. It was everything…I remember saying, Oh my God. Sit back and listen to this!"32

After 22 sessions in four different studios, Brian's masterpiece was finally completed, but straight away it ran into trouble when Capitol executives became concerned with the lyrics' psychedelic overtones, accusing Brian of having based the production on his LSD experiences, although Brian clarified that it was marijuana: "I made [the record] on drugs; I used drugs to make that.. I learned how to function behind drugs, and it improved my brain… It made me more rooted in my sanity.289 He later recalled: "We talked about good vibrations with the song and the idea, and we decided that on the one hand you could say…those are sensual things. And then you'd say, "I'm picking up good vibrations," which is a contrast against the sensual. That's what we're really talking about."123

Ahead of its release, Brian told journalist Tom Nolan that the new "monster" single would be about "a guy who picks up good vibrations from a girl," going on to explain: "It's still sticking pretty close to that same boy-girl thing, you know, but with a difference. And it's a start, it's definitely a start."240 In a press release, Derek

Taylor stated: "Wilson's instinctive talents for mixing sounds could most nearly equate to those of the old painters whose special secret was in the blending of their oils. And what is most amazing about all outstanding creative artists is that they are using only those basic materials which are freely available to everyone else."291

To promote the single several promo films were shot - the first showing the band in Monkees-fashion at a fire station and roaming the streets of LA, while another featured the band rehearsing at Western.

"Good Vibrations" was finally released as a single in the US on October 10th, replacing the New Vaudeville Band's "Winchester Cathedral" to become their third #1 on the Hot 100 after "I Get Around" and "Help Me Rhonda," and their first million-selling single in that country. It would also be their last chart-topper there until "Kokomo" twenty years later, setting the record for the longest gap between #1 hits on the Hot 100. Over in the UK, it replaced the Four Tops' "Reach Out, I'll Be There" to score their first #1, and by doing so giving a much-needed boast to what was perceived as a dip in their long-standing popularity.

Cash Box described it as a "catchy, easy-driving ditty loaded with the Boys' money-making sound,"292 while *Billboard* wrote that "the group has a sure-fire hit in this off-beat and intriguing rhythm number. Should hit hard and fast."293 Scott Interrante, writing for *Pop Matters,* described how the song "changed the way a pop record could be made, the way a pop record should sound, and the lyrics a pop record could have…It's influence on the ensuing psychedelic and progressive rock movements can't be overstated, but its legacy as a pop hit is impressive as well."294 Rick Swan wrote: "Smart, original, and surprising, 'Good Vibrations' if not perfect, is as close as one human can get."21 *Smile* historian Domenic Priore described the song as "unlike anything previous in the realms of classical jazz, international, soundtrack, or any other kind of recording,"8 while musicologist Charlie Gillett called it "one of the first records to flaunt studio production as a quality in its own right, rather than a means of presenting a performance."295

Brian called his masterpiece "the summation of my musical vision. A harmonic convergence of imagination and talent, production values and craft, songwriting and spirituality."76 Without doubt, he had been good to his word in giving us his "pocket symphony to God."

2. Surf's Up *(Surf's Up 1971)*
(Brian Wilson, Van Dyke Parks)
Recording (Smile)
07/10/66 Western Recorders, LA (tracking for "Child Is Father Of the Man", piano overdub)
11/10/66 Western Recorders, LA ("Child" version 2 - logged as "Cabin Essence")
12/10/66 CBS Columbia Studio, LA ("Child" tracking, mixing)
04/11/66 Western Recorders, LA ("Surf's Up" 1st movement tracking)
07/11/66 Western Recorders, LA (horns overdubbed)
08/11/66 Western Recorders, LA (1st movement tracking, percussion overdubs)
02/12/66 CBS Columbia Studio, LA ("Child" vocals)
05/12/66 Western Recorders, LA (possible vocals)
15/12/66 CBS Columbia Studio, LA ("Surf's Up" lead vocal overdub, piano overdub)
15/12/66 Brian's home, Bel Air (filming for Oppenheim's documentary *Inside Pop*)
17/12/66 Brian's home, Bel Air (re-filming Brian's performance for *Inside Pop*)
23/01/67 Western Recorders, LA (tracking session - additional strings & horns)
08/02/67 CBS Columbia Studio, LA (further tracking)

10/04/67 Sunset Sound Recorders, LA ("Child" version 3 vocals)
Recording (Surf's Up)
18/06/71 Sunset Sound Recorders, LA (new track for 04/11 version)
19/06/71-23/06/71 Sunset Sound Recorders, LA (overdubs)
06/67-07/71 Beach Boys Studio, Bel Air (new arrangement)
Producer - Brian Wilson
Engineers - Chuck Britz (Western), Stephen Desper (Bel Air), Ralph Valentin? (Columbia)
Band members
Brian Wilson (lead vocal, piano on 2nd movement, backing vocals); Carl Wilson (lead vocal on 1st movement, backing vocals, Hammond organ, shaker, possibly Moog synth); Mike Love (backing vocals); Dennis Wilson (backing vocals); Al Jardine (lead vocal on outro, backing vocals); Bruce Johnston (backing vocals)
Session musicians *(04/11/66)*
Jimmy Bond (upright bass); Arthur Brieglab (French horn); Roy Caton (trumpet); Frank Capp (car keys, hi-hat); Al Casey (electric baritone guitar); David Duke (French horn); Carol Kaye (Fender bass); George Hyde (French horn); Al De Lory (upright piano); Nick Pellico (glockenspiel); Claude Sherry (French horn)
Guests
Marilyn Wilson (backing vocals); Jack Rieley (backing vocals); Bill De Simone (backing vocals on outro); Steve Desper (Moog programming)
Album released - 30/08/71
Film/TV performances
17/12/66 *Inside Pop: The Rock Revolution* CBS News Special (broadcast 25/04/67)
25/02/72 *Grand Gala Du Disque Populaire* RAI Amsterdam

It was one summer evening in 1966 when two young men sat down together at a grand piano with their feet in a sandbox littered with dog faeces. One was 24-year-old Brian Wilson, and the other was a bespectacled lyricist, two years his junior, called Van Dyke Parks. In the space of an hour, apparently high on drugs, they had written their second song together and what would become, not only one of the Beach Boys' greatest songs, but undeniably one of their most complex recordings for the legendary *Smile* project.

"Here is a man lost in the muse, recalling abstract lyrics from deep within his consciousness"

Brian recalled: "We wrote the song in one night, staying up until six in the morning. It opened on a minor seventh - unlike most of our songs, which open on a major - and from there it just started building and rambling, a lot of chord changes and things. I thought it rambled beautifully and said a lot at the end. A children's song, a song of freedom...But it was easy to write. I'd write a melodic line and Van Dyke would come up with some words for it right away. And when we finished it, he said, 'Let's call it 'Surf's Up', which is wild because surfing isn't related to the song at all. Special? That's right. Van Dyke and I really kind of thought we had done something special when we finished that one"[8, 11]

When the band flew back from their European Tour on November 15th 1966 they had barely a day off before commencing an eight-day tour of the US. During their short stay Brian had informed the jetlagged guys that the next album *Smile* and the single "Heroes and Villains" were expected by Capitol to be completed by Christmas.

Parks recalled the inspiration behind the song's title: "When Dennis came back from the Royal Albert Hall, he came in and we had everything but those six syllables of 'Surf's Up' that contained the title. He cried. They said they got laughed off the stage for their button-down pinstripe shirts and their Kingston Trio image, how passé they seemed to be. He was weeping - or he was weeping because he loved the song so much. He said, "What's the name of that song? Brian looked at me and said, "What are we gonna call the song?, and I said, "We're gonna call it "Surf's Up," because of the surfing image. Although it was the most gauche factor, and although maybe Brian thought it was the most dispensable thing, I thought it was very important to continue to use the name and keep the elephant in the room - to keep the surfing image, but to *sensitise* it to new opportunities. One of these would be an eco-consciousness; it would be speaking about the greening of the Earth, aboriginal people, how we had treated the Indians, taking on those things and putting them into the thoughts that come with the music. That was a solution to the relevance of the group, and I wanted the group to be relevant."8

Unfortunately, Parks' recollections are as confusing as his lyrics. Not only did the Beach Boys not play the Royal Albert Hall on that tour, but that AFM (American Federation of Musicians) track sheets indicated that the song had already been given the title before the band returned from the UK).11

Park's lyrics were heavy on patrician period imagery, with horse-drawn carriages, opera glasses and diamond necklaces. In 1966 Brian told journalist Jules Siegel that the intention was to have the "central character at a concert amidst an aristocratic crowd clinging to systems and beliefs that must inevitably fall. The scene dissolves to a dream of ancient times and grand battles at sea. Yet for all the suffering through the ages, the jaded protagonist cannot even shed a tear. In the end, God points the way: return to the pure love one feels as a child."10

Parks also quotes the titles of short stories by Edgar Allan Poe (*The Pit and the Pendulum*) and Guy de Maupassant (*The Diamond Necklace*). Siegel goes on to offer an explanation for the lyric, "*columnated ruins domino*" as symbolising the collapse of "empires, ideas, lives and institutions."280 The phrase, "*Are you sleeping, Brother John?*" is a reference to the children's song "Frère Jacques," while "*The Child Is Father of the Man*" is a quote from William Wordsworth's 1802 poem, *My Heart Leaps Up*.

Songwriter Jimmy Webb saw the song as a "premonition of what was going to happen to our generation and…to our music - that some great tragedy that we could absolutely not imagine was about to befall our world,"211 while Domenic Priore, the last word in *Smile* historiology, described it as just "a plea for the establishment to consider the wisdom coming out of youth culture in 1966."8 Paul Williams looked at the song as "a pivot on which everything that's come before in the song wheels and turns, and maybe…everything the Beach Boys and Brian have sung and played and done up to this moment."281

Sylvie Simmons, writing for *Mojo*, gives one of the best interpretation of the lyrics: "The recording opens with a twilit, ambient calm, the melody line echoing the slow rise and fall of waves before it peaks in *'columnated ruins domino.'* Those three words manage to evoke innocence, isolation and spirituality, as the choirboy vocal hitting the high F turns 'domino' from a game tile into God, and the 'columnated ruins' conjure a monastic walkway. A dash of Gershwin horns transports us to the city and into a theatre, where some kind of performance is going on. Then, *'Are you sleeping, Brother John'*...transports us back in time and also back again to our cloistered priory. The remembrances of things past conclude, correctly, that *'the laughs come hard in Auld Lang Syne'* a song about old friends. The raised glass is followed by a shard of operetta until the tide turns again and calm returns, through the magic of another *'children's song.'* And 'Surf's Up' rides out on a host of Beach Boys harmonies singing the Wordsworth coda..."25

At Western on November 4th Brian recorded the first instrumental track for what was listed on the AFM sheet as "1st Movement." Six session musicians were present. Several overdubs followed a few days later, with one session dedicated to a humorous experiment with horn effects and labelled "George Fell Into His Horn," a reference to sessionist George Hyde. On November 8th, the master tape of the instrumental track for "1st movement" was completed.

Moving to Columbia Studio the following month, vocal sessions were carried out on the "Child Is Father Of the Man" segment, and on the 15th Brian overdubbed his vocals and piano. That same afternoon television producer and musician David Oppenheim, a friend of Leonard Bernstein, arrived to film the band working on their new album for the CBS documentary, *Inside Pop: The Rock Revolution.*

According to David Leaf, the documentary was originally supposed to be focused on Brian. Oppenheim told Steven Gaines: "Some person in New York was very high on Brian Wilson. I was very curious about him and his music." When he came to Brian's Laurel Way home, he recalled: "Brian was looking at the tv set with the volume off and just the colour, detuned, and lots of vegetables around...It was a strange insulated household, insulated from the world by money...a playpen of irresponsible people."123

Although an interview was planned, the filmmakers were not able to get much out of him and any footage was discarded. For the second part of the documentary Brian was filmed singing "Surf's Up" at the piano, and although the singing was deemed adequate, the visuals were not, and filming was re-scheduled for two days' time, this time at Brian's home. The stunning one-take performance on a grand piano, complete with candelabrum and hosted by Bernstein himself, was aired nationwide in April 1967, giving viewers their first glimpse of Brian performing part of the song that many would say was the creative pinnacle of his career. In a voice-over, Oppenheim described the song as "poetic, beautiful in its obscurity...one aspect of new things happening in pop music today. As such, it is a symbol of the change many of these young musicians see in our future."10

Domenic Priore wrote: "The filmed performance of 'Surf's Up' displays a man possessed by music, heart and soul, and with an interior, spiritual connection to the words he is singing. Here is a man lost in the muse, recalling abstract lyrics from deep within his consciousness."8

In February, Brian was back at Columbia for further tracking sessions, the recording of which would later feature in the June 1971 re-working of the song, but by April the song would not feature in the last remaining sessions for *Smile,* which would be abandoned altogether in May.

In 1999 Brian's former assistant Michael Vosse wrote that the song was to be *Smile's* closing track and followed by a "choral anthem," and just to add more mystery, Byron Preiss said that the song was first intended to be part of "The Elements Suite" and briefly considered to paired up with "Love To Say Da Da."[282]

Apparently nothing has yet been found of a full-developed recording of the song's "2nd Movement," although rumoured to exist. Brian admitted many years later that he didn't remember recording it. Maybe the session was mislabelled or even cancelled, but it remains just one more holy grail for both music scholars and fans.

So why wasn't "Surf's Up" included on their next album, *Smiley Smile*? Brian said that his decision to keep the song unreleased had "nearly broke up" the band.[279] One reviewer regretted the decision to keep it off the album, saying that the song was "better than anything that is on the album and would have provided the same emotional catharsis as that 'A Day In the Life' provides for 'Sgt Pepper.'"[8]

In a 1970 interview Brian said that the song was "too long to make it for me as a record, unless it was an album cut, which I guess it would have to be anyway. It's so far from a singles sound. It could never be a single."[11]

Early the following year, the Beach Boys were recording their second album for Warner with the short-lived tentative name of *Landlocked*. In an interview for *Rolling Stone*, their new manager Jack Rieley explained how he came up with the title: "It represents departure. It was meant as a demarcation line, separating striped-shirted bullshit that had become irrelevant, an object of public scorn, from artistry, new creativity and great new songs..."[11] With the idea of using existing recordings, what were proposed by the band were referred to by Rieley as "forgettable." He suggested to Brian that "Surf's Up," a song he had long admired, be included.

But it wasn't until early June that Brian suddenly gave his approval for Carl and Rieley to re-record the song, after telling Rieley, "Well, ok, if you're going to force me, I'll...put [it] on the album, and then confirmed it with Warner boss Mo Ostin.[11]

For the next month or so, Brian, Carl and Rieley retrieved and examined the *Smile* multi-tracks from Capitol's vault, mainly in search of the "Surf's Up" masters. Taken to Carl's home, he and Rieley (and Brian, too, on a couple of occasions) listened to all the outtakes and snippets and even without the help of an engineer began repairing and splicing the tapes. What they found was that the song had survived in several unconnected sections, and the task now was reconstructing it. The three sections were as follows: the first (0:00-1:36) was based on the February 8th 1967 backing track; the second (1:37-3.09) on Brian's vocal-piano part recorded for *Inside Pop* on December 15th 1967; and the third (3:09-4:11) based on the "Child Is Father Of the Man" recording of December 2nd 1966).[11] The four-track recording from February 8th was transferred onto Brian's 16-track machine. An attempt to record an entirely new instrumental track from scratch was abandoned as sounding inferior to the original, so it was decided to use the February 8th track with two organ overdubs.

When it came to the vocals for the first section, Rieley asked Brian if he wanted to re-record them, but Brian insisted that a reluctant Carl did them. Rieley recalled: "Carl didn't want to sing the lead in the first portion of the record. He just didn't want to." Carl agreed with everyone else that Brian had to do it. However, Carl conceded, and Rieley recalled how "he hit that high note...and he really did it well. He read the lyric beautifully..."11 Section two was the unused recording of the song made at Columbia for the documentary on December 15th. Without hardly any alterations, a Moog synthesiser bass was overdubbed for this and part of section three. Carl then added his vocals, blending his voice with Brian's in perfect harmony, and created backing vocals. Section three was the vocal "Child" refrain taped on December 2nd, once more transferred to the 16-track tape, with vocal "ooohs" added for the final mix. Rieley recalled how the final "child" tag was accomplished: "[It] was something which we all got involved in. I know Al had an important part in that, Carl sings a couple of parts, so do Mike and Bruce. Even I'm on it. So is a guy who worked for us part-time...It was a lot of fun doing [that].11

With the song ready for mixing, there was one last surprise. After listening to the recording from his bedroom above, Brian came down in his pyjamas and told them to halt the mixing and add one more part to the ending. Given a mic and some headphones, Brian then arranged the beautiful "Child" coda, as if, as Keith Badman, surmised, "it was always in Brian's mind from the song's conception, forgotten until now."11 According to Steve Desper, Brian sang the part "and then ran out." In 1996, Rieley wrote that Brian had "stated clearly that it was his intent all along for Child to be the tag for 'Surf's Up.'"106 One further double-tracked line was then added -"*a children's song, and we listen as they play?/their song is love, and the children know the way.*" Desper credited Brian with the line, although Rieley credited himself.

And that was it. Another masterpiece was in the can, and the album accordingly renamed *Surf's Up*.

Despite the acclaim that followed, Brian would later admit his displeasure about it all. In a 1995 radio interview he said: "I'm embarrassed, totally embarrassed. That was a piece of shit. Vocally it was a piece of shit. I was the wrong singer for it in the first place...And in the second place, I don't know why I would ever let a record like that go out like that."11 A few years later, he seemed to have mellowed a little, saying his voice "was a little bit limited. It's not my favourite vocal I ever did, but it did have heart."69

With the album's release in August 1971, there must have been many listeners who were unaware that the title track was in fact a *Smile* remnant, and when released as a single three months later, it failed to chart. But the reviews were as expected. *Rolling Stone* confirmed that the song lived up to its legend, calling it "dazzling" to a fault,283 while *Melody Maker's* Richard Williams lamented that "had it been released back at *Pepper*-time...might have kept many people from straying into the pastures of indulgence and may have forced them to focus back on truer values. I've rarely heard a more perfect, more compete piece of music. From first to last it flows and evolves from the almost lush decadence of the first verses to the childlike wonders and open-hearted joy of the final chorale."11

The *New York Times* agreed that the song "bears easy comparison with the best of the Beatles' *Sgt Pepper* songs,"11 with the *Guardian* comparing it favourably to songs from *Pet Sounds,* stating: "It's subtle shifts of pace and timing, and delicate harmony singing, put it in the top flight of Beach Boys' numbers."284 Both *Cash Box* and *Record World* described the song as a "masterpiece,"285,286 while more recently *Mojo* placed it at the top of their 50 Greatest Beach Boy Tracks, stating: "Parks described the song as 'durable goods' and he was right. Not so much timeless, but a song out of time, an elegy whose richness and mystery only deepens with age."25

Philip Lambert celebrated the song as being the "soul" of *Smile* and the "sum total of its creators' most profound artistic visions [with its] perfect marriage of an eloquent lyric with music of commensurate power and depth."9 But it was Rick Swan who summed it up perfectly: "Starved of *Smile* for what seemed like forever, fans expected the sun, the moon, the secret of eternal life, and all they got was a song. But what a song, a thrilling journey through an alternative musical galaxy, filled to overflowing with Brian's musical innovations and Van Dyke's frisky apocalyptic vision."21

1. God Only Knows (*Pet Sounds* 1966)
(Brian Wilson, Tony Asher)
Recording
08/03/66 Western Recorders, LA (tracking - take #20 master)
09/03/66 Western Recorders, LA (strings overdubbed)
10/03/66 CBS Columbia Studio, LA (Carl's lead vocal & group vocal harmonies overdubbed, vocal inserts)
12/03/66 Western Recorders, LA (alternative mixes with sax solo & a capella end tag)
13/03/66 Western Recorders, LA (mixing)
22/03/66 Western Recorders /CBS Columbia Studio, LA (alternative mixes inc Brians lead vocal)
11/04/66 CBS Columbia Studio, LA (Carl's lead vocal & group harmonies overdubbed; vocal inserts)
Producer - Brian Wilson
Engineers - Chuck Britz (*Western*), Ralph Valentin (*Columbia*)
Band members
Carl Wilson (lead vocal, 12-string electric guitar); Brian Wilson (backing vocals); Bruce Johnston (backing vocals)
Session musicians/Guests
Hal Blaine (drums); Carl Fortina (accordion); Jim Gordon (plastic orange juice cups); Bill Green (flute & alto flute); Leonard Hartman (clarinet & bass clarinet); Jim Horn (flute & alto flute); Carol Kaye (12-string electric guitar); Larry Knechtel (harpsichord); Jay Migliori (clarinet); Frank Morocco (accordion); Ray Pohlman (electric bass guitar); Don Randi (tack piano with taped strings); Alan Robinson (French horn); Lyle Ritz (upright bass); Tony Asher (possibly sleigh bells); The Sid Sharp Strings (2 violins, 1 cello, 1 viola); Terry Melcher (tambourine)
Album released - *16/05/66*
US single released - 18/06/66 b-side to "Wouldn't It Be Nice" Capitol 5706 #8
UK single released - 22/07/66 b/w "Wouldn't It Be Nice" Capitol CL 15459 #2
Film/TV performances
25/04/66 *Top of the Pops* BBC-1 London (promo film shot at Lake Arrowhead, Hollywood (broadcast 04/08/66)
15/12/67 *UNICEF Christmas For the Children of the World* TFI Paris (broadcast on BBC-1 London 27/12/67)
25/08/67 *Lei'd in Hawaii* (footage taken from the concert shown on various documentaries)
14/12/68 *Twien*, Theater De Brakke Grond, Amsterdam (broadcast 23/12/68)
16/06/69 Olympia Theater Paris TFI (filmed concert)
21/01/77 Capital Centre, Washington DC
21/06/80 Knebworth England concert (later released on CD/DVD)

Placing this ahead of what many consider to be some of the Beach Boys' greatest achievements may appear a little indulgent on my part. And it surely is. But I would choose in a heartbeat what some have called a beautiful suicide song over all the technical brilliance and avant garde experimentation that Brian will no doubt be best remembered for.

To have a pop song that mentioned God was always going to be controversial at the time, but to begin a song that gets to the heart of real emotion with the words "*I may not always love you*," turns a would-be standard love paean into one of poignant vulnerability and self-doubt. Of course, this was nothing new for Brian. He had dipped into his confessional box of teenage angst in the past with songs such as "Lonely Sea," "Please Let Me Wonder," and "In the Back of My Mind," but never more heartbreakingly beautiful and spiritual as this. Although described by some commentators as a suicide song, it was never intended as such by the writers.

Musicologist Philip Lambert wrote: "[Brian] felt he was reaching deep into his soul to produce music of a timeless quality, to send a message that was both bravely personal and broadly general. He wanted to bring forth a universal love that he felt uniquely qualified to realise and that he felt music was uniquely suited to express."9 Kingsley Abbott describes the song as marking "a vulnerability and maturity miles ahead of the earlier paeans to fun in the sun."75

"If music is God's voice, He is speaking here with transcendent eloquence"

Tony Asher, the advertising copywriter and musician who Brian employed as lyricist for many of the *Pet Sounds* tracks, described the song as their most effortless collaboration: "There's something about its simplicity, its naïveté, maybe, that people respond to."72 According to Brian, Asher "had a musical influence on me somehow. After about ten years, I started thinking about it deeper, [and] I remember him talking about 'Stella by Starlight' and he had a certain love of classical songs." The music he referred to was the 1944 standard by Victor Young from the movie *Uninvited*. Brian recalled: "That was a vision that Tony and I had. It's like being blind, but in being blind, you can see more. You close your eyes; you're able to see a place or something that's happening."72

In Brian's since-discredited 1991 memoir, he claimed that the song was derived from a John Sebastian composition for the Lovin' Spoonful, reputedly the vocal layering of "You Didn't Have To Be So Nice," but both Sebastian and Asher failed to see any connection.

While writing the song, having the word "God" in the title became a topic for discussion. Asher recalled that from a commercial point of view, Brian had told him: "You're not going to get any airplay on this song" and he saw his point. Conservative radio stations, particularly in the US South, were unlikely to play songs with words like damn or hell in the lyrics, so the use of God stood a good chance of also being banned. Brian didn't want to be the first one to try it. The only previous song to chart with it in the title was Johnny Burnette's "God, Country And My Baby," a #18 hit in 1961. According to Asher, he "really had to fight with him to retain that title."122

The opening line, "*I may not always love you*" was also the cause of disagreements between the writers, as Asher recalled: "I liked the twist, and fought to start the song that way. Working with Brian, I didn't have a lot of fighting to do, but I was certainly willing to fight for the end for that."74

Eventually, Brian agreed to keep God in the title after being persuaded by others that, according to Asher, it would give him an "opportunity to be really far out [because] it would cause some controversy, which he didn't mind."72 There was also the growing decline of traditional religion in the country to be considered.

Brian and Carl frequently mentioned the spiritual qualities of *Pet Sounds* and "God Only Knows" in particular in a number of their interviews. Around the time of its recording Carl remarked: "We believe in God as a kind of universal consciousness. God is love. God is you. God is me. God is everything right here in this room. It's a spiritual concept, which inspires a great deal of our music."11

In an interview with David Leaf, Brian discussed the spiritual aspects of *Pet Sounds*: "Carl and I were in prayer together. We'd pray together, and we prayed for light and guidance through the album. We kind of made it a religious ceremony... It's like a gift. He gives you the gift of being able to feel something, you know, to feel this overall feeling, you know? And then when you convert it into music, that's the creative process...I believe that music is God's voice."9

Brian would later claim he sat down at the piano and wrote the song to emulate the high standard set by the Beatles' ground-breaking album *Rubber Soul*, which had been released in the US just three months before.

Marilyn Wilson recalled: "The first time I heard ["God Only Knows"] Brian played it to me at the piano. And I went, 'Oh my god, he's talking about God in a record.' It was pretty daring to me. And it was another time I thought to myself, 'Oh boy, he's really taking a chance.' I thought it was almost too religious. Too square, at that time. Yet it was so great that he would say it and not be intimidated by what anybody else would think of the words or what he meant."72

Jim Fusilli noted that in 1964 Brian had written a note to his new bride with the closing line, "Yours 'til God wants us apart."130 Although Brian would go on to say that the song was not written for anyone in particular, Marilyn responded, "I'm the only one here, so it must be about me. Then I would think, 'No it wasn't.'"72

Marilyn saw the song as autobiographical from Brian's point of view: "He knew that I was there and I would never leave him, so he knew that he could abuse me, even though he didn't try to. I was never number one, I was always two or three. But if I would leave in some kind of a way, he would get totally distraught. I was his anchor. Music was always number one. I didn't mind that. I just wanted to be number one as a mate and in his love life. Music was who he was. I related to it. That's how we related. The music was so beautiful. You can't compete with something that's part of you. That was not competition."72

Work began on the song at Western's Studio 3 on March 8th 1966, one of the last tracks recorded for the album. With Carl along to play his 12-string electric guitar, some 20 session musicians were hired for the day. These and other LA musicians would go on to be dubbed "The Wrecking Crew" by drummer Hal Blaine, but not until 1990. Guitarist Carol Kaye explained: "None of us ever called ourselves the Wrecking Crew back in the 60's - that was totally unheard of. Some musicians don't like the term; we were all independent, freelance professionals, and were totally interchangeable in all the studio work we did."72.

Bruce was also on hand in the studio, and later remarked: "I didn't realise just how great *Pet Sounds* was going to be until I witnessed this session.11 Among the stand-out features were Alan Robinson's French horn that bookends the track; Jim Gordon's backwards clip-clop percussion with plastic orange juice cups; Carl Fortina and Frank Marocco and their layered accordions; the Christmas sleigh bells credited on the log sheet to Tony Asher; Hal Blaine's closing drum triplets; Bill Green's flute playing two low-range melodic phrases toward the end, and Don Randi playing quarter notes on a piano with a strip of masking tape over the strings.

With musicians struggling to play what turned out to be the iconic instrumental break, pianist Don Randi said, "Brian, why don't we do it short?" - suggesting they play the parts in staccato rather than full quarter notes. Loving the sound, Brian agreed to the change. The three-track recording of the instrumental was then bounced to just one channel of an eight-track tape at Columbia to allow room for further overdubs. It still remains one of the most listened to of the many studio chats recorded during the making of the album.

Following string overdubs, the vocals began at Columbia on March 10th. Although Brian admitted he originally wanted to sing lead, he gave it Carl: "I was looking for tenderness and a sweetness which I knew Carl had in himself as well as in his voice. He brought dignity to the song and the words, through him, became not a lyric, but *real* words."297 Carl recalled later: "[Brian] says it fits my beautiful spirit. I know I shouldn't be embarrassed by a compliment but for so many years there was little communication between us three brothers, because we were…all near the same age and we were young and we were thrown into an adult world rather suddenly."11

Jim Fusilli commented on Carl's lead: "His voice is so soft and sweet, so young with a suggestion of mature apprehension. When Brian sang it, it was sweet and youthful too, but that hint of tentativeness isn't there, and his voice is brassy and a smidge too strong when he shifts to falsetto. Carl sounds like a little angel."130

Subsequent mixes included a discarded saxophone solo for the bridge and an alternative a capella ending that included the voices of Marilyn, Diane Rovell and Terry Melcher. According to Carl, "Everybody got in on it. It was like, 'Come on out here into the studio.' Brian would make up a little part. That was fun; we listened to it endlessly."10

The final vocal overdubs took place at Columbia on April 10th with Carl again on lead and Brian coaxing him: "Don't do anything with it. Just sing it real straight. No effort. Take a breath. Let it go easy."85 The coda was scaled down to just three lines sung by Brian and Bruce, with one of Brian's lines duplicating the part that had been played on French horn. Bruce recalled: "We were at the Columbia Records studio, overdubbing the vocals on an eight-track machine. After Carl finished singing the lead and centre harmony parts he was tired, and Brian sent him home. But we had extra time - and open tracks. Brian and I stayed, and the two of us overdubbed additional vocal parts on the ending, with him singing the top and bottom parts, and me singing the middle. It works because it caused a perfect vocal-to-track balance, and it's not too top-heavy. It's brilliant- a fine example of 'less is more.'85

One of the many highlights of the song is the much-revered bridge. Following Randi's staccato piano part, bass, tambourine, wood blocks, violin and cello create a sonic tapestry to underpin what can only be described as the band's greatest-ever vocal moment, as Charles Granta describes: "The primary vocal line features Carl, Brian and Bruce singing a breathy, melodic 'sigh' - a fluid phrase evocative of the French horn theme...Superimposed over this are two lines: a series of syncopated 'do-do-do-do-do-do-dos' and 'ba-ba-ba-ba-ba-ba-bas' that provide contrasting rhythmic support. The interplay and blending of these separate vocal parts - sung by only three voices - is ingenious. Then the 'do-do-do-do-do-do-dos' that began as staccato notes swiftly merge into the overall 'sigh' of the primary vocal, which forms the backdrop for the pulsating 'ba-ba-ba-ba-ba-ba-ba' line. The tension builds, climaxing with a soaring glissando that resolves all three vocal parts to one single vaporous sigh."[72]

Sounds complicated, indeed, but Brian had just created one of the most dazzling harmonies, not just in his career, but in all of pop music.

Jim Fusilli also described this magical moment: "The vocal arrangement on the bridge is brilliant, and it masks the dilemma. Carl, Brian and Bruce reprise the theme played by the French horn over some doo-wop sounds, and the three principal voices, seemingly coming from different planes, build, build and eventually swoop down, creating a sound very much like a romantic sigh. This startling glissando meets the string quartet and glides flawlessly into the verse."[130]

In his 2016 memoir Brian commented on the vocal rounds: "I liked all those song that used rounds, like 'Row, Row, Row Your Boat' and 'Frère Jacques.' I liked rounds because they made it seem like a song was something eternal."[35]

Apparently Brian had wanted to release "God Only Knows" as a Carl Wilson solo single, and "Good Vibrations" as the band's next single, but problems he was having with the latter recording and pressure put on him by Capitol for a new single persuaded him to put it out under the Beach Boys' name.

Two months after the album's debut "God Only Knows" was released in the US as the flip-side to "Wouldn't It Be Nice," (surely one of the greatest value-for-money 45's in pop history). With the A-side peaking at #8 on the Hot 100, "God Only Knows," possibly due to radio stations being hesitant to play it due to the word "God," stalled at #39. In other countries the sides were reversed. In the UK it emulated the parent album by reaching #2, held off the top spot by the Beatles' "Yellow Submarine/Eleanor Rigby." Towards the end of the year a "God Only Knows" EP was issued to coincide with the band's first tour there, and included "Here Today," "Sloop John B," and "Wouldn't It Be Nice."

A promotional film for the song was made for the BBC and directed by the band's publicist Derek Taylor. Although later edited, it featured snippets of two other songs, "Here Today" and "Wouldn't It Be Nice," and showed the boys (without Bruce) in the woods at Lake Arrowhead wearing horror masks and playing Old Maid.

Record Mirror called "God Only Knows" a "very pretty rockaballad with low key chanting...a meaningful love lyric teens will find irresistible,"[298] while *Cash Box* called it a "slow-shufflin' tender, romantic ode about a guy who is so much in love that he doesn't think that he could go on without his gal."[299] Tony Asher reflected: "This is the one that I thought would be a hit record, because it was so incredibly beautiful...I guess that in the end [it] is the song that most people remember, and love the most."[72]

In more recent times, the song has been embraced across the world and become a bona fide standard, often ranked high in lists of the greatest records of all time, and praised by both fellow artists and the most esteemed of music reviewers. It was the song that famously made Paul McCartney cry, and John Lennon, Barry Gibb, Elton John, and Pete Townsend are just a few who have sung its praises. Session man Don Randi once warned what would happen if music students were required to perform the song a capella - "There'd be a lot of suicides."[21]

The late American jazz singer-songwriter Margo Guryan, whose 1968 album *Take a Picture* was written as a direct result of listening to "God Only Knows," recalled: "To say that my life changed in two minutes 46 seconds would not be exaggerating. It taught me how songs could be structured by allowing the bassline to determine the chord choice rather than the other way round. I listened to it over and over again, learned the words, sang with it, immersed myself in it, and I began to understand."[75] In another interview she recalled: "I thought it was just gorgeous. I bought the record and played it a million times…That's really how I started writing that way. I just decided it was better than what was happening in jazz."[300]

Critic Dan Caffrey wrote that the song "has resonated with generations of music fans simply because of its concept…The entire world will listen to it for years to come,"[17] while Jim Fusilli referred to it as "a mature proclamation of love and another desperate plea. And it's a distillation of what much of *Pet Sounds* is about: the sense that if we surrender to an all-consuming love, we will never be able to live without it. And, though, we're uncertain that the reward is worth the risk, we yearn to surrender."[130]

Rather than calling it a suicide song, Philp Lambert described it more accurately: "[An] extreme love song, full of a blinding intensity of passion and feeling, and not a little insecurity and desperation as well," and how by listening to the glorious coda, "rapt listeners lose themselves in the intricate elegance of the vocal interplay, perhaps imagining a heavenward ascent, allowing themselves to escape the confines of earthly life, to be transported to a better place. If music is God's voice, He is speaking here with transcendent eloquence."[9]

Sir Paul McCartney also recalled what the song meant to him: "It's a really, really great song - it's a big favourite of mine…Its very deep…very emotional, always a bit of a choker for me, that one. There are certain songs that just hit home with me, and they're the strangest collection of songs…but that is high on the list, I must say."

Final words

To look back on the career of the Beach Boys, especially great albums like *All Summer Long, Today!, Surf's Up,* and *Sunflower*, it is hard (maybe even pointless) to do so without paying homage to the impact of *Pet Sounds*, and the 13 incredible tracks that are all included in this list. To close this work, I've chosen two wonderful quotes that give you some indication of what it meant to people on hearing the album for the very first time. First we have Brian's long-suffering wife Marilyn: "The first time I heard *Pet Sounds* was a special night. The album was done, finally finished. [Brian] brought it home on that big acetate, and he set the mood. We were on our king-sized iron brass bed and headboard; we had the lights down low. He played it, and it was one of the most moving experiences you could ever imagine. As I heard each song, one by one, it was 'Gasp.' It was so beautiful, one of the most spiritual times of my whole life. We both cried. Right after we listened to it, he said he was scared that nobody was going to like it. That it was too intricate...*Pet Sounds* is an album from a very frustrated man. It's such a complicated thing. Some people want to get up and exercise; all Brian could do is live and breathe music. That's all he thought about, coming from every pore in him. He doesn't just think of music; his body was just music. Nobody will ever know the emotional meaning in every single line of that record."[72]

Over in England, the Beatles' eminent record producer Sir George Martin also recalled what effect the album had on him and the band: "We thought we knew it all, and then we heard this record and it just blew us away...If there is one person that I have to select as a living genius of pop music, I would choose Brian Wilson. His invention and creativity with the Beach Boys reached a level that I always found staggering and *Pet Sounds* must rank as one of the highest achievements in our genre. Certainly, Brian pushed the frontiers a bit further and gave the Beatles and myself a good deal to think about in trying to keep up with them. His initiative was a marvelous combination of really original music compositions, a wonderful sense of instrumental sound, and a great understanding of record production. I guess you can say I'm a fan."[72]

Like George, I'm also a fan, and have been for most of my seven-decade long life. But, of course, it should not be all about Brian. The Beach Boys were a band of incredibly gifted artists, each and every one contributing to their immense success, with or without their illustrious leader, and succeeding in keeping the ship afloat while Brian's mental health struggles kept him away from the studio. So, for Carl, Dennis, Mike, Al, Bruce, David, Ricky and Blondie, and a host of others outside of the band, the parts they all had to play in the story, no matter how significant or not, should always be deeply appreciated.

Unlike many fellow artists of their generation, the Beach Boys' music will live on for many decades to come, maybe even into the next century and whatever new technology that may bring to enhance our listening pleasure. Students will continue to study their chord structure and vocal harmonising in ways not known to us now, but whatever that may be, there will still be the thrill of hearing some of their songs for the very first time and, like us today, be enchanted by that same enormous power and inspiration their music still has to give.

Sources

1. Doe, Andrew G & Tobler, John, *Brian Wilson and the Beach Boys: The Complete Guide to their Music* 2004
2. Sharp, Ken, *Christmas With Brian Wilson,* Record Collector Jan 2006
3. Murphy, James B, *Becoming the Beach Boys 1961-1963* 2015
4. Hickey, Andrew, *The Beach Boys on CD 1961-1969* 2011
5. Matijas-Mecca, Christian, *The Words and Music of Brian Wilson* 2017
6. Leaf, David, *Surfin Safari/Surfin USA* CD liner notes 1990
7. Priore, Domenic, *Look! Listen! Vibrate! Smile!* 1995
8. Priore, Domenic, *The Story of Brian Wilson's Lost Masterpiece Smile* 2005
9. Lambert, Philip, *Inside the Mind of Brian Wilson* 2007
10. Dillon, Mark, *Fifty Sides of the Beach Boys* 2012
11. Badman, Keith, *The Beach Boys: The Definitive Diary of America's Greatest Band* 2004
12. *Behind the Smile Sessions*, Aquarium Drunkard Oct 12 2011
13. Hermes, Will, Rolling Stone June 5 2012
14. Hamm, Ryan, Under the Radar June 19 2023
15. Petridis, Alexis, *The Beach Boys: That's Why God Made the Radio*, The Guardian May 31 2012
16. Phillimore, Alex, Beats Per Minute July 12 2012
17. Caffrey, Dan, Consequence of Sound June 5 2012
18. Rock Cellar Magazine Sept 2013
19. Abbott, Kingsley, *Back to the Beach: A Brian Wilson and the Beach Boys Reader* 2003
20. Record World May 5 1979
21. Swan, Rick, *The Beach Boys - All the Songs* 2018
22. Doggett, Peter, Record Collector Sept 1990
23. The Rolling Stone Album Guide 1992
24. Greenwald, Matthew, AllMusic
25. *50 Greatest Beach Boys Songs*, Mojo June 2012
26. Leaf, David, *Friends/20/20* CD liner notes 2000
27. Billboard June 9 1962
28. Wilson, Brian, *Wouldn't It Be Nice - My Own Story* 1991
29. White, Timothy, *The Nearest Faraway Place: Brian Wilson, the Beach Boys and the southern California experience* 1994
30. Cash Box Feb 20 1965
31. Rolling Stone May 31 1979
32. Carlin, Peter Ames, *Catch a Wave: The Rise, Fall & Redemption of the Beach Boys' Brian Wilson* 2006
33. Sharp, Ken, *Al Jardine Interview*, Goldmine June 28 2000
34. Elliott, Brad, *Surf's Up: The Beach Boys on Record 1961-1981* 2003
35. Wilson, Brian & Greenman, Ben, *I Am Brian Wilson: The Genius Behind the Beach Boys* 2016
36. Beard, David, *The Beach Boys' Today,* Beachboys.com Mar 8 2022
37. Interrante, Scott, Pop Matters Nov 2020
38. Sharp, Ken, *Bruce Johnston on the Beach Boys' Enduring Legacy*, Rock Cellar Magazine Sept 2013
39. Record World Apr 21 1973
40. Crawdaddy May 1977
41. Felton, David, *The Beach Boys: The Healing Power of Brother Brian*, Rolling Stone Nov 4 1976
42. Petridis, Alexis, *The Beach Boys' 40 Greatest Hits Ranked!* The Guardian Jan 27 2022
43. Stebbins, Jon, *Dennis Wilson - The Real Beach Boy* 2000
44. Leaf, David, *Little Deuce Coupe/All Summer Long* CD liner notes 1990
45. Beviglia, Jim, *The Beach Boys' Disney Girls,* American Songwriter June 10 2018
46. Baker, Sonny, *The 50 Greatest Beach Boys Songs*, Mojo June 2012
47. Sharp, Ken, *Alan Jardine: A Beach Boy Still Riding the Waves*, Goldmine June 28 2000
48. Linet, Mark, *The Smile Sessions* booklet 2011
49. Love, Mike, Beat International Feb 1988
50. Rolling Stone Feb 24 1968
51. Jolly, Nathan, *200 Sad Songs*, Wordpress.com June 30 2016

52. Harrison, Daniel, *After Sundown: The Beach Boys' Experimental Music* 1997
53. Blum, Jordan, Pop Matters Sept 23 2013
54. Faust, Edwin, Stylus Magazine Sept 22 2003
55. Uncut magazine Sept 2021
56. Preiss, Byron, *The Beach Boys: The Authorised Biography of America's Greatest Rock and Roll Band* 1979
57. *Michael Vosse Talks About Smile*, Fusion Apr 14 1969
58. *Smile, Brian and Pull Those Strings*, Teen Set Mar 1967
59. Petridis, Alexis, *The Smile Sessions Review*, The Guardian Oct 27 2011
60. Atkins, Jamie, *Wake the World: The Beach Boys 1967-73*, Record Collector July 2018
61. Elliott, Brad, *Pet Sounds track notes*, Aug 31 1999
62. Melody Maker May 21 1966
63. Sharp, Ken, *Brian Wilson - God's Messenger*, American Songwriter Jan 2 2009
64. Leaf, David, *Party/Stack O Tracks* CD liner notes 1990
65. McParland, Stephen J, *Our Favorite Recording Sessions* 2000
66. McParland, Stephen J, *The California Sound: An Insider's Story* 2000
67. Chidester, Brian, *Busy Doin' Somethin' - Uncovering Brian Wilson's Lost Bedroom Tapes* Paste magazine Mar 7 2014
68. Record Collector Oct 17 2017
69. White, Timothy, *Sunflower/Surf's Up* CD liner notes 2000
70. Miller, Jim, Rolling Stone Oct 1 1970
71. Greenwald, Matthew, AllMusic July 24 2022
72. Leaf, David, *Pet Sounds Sessions* booklet 1997
73. Kent, Nick, *The Last Beach Movie Revisited: The Life of Brian Wilson* 1995
74: Granata, Charles L, *Wouldn't It Be Nice: Brian Wilson and the Making of the Beach Boys' Pet Sounds* 2003
75. Abbott, Kingsley, *The Beach Boys' Pet Sounds: The Greatest Album of the Twentieth Century* 2001
76. Songfacts.com
77. Record World Feb 28 1970
78. Billboard Feb 28 1970
79. Cash Box Feb 28 1970
80. Hann, Michael, The Guardian Sept 22 2011
81. Billboard Oct 31 1964
82. Cash Box Oct 31 1964
83. Petridis, Alexis, *The Beach Boys' 40 Greatest Hits Ranked!* The Guardian Jan 27 2022
84. Curnutt, Kirk, *Icons of Pop Music: Brian Wilson* 2012
85. Granata, Charles L, *I Just Wasn't Made for These Times - Brian Wilson and the Making of Pet Sounds* 2003
86. Jopling, Norman, Record Mirror July 2 1966
87. Mason, Stewart, AllMusic
88. Little, Michael, *Graded on a Curve*, The Vinyl District Aug 2014
89. Webb, Adam, *Dumb Angel: The Life and Music of Dennis Wilson* 2001
90. Frome, Lynette, Reflextion 2018
91. Mansonblog.com
92. *1967 Sunshine Tomorrow* liner notes 2017
93. Sharp, Ken, *Love Among the Ruins* Goldmine 1992
94. Williams, Paul, *Brian Wilson and the Beach Boys - How Deep Is the Ocean?* 1997
95. Billboard Oct 21 1967
96. Cash Box Oct 21 1967
97. Rolling Stone Feb 24 1968
98. Himes, Geoffrey, Musician Magazine Dec 16 1982
99. *The Life of Rieley*, Record Collector Sept 6 2013
100. Record World Oct 17 1970
101. Pitchfork July 18 2000
102. Ledgerwood, Michael, Disc &Echo Dec 1970
103. *A Conversation With Brian Wilson*, Oui Dec 1976
104. New Musical Express, May 7 1967
105. Kubernick, Harvey, Best Classic Bands 2007

106. *Jack Rieley's Comments and Surf's Up*, Smileysmile.net Dec 1 2010
107. Wilson, Brian, *Beach Boys' Classics Selected by Brian Wilson* liner notes 2002
108. Washington Post Feb 17 2017
109. Record World July 1 1972
110. Aquarium Drunkard Mar 14 2017
111. Abrams, Johnny, *Holland* Rocksucker.co.uk June 18 2012
112. Rocksucker.co.uk Oct 25 2011
113. Record Collector Jan 1995
114. Greenwald, Matthew, AllMusic July 17 2014
115. Cash Box Aug 29 1964
116. Leaf, David, *Today/Summer Days* CD liner notes 1990
117. Interrante, Scott, Pop Matters June 2014
118. Hann, Michael, The Guardian Apr 27 2012
119. Mitchell, Matt, Paste July 17 2023
120. YouTube interview July 30 2022
121. The Stephen Desper Thread Oct 3 2016
122. Leaf, David, *God Only Knows: The Story of Brian Wilson, the Beach Boys and the California Myth* 1978
123. Gaines, Steven, *Heroes and Villains: The True Story of the Beach Boys* 1995
124. Kempke, Erik, Pitchfork Aug 15 2000
125. Diken, Dennis, *15 Big Ones/Love You* CD liner notes 2000
126. Jardine, Alan, *The Beach Boys' Alan Jardine: My Life In Music*, Uncut July 18 2022
127. Daro, Lorren, *Brian and LSD*, Collapse Board May 28 2012
128. Valania, Jonathan, *Bittersweet Symphony*, Magnet Aug-Sept 1999
129. *Good Vibrations? The Beach Boys' Mike Love Gets His Own Turn*, Goldmine Sept 18 1992
130. Fusilli, Jim, *Pet Sounds* 2005
131. Holdship, Bill, *The Beach Boys - The Making of Pet Sounds*, Mojo Jan 2007
132. D Strauss, New York Observer Dec 8 1997
133. Prince, Patrick, *Brian Wilson Gives a Brief Summary of Hit Songs*, Goldmine Mar 2 2011
134. Cash Box Feb 20 1965
135. Billboard Feb 20 1965
136. Greenwald, Matthew, AllMusic
137. Paste, July 17 2023
138. Cash Box Aug 29 1964
139. Jopling, Norman, Record Mirror, July 2 1966
140. Stebbins, Jon, *The Beach Boys FAQ: All That's Left To Know About America's Band*, Backbeat 2011
141. Shapiro, Stanley, Shindig Oct 20 2021
142. Doe, Andrew, Don't Forget the Songs365, wordpress.com Sept 3 2013
143. Sclafani, Tony, Pop Matters Nov 1 2007
144. Shapiro, Stanley, Shindig Oct 20 2021
145. Shindig July 14 2002
146. *1000 Days That Shook the World: The Psychedelic Beatles*, Mojo 2002
147. Guarisco, Donald A, AllMusic
148. Kyle, Joseph, The Recoup Aug 31 2018
149. Negron, Chuck, *Three Dog Nightmare* 1999
150. Lenser, Barry, Pop Matters May 15 2014
151. Perone, James E, *The Album: A Guide to Pop Music's Most Provocative, Influential and Important* Creations, 2012
152. Record World, Oct 8 1966
153. Paste, July 17 2023
154. McIntosh, Dan, Songfacts.com July 23 2022
155. Sharp, Ken, Goldmine Mar 2 2011
156. Petridis, Alexis, *1000 Albums To Hear Before You Die*, The Guardian Nov 17 2007
157. Uncut, Mar 2008
158. Billboard, Apr 10 1965
159. Cash Box Apr 10 1965
160. AllMusic July 23 2022
161. Songfacts.com

162. Smith, Lee V, Inside Atlanta Mar 2021
163. Nolan, Tom, Rolling Stone Nov 11 1971
164. The Uncool July 10 2012
165. Maxwell, Emily, American Songwriter Apr 27 2015
166. Cash Box, Dec 16 1967
167. Rolling Stone Feb 24 1968
168. Leaf, David, *Surfer Girl/Shut Down Vol 2* CD liner notes 1990
169. Endless Summer tv series 1989
170. Sharp, Ken, Goldmine July 23 2022
171. Zollo, Paul, *Sleighbells in the Summer: Brian Wilson*, Song Talk, Fall 1988
172. *Al Rejoins the Beach Boys,* New Musical Express Aug 14 1964
173. Murphy, James B, *Judy Bowles Interview*, Becoming the Beach Boys Jan 22 2011
174. Cash Box July 27 1963
175. Kubernick, Harvey, *Brian Wilson Remembers: An Indepth Interview with the Beach Boys' Resident Genius,* Best Classic Bands July 3 2021
176. Doggett, Peter, *Holy Man and Slow Booze: Dennis Wilson*1997
177. Locey, Bill, *Leader of the Jam* Jan 13 2005
178. Kent, Nick, *The Dark Stuff: Selected Writings on Rock Music 1972-93* 2007
179. Benci, Jacopo, Record Collector Jan 1995
180. Rock Cellar Magazine June 18 2018
181. Greenwald, Matthew, AllMusic July 26 2014
182. Miller, Jim, Rolling Stone Oct 1 1970
183. *How the Beach Boys Became the Godfathers of Dream Pop*, udiscovermusic.com June 20 2023
184. Golsen, Tyler, Far Out Apr 12 2023
185. Cash Box, July 17 1965
186. Roberts, Michael, *Listening To the Distant Echoes of a Pop Genius*, Westworld Sept 14 2000
187. Rusten, Ian & Stebbins, Jon, *The Beach Boys in Concert* 2013
188. Love, Mike, *Good Vibrations - My Life as a Beach Boy* 2016
189. Interrante, Scott, *When I Grow Up,* Pop Matters June 4 2014
190. Simpson, Dave, *The Beach Boys' Mike Love* The Guardian July 5 2012
191. Songfacts.com
192. Tobler, John, *The Beach Boys* 1978
193. Valentine, Penny, Disc & Echo July 20 1968
194. Record World July 20 1968
195. Cash Box July 13 1968
196. Brent, Mark, *I Just Wasn't Made For These Times*, Backbeat 2005
197. Guarisco, Donald A, AllMusic May 9 2012
198. *Art Rock Legend Brian Wilson in Studio Q*, YouTube Sept 26 2011
199. *Beach Boys Hit Inspired by Utah Girl Having All the Fun*, ksl.com Feb 11 2007
200. White, Timothy, Billboard June 1996
201. Cash Box Feb 8 1964
202. *Brian Wilson on the Little Girl I Once Knew*, YouTube Apr 2 2020
203. Interrante, Scott, Pop Matters June 20 2022
204. Cash Box Nov 20 1965
205. Melody Maker Dec 11 1965
206. Pop Matters Sept 11 2008
207. Gidman, Gary, *Make It Good: The Songs of Dennis Wilson*, Mar 1984
208. Greenwald, Matthew, AllMusic
209. Leaf, David, *Requiem for a Beach Boy* 1985
210. *Thoughts of You: Dennis Wilson's Pacific Ocean Blue*, textura.org Oct 2008
211. Lambert, Philip, *Good Vibrations: Brian Wilson and the Beach Boys in Critical Perspective,* 2016
212. Greenwald, Matthew, AllMusic Jan 6 2015
213. Desper, Stephen, *The Beach Boys' Studio Disasters*, smileysmile.net Sept 23 2018
214. Sharp, Ken, *Mike Love of the Beach Boys: One to One*, Rock Cellar Sept 9 2015
215. Rolling Stone, July 27 2016
216. Rolling Stone, July 27 2016
217. Kotal, Kent, *The True Story Behind the Beach Boys' Classic Song The Warmth of the Sun,*

Forgottenhits.com. June 16 2015
218. Panfile, Greg, *Mind of Brian* 2016
219. Cash Box Oct 31 1964
220. Guarisco, Donald, AllMusic June 10 2016
221. Esch, Jim, AllMusic Mar 92012
222. Joling, Norman, Record Mirror, July 2 1966
223. Cash Box May 16 1964
224. Sellars, Jeff, *God Only Knows -Faith, Hope and Love and the Beach Boys* 2015
225. White, Timothy, *The Passion of Pet Sounds*, Billboard Oct 12 1996
226. Cash Box Mar 5 1966
227. Goldstein, Richard, Village Voice Feb 16 1967
228. Disc & Music Echo, Mar 21 1967
229. New Musical Express, Mar 21 1967
230. Disc & Music Echo, May 6 1967
231. Billboard, July 29 1967
232. Cash Box, July 29 1967
233. Valentine, Penny, Disc & Music Echo July 29 1967
234. Fornatele, Peter, WNEW-FM Nov 3 1976
235. Turner, Dale, *The Low Down on the Low End: Brian With Carol Kaye*, Bassics June-July 2000
236. Jopling, Norman, Record Mirror July 2 1966
237. Cash Box, July 16 1966
238. Pitchfork, *The 200 Best Songs of the 1960s*, Pitchfork, Aug 18 2006
239. Rock & Roll Mini Series 1995
240. Sanchez, Luis, *The Beach Boys' Smile*, 2014
241. Rooksby, Rikky, *Inside Classic Rock Tracks* 2001
242. Richardson, Mark, *The 200 Greatest Songs of the 1960s*, Pitchfork 2010
243. Cash Box, May 16 1964
244. Sharp, Ken, *Best individual Artist: Brian Wilson*, Goldmine Mar 2 2011
245. Boucher, Geoff, Los Angeles Times Aug 12 2007
246. Hedegard, Erik, *The Ballad of Mike Love*, Rolling Stone Feb 17 2016
247. Runtagh, Jordan, *The Beach Boys In Ther Own Words*, People June 8 2018
248. Record World, July 17 1965
249. Cash Box, July 17 1965
250. Boucher, Geoff, Los Angeles Times June 27 1997
251. Playboy Dec 1984
252. Goldmine 2011
253. Mojo
254. Songfacts.com
255. Andrewromano.net May 2012
256. Unterberger, Richie, AllMusic Apr 25 2011
257. Christgau, Robert, Village Voice May 1970
258. Billboard Sept 12 1964
259. Cash Box Oct 19 1963
260. Paytress, Mark, *A Passage to India*, 1000 Days of Revolution, Mojo 2003
261. Leaf, David, *Smiley Smile/Wild Honey* cd liner notes 1990
262. Pewter, Jim, Brian Wilson Interview, KRTH Radio Nov 1976
263. Cash Box Mar 9 1963
264. Paste magazine July 17 2023
265. Brian Wilson on Friends, YouTube July 30 2022
266. Cash Box Apr 13 1968
267. Rolling Stone Aug 24 198
268. Guarisco, Donald, AllMusic July 26 2022
269. New York Times Apr 6 2000
270. The Quietus, May 22 2023
271. Atkins, Jamie, *Dennis Wilson's Best Beach Boys Songs*, undiscovermusic.com Dec 4 2022
272. Greenwald, Matthew, AllMusic Dec 11 2012
273. *Thoughts of You: Dennis Wilson's Pacific Ocean Blue*, textura.org Oct 2008
274. Shindig Sept 2021

275. Ward, Thomas, AllMusic
276. Billboard, Apr 10 1965
277. Cash Box, Apr 10 1965
278. Peters, Tony, *Beach Boys Smile Sessions*, Oct 17 2011
279. Highwater, Jamake, *Rock and Other Four Letter Words* 1968
280. Siegel, Jules, *Goodbye Surfing, Hello God* Cheetah Oct 1997
281. Williams, Paul, *Back to the Miracle Factory*, 2002
282. *Michael Vosse Talks About Smile*, Fusion Apr 14 1969
283. Rolling Stone Oct 14 1971
284. Cannon, Geoffrey, The Guardian Oct 29 1971
285. Cash Box, Dec 4 1971
286. Record World Dec 4 1971
287. *Mike Love Not War: Q&A With a Beach Boy,* July 5 2012
288. Pinnock, Tom, *The Making of Good Vibrations*, Uncut June 2012
289. Varga, George, *Brian Wilson Talks Pet Sounds 50 Years Later*, San Diego Union-Tribune June 26 2016
290. Brend, Mark, *Strange Sounds: Offbeat instruments and Sonic Experiments in Pop* 2005
291. Taylor, Derek, Hit Parader, Oct 5 1966
292. Cash Box Oct 15 1966
293. Billboard Oct 15 1966
294. Interrante, Scott, *The 12 Best Brian Wilson Songs*, Pop Matters May 2015
295. Gillett, Charlie, *The Sound of the City: The Rise of Rock and Roll*, 1984
296. Cunningham, Don & Bleiel, Jeff, *Add Some Music To Your Day*, 1999
297. Jones, Peter, *Brian Tells About His Music…*Record Mirror Aug 13 1966
298. Record World July 23 1966
299. Cash Box July 16 1966
300. Broom, Eric, Mean Street Sept 2001
301. Abrams, Jonny, *Today!* Rocksucker.co.uk Nov 7 2011
302. Abrams, Jonny, *Sunflower* Rocksucker.co.uk June 17 2012
303. Was, Don, *Brian Wilson: I Guess I Just Wasn't Made For These Times*, DVD 1995
304. Disc & Music Echo, May 31 1969
305. Letovski, Irv, Los Angeles Times Oct 23 1991
306. Prince, Patrick, *The Beach Boys Beginnings Examined Through Book*, Goldmine Jan 26 2016
307. D'Arcy, Matt, *Birth of the Beach Boys*, Combo Musical Weekly, Jan 1 1965
308. Scoppa, Bud, *Good Vibrations: The full story of the Beach Boys*, Uncut June 2022

Further Reading

Abbott, Kingsley, ed. *Back to the Beach: A Brian Wilson and The Beach Boys Reader* (1997)
Abbott, Kingsley, *The Beach Boys Pet Sounds: The Greatest Album of the Twentieth Century* (2001)
Anstey, Robert G, *The Beach Boys: The Musical Evolution of America's Band* (2004)
Anthony, Dean, *The Beach Boys* (1985)
Badman, Keith, *The Beach Boys: Definitive Diary of America's Greatest Band on Stage and in the Studio* (2004)
Barnes, Ken, *The Beach Boys: A Biography in Words and Pictures* (1976)
Blaine, Hal & David Goggin, *Hal Blaine and the Wrecking Crew* (1990)
Carlin, Peter A, *Catch A Wave: The Rise, Fall & Redemption of the Beach Boys' Brian Wilson* (2006)
Cunningham, Don & Jeff Bleiel, *Add Some Music To Your Day: Analysing and Enjoying the Music of the Beach Boys (* (2000)
Curnutt, Kirk, *Brian Wilson* (2012)
Dillon, Mark, *Fifty Sides of the Beach Boys* (2012)
Doe, Andrew & John Tobler, *The Beach Boys: The Complete Guide to Their Music* (2004)
Elliott, Brad, *Surf's Up! The Beach Boys On Record 1961-1981* (2003)
Fusilli, Jim, *The Beach Boys' Pet Sounds* (2005)
Gaines, Steven S, *Heroes & Villains: The True Story of the Beach Boys* (1995)
Granta, Charles L, *I Just Wasn't Made For These Times: Brian Wilson and the Making of Pet Sounds* (2003)
Lambert, Philip, *Inside the Mind of Brian Wilson: The Songs, Sounds and Influences of the Beach Boys' Founding Genius* (2007)
Lambert, Philip, ed. *Good Vibrations: Brian Wilson and the Beach Boys in Critical Perspective* (2016)
Leaf, David, *The Beach Boys and the California Myth* (1985)
Leaf, David, *The Beach Boys* (1985)
Love, Mike & James Hirsch, *Good Vibrations: My Life as a Beach Boy* (2016)
Matijas-Mecca, Christian, *The Words and Music of Brian Wilson* (2017)
McParland, Stephen J, *Our Favourite Recording Sessions: In the Studio With Brian Wilson and The Beach Boys 1961-1970* (2000)
McParland, Stephen J, *Smile, Sun, Sand & Pet Sounds* (1999)
McParland, *The California Sounds: The Musical Biography of Gary Usher* Vol 1 (2000)
Morgan, Johnny, *The Beach Boys: America's Band* (2015)
Murphy, James B, *Becoming the Beach Boys 1961-1963* (2015)
Preiss, Byron, *The Beach Boys: The Authorised Biography of America's Greatest Rock and Roll Band* (1979)
Priore, Domenic, *Look! Listen! Vibrate! SMILE!* (1998)
Priore, Domenic, *The Story of Brian Wilson's Lost Masterpiece* (2005)
Rusten, Ian & Jon Stebbins, *The Beach Boys in Concert: The Complete History of America's Band On Tour and On Stage* (2013)
Sellars, Jeff, ed. *God Only Knows: Faith, Hope, Love and the Beach Boys* (2105)
Siegel, Jules, *Goodbye Surfing, Hello God!* (2011)
Stebbins, Jon, *The Beach Boys FAQ: All That's Left To Know About America's Band* (2011)
Stebbins, Jon & David Marks, *The Lost Beach Boy: The True Story of David Marks* (2010)
Swan, Rick, *The Beach Boys: All the Songs* (2018)
Tobler, John, *The Beach Boys* (1977)
Webb, Adam, *Dumb Angel: The Life and Music of Dennis Wilson* (2000)
White, Timothy, *The Nearest Faraway Place: Brian Wilson, the Beach Boys, and the Southern California Experience* (1994)
Williams, Paul, *Brian Wilson & The Beach Boys: How Deep Is the Ocean?- Essays and Conversations* (1997)
Wilson, Brian & Todd Gold, *Wouldn't It Be Nice: My Own Story,* (1991) * since discredited
Wilson, Brian, *I Am Brian Wilson: A Memoir* (2016)
Wise, Nick, *The Beach Boys in Their Own Words* (1994)